From an Other to the other

Jacques Lacan

From an Other to the other

The Seminar of Jacques Lacan
Book XVI

Edited by Jacques-Alain Miller

Translated by Bruce Fink

polity

Originally published in French as *D'un Autre à l'autre. Le Séminaire de Jacques Lacan, Livre XVI.* © Éditions du Seuil, 2006

This English edition © Polity Press, 2024

Polity Press
65 Bridge Street
Cambridge CB2 1UR, UK

Polity Press
111 River Street
Hoboken, NJ 07030, USA

ISBN-13: 978-1-5095-1005-4 hardback

A catalogue record for this book is available from the British Library.

Library of Congress Control Number: 2022951306

Typeset in 10.5 on 12 pt Times NR MT
by Cheshire Typesetting Ltd, Cuddington, Cheshire
Printed and bound in the UK by CPI Group (UK) Ltd, Croydon

The publisher has used its best endeavours to ensure that the URLs for external websites referred to in this book are correct and active at the time of going to press. However, the publisher has no responsibility for the websites and can make no guarantee that a site will remain live or that the content is or will remain appropriate.

Every effort has been made to trace all copyright holders, but if any have been overlooked the publisher will be pleased to include any necessary credits in any subsequent reprint or edition.

For further information on Polity, visit our website:
politybooks.com

Contents

JOUISSANCE: ITS REAL

JOUISSANCE: ITS LOGIC

EVACUATION

APPENDICES

Figures

Translator's Note

Numbers found in the margins here correspond to the pagination of the 2006 French edition of Lacan's Seminar XVI *D'un Autre à l'autre*, edited by Jacques-Alain Miller and published by Éditions du Seuil in Paris. All references here to Lacan's *Écrits* (Paris: Seuil, 1966) are to the pagination of *Écrits: The First Complete Edition in English* (New York & London: W. W. Norton & Co., 2006). When I refer to Lacan's Seminars, I provide the pagination of the English editions, when they exist; when they do not, I give the page number(s) in the French editions. All the extant Seminars except Seminar VI were published in French by Éditions du Seuil in Paris. Seminar VI was published by La Martinière / Le Champ freudien. Seminars that have yet to be published in French are indicated by volume number and date of class. References to Freud's work here are always to *The Standard Edition of the Complete Psychological Works of Sigmund Freud* (24 volumes) published in London by Hogarth Press, abbreviated here as SE, followed by the volume number and page(s). Words followed by an asterisk (*) are found in English in the original. Text in square brackets has been added by the translator.

I thank Héloïse Fink and Rolf Flor for their assistance with the French and German, respectively.

Book XVI

From an Other to the other

INTRODUCTION

I

FROM SURPLUS VALUE TO SURPLUS JOUISSANCE

> The essence of psychoanalytic theory
> is a discourse without speech [*parole*].

On the board

We have come together again this year for a Seminar the title of which, *From an Other to the other*, I chose in such way as to convey the main landmarks around which I will revolve this year. This discussion will be crucial, for we must define the status of the discourse known as "psychoanalytic discourse," whose emergence in our era entails so many consequences.

A label has been placed on the way in which this discourse proceeds [*le procès du discours*]. "Structuralism," it has been called – a term that did not require much ingenuity on the part of the publicist who suddenly coined it a few months ago, in order to encompass a certain number of writers whose work had already long since sketched out several of the avenues of this discourse.

I just mentioned a publicist. You are all aware of the play on words I have allowed myself around *poubellication* [a combination of *poubelle* (garbage can or rubbish bin) and *publication*; henceforth: "rubblication" or "poo-blication"]. A certain number of us have thus been dumped into the same trash can thanks to he whose job it was to do so. I could have found myself in worse company. Indeed, I can hardly be uncomfortable about those with whom I find myself lumped, they being people for whose work I have the highest regard.

In this era dominated by the genius of Samuel Beckett, we know quite a bit about garbage cans [see *Endgame*]. Having been a member of three psychoanalytic societies over the course of the past 30 years, in stints of 15, 10, and 5 years, I personally know a fair amount about what it means to cohabitate with trash.

As for structuralism, we can understand the uneasiness certain people feel – owing to the way in which others think they can handle our shared habitat from the outside – and their wish to leave it behind a bit in order to limber up their legs.

Nevertheless, since an impatience to do so has apparently come over certain people, I have realized that perhaps I'm not so badly off in this wastebasket category after all.

1

Structuralism can only be identified, or so it seems to me at least, with something that I will quite simply call "seriousness."

Be that as it may, structuralism in no way resembles a *philosophy*, if we use that word to designate a worldview or even some way of grounding intellectual positions, whether on the right or on the left.

If, as a psychoanalyst, I had tried in any way to introduce what is ridiculously called a "psychoanalytic anthropology," it would suffice, in order to refute me, to recall, at the very threshold of this domain, the constitutive truths psychoanalysis brings with it. They concern those that Genesis tells us God created – man and woman – although one also finds "God created him" [*Dieu le créa* instead of *Dieu les créa*]. God only knows why!

Psychoanalysis tells us that there is no union of man and woman

- without castration determining, at the level of fantasy, the reality of the [female] partner for whom castration is impossible, and
- without castration playing its part in a sort of concealment [or: receiving or possessing of stolen goods, *recel*] that posits castration as truth in the [male] partner to whom it is spared in reality, except in cases where things accidentally go too far.

The impossibility of carrying out castration comes to be posited as determining her reality, whereas the worst possible thing castration threatens him with has no need to occur to be true, in the sense in which the term leaves one no recourse.

This reminder alone implies that, at least in the field that appears to be ours, there is no harmony, no matter how we designate it. Owing to this, we must obviously ask ourselves what sort of discourse can suit this field.

Will we have to raise here the question with which all of philosophy begins? Compared to so many other fields of knowledge [*savoirs*], which are lacking in neither value nor efficacity, what would make *this* discourse – which is self-grounded and based on a criterion that thought appropriately gauges – deserve to be called *epistéme*, science?

In the attempt to bring thought into tune with itself, we are encouraged to be more prudent, if only, first of all, through the challenge I have just sketched out: truth's challenge to reality [*réel*]. The notion of the unconscious confronts us with a rule [or: yardstick, *règle*] of thought that must be grounded on the basis of non-thought as something that could be its cause.

It is only to the extent that statements lie outside of meaning [*hors-de-sens*] – and not on the basis of their meaning, as people think and as all of phenomenology assumes – that I am qua thought. My thought is not adjustable [*réglable*] at will, whether we add the word "alas" or not. It is regulated [or: ruled, *réglée*]. When I take action, I do not try to express it but rather to cause it. Yet it is discourse, not action, that is at stake here. In discourse, I need not follow its rule [*règle*] but, instead, find its cause. Thought's being is found in *l'entre-sens* [between meaning, between senses, and, perhaps, the direction in which one enters] – you can hear that as obscenely as you like.

That which serves as [thought's] cause, because it goes [*passer*] through my mind, purely and simply allows what was qua being to go through [*passer*]. This is owing to the fact that, where it came from, it has already and always passed through, producing thought effects.

"It is raining" [*Il pleut*] is a thought event whenever it is enunciated, and its subject is first and foremost this "it" [*il*], this *hile* [meaning hilum, but pronounced in French just like *il*], I would say, that it constitutes in a certain number of significations. Which is why this it [*il*] is comfortably found anew in everything that follows. "It is raining" [*Il pleut*] can, for example, be followed by "first truths, [or] it's too much [*il y a de l'abus*]." Above all, if we confound rain qua meteor and *aqua pluvia*, rainwater, the water one collects, the meteor lends itself to metaphor. Why? Because it is already made up of signifiers. "It is raining." The being of thought is the cause of a thought insofar as it is outside of meaning [*hors-de-sens*]. It was already and always the being of a prior thought.

Now making use of this structure renders impossible the touting of any sort of infallibility [*infallibilité*]. It relies on the crack [or: failure, *faille*] alone, or rather on how it proceeds [or: develops, *procès*]. There is, indeed, a cracking process [or: development of the failure, *procès de la faille*], and it is the process on which making use of structure relies. But it can only rely on it by following it, which is in no wise to go beyond it – unless this allows it to be grasped in the consequence that is set in stone at the very point at which the repeating of the process stops. Which implies that it is its interruption [*temps d'arrêt*; see *Écrits*, p. 166] that determines the result.

This, I would add discreetly in passing, explains why all art is defective. It derives its power from collecting what is hollowed out at the point at which its failure [or: breakdown, *défaillance*] occurs. This is why music and architecture are the supreme arts. I am using the word "supreme" here in the technical sense, as the maximum at the basal level, producing the relation between the harmonic number and time and space, from the vantage point of their incompatibility. Indeed, as we now know, the harmonic number is no more than a sieve – it retains neither the one nor the other, neither time nor space.

This is what structuralism takes seriously. It takes knowledge qua cause seriously – cause in thought with, most often, it must be said, a delusional aim.

Don't be scared. These are introductory comments, reminders of certainties, not truths.

Today, before presenting the schemas with which I intend to begin, I would like to mention that, if there is already something you can hold on to, it is what I took the trouble to write on the board earlier: "The essence of psychoanalytic theory is a discourse without speech."

This is the essence of the theory. The essence of psychoanalytic theory is the functioning of discourse, specifically insofar as – and this may strike you as new or at least paradoxical – I say that it is "without speech."

What is the status of theory in the psychoanalytic field? On this point I hear strange echoes around me. Misunderstanding abounds. By positing a whole field of thought as [involving] manipulation, I seem to be calling traditional principles into question, and this leads people to translate what I am saying as some such nonsense as "theoretical impossibility" – which is especially surprising in that this is done in nearby places and by people who are close to me.

One day I stated – in a context that made what I meant quite clear – that "there's no such thing as a universe of discourse" [Seminar XIV, class given on November 16, 1966]. This apparently led some, shortly thereafter, to conclude, "Then why bother?"

Yet my statement was not the least bit ambiguous. It is hard to see how the fact that one can state (which I did) that discourse has no point of closure can lead people to conclude that discourse is impossible, or even slightly devalued thereby. Far from it. Which is precisely why this discourse is in your hands. You have a responsibility to direct it well, taking into account what the statement that "there's no such thing as a universe of discourse" means.

There is thus, in this regard, nothing for me to correct. I must simply return to it to take the following steps, by laying out the consequences of the discourse I have already delineated. I will perhaps also have to return to what makes it such that – despite being as attached as an analyst may be to the conditions of this discourse – one can thus show where it breaks down [*défaillance*] at any moment.

Before turning to this, allow me a bit of music.

2

There was a point in time at which I used pots as an example, but people made such a fuss about it that I decided to leave it out of my *Écrits*.

A pot is the tangible image of a notion; it *is* in some sense a signification that is shaped by itself.

Manifesting the appearance of a form and a content, a pot makes us think that it is the content that is the signification, as if thought here manifested a need to imagine that it [thought] must contain something else – which the expression to "contain oneself" designates when it bears on an impetuous act. I called it a "mustard" pot in order to point out that, far from necessarily containing any, it is precisely because it is empty that it takes on its value as a mustard pot. This is because the word "mustard" is written on it. But mustard [*moutarde*] means that the pot is in a hurry [*moult lui tarde*] to accede to its eternal life as a pot, which begins from the moment it has a hole in it.

Indeed, it is in this form that we find it throughout the ages in archaeological digs, when we look in graves for something that can attest to the state of a civilization. The pot has a hole in it in homage, it is said, to the dead and so that the living cannot use it. That, of course, is one reason. But there is perhaps another – namely, that the pot is designed to produce this hole, in order that the hole be produced. This is what is illustrated by the myth of the Danaids. It is with a hole in it that a pot, when we have retrieved it from its gravesite, stands proudly on the collector's shelf. In this moment of glory, its status is akin to God's: it is in this glory that it reveals its precise nature. 16

The structure of a pot – not its matter – appears here as what it is, namely the correlate of the functioning of a tube or drum. If we go looking for precursors for it in nature, as in horns and conch shells, we will see that their essence – namely, their ability to produce sound – is still there after life has been extracted from them.

Whole civilizations are no longer represented to us by anything other than these little pots, which take the form of a head or of some animal, covered in myriad signs that are impenetrable to us, in the absence of documents connected to them.

Here we sense that the signification or image is truly on the outside, and that what is on the inside is precisely what lies in the grave where we find it – namely, precious materials and substances, perfumes, gold, frankincense, and myrrh, as they say.

The pot explains the signification of what is there at what level. At the level of a use value, or rather, let us say, of an exchange value with another world and another dignit(ar)y. At the level of an homage value.

The fact that the Dead Sea Scrolls were found in pots reminds us that it is not the signified that is inside but rather the signifier. It is with the latter that we deal when it comes to what is important to us – namely, the relationship between discourse and speech in psychoanalytic efficiency.

Having arrived at the point of offering what will serve you as an image of the unit(y) [*l'unité*] of theoretical function in the approach that is properly or improperly called structuralist, I will ask you to allow me a shortcut.

I will call on Marx, who it was hard for me – bothered as I was about it for a long time – not to bring in sooner in a field where he certainly has his place. As Marx does [regarding surplus value], I will indicate the place where we must situate the essential function of object *a*.

First I will remind you what has been clearly brought out, and not far from here, by recent studies, commentaries on Marx that were – until this was denied by their author – designated as structuralist. The author asks what the object of capital is. We shall see what psychoanalysis allows us to correspondingly enunciate.

17

Marx begins from the functioning of the market. What is new in his approach is how he situates labor. It is not that labor is new, it is that it is purchased, that there is a market for labor. This is what allows Marx to demonstrate what is inaugural in his discourse: surplus value.

It turns out that this approach implies the revolutionary action with which you are all familiar. Or rather, with which you are not very familiar, for is not clear that the taking of power has resolved the subversion of the subject – of the capitalist subject – which had been expected to ensue from this action, or that it has in fact had bountiful consequences, even in the eyes of the Marxists who had to reap them. But for the time being, that is of little importance to us. What is important is what Marx designates and what his approach means.

Whether commentators on Marx are structuralists or not, they seem to have demonstrated that Marx himself was a structuralist. For it is clearly on the basis of what he was as a thinking being, at the point determined by the predominance of the labor market, that the function – which is admittedly obscure, given the confusion found in the commentaries – of surplus value proved to be the cause of his thought.

The fact that discourse is identical to its conditions will hopefully be clarified by what I will now say about the psychoanalytic approach.

Just as labor was not new in the production of commodities, the renunciation of jouissance – whose relationship to labor I need not define any further – is far from new. Indeed, right from the outset – and as opposed to what Hegel says or seems to say – it is the renunciation of jouissance that constitutes the master, who clearly intends to make it the motor force of his power. What is new is that there is a discourse that articulates this renunciation, and that brings out in it what I will call the function of "surplus jouissance" [*plus-de-jouir*]. That is the essence of psychoanalytic discourse.

This function appears owing to the very existence of discourse. It demonstrates that the renunciation of jouissance is an effect of discourse itself. To delineate things, we must in fact assume that there is a market in the field of the Other that totalizes merits and values, that assures the organization of choices and preferences, and that implies an ordinal and even a cardinal structure.

Discourse possesses the means of enjoying [*jouir*] insofar as it involves the subject. There would be no "reasons of subject" – in the sense in which one says "reasons of state" – if, in the Other's market, there were not the following correlate: a surplus jouissance is established that is captured by certain people.

In order to demonstrate how surplus jouissance is related to enunciation, how it is produced by discourse, and how it appears as an effect would no doubt require detailed commentary. But it is not something that is all that new to your ears if you have read my work, for it is the topic of my paper "Kant with Sade" [in *Écrits*]. I demonstrate there the total reduction of surplus jouissance to the act of applying to the subject the term *a* of fantasy through which the subject can be posited as self-caused [*cause-de-soi*] in desire.

This year I will elaborate on this point by returning to Pascal's wager, which provides an excellent illustration of the relationship between renunciation of jouissance and wagering as a dimension. The whole of life is reduced therein to an element of value. A strange way to inaugurate the market of jouissance in the field of discourse!

18

But doesn't it follow easily from the function of goods allocated to the dead inscribed in history that we saw earlier?

Thus this is not what is currently at issue. We are dealing with theory insofar as it frees itself from [*s'allège de*] the function of surplus jouissance. The production of an essential object is played out around surplus jouissance, an object whose function we must now define: object *a*.

The crudeness of the echoes my introduction of this term has received is and remains for me the guarantee that it has the efficacity I bestow on it. Recall Marx's famous passage in which, while developing his theory, he relished the opportunity to see surface the living incarnation of misrecognition.

I have enunciated that "the signifier is what represents a subject to another signifier." That is a definition. A definition must be correct and a teaching must be rigorous. At a time when psychoanalysis is called upon to answer for something – something you should not believe I have any intention of eliding, which is the crisis of the relationship between students and the university system – it is intolerable and unthinkable that people content themselves with saying that there are things about a field [*un savoir*] that one can in no way define. If psychoanalysis cannot be enunciated as a field of knowledge and be taught as such, it has no business being where that is the only thing that counts.

19   If the knowledge market is quite rightly shaken up by the fact that science brings it the unit of value [or: course credit, *unité de valeur*] – something that allows it to sound the status of its exchange right down to its most radical functions – it is certainly not so that psychoanalysis can present itself by throwing in the towel, when it can perfectly well articulate something about it. Every term that is employed on this topic – like "non-conceptualization" or the evocation of some sort of "impossibility" – merely designates the ineptitude of those who promote it. The strategy with the truth, which is the essence of therapeutics, undoubtedly cannot reside as such in any specific intervention known as interpretation. In practice, all sorts of specific functions and variable lucky games can undoubtedly be opportune. Still, this is not a reason to misrecognize that they have no meaning unless they are situated at the precise point at which it is the theory that gives them their weight.

This is clearly what is at stake.

Surplus jouissance arises from the renunciation of jouissance owing to the effect of discourse. It is what gives object *a* its place. Insofar as the market defines any object whatsoever of human labor as a commodity, this object bears within itself some element of surplus value.

Surplus jouissance is thus what allows us to isolate the function of object *a*.

3

What do we do in analysis if not set in motion a discourse through the fundamental rule of psychoanalysis? What does the subject put in abeyance [*suspend*] in this discourse? His function as a subject. The subject is excused here from sustaining his discourse with a [claim like] "I am saying." It is one thing to speak and another to assert, "I am saying what I just stated." The subject of the statement says, "I am saying"; he says, "I am asserting," just like I am doing here in my teaching. I am articulating this speech. It is not poetry. I am saying what is written here, and I can even repeat it, which is essential, varying it by adding that I wrote it.

In analysis, the subject is excused from maintaining what he states. Will he thereby attain that purity of speech, that "full speech" which I spoke about during my evangelizing phase? Who was my so-called "Rome Discourse" [see "Function and Field of Speech and Language"] addressed to if not to those whose ears were most unwilling to hear it? I will not characterize what made those ears so impermeable, for it would be to pass judgment in a way that could only be offensive. 20

But consider the following. When speaking of "the Freudian Thing," I just so happened to give free rein to something that I myself called a prosopopoeia. It involved the truth stating the following:

> To you I am thus the enigma of she who slips away as soon as she appears, you men who try so hard to hide me under the tawdry finery of your proprieties. Still, I admit your embarrassment is sincere –

recall that I pointed out the function of the term "embarrassment" [or: quandary, *embarras*] on a separate occasion –

> for even when you take it upon yourselves to become my heralds, you acquire no greater worth by wearing my colors than your own clothes, which are like you, phantoms that you are. Where am I going, having passed into you? And where was I prior to that? Will I perhaps tell you someday? But so that you will find me where I am, I will teach you by what sign you can recognize me. Men, listen, I am telling you the secret. I, truth, speak. [*Écrits*, p. 340]

I did not write "I am saying [so]." If what speaks appeared, the analysis would certainly be over [*close*], as I ironically wrote. But this is precisely what does not happen, or what deserves to be punctuated differently when it does.

Let us return to the status of the subject who is called into question here.

Through an artifice, he is asked in analysis not to be he who maintains what is proffered. One mustn't believe, however, that the latter disappears, for the psychoanalyst is there to represent him – I mean, in order to sustain him while he is unable to find anew his bearings as regards the cause of his discourse. This is why we must now turn to fundamental formulations, specifically the one that defines the signifier as what represents a subject to another signifier.

I am surprised that no one has yet observed that its corollary is that a signifier cannot represent itself to itself. Naturally this is not new either, for it is implied by what I have articulated regarding repetition [see, for example, Seminar XI, classes 2–5]. But we must pause here for a moment in order to see it in action: what can the "itself" of the signifier mean in this sentence?

Note that when I talk about the signifier, I am talking about something opaque. When I say that we must define the signifier as what represents a subject to another signifier, I mean that no one will know anything about it except the other signifier. And the other signifier is headless, since it is a signifier. Here the subject is stifled and effaced at the very moment he appears. How can some facet of this subject, who disappears as soon as he emerges – produced by a signifier in order to immediately fade [*s'éteindre*] in another – be constituted and ultimately manage to get itself viewed as a *Selbstbewußtsein* [self-consciousness or self-awareness], in other words, as something that is content to be identical to itself? This is what we must now consider.

In whatever form the subject arises in its presence, he cannot reunite with his signifying representative without a loss occurring in the identity that is known, strictly speaking, as object *a*. This is what Freud's theory says about repetition. Which means that, regarding recourse to jouissance – in which, owing to the sign, something else comes to occupy its place, namely, the trait that marks it – nothing is identifiable. Nothing can arise here without an object being lost.

A subject is what may be represented by a signifier to another signifier. Isn't this modeled on the fact that, in what Marx deciphers, namely economic reality, the subject of exchange value is represented with respect to use value? It is in the gap [or: slippage, *faille*] [between exchange value and use value] that what is known as surplus value arises and falls away. The only thing of importance to us here is this loss. No longer identical to himself, the subject no longer enjoys. Something is lost that is known as surplus jouissance. It is strictly correlated with the coming into play of what henceforth determines everything about thought.

It is no different when it comes to symptoms. What is at stake in symptoms if not the greater or lesser ease with which the subject revolves around something that we call surplus jouissance, but that he is quite incapable of naming? Unless he goes around it, he cannot proceed to do anything involving not only his relationships with his fellow men, but even his most profound relationship, the one with life itself [*vitale*]. Economic references and configurations are all the more serendipitous than those Freud had at his disposal from the realm of thermodynamics, which were more remote in this case, although not entirely unsuitable.

This is thus the element that can allow us to make headway in analytic discourse. In the definition of the subject as caused by the relationship between signifiers, we have theoretically posited – *a priori* and without any need for a long recursion in order to consti- 22
tute its premises – something that prohibits us from ever grasping him.

This is also the occasion to perceive what gives the subject the unity – let us provisionally call it preconscious, not unconscious – that has heretofore allowed us to consider him to supposedly have everything he needs [or: to supposedly suffice unto himself, to supposedly be self-contained, *prétendue suffisance*]. Far from that being the case, it is around the formula ($ ◊ a) – that is, around the being of *a*, of surplus jouissance – that a relationship is constituted that, up to a certain point, allows us to see a soldering occur: that precipitation or congealing which is such that we can unify a subject as the subject of an entire discourse.

I will put on the board a schema that illustrates what is involved here.

The first formula indicates that a signifier, S_1, represents the subject – barred S, who can never but elude himself [or: never be able to grab hold of himself, *qui jamais ne saura se saisir*] – to another signifier, S_2.

$$\frac{S_1}{\$} \rightarrow S_2$$

The second formula indicates that any signifier in the chain, in this case S_3, can be (cor)related to something that is still merely an object, little *a*, which is created [or: manufactured, *se fabrique*] in the relationship to surplus jouissance.

$$S_3 ◊ a$$

By entering into the workings of the organism, the object is able to take the shape of those vanishing entities whose list I have already provided, which runs the gamut from the breast to feces, and from the voice to the gaze. These are all created by the discourse concerning the renunciation of jouissance. The mainspring of this creation is the fact that surplus jouissance can be produced around them.

As I already told you regarding Pascal's wager: even if there were only one single life beyond death that we could win by wagering, we would have to work enough in this life to know how to conduct ourselves in the next.

The mainspring of this work – like the exchange to which the wager proceeds with something we would (like to) know is worthwhile – is a function which is correlated with surplus jouissance and which is that of the market. It is at the very basis of the idea Pascal explored, with the extraordinary blindness, it seems, of someone who lived at a time when the market function first began to skyrocket. Although he inaugurated scientific discourse, let us not forget that he also – even at the most extreme moments of his retreat and his conversion – wanted to found a company of Parisian omnibuses. Pascal knew not what he was saying when he spoke of a happy life, but we see its incarnation here. What else can be grasped in the term "happy" if not the very function that is incarnated in surplus jouissance?

We thus have no need to wager about the next life to know what it is worth where surplus jouissance shows itself nakedly. This has a name: perversion. And this is why holy women have perverted sons. There is no need for the next life for the transmission of an essential play of discourse to occur between such a woman and her son.

The following schema allows us to conceptualize how what is involved in the production of *a* plays out [*se joue*] in fantasy.

$$\frac{\$}{a} \qquad \frac{\$ \lozenge (\$ \lozenge (\$ \lozenge a))}{a}$$

The reiteration of the signifier that represents the subject, barred S, in relation to himself, is correlated with *a*, which is placed below the bar here. Inversely, the relationship between the subject and the object thereby takes on consistency in ($ \lozenge a$), in which something arises which is no longer either subject or object, but which is known as fantasy. The other signifiers – forming a chain, linking up, and thereby congealing in the effect of signification – can introduce metonymy as an effect that solders the subject together.

For example, in the sentence "a child is being beaten" [or: someone is beating a child, *on bat un enfant*] – whether the subject is situated in the moment of "a child," of "being beaten," or of "someone" [*on*] – the subject becomes something equivalent, a unified [*solidaire*] being to which we are inclined to give an all-purpose image in discourse, as if there could be a subject of all signifiers.

If, owing to the fundamental rule of psychoanalysis, something can be sufficiently loosened up in this chain so that revelatory effects occur, how can we characterize this fact so as to give it its full import? In order to provide an image for the appearance of truth in analytic experience, I characterized it with a mythical "I am speaking" [or: "I speak," *Je parle*]. It is the ideal (one), no doubt, but we must now understand that the truth thus brought out is taken up and suspended between the two registers that I am adumbrating as limits in the title of my Seminar this year: the Other and little *a*.   24

What is the Other? It is the field of truth that I defined as the locus in which the subject's discourse takes on consistency and in which it is proffered in order to offer itself up to be refuted or not. The problem arose for Descartes to know whether there is or is not a God who guarantees this field. Today this problem has totally evaporated, owing to the fact that there is no possibility of a totally consistent discourse in the field of the Other.

Please excuse me for not having time to demonstrate it today. Let it suffice for me to indicate that it is demonstrable. I hope to explain it to you next time, especially as related to the subject's existence. It is a demonstration that I already once very quickly wrote on the board. It is easily found in the first chapter of [any book on] what is known as set theory. Yet it will be necessary, at least for some of you here, to demonstrate in what way it is relevant – in the elucidation of the function of our discourse as analysts – to present a function that is extracted from a logic that one would be mistaken to believe that to call it mathematical is to exclude it and consign it to the next classroom over.

If the consistency of what is known as truth cannot be assured anywhere in the Other, where then is truth if not in what *a*'s function assures [*en réponde*]? On another occasion, I thus already laid out the status of truth's cry.

"I, the truth," I wrote, "speak" [or: "am speaking," *parle*]. And I do so purely to embarrass you. This is what truth can say to move us. But this is not what someone suffering cries out, because he *is* that truth. The latter must know that his cry is but a silent cry, a cry in a vacuum, a cry that I once illustrated using Munch's famous engraving [*The Scream*; see Seminar XII, class given on March 17, 1965].

What in the Other can respond to the subject at this level? Nothing other than what constitutes his consistency and his naïve faith in what he is as an ego. Namely, his true stay: his creation [*fabrication*] as object *a*. The only thing across from the subject is the one-extra [*l'un-en-plus*] among so many others, who can in no way answer truth's cry, if not to say that it is quite precisely its equivalent: non-jouissance, misery, distress, and solitude. Such is *a*'s counterpart, the counterpart of the surplus jouissance that constitutes the subject's coherence qua ego.

25   There is nothing to add – unless I wish to leave you today on a lighter note, and in order to do so I mention the words of an old king from Ecclesiastes, a king who saw no contradiction between being the king of wisdom and having a harem.

All is undoubtedly vanity, he tells us, so enjoy the woman you love. In other words, make a ring of the hollow or emptiness that is at the center of your being. There is no neighbor if it is not the very hollow that is in you, your own emptiness.

This relationship is assuredly guaranteed solely by the figure that undoubtedly allowed Freud to make his way down this perilous path, enabling us to clarify relations that could not have otherwise been bearable without this myth, divine Law, that leaves the jouissance between man and woman in its entirely primitive state. We must say the following: "Give her what you do not have, because the only thing that can unite you with her is her jouissance."

It is on that note – a simple, total, religious enigma akin to what is broached only in the Kabbalah – that I will release you today [literally: certify your account books today, *je vous donne quitus*].

November 13, 1968

THE INCONSISTENCY
OF THE OTHER

THE KNOWLEDGE MARKET
AND TRUTH (ON) STRIKE

Structure is real(ity)
On a discourse that has an impact
Language and logic
The worker's frustration
Renouncing jouissance

Last time, which was a premiere, I referred to Marx by introducing a new notion alongside that of surplus value.

I first presented the relationship between the two notions as "homologous," with all the reservations this term brings with it.

Surplus value is called *Mehrwert* in the language in which it was, not named for the first time, but in which its essential function was first discovered.

I have written the word on the board, for Lord only knows what would happen if I merely pronounced it here, given my audience, especially the psychoanalysts among them, being recruited among what are known as double agents, whether by nature or heredity. I would soon hear it said that I had talked about the "green mother" [*mère verte*] and that I was reverting to well-trodden paths. After all, some people use my phrase "It is speaking" [*ça parle*] as though it referred to the subject's supposedly obstinate desire to return to the comfort of his mother's womb!

I thus attached, superimposed, and plastered the notion of surplus jouissance [*plus-de-jouir*] onto the flipside of surplus value.

Plus-de-jouir is the way it was put in the language in which it was said for the first time – in other words, in French – at the last class. To put it in the language that inspired me to coin it, I would call it *Mehrlust*, assuming no Germanist in the audience objects.

Naturally, I did not proffer this term without discreetly referring, allusively as I sometimes do, to the person whose research and thought led me to it – and why wouldn't it have? – namely, Althusser.

As typically happens, in the hours that followed, people chattered about it in the cafés in which they gather to chew the fat regarding what is said here. You can't imagine how flattered I am, even thrilled. In truth, I don't disavow what was said on that occasion, since I began my class last time by mentioning the rubblication or publitrashing [*poubellicant ou poubellicatoire*] factor, however you'd like to call it, of structuralism.

I alluded to the fact that, according to the latest news, Althusser is not all that comfortable with [the label of] structuralism. And I simply pointed out that, regardless of what he does or doesn't accept, it seems quite clear to whoever reads his work that his discourse makes Marx into a structuralist, and specifically in the sense that he underscores Marx's seriousness.

You would be wrong to believe that the feeling, of whatever type, that rallying around a flag may give rise to [in someone] is what is essential here.

I would like to return to structure.

1

Structure should be taken in the sense in which it is most real, in which it is reality [*réel*] itself.

That, at least, is what I say, and what I have highlighted on other occasions. When I have drawn topological schemas on the board and even manipulated them, I have underscored the fact that I was not in any sense speaking metaphorically.

Only one of the following two things can be true: either what we are talking about in no wise exists, or, if the subject – such as I am describing him – exists, he is constituted precisely like the things I put on the board. On the condition, that is, that you understand that these little images, which are all one can use to represent him on a page, are designed only to illustrate certain connections that cannot be pictured, but that can be written without any problem.

Structure is thus real. This is generally determined by convergence toward an impossibility. Which is why it is real.

I am talking about structure today solely because I am forced to by the café gossip, but I shouldn't have to talk about it, since I say it. What I say establishes [or: lays out, *pose*] structure because it aims at the cause of discourse itself, as I said last time.

Implicitly, and like anyone who teaches, wanting to serve that function, I defy, in theory, anyone to refute me by a discourse which accounts for discourse otherwise than I have just done – namely, and I am repeating this for the deaf, that what discourse aims at is the cause of discourse itself.

People are free to account for discourse otherwise – for example, as expression or as a relationship to content for which one invents a form. But I would then point out that it would be unthinkable to situate psychoanalytic practice in it in any way whatsoever, even as charlatanism. It should be understood that what is at stake is whether or not psychoanalysis exists.

But, on the other hand, there is something by which psychoanalysis indisputably asserts itself. For it is a symptom of the point in time we have arrived at in what I will provisionally call civilization.

This is no joke. I am not talking about culture. Civilization is far more vast. It is, moreover, merely a matter of convention. We will try to situate culture in the current use people make of the term at a certain level that I will call "commercial."

Let us return to my discourse, and to what I mean by a discourse that is worthwhile. To employ a metaphor that I have used several times to get my point across, I will compare discourse to a cut made by scissors in the material I talk about when I speak about the subject as real [or: about the reality of the subject, *le réel du sujet*].

Owing to the way in which the scissors cut into structure, the latter is revealed for what it is. If the scissors cut one way, relationships change, such that what couldn't be seen beforehand can be seen afterward. Although saying that it is not a metaphor, I illustrated this cut using a Möbius strip; I cut it in such a way that it turned into a strip that was nothing like what it had been before. The next step we need to take is to realize, on the basis of this transformation, that the whole of the Möbius strip resides in the cut.

This is a way of employing as little metaphor as possible. Let us say that, in theory, there is no point talking about anything other than the reality [*réel*] on which discourse itself has an impact. Call that structuralism – or not. It's what I called the condition of seriousness last time.

This condition can be required especially in a technique, that of   32
psychoanalysis, that claims that, in it, discourse has an impact, since the patient submits in an artificially defined way to a certain rule-bound discourse solely in order that it have an impact.

Nothing can prevail against this, and certainly not remarks claiming that I neglect the energetic dimension, a claim found in books whose very text is cobbled together from [*raclé de*] my own discourse. I pay no attention to such things when they are polemical. But we find ourselves here at the heart of the subject, since, as I pointed out last time, I replaced this rousing reference to energetics

– rousing above all to those who don't even know what it means –
with a reference to political economy, which in our times can hardly
be accused of being less materialist.

But let us not disdain energetics here. If we apply what I just said,
in order for energetics to be related to our field, discourse would
have to have an impact on it. And it does. I'm talking about true
energetics and physics inasmuch as it plays a role in science.

Long before such laughable objections were published, I had
highlighted – in classes the parties involved may well have attended,
since they made use of them later in their own lectures – the fact that
energetics is only conceivable as a consequence of discourse. It is not
because it falls under the heading of physics that it isn't clear that
there is no way to begin to formulate the principle of all energetics,
in the literal sense of the term – namely, the reference to a constant,
which is precisely what is known as energy, with respect to a closed
system, which is another essential hypothesis – unless one plots with
signifiers the ranges and levels with respect to which the initial function of work, as understood in physics, can be assessed. The fact
that, with that, one can create a physics that functions is the proof
that a discourse can have consequences.

This simultaneously means that physics implies the existence
of a physicist. And not just any old physicist, but a physicist who
employs the right discourse, in the sense in which I just articulated
it – in other words, a discourse that is worth proffering and that is
not merely a heartbeat, like energetics becomes when it is used as
delusionally and ridiculously as it is when people turn the notion of
libido into a life drive.

To say that there is no physics without a physicist is not to ground
it on an idealist postulate. I hope that no one here would formulate
that objection, which would be rather farcical in the context of what
I just stated, since I am in the process of saying that it is physics
as a discourse that determines the physicist and not the other way
around. There were no true physicists until this discourse came to
the fore.

This is the meaning I attribute to the kind of discourse that is
acceptable in science.

Except that there is, of course, the realist argument. It seems irre-
sistible to imagine that nature is always there, whether we are there
or not, we and our science, as if our science were our own and we
were not determined by it.

I am absolutely not debating that. Nature is there. What differentiates it from physics is that physics is worth talking about,
discourse has an impact on it, whereas, as everyone knows, no discourse has any effect on nature, which explains why we love it so.

Being a natural philosopher has never, at any time, guaranteed that one was a materialist, or scientific either.

But if physics clearly gives us a model of a discourse that is worthwhile, the necessities of our discourse must be traced further back.

2

Every discourse presents itself as chock-full of consequences, consequences that are obscure. In theory, nothing we say fails to entail consequences. Yet we don't know which ones.

I will take things up again at the level of language in order to clearly designate the limits.

We find in language a syntax incarnated by a large number of languages that, owing to a lack of audacity, we call "positive" languages. Since I just made a comment about nature that I suspect probably did not appear irrelevant to you, why not call them "natural" languages? This would allow us to see what linguistics involves more clearly, and what allows us to situate linguistics within scientific discourse.

Whatever priority we grant language because we forget that it is a natural reality, every scientific discourse on language begins by eliminating its material(ity) [or: paring down its matter, *réduction de son matériel*].

We thereby highlight a functioning in which consequences are grasped – I would go even further, in which the very notion of consequences is grasped, with its varieties, the necessary and the contingent, for example.

By eliminating its matter, we bring about a discursive split. This is what makes what I first assert worthwhile – namely, that there's no such thing as a metalanguage, which is true in the field of natural language.

Why do people eliminate its matter? As I just told you, it is in order to highlight a functioning in which consequences are grasped. Once you grasp the consequences, you articulate them in something that you have every right to consider to be a metalanguage – apart from the fact that "meta" can only lead to confusion. This is why I preferred to confine myself to saying that detaching, in discourse, what must be called by its rightful name, logic, is always conditioned by an elimination of matter and by nothing else.

Without going any further into this, I will illustrate it for you. Eliminating material means that logic began at the precise moment in history at which someone deliberately substituted a simple letter for certain linguistic elements functioning in their natural syntax.

34

That inaugurated logic. It was when someone introduced an A and a B into an "if this, then that" sentence that logic began. It was only from that point on that one could posit a certain number of axioms and laws of deduction regarding the use of A and B which deserve to be called "meta-linguistic," or if you prefer "para-linguistic," articulations.

Thus, just as there is no physics that extends, like God's goodness, to all of nature, there is no logic that encompasses all of language.

The fact remains that it is either a delusion and absurd madness to pay even the slightest attention to psychoanalysis, or what it enunciates is that everything you are – including what you are qua feeling and not just thinking, and there is no reason to despise this term (for is thinking the exclusive privilege of intellectualistic intellectuals who, as everyone knows, are the scourge of our lowly world and above all of our sorry psychoanalytic world?) – falls under the consequences of discourse.

35

Even your death, I mean the paltry [or: insignificant, *falote*] idea you may have of it, is inseparable from what you can say it to be – and I don't mean "say it naïvely." Even the idea you have of your death, which I called "paltry" because it doesn't have much weight to you, is inseparable from the maximal discourse you can construct about it. This is why the feeling you can have about your death cannot but be paltry.

You cannot even begin to speak about your death naïvely. I am not alluding here to the fact that primitive peoples are thought to be naïve and that's why they talk about death in such a funny way. The fact that to them death is always due to some mischief [or: scam, *truc*], a poisoning, a spell that has been cast, or something that is out of whack – in short, accidental – in no way proves that they talk about it naïvely. You think it's naïve? It's just the opposite. And this is why they are subject to the same law – namely, that the feeling they have about their death is inseparable from what they can say about it. QED.

Someone – among those who could learn a bit here and stop talking nonsense – left earlier because he thinks I am uttering banalities. But they must be necessary to say, otherwise why would I take the trouble, after everything I just said about the fact that a discourse either has an impact or it doesn't? The impact of my discourse, in any case, is that he walked out, which is telling.

This is clearly why it is essential that we analysts have a few people trained in what is known, for some reason, as "mathematical logic."

The name denotes an old discomfort. As if there were any other kind of logic! Mathematical logic is logic *tout court*. It turns out to be of interest to mathematicians, and that distinguishes it from Aristotelian logic which, obviously, did not interest mathematicians much. The fact that it interests mathematicians constituted progress in logic, of course. To call a spade a spade, mathematical logic is altogether essential to your existence in reality, whether you know it or not.

It is precisely because you don't really know it that things happen from time to time that shake things up – I am referring to recent things [the May 1968 uprising]. People expect me to talk about them. I will talk about them, I will talk about them. It all depends on how long it takes me to lay out what I have prepared for you today. I would like to reach a little climax before leaving you, but it's not clear I will because what I bring you here is never very precisely timed. 36

That is not the point. Whether you know it or not, I obviously just alluded to the fact, since . . . [text missing?] I said, "Whether you know it or not." The bizarre question that arises here is whether mathematical logic has always had the consequences on your existence as a subject that I just said it has, whether you know it or not. How could that be the case before the kind of logic known as mathematical logic made its appearance in the world? This is the question whether God exists.

I already pointed this out, but I will repeat it, as one can never repeat oneself too often. Was mathematical logic in God's mind before you were affected by it in your existence as a subject, meaning that your existence was already conditioned by it?

The problem is important because it is here that we take the step forward that consists in realizing that a discourse has an impact. Something must have already verged on the effects of discourse before the discourse of mathematical logic could be born. In any case, even if we can already locate, in our existence as a subject, something that we can retroactively attach to some effect of logical discourse in this existence, it is clear and must be firmly kept in mind that these are not the same consequences as those that have manifested themselves since the discourse of mathematical logic was proffered.

The necessary and the contingent are situated in the discourse that is in fact proffered.

This is why I cannot see how referring to structure means that we supposedly overlook the dimension of history.

3

It simply depends on the kind of history we are talking about.

History as it is included in historical materialism seems to me in strict accordance with structural requirements.

Did surplus value exist before abstract labor [or: work, *travail*] – by which I mean the kind of labor from which this abstraction was isolated as a social average [or: common denominator] – arose owing to what I will call the "absolutization" of the market? I won't guarantee the accuracy of the word, but I wanted to proffer a word that packs a punch.

It is highly probable that the absolutization of the market was a precondition for the appearance of "surplus value" in discourse. The absolutization of the market is difficult to separate from the development of certain linguistic effects, which is why I introduced "surplus jouissance." It took the absolutization of the market, which went so far as to encompass labor itself, for surplus value to be defined as follows.

We pay for labor with money, since we are in a market [economy]. We pay its true price, as defined on the open market by the function of exchange value. There is nevertheless value that is not paid for in what appears as the fruit of labor, for the true price of this fruit resides in its use value. This unpaid labor – although it is remunerated fairly according to the consistency of the market in the functioning of the capitalist subject – is surplus value.

Surplus value is thus the fruit of the means of articulation that constitute capitalist discourse. This is what results from capitalist logic.

Now, articulated in this way, this discourse leads to a certain position of the "I" in the system. When this "I" is in the place of the worker, which is ever more generally the case, the position implies demanding something related to the worker's frustration, in quotes.

It is strange, it must be said, that the one leads to the other, for it merely involves the consequences of a perfectly well-defined discourse in which the worker inscribes himself qua "I." I am saying "I." Note that I did not say "subject," whereas I mentioned the capitalist subject.

I am proceeding slowly. We will meet again, I hope, apart from those who leave in the middle of class, and you will see that it is no accident that I said "subject" in one case and "I" in the other. We will see this again at a certain level, which you should have long since been aware of because it is a level of my graph of desire. I constructed it over ten years ago before an audience of asses. They still haven't figured out where *I* is located on the graph. I really must explain it to them. In order to do so, I must prepare. We are plowing [the fields] here. It is hard work. Let us hope that, before the end, I will be able to tell you how work is situated in the teacher's discourse.

It is thus strange and interesting that this leads to the idea of frustration, with the demands that stem therefrom, and the little reconstructions that are characterized as "revolutions." I cannot fail to mention now that the dimension introduced at this precise point is conflictual.

I said that it was strange and interesting, which should at least incite you to recognize this dimension, shouldn't it? It is difficult to designate it in any other way than with the words "strange" and "interesting," but "strange" is a word that points to truth.

Truth cannot be grasped right off the bat. I already presented it once in its junction with knowledge, a junction whose topology I tried to sketch out because it is difficult to talk about anything whatsoever in psychoanalysis without presenting it. This clearly indicates how prudent one must be, for Lord knows what sort of idiocies I've heard circulating on the topic. We are going to try to zero in on this junction a bit more closely.

Let us begin with the fact that capitalist reality doesn't have such a bad relationship with science. It adjusts to it quite well. And it seems like it could go on functioning like that for at least a while.

I said "reality," not "the real." I also spoke about what has been constructed on the basis of the capitalist subject, about what has been generated at the level of the fundamentally integrated demand for the recognition of surplus value – otherwise Marx's discourse has no meaning – and about what constitutes the specifically scientific impact on something having to do with the subject.

Capitalist reality thus adapts quite well to science, at a certain level at least. People put objects into orbit that are quite well made and even inhabitable.

On the other hand, at the closest level – the one where revolution and the political forms it gives rise to are sparked – it is not clear that something has been entirely resolved at the level of the frustration I designated as being the level of a truth.

The worker is undoubtedly the sacred site of the conceptual element that constitutes the truth of the system, and that emerges when knowledge – which holds together all the more perfectly because it is identical to its own percept in being [*son propre perçu dans l'être*] – rips apart somewhere. Let us thus take a step that is permitted by the fact that we are undoubtedly dealing with the same substance here. Let us see what this structural fabric feels like, and cut it with our scissors.

39

It involves knowledge. It is in relation to knowledge, in its scientific form, that I just prudently assessed the status of relations between two realities that are opposed in our political world.

Although earlier it may have seemed that I began my discourse with it, knowledge is not work. It may at times be acquired by working, but it can also be handed to you on a silver platter. Knowledge is ultimately what we call the price [or: prize, *prix*]. The price is sometimes incarnated in money, but knowledge, too, is worth money – indeed, ever more money. This is what should tip us off. This price is the price of what? It is clear – it is the price paid for renouncing jouissance.

It is by giving up jouissance at the outset that we begin to know a little bit about it, without there being any need for work to do so. It is not because work involves renouncing jouissance that every renunciation of jouissance is accomplished solely through work.

You have an epiphany that allows you to hold yourself back or contain yourself. I alluded to this last time in order to define thought. If you stop to think for a spell, you can perceive, for example, that woman does not live on bread alone, but also lives on your castration, assuming you're male. Knowing that, you will live your life more sure-footedly. It has use value.

Knowledge has nothing to do with work. But in order for something to be clarified here, there must be a market, a market of knowledge. Knowledge must become a commodity. This is happening all too quickly, and we had no clue about it before. We should at least have had an inkling about it when we saw the form that things were taking, and the free-for-all that has been occurring for some time at universities.

40   There are things I have spoken about in passing, from other perspectives. For example, that there's no such thing as intellectual property, which doesn't mean there's no such thing as theft. This is even how property begins [see Proudhon's 1840 book *What is Property?*]. All of that is very complicated, as it only began, naturally, when people began to be paid to give lectures abroad. I mean to say that foreigners started paying people to give them. And you see, this is beginning even in France. So now one can award a Make-Me-Sick [*Haut-le-Coeur*] Prize, as I once dubbed it in a small circle of friends, to whomever manages to command the highest speaker fees.

But this is merely anecdotal. Knowledge does not form a market owing to men's corruption or imbecility. It has long been known that the Sorbonne is the epicenter of this sort of negative quality or weakness. This has been known throughout history. In Rabelais' time, they were already bastards, just as they were at the time of the

Jansenists. It never fails – they are always on the right side, in other words, on the wrong side.

There's nothing new about that. I tried to locate the root of what people ridiculously call the "events" [a reference to May 1968]. There are no events to be found here. But I will explain that to you another time.

The very process by which science becomes unified, insofar as it is grounded in a consistent discourse, reduces all fields of knowledge [*tous les savoirs*] to a single market. This is the central reference for us here. It allows us to conceptualize how there can be something which – while paid for at its true price as knowledge according to the norms that are constituted on the basis of the science market – is nevertheless obtained for free. It is what I called surplus jouissance.

Owing to knowledge, we finally perceive that jouissance is organized and can be established as sought after and perverse. This is not new, but it is only revealed on the basis of the homogenization of fields of knowledge on the open market.

What thus represents here the discontent in civilization, as it is put? It is a surplus jouissance obtained by renouncing jouissance, the principle of the value of knowledge being respected.

Is knowledge a commodity [*bien*]? The question arises because its correlate is the following: *non licet omnibus*, as I already said, *adire Corinthum* [not everyone can go to Corinth]. Not everyone has access to surplus jouissance.

What is or isn't paid for in this context? Labor, as we saw earlier. But what is involved here? What I pointed out earlier as regards what arises that is conflictual in the function of surplus value puts us on the scent. It is what I already called truth.

The symptom is the way each person suffers in his relationship to jouissance, because he thrusts himself into it [*s'y insert*] via the function of surplus jouissance – the symptom appearing on the basis of the fact that there is no longer anything but an average, abstract social truth.

This is what results from the fact that knowledge is undoubtedly always paid for at its true price, but below the use value that this truth generates – for others than those who are in the right, as always. It thus entails the function of surplus jouissance. And this *Mehrlust* mocks us, because we don't know where it is hiding.

Which is why your daughter is mute, my dear friends. This is why the shit hit the fan in May [1968].

It was a grand *prise de parole* [speaking out or taking the floor], as it was put by someone who has a non-negligible place in my field. *Prise de parole*? I think we would be wrong to consider this *prise* homologous to any sort of taking [or: storming, *prise*] of the Bastille

41

[during the French Revolution]. More like a pinch [*prise*] of tobacco or taking drugs, in my view.

It was the truth that positively manifested itself on that occasion. A collective truth, but in the sense in which a [general] strike seemed quite consonant with this truth.

A strike is just the kind of relationship that welds the collective to labor. Indeed, it is the only one that does so. We would be quite mistaken to believe that a guy who works on an assembly line is working collectively. He is the one who is doing the work, all the same. In a strike, work's collective truth manifests itself. But what we saw in May was a truth strike.

There, too, the relationship to truth was obvious. The truth was scrawled on the walls. You should naturally recall something I had fortunately pointed to three months earlier: the truth of idiocy [*connerie*] is not without raising the question of the idiocy of truth.

There were even idiocies that one might have thought came from Lacan's discourse. They were almost identical. It was accidental, of course. It was obviously based on the fact that when you take things out of context, they may be true, but they may also sound idiotic. Which is why I prefer a discourse without speech.

42   The strange thing was what we saw by way of a passionate questioning, the questioning that arose in the soul of someone I will call – I will sketch him out for you – the communist clergyman, he whose goodness knows no bounds in nature either. We can expect to receive moral commentary from him, the kind that comes with age.

I gave one of them the name Mudger Muddle. I coined the moniker myself. It evokes a crocodile wallowing in the mud, and the fact that, with a delicate tear, he draws you into his well-meaning world. I met Mudger Muddle on the sidewalk of the boulevard Saint-Germain [in Paris]. He told me he was searching for Marxist theory and that he was inundated by the happiness all of that exuded. But it didn't occur to him that happiness can come from a truth strike. Given how heavily truth weighs on us at every instant of our existence, how happy we would be to no longer have any other relationship with truth than a collective one!

The truths that were scrawled on the walls were sometimes idiotic, as I mentioned. No one notices that they are in my discourse, too. That's because in mine they are frightening. On the walls, they were frightening too. So much idiocy gives rise to unparalleled fear. When collective truth comes out, we realize that all discourse can go down the drain. Since then, things have fallen back into place somewhat. But they are simmering. That's why capital has been fleeing the country.

Since I have taken the risk today of providing my own interpretation of what people call the "events," I would like to tell you: "Don't believe that this has put an end to the process." It is out of the question, for the time being, that the knowledge market will dry up. You yourselves will act in such a way that it will be established ever more solidly. Course credits [*unités de valeur*], those new little sheepskins they want to award you, [will ensure] that. They are the sign of what knowledge will progressively become in the market known as the university system. Truth may have spasmodic functions there, but it won't settle [*réglera*] your existence qua subject for each of you.

As I reminded you last time, I was very kind to truth in an article I wrote ["The Freudian Thing"]. I had it make the most intelligent remarks I could attribute to it, borrowing them from what I say when I do not speak the truth. In other words, no discourse can speak the truth. A discourse that holds up [*tient*] is one that can hold up rather a long time without you having to ask it to account for its truth.

Wait with your backs to the wall to combat those who will present themselves saying, "You know, don't you, that you can't say anything about psychoanalysis." That is not the tenor of what you should demand if you want to master the world with the value known as knowledge. If a discourse dodges the question, there is only one thing for you to do: ask it to explain why. A discourse that does not explain itself is a vain discourse.

Don't believe that the fact of saying that "all is vanity," which is what I left you with last time, is anything other than a lure, one with which, as I told you, I wanted to let you leave with your souls at peace until we met again.

The discourse I am proffering will lead us together to turn next time to those who, right from the very outset, posit the essential vanity of all discourse.

November 20, 1968

III

TOPOLOGY OF THE OTHER

Ordered pairs

Last time, we arrived at a point about which I must provide a few clarifications that I will call topological.

I am not taking up topology for the first time here, but I must link it to what I have introduced this year in a form that designates the relationship of knowledge to something that is certainly more mysterious, albeit more fundamental. The danger is that it be taken as the function of a content [*fond*] in relation to the field of a form, whereas it involves something quite different.

Namely, jouissance.

1

It is only too clear that jouissance constitutes the substance of everything we talk about in psychoanalysis.

Jouissance has such an import here that it allows us to introduce the strictly structural function of surplus jouissance. This is why it is not formless.

I presented surplus jouissance in my recent classes as homologous to Marx's surplus value. To say "homologous" is clearly to say that they are not analogous. They are the same. They are cut from the same cloth, insofar as what is involved is the cut made by the scissors of discourse.

Everyone who has been attending this Seminar for some time realizes that the relationship between surplus jouissance and surplus value revolves around the function of object *a*.

I invented object *a*, in a certain sense, just as one can say that Marx's discourse invented things. What does that mean? What Marx discovered was surplus value. We can't say that object *a* had never been broached before my own discourse did so, of course, but it was broached in a frankly inadequate way, as inadequate as was the definition of surplus value before Marx's discourse rigorously highlighted it.

The point is not to underscore their equivalence as discoveries, but rather to raise the question of what the discovery itself allows us to think, if I define it first and foremost as the *effect* of a discourse – for we are not talking about theory here, in the sense in which it covers something that becomes apparent at a given moment in time.

Object *a* is an effect of analytic discourse, and in this respect what I say about it is nothing but this very effect. Does this imply that it is merely an artifice created by analytic discourse? That is the question I am asking, and it is consistent with the deepest aspect of the question I am raising about the analyst's function.

There would be no analytic discourse, nor any revelation of the function of object *a*, were the analyst himself not this effect. I would go even further: were the analyst himself not the symptom that results from the historical impact of a transformation of the relationship between knowledge – insofar as it determines the subject's position – and jouissance as an enigmatic content [or: backdrop, *fond*]. The question of artifice is modified, held in abeyance, and mediated by the fact that what was discovered in an effect of discourse already appeared as the effect of discourse in history.

In other words, psychoanalysis only appeared qua symptom because a turning point regarding knowledge in history – I am not saying in the history of knowledge – or regarding the impact of knowledge in [the course of] history, was reached. That turning point distilled out, as it were, the function defined by object *a* in order to offer it up to us, in order to place it within our grasp.

My Italian translator – whom I will not embarrass if I speak about her, since she missed her plane this morning and is not here today – is the only one who clearly realized, a while ago already, that the function of surplus value was identical to that of object *a*. Why didn't more people realize it, unless they did so without telling me? It's strange.

What is strange is tempered, of course, when we grasp, in the heat of the moment, as I do – it is my fate – the difficulty of making headway in analytic discourse, resistance increasing the further we go.

My Italian translator's realization was all the more striking because it occurred to someone who is from a much younger generation. Isn't it odd that I can frequently touch all the more easily and have effortless exchanges with those in the next generation, whose average age, which I quickly calculated, is roughly 24?

I certainly won't say that this is an effect of my discourse, but an effect of the growing difficulty generated by what I called the absolutization of the knowledge market.

I wouldn't say that, at 24, everyone is Lacanian. But it is clear that none of the difficulties I encountered over the years in conveying my discourse occur, at least not in the same place, when I am dealing with those who – not even being psychoanalysts – approach problems of knowledge from the most modern angle and who are, let us say, somewhat open to the field of logic.

This generation has set about studying my *Écrits*, obtaining diplomas and writing dissertations about them. In short, my writings have been put to the test of academic transmission. I have heard about this and have already seen the fruits of their labors. Thus I have recently noted, not that I was surprised by this, the difficulty these young authors have extracting from my *Écrits* a formulation that is acceptable and classifiable in what academia offers them by way of categories.

What certainly escapes them most in my *Écrits* is precisely what constitutes their weight and crux, which undoubtedly holds the attention of my readers, who are so surprisingly numerous. Namely, the dimension of work that is represented in them. I mean that each of those writings represents something that I had to move, push, and haul away, from the standpoint of resistance.

That resistance was not individual in nature. It concerned the very existence of generations.

When I first began to teach, my audience, caught up in a relationship to knowledge that was a relationship that was giving way, came from an older generation than today, and turned out to be already trained in all sorts of ways. Nothing was more difficult than to situate them at the level of this announcing and denouncing experience that is psychoanalysis. This is why I articulate what I am trying to articulate today in the hope that the younger generations who lend me their ears will encounter what, in fact, presents itself as a discourse.

Let us not, however, expect in any way that the discourse unfolding here will turn into a staking out of a position that is removed from what truly operates in the progress of analytic discourse. What I say about the subject as the effect of discourse completely rules out the possibility of my discourse constituting a system. On the contrary, what makes this discourse difficult is that it must indicate, by its very way of proceeding, how it is itself commanded; it must indicate – by subordinating the psychoanalytic subject, whom I am sustaining here – what commands it and concerns all knowledge.

As everyone knows, my position is identical in many ways to that of epistemology, as it is called. A question arises here that can be formulated as follows: What is the status of the desire that sustains, in the most hidden way imaginable, mathematical discourse – the discourse that is apparently the most abstract?

The difficulty is nevertheless of a totally different order at the level where I must situate myself. While we must hold in abeyance the question of what motivates mathematical discourse, it is nevertheless clear that each of its operations is designed to plug up, elide, sew up, and suture the question of desire at every moment. Recall the function of suture that we already discussed here, four years ago. What is involved, on the contrary, in analytic discourse is to give its full presence to the function of the subject – reversing the attempt to eliminate him that inhabits logical discourse – in order to perpetually center things on what constitutes a gap.

This is all the more problematic as we can in no way make up for this gap if not by artifice, and we must thus carefully indicate what we are doing when we allow ourselves to designate this lack, an effect of the signifierness [*signifiance*] of something which, claiming to signify it, cannot, by definition, be a signifier.

I use the symbol S(Å), the signifier of barred capital A, in order to designate this lack. As I have often said, this lack is a lack in the signifier. What does that mean? What does this lack in the signifier represent?

We can perfectly well admit that this lack is specific to our errant fate. But where we designate lack as such, it has always been the same. If there is thus something that ties us to history, it is to reckon how men have managed to fend it off for so long.

This is not the question that I wish to raise with you today. On the contrary, we are here to talk about topology, as I said.

49

2

If there is one formulation that I have insistently repeated recently, it is the one that roots the subject's determination in the fact that a signifier represents him to another signifier.

This formulation has the advantage of situating the subject in the simplest, most minimal link [or: connection, *connexion*] that can be posited, that between signifier 1 and signifier 2. On that basis, one can no longer lose sight of the subject's dependence for even a single instant.

The relationship between signifier 1 and signifier 2 will not fail to resonate for those who have some familiarity with what are known as "ordered pairs" in logic, [more specifically in] set theory.

One might hope that informed seminar participants are no longer rare here, and that it is important to provide this theoretical reference, even if, for the time being, I can merely mention it, with the understanding that I will comment on it later, should anyone ask me to.

What I refer to as my discourse didn't start yesterday, and our path this year, as I told you last time, leads us to the [cutting] edge of what I have already constructed, at the level of experience itself. I constructed it in the course of work which, I would say, consisted in bringing into my discourse, in this provocative "I am saying," those who were willing to overcome the obstacles they encountered owing to the fact that this discourse began at the heart of an institution [the Société Française de Psychanalyse] that was specifically designed to interrupt it.

I endeavored to construct this discourse in its fundamental relationship to knowledge in the form – that a number of those who opened my book found on a certain page [*Écrits*, p. 817] – designated by the name "graph [of desire]."

It has already been ten years since this work came to fruition in my Seminar on *Formations of the Unconscious* [Seminar V]. To clearly indicate how it arose, I would say that it began with a commentary on *Witz*, as Freud called it – in other words, jokes [or: puns].

In returning to the point at which I left things last time, I did not directly consult that Seminar, but rather the summary of it that was published in the *Bulletin de psychologie* [XI, 4–5, 1 (January 1958), pp. 293ff]. The summary is quite reliable, even if it isn't perfect, I must say. Without having to resort to unpublished notes, you can find proof there that things were already well situated in 1957/58, in the Seminar that followed the one I had given the year before on *The Relationship to the Object* [Seminar IV, *La relation d'objet*].

That period seems quite prehistoric with respect to the explicit emergence of object *a*. The latter was only prefigured at that time in the function of the metonymic object, but it was already clearly prefigured for anyone who heard what followed.

In the first section of the summary of that Seminar, which covers the classes given on November 6, 13, and 20, 1957, we find a first drawing that looks like this:

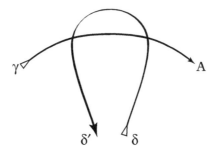

Figure 3.1: A First Sketch of the Graph of Desire

We have here a line that begins at δ and ends at δ'. It suffices to see how I drew the curve, with a little pyramid at the beginning, at δ, and an arrow at the other extremity, at δ', for it to be clear that the curve does not start at δ' and go in the opposite direction. But no matter. Apart from this detail, the summary is still of value.

For it shows that this first sketch of the graph functions in such a way as to depict [*inscrire*], as has become obvious since then, the status of a unit of the signifying chain, inasmuch as it only culminates where it intersects the intention – expressed in the future perfect tense – that determines it. If, starting here, something is established, which is, let us say, the want-to-say [or: mean-to-say, *vouloir-dire*], the discourse that will unfold will only culminate by meeting up with it – in other words, will only take on its full import in the way designated here, that is, retroactively.

One can thereby provide a first reading of A taken as the Other or locus of the code. A harbors the treasure trove of language that we must assume to already be there in order for elements to be intentionally extracted from it, elements that come to be written one after the other, unfolding in the form of a series – S_1, S_2, S_3, etc. – otherwise stated, in the form of a sentence that keeps looping back on itself until something is realized and closed therein.

What would have been more natural than to have articulated, if only dialectically, back then that this schema represented the signifier and the signified? After all, when I consider how long this march forward took, why wouldn't I tremble now at the thought that I had allowed myself to say something so dumb? Thankfully, I didn't, and we find, at the hand of the scribe who, despite his oversights, nevertheless clearly included what was essential at the time: "My schema represents, not the signifier and the signified, but two states of the signifier" [p. 520].

"The circuit" – I won't repeat how he states it, since he gets it backwards, but it is obviously this circuit here, δAγδ' – "represents the signifying chain insofar as it remains permeable to the effects of metaphor and metonymy. This is why I take it to be constituted at the level of phonemes. The second line" – the one that begins shy of γ and continues beyond A – "represents the circle of discourse, everyday discourse constituted by semantemes that obviously do not have a one-to-one correspondence to the signified, but are defined by usage."

You can sense how much this edifice, at the point at which I constructed it, was conditioned by the necessity of establishing the status of the forging of the word "famillionairely." It remained to be perceived that unconscious formations, insofar as they can at times produce puns, provide the most obvious access to the functioning of discourse. The word "famillionairely" could obviously be produced only because something that played out at the level of phonemes and something that fell within the ambit of the most everyday discourse intersected in a precise and structurally definable interference.

Who told the story in which the word first appeared [*Travel Pictures* (New York: Archipelago Books, 2008)]? It was essential that it not be Heinrich Heine. It was Hirsch Hyacinth, another H. H., who in speaking about Salomon Rothschild, intended to say that the man welcomed him in an altogether familiar way. That was how the word "familiarly" entered into the circle of discourse. But, adding phonemes to the word, Hirsch Hyacinth ended up saying that the man welcomed him "famillionairely." He thereby created a priceless formulation, which affects everyone. To put it simply, this familiarity had an aftertaste of millions, as Freud expressed himself somewhere, but no one laughed, for it was not a pun. Yet when it appeared in the form of "famillionairely," laughter ensued.

Let us inquire, all the same, why laughter didn't fail to ensue. It did not fail to ensue quite precisely because a subject was involved in it. But we still need to know where to situate him.

Freud articulated it. This subject always functions within a three-fold register. There is no such thing as a joke without the presence of a third party. A joke does not consist in something told by one interlocutor to another – namely, in the moment at which Hirsch Hyacinth told the story to his pal – but in the moment at which his pal finds himself elsewhere, about to tell the story to a third party. This triplicity is preserved when the third party, in turn, repeats the message [to a fourth]. In effect, the message only bears on the new listener to whom it is told, insofar as Hirsch Hyacinth, remaining alone, questions, from his position, the status [of he who tells the story to a new party].

What is the crux of this "famillionarity"? It will escape everyone who transmits it. It involves the precise innovation I introduced into our discourse and that I will not hesitate on this occasion to transplant into this field – namely, the capitalist subject.

What is the function of those who do not fit into the categories constituted by what is so inadequately captured by the notion of the exploitation of certain men by others – I mean those who are not located at one or the other of the two extremes of the chain of exploitation? What are they, if not employees? If this *Witz* makes people laugh, it is clearly because each of the interlocutors who meet up along the path of this pretty little joke consider themselves, without knowing it, to be concerned by it as employees, or, if you prefer, as part of the service sector.

It is not irrelevant that Heinrich Heine tells us he heard this from Hirsch Hyacinth, but let us not forget that, after all, if Hirsch Hyacinth existed, he was also Heinrich Heine's creation. I described his possible relations with the Baroness Betty [Salomon von Rothschild] in enough detail to be able to say that, if someone who hears what simply seems to be a pun or witticism laughs at it, it is insofar as he is fascinated by a certain form of wealth – and not just any old form – and by certain modes of its impact on a relationship that does not merely involve social oppression, for every subject has an interest in the knowledge that commands his position.

The reason I am reminding you of this structure is to highlight the rigorous way in which I laid out the circle of discourse, right from this first approximation concerning the subject's function. This paved the way for the true function of what completes it, namely the fact that nothing can be articulated about it unless it is provided with a second floor [or: second story, *deuxième étage*] – which only presents itself in this way, moreover, because of the two-dimensionality of paper (for one could also describe it the other way around [*à l'envers*]) – insofar as it is attached to the function of A that we must explore today.

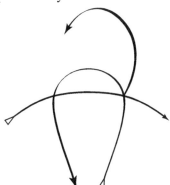

Figure 3.2: The Bait

We are interrogating the function of A because there is no part of discourse that does not in and of itself interrogate it, and I have said in what way – one that is so well articulated, so well brought out by analytic discourse itself – in the way I introduced the bait, so to speak, by clipping on to the simplified graph a question mark that rises above it. In referring to Jacques Cazotte's *The Devil in Love*, I termed it "*Che vuoi*? What does He want? What does the Other want? I wonder."

The twofold nature of the relationship to the Other is such that we split this line, a line which on the lower floor now presents itself as discourse, or to put it more purely, enunciation; the upper line is already constituted as demand, as the following figure shows:

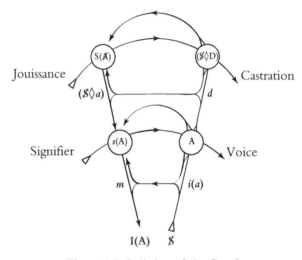

Figure 3.3: Splitting of the Graph

On the right, we find (S ◊ D), the barred subject placed in conjunction – a conjunction defined by what I provisionally called a "lozenge" – with articulated demand as such. On the left, homologously to the function $s(A)$ – in other words, to what is produced qua subject effect in enunciation – there is the index or indication S(Å).

I need not give this indication a first gloss, for I have already commented on it in several ways, but I must, rather, investigate it anew from the perspective I am introducing today. In order to do so, I must start from the point at which the subject is defined as being what one signifier represents to another signifier – namely, from the lowest level of what presents itself here as a ladder.

It is not simply by superimposing the imaginary on the symbolic that I indicated here, at $i(a)$, the image of a, the presence of the object that at the time I simply called the "metonymic object," in order to make it line up with something that is its image and reflection, namely *m*, the ego [*m* for *moi*, ego].

In a homologous position, we find the interrogating of the Other's desire, *d*(A), which is apparently the mainspring of imaginary identifications here. This is why I have used red chalk to draw it, but we will see that it, too, is articulated in a symbolic mode. Here, on the left, the formula of fantasy appeared for the first time, as you know, in the form ($ ◊ *a*).

It is now clear that the chain that travels backwards [δ → A → γ → δ'] is the signifying chain. This is so because A already contains the first articulation of the status of the signifier's function insofar as it determines the subject – namely, the relationship between signifier 1, S_1, and the minimal form that I called the ordered pair ($S_1 → S_2$), to which the statement that the signifier is what represents a subject to another signifier confines itself.

This other signifier, S_2, specifically represents knowledge in this fundamental link [*connexion*], insofar as it is the opaque term in which the subject manages to lose himself, as it were, or in which he is extinguished, something I have always termed "fading." In this genesis of the subject, knowledge initially presents itself as the endpoint at which the subject is extinguished.

This is the meaning of what Freud called *Urverdrängung* [primal repression], which is merely a supposed repression, for it is explicitly formulated as not being a repression, but as being a core that, even though it consists of knowledge, is already beyond the subject's reach. This is what the notion of *Urverdrängung* signifies, inasmuch as it makes it possible for an entire signifying chain to join up with it. This implies the following enigma, the following true *contradictio in adjecto*: the subject qua unconscious.

At this early, or sufficiently early, moment in the articulation of the [teaching] discourse that I find myself in the position of propping up in analytic experience, you see that I already asked who can say, "I say [or: I am saying]," at the level of discourse's unconscious formation, a pun in this case. This shows you that, right from the beginning of this [teaching] discourse, I laid out the precise distinction between discourse and speech that you find anew in the key formulation I wrote on the board in the first class of this year, concerning a discourse without speech, which is the essence, as I said, of analytic theory.

It is at this juncture that what I must propose this year will come in. In "From an Other to the other," who must we allow to speak?

It is not speech here, and I haven't yet shown you the essentially ungraspable person I called truth, even though I already brought it into play by reminding you [in the first class] of the discourse I attributed to it [in "The Freudian Thing"]. If I had it say, "I am speaking," it is, as I emphasized, because what is at stake is something other than what it says.

I am mentioning this here in order to note that truth is in the background, and that it awaits us as regards what we must say about the function of discourse.

Let us now turn to this function.

3

What is involved in the signifying chain – the same one I am always talking about – is thus the relationship between one signifier and another signifier.

Let us confine ourselves to recalling that, right from its very first step, set theory stumbles upon the paradox known as Russell's paradox.

I need not dissimulate the fact that, by presenting it to you right from the get-go, I am artificially sparing myself the task of introducing it via set theory. If I had to remind you of the foundations of set theory, it would take me quite some time – to do it properly would require a rather extensive discussion.

In a certain definition, which is that of sets, what do we do with a relationship of connection [or: linking up, *relation de connexion*], which is closest to the signifying relationship? As nothing is indicated in the first definition of the function of the signifier if it is not that the signifier represents the subject in its relationship to another signifier, we can define this relationship as we like. The simplest term is that of "membership" [*appartenance*].

This would suffice to confirm for us, if many other features did not, that in mathematical logic it is set theory that is best positioned to deal with this simple connection, not to say formalize it. Many linguists have realized this.

Let me remind those of you who have heard a bit about set theory of its first step. If we take as a class all the elements of such a connection, insofar as one can indicate that none of them is a member [or: element] of itself, this leads to a paradox – one that can be demonstrated.

Let me repeat that I am merely hinting at an introduction here. To fill it out would lead us into far odder statements. I will perhaps do so today if time permits, or perhaps we can do so later. In the meantime, I am going to proceed differently. I will rely on my graph alone, and I will try to show you in a thoroughly formal way what we are led to by the formulation that "a signifier represents the subject only to another signifier" if we use the elements that the graph itself immediately offers us.

We are going to take S as the signifier and A as the other signifier.

$$S \rightarrow A$$

Figure 3.4: The Ordered Pair S → A

Since I initially called A the locus or treasure trove of signifiers, aren't we in a position to question what it means to posit, qua signifier of a relationship, a signifier that intervenes in that very relationship? In other words, if it is important, as I emphasized, that the alterity of the other signifier be the only thing that intervenes in the definition of the signifier, can designating the relationship (S → A) with this very signifier, A, alterity of the Other, be formalized in a way that leads somewhere?

A

Figure 3.5: A Designating the (S → A) Relationship

In order to reassure those who may be bothered by this way of posing the problem, let me mention that it is not at all foreign to what constitutes the point of departure of a certain strain of formalization in mathematical logic.

This would require me to adequately explain the difference between the definition of sets and that of classes. The question is so well formulated at the level of mathematical logic – and I only wish to Heaven we took more of an interest in it because problems are resolved there – that there is a point at which mathematical logic indicates that there is no class of sets that do not include themselves. You see here, in this drawing, an example in which this is at least indicated.

58

But we must do something other than mathematical logic, for our relationship to the Other is a more burning relationship, one involving demand.

Owing to the demand addressed to the Other, it turns out that the Other already in some sense includes everything with which it links up. Yet if this were so, there would be a dialogue, whereas I very precisely proffered at the end of last year's Seminar that there is no such dialogue. This is what makes it such that, in this rudimentary way and as if in the margins of set theory, I am investigating whether or not the Other can be conceptualized as a closed code, on the keyboard of which one need but press in order for discourse to be established without gaps and totalized.

I could have put a *b* in the place of S, which would have allowed you to realize that we are at the *b a ba* [the ABCs or most elementary stage] of the investigation. But right from this elementary stage, you will see how this question deepens, topologically speaking.

I have raised the question in this way to make it clear that the A that figures in the ordered pair that constitutes this set should be viewed as identical to the A that designates the same set. The relationship of S to A, (S → A), is thus going to be written (S → (S → A)), if I substitute for A what A is, insofar as it is the signifier of the set constituted by the relationship of S to A. This is quite typical in any exposition of a theory of sets.

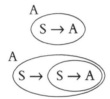

Figure 3.6: First Rewriting

You thus see what this leads to. We end up with a series of circles that I am drawing – I don't know what they are, but they allow us to designate a specific set and make it function – and an indefinite repetition of S, without us ever being able to stop A's retreat [*recul*], as it were.

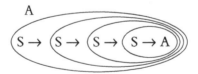

Figure 3.7: Serial Rewriting

But don't get it into your head that A is spatially reduced and vanishes. Nothing is indicated here that would involve an infinitesimal reduction of the distance or some extrapolation of a limit [*passage à la limite*]. What is involved is merely the specifically elusive nature of A, even though it always remains the same. A's elusive character should not surprise us, for we have made A into the locus of *Urverdrängung* [primal repression].

This elusiveness allows us to see precisely what I was questioning a moment ago – namely, the status of the circles I have drawn. If A makes them multiply in this way, it is simply because we can always write A outside and inside. The circles do nothing more than index this identity.

Otherwise stated, the circle that is, in a sense, the most advanced in what arises from this notation of dissymmetry, will always, in the end, join up with the initial circle. This leak, which is such that it is on its very inside that an envelope finds its outside, is nothing but what I formerly drew in the topological form of a projective plane, which is materialized for our eyes by a cross-cap [see Seminar IX]. Do you sense the kinship between them?

The fact that capital A as such has within itself a gap – which is based on the fact that one cannot know what it includes, if it is not its signifier – is the decisive point where we see the status of the gap in knowledge emerge. Inasmuch as the possibility of the subject, insofar as he formulates himself [or: is formulated, *se formule*], is linked to the Other as locus, it is crucial to know that what would serve him as a guarantee – namely, the locus of truth – is itself a locus with holes in it.

In other words, we perceive here that the question "Does God exist?" – which we already know comes to us from a fundamental experience, which is no accident, nor is it a precarious production of priests – takes on its import solely because it is based on a more fundamental structure that concerns knowledge. Can we say that, in the locus of knowledge, knowledge somehow knows itself? This is how I have always tried, for those who understand me, to resituate the question of God's existence, which can only be the object of a wager. The following question can truly be articulated, for however we prop up the function of knowledge, we can only prop it up, as experience tells us, by articulating it with signifiers: "Does knowledge know itself or is it full of gaping holes [*béant*] owing to its very structure?"

There is something even simpler. Since the innermost circle joins up with the outermost and meets up with itself, albeit inside out, I could have used the Klein bottle to help you get your bearings. It would have taken on meaning as an index of the difficulty involved here. I have drawn it on the board often enough here for some of you here to remember it.

What it entails is that this structure – insofar as we can give it some imaginary prop, which is why we must be particularly careful in doing so – is nothing other than object *a*, because object *a* is the hole that is designated at the level of the Other as such when it is called into question in its relationship to the subject.

Let us try now to grasp the subject where he is represented. Let us try to extract S, the signifier that represents the subject, from the set constituted by the ordered pair. Here it is easy to find ourselves on familiar ground. What are we doing by taking up the Ss if not extracting from set A all the signifiers about which we can say that they do not contain [or: include or list] themselves? This is Russell's paradox.

You need but look at the first pages of any theory, whether naïve or not, of sets to see that this is perfectly well illustrated in the articulation of the sophism. The class of all catalogs that don't include themselves cannot in any way be situated in the form of a set, precisely because it cannot figure in the elements that are already inscribed in this set. It is distinct from them.

I have already discussed this topic many times. It is well known and trivial. There is no way to include in a set what you might extract from it by designating it as a set of elements that do not include themselves. I won't draw this on the board, but will confine myself to saying that, by simply asking the question whether S is in A, by simply isolating the set of all Ss – insofar as S, unlike A, does not include itself – you end up not knowing where to locate this set. Try it yourself. If it is outside, it is inside. If it is inside, it is outside.

In other words, any discourse that claims to be founded essentially on the relationship to another signifier cannot be totalized in any way whatsoever qua discourse. Indeed, the universe of discourse – I am not talking here about the signifier, but about what is articulated qua discourse – will always have to be extracted from any field that claims to totalize it.

In still other words, the more you wonder whether any S, initially posited as being in the relationship S(A), is a member [or: element] of set A, you will see that, unlike in the schema on the board, that S will necessarily be excluded from A. The same will be true for the next S that you wonder about. The Ss will always exit, providing the essence of what is tantamount to metonymy in the continuity of the signifying chain – namely, the fact that every signifying element extracts itself from every conceivable totality.

This is undoubtedly a bit dense and, in ending today, I apologize for that. But note, lastly, the process that arises from these successive exits from the envelopes that are never infertile without ever encompassing themselves. What is tangible here regarding the subject's division arises precisely from the point that, employing a spatial metaphor, we call a hole, insofar as it has the structure of a cross-cap or Klein bottle. This point is the center at which *a* is posited as absence.

61

If this suffices to strike you and hold your attention, you will see that what follows will spell out what this implies about the place of analytic investigation between the chain of demand and the chain of enunciation as we see it on the graph.

The subject of enunciation is only enunciated as "he," whereas what appears, not only by way of demand, but by way of the relationship of demand to the chain of enunciation, appears as "I" and "you."

This will be the topic of our next class.

November 27, 1968

IV

FACTS AND WHAT IS SAID
[*LE FAIT ET LE DIT*]

Laughter and elision
There is no theory of the unconscious
Suffering and truth
"I am what I is"
The ordered pair revisited

Let us get straight to work since we are running behind today.

Our last class revolved around the Other, what I call "the Other with a capital O." It ended with me proposing certain schemas whose somewhat fascinating appearance alone I said we should not dwell on, for they should be linked to a logical articulation, the one involving the relationship between one signifier and another.

In order to draw out the consequences of this relationship, I endeavored to articulate it by beginning with the function of ordered pairs as laid out in set theory. At least I tried, on this logical basis, to convey to you the crux of the interest I hope we all have in hearing the following point clearly articulated: the Other, the Other with a capital O – in its function, such as I have already broached it – encloses no knowledge about which we can presume, let us say, that it will someday become absolute.

Note that, by saying "presume," I am gesturing toward the future, whereas I usually gesture toward the past by enunciating that referring to the Other props up the erroneous notion that knowledge is already there [in the Other].

I will not begin with that, but I wanted to mention it, for I will return to it later.

1

It is extremely important for what is to come that the Other be called into question here.

There is nothing subversive about the statement that the Other does not enclose any absolute knowledge that is either already there or to come.

I recently read somewhere the expression "subversion of knowledge," situated at an ideal point which shall, moreover, stay off in its corner [*coin*], as it were. This expression was supposedly proposed under my aegis. Yet I have absolutely never stated anything of the kind. Such slippages can only be considered highly regrettable, attesting as they do to a bogus use that is made of bits and pieces of my discourse that are not even properly detached, or rather a re-assemblage of terms that I would never have dreamt of assembling, in view of having them function in a market that would not be at all happy if it began to colonize academia.

Why is knowledge subverted just because it can't be made absolute, when the claim that it can be absolute, wherever it shows its head, or wherever it has shown its head, has always been *laughable*?

This word brings us to the heart of the matter, by which I mean the new path I am taking using puns inasmuch as they provoke laughter. They provoke laughter, in short, insofar as they are properly linked to the gap inherent in knowledge.

If you will allow me to go off on a brief tangent, I will mention in this connection the first chapter of Part III of [Volume I of] Marx's *Capital*, "The Production of Absolute Surplus Value," which is chapter 7, "The Labor Process and the Valorization Process."

In these few pages, we find something that I did not have to wait for recent studies on Marx's structuralism to notice, but that had struck me when I was around twenty. This old volume that you see here, which is falling apart – I remember reading it on the way to the hospital in the vehicle I had at the time, namely, the subway.

Marx introduces surplus value [*plus-value*] – he introduces it a bit more [*un peu plus*], a bit more-value [*un peu plus-value*], it wouldn't have taken much for him not to introduce it at all [*un peu plus il ne l'introduisait pas*], neither surplus nor value, I'm messing with your minds [*ni plus ni value j't'embrouille*] – after debonairly allowing the capitalist to say his piece. Marx allows him to justify his position regarding the point at issue – namely, the service he renders to the man who has but a rudimentary tool, a jointer plane, with which to do his work, by putting at his disposal a lathe and a milling machine. Thanks to this, the man will be able to work wonders, and there will be a fair exchange of good and even faithful service.

Marx allows plenty of time for this plea – which seems like the most honest discourse in the world – to be laid out. But he points out that the ghostlike character across from him, the capitalist, then laughs [*Capital*, Vol. 1 (New York: Vintage Books, 1976), p. 300].

It was this superfluous detail that struck me when I first read the passage. It seemed to me at the time that this laughter was closely related to the essence of surplus value which Marx then proceeded to unveil.

"Go on, mischievous fellow," Marx [as much as] says to the capitalist. "Keep providing the worker with the means of production that you happen to possess. But you won't pay him any more for the work he does with your lathe and milling machine than you did for what he made with a simple plane [or: jointer, *varlope*]. As least with his plane he could assure his own subsistence."

What I am highlighting in passing has never been noted before, naturally, and I was unable to mention it myself when I began constructing the graph [of desire] on the basis of puns. I am referring to the conjunction of laughter with the radically avoided function of surplus value, whose relationship to the characteristic elision that is constitutive of object *a* I have already sufficiently indicated. The jump, shock, a little bit more, a little bit less I spoke about earlier, the sleight of hand or prestidigitation that hits you in the gut when you hear a pun – all of that revolves around the fundamental relationship between laughter and elision.

In short, here as elsewhere – I mean in the foundational function that is hidden in the relationship between production and work, as elsewhere, in another relationship that is more profound to which I am trying to lead you on the basis of surplus jouissance – there is something like a fundamental joke that is, strictly speaking, based on the joint into which we must jam our crowbar, when we are dealing with relations involved in the experience of the unconscious understood in its most general function.

This nevertheless does not imply that there can be any sort of theory of the unconscious. Trust me, I am not aiming at anything of the kind.

I will return to [or: revise, *reprendre*] that statement since it, too, can give rise to improper formulations. There is, assuredly, a theory of psychoanalytic practice. But a theory of the unconscious? No, unless one intends to extend the scope of the theory of analytic practice which, regarding the unconscious, gives us what can be taken from it in the field of this practice and nothing else.

To talk about a theory of the unconscious is to open the door to a ridiculous deviation that I would like to block, which has already paraded for years as "applied psychoanalysis," and which has allowed for all sorts of abuses, especially in the fine arts. It is a travesty along psychoanalysis' way, which has led to a hole I find dishonorable. I won't go into it any further.

Let us return to the topic at hand [prior to this tangent].

The Other merely provides the subject's fabric [*étoffe*] – namely, his topology, that by which the subject brings with him a subversion, certainly, but one that is not solely his own. What is at issue is "the subversion of the subject" – as I labeled it and put it in the title of one of my writings – with regard to what people had said about him prior to that time. Yet the subversion at stake here is the one the subject brings with him, of course, but which the real – which in this perspective is defined as the impossible – makes use of [*se sert*]. Now, at the precise point at which he is of interest to us, there is no subject except on the basis of a speech act [or: on the basis of an instance of speaking (or: saying), *il n'y a de sujet que d'un dire*].

I am thus proposing two references: one to the real and one to speaking [*au dire*]. Here you may still be uncertain and wonder, for example, whether this is no more than what has always been imagined about the subject.

We must thus realize that the subject is the effect and consequence [*dépendance*] of this saying. There is no subject except on the basis of a speech act. This is what we have to home in on [*serrer*] correctly in order not to detach the subject. To say, moreover, that the real is the impossible is also to enunciate that the real is the tightest homing in on saying [or: speech's tightest grip, *le serrage le plus extrême du dire*], insofar as saying introduces the impossible and doesn't simply enunciate it.

Some may find this dubious, as the subject would seem therefore, in a sense, to be no more than the ever-mobile [*volant*] subject of discourse, the deployment of a cancer growing in the middle of the world, a world in which a junction occurs that nevertheless brings this subject alive. But it is not just any old thing that constitutes a subject. We have to be careful here to take things up anew in such a way as not to fall into the confusion of turning this subject back into the thinking subject.

Regardless of the pathos of the signifier – I mean owing to the signifier – this pathos does not in and of itself constitute a subject. What defines this pathos is quite simply, in every case, what is known as a fact [*un fait*]. Here lies the gap where we must explore what our experience produces, which is something other than and something that goes much further than the being who speaks insofar as we are talking about humans.

67

More than one thing in the world is liable to be affected by the signifier [*est possible de l'effet du signifiant*]. Nothing in the world ever truly becomes a fact [or: constituted, *fait*] without the signifier articulating it. No subject ever comes along unless the fact [of his existence] is said. We must work between these two boundaries.

The facet of a fact that cannot be said is designated – albeit in the [act of] saying itself – by its absence, and that is truth. This is why the truth is always insinuated, but can be written, too, in a perfectly well calculated way where it has its only place: between the lines. Truth's substance is precisely what suffers from the signifier – that goes very far – what suffers owing to its very nature, let us say. When I say that this goes very far, [I mean that] it goes very far in nature.

For a long time, people seemed to accept what was known as mind [or: spirit, *l'esprit*]. It is an idea that became a bit passé – although nothing is ever as passé as you think – because it turns out that it is never anything but the signifier itself that is involved in what goes by the name of mind, and this overturns quite a lot of metaphysics.

What relation is there between what we do and metaphysics, and what would a questioning of metaphysics that does not wish to forgo the benefit of its experience look like, when what remains of metaphysics in a certain number of points and zones is more varied or plentiful than one might think at first glance, and of quite varied quality? It is also important to know what "structuralism" must accomplish. The question is raised in a collection that just came out – I saw the galley proofs and don't know if it is available yet – entitled *Qu'est-ce que le structuralisme?* [("What Is Structuralism?") Paris: Seuil, 1968]. It was edited by my friend François Wahl, who called certain people to arms. I advise you to read it, for it brings a number of questions into focus, and it is assuredly quite important to distinguish what we are doing from metaphysics.

Yet, before doing so, it is worth mentioning that we must not lend too much credence to the dispelling of illusions [*désillusion*] that is announced there. Dispelling the illusion of mind is not a complete triumph if it merely transfers to matter – superstitiously characterized as an ideality – the same impassive substance that people used to locate in the mind. I said "superstitiously" because one can do its genealogy; it goes back, oddly enough, to the Jewish tradition. One can, in fact, highlight what a certain transcendence of matter owes to what is said in the Scriptures – singularly unnoticed, of course, but altogether clear – about God's corporeality.

I was going to discuss this in my Seminar on *The Names-of-the-Father*, which I have since crossed off my list [*sur lequel j'ai fait une croix*] – "cross" being the operative word! – and I cannot return to it today.

68

This materialist superstition – adding the word "vulgar" to "materialism" changes nothing – richly deserves the love it receives from one and all, because it is clearly what has been most tolerant up until now of scientific thought. But we must not believe that the tolerance in question will last forever. It would be enough for science to come down a bit hard on it for it not to last.

It is not unthinkable when we consider how touchy an honorable member of the Russian Academy of Sciences became one day when I remarked that the word "cosmonaut" struck me as a misnomer, because nothing in fact seemed less cosmic than such a man's trajectory. He was immediately troubled, bridling on hearing a quip that was, good Lord, so gratuitous. Whatever you may call it – it is not clear, after all – whether you call it God, in the sense of the Other, or Nature, which is not the same thing, it is nevertheless to one of those two that we must attribute a prior knowledge of Newton's law for us to be able to speak of the cosmos and of cosmonauts. That's all I wanted to say.

This is where we sense how much metaphysical ontology continues to be concealed even in the most unexpected of places.

Let us return to what is at issue for us.

2

What justifies the rule that grounds psychoanalytic practice, the one known quite simply as free association?

"Free" means nothing other than "dismissing the subject." We aren't necessarily successful in dismissing the subject. It is not always enough to dismiss someone for him to leave.

What justifies our rule is that a subject does not speak the truth, yet suffers from it.

Let me label here an occurrence of what I will call phenomenological infatuation.

I have already mentioned one of the minor monuments found in a field in which statements are made that seek to corner the market on ignorance. *L'Essence de la manifestation* ("The Essence of Manifestation") is the title of a book that has been well received in academia, whose author I need not name since I am about to call him conceited. The essence of his own manifestation, in any case, is the power with which on a certain page he articulates that, if there is something we can be sure of, it is that suffering is nothing more than suffering. It always has an impact when someone tells you that – it's enough to have had a toothache and to have never read Freud to find that quite convincing.

We can thank such intellectuals [*clercs*], that's the word for them, for promoting what shouldn't be said [*l'à-ne-pas-dire*] in order to allow us to clearly demarcate what truly should be said.

Saying that, I too am a bit traditional, I think, for I am providing too much justification for his error, and this is why I will add, in passing, that in saying so, I don't entirely believe it. But to lay out what is at issue, I would have to launch into an apology for sophists, and God only knows where that might lead.

Be that as it may, the difference is as follows: if what we analysts do has an effect it is precisely because suffering is not suffering. To say what must be said, we must say that suffering is a fact. That sounds almost the same, but it is not at all identical, at least if you clearly understood what I said earlier about what a fact is.

Let us instead be more modest. There is suffering that is a fact – in other words, that harbors an act of speaking [*un dire*] within itself. It is owing to this ambiguity that we can refute the idea that its manifestation cannot be surpassed. Suffering wants to be a symptom, which means truth.

Broaching this for the first time requires that I temper the effects of discourse, so I will make suffering say, just like I did before for truth, "I speak," although in different terms for each of them, and with a tone that is not the same. I am mentioning this merely because I recently highlighted this point. Let us try to be more rigorous as we proceed.

70   Suffering has its own language and it is quite unfortunate that anyone at all can speak it without knowing what he is saying. But it is, after all, what is unconscious in every discourse. As true discourse is a discourse without speech, as I wrote on the board at our first class this year, once your discourse is rigorously enunciated, anyone can repeat it after you without much consequence. This is one of the dangers of the situation.

Let us thus leave suffering aside, and as regards truth, let us indicate what we shall have to bring into focus in what follows.

Truth says "I," and this defines two upper thresholds [or: outer limits (or maximal ranges), *champs limites*]. The first is the one in which the subject can only be located as the effect of the signifier, the one in which there is a pathos of the signifier with no link yet established in our discourse to the subject. This is the field of facts. And secondly, there is what interests us, something that has never been touched on except on Mount Sinai, namely, that which says "I."

I apologize for saying "on Mount Sinai" – it just slipped out [literally: it just came out of me from between my legs, *il vient de me sortir d'entre les jambes*]. I did not intend to rush toward Mount Sinai, but since it just tripped off my tongue, I should justify why it did.

I had begun – around this little hole (which remains gaping) in my discourse known as The Names-of-the-Father – to investigate the translation of the words *'ehyeh 'ăšer 'ehyeh*. I'm afraid I don't pronounce Hebrew well.

Greek metaphysicians translated it as "I am the one who is" [*Je suis celui qui est*] because, of course, they had a need for being. But that is not what it means. Other people proposed intermediate terms like "I am the one who am" [*Je suis celui qui suis*]. This one received Rome's blessing, but it doesn't mean anything. I myself pointed out that it should be understood as "I am what I am." Indeed, that at least has the value of a punch in the face. You ask me my name and I answer, "I am what I am," and you can go fuck yourself. Which is what the Jews have been doing ever since.

I have been thinking anew about how to translate it, but I didn't plan to speak to you about it today. Yet since Mount Sinai came out regarding the truth that says "I," since it happened, let's go for it. I believe it must be translated as "I am what I is."

If Mount Sinai slipped out like that, it was in order to illustrate for you what I mean to investigate regarding the status of the "I," insofar as the truth says "I."

Naturally, in the little Parisian cafés where people gossip, rumor would soon have it that, like Pascal, I have chosen the God of Abraham, Isaac, and Jacob. Let such souls, on whichever side they situate themselves in welcoming this news, set their knee-jerk reactions aside, for the truth says I, but the inverse is not true – not everything that says I is truth. Where would we be if this were not the case?

Which doesn't mean these remarks are completely superfluous. You should realize that by calling into question the function of the Other on the basis of the very crux of its topology, what I am shaking up is what Pascal called the God of the philosophers. It is not an overly pretentious goal – it is truly the issue of our times.

Now, it is no small matter to call the philosophers' God into question because it has hitherto been quite hard to eradicate, in the way I alluded to earlier. It is clearly present in myriad modes of transmitting the knowledge that I have been telling you has not been subverted in the slightest – even and all the more so, by calling into question the Other who is supposed to be able to totalize it. That was the meaning of what I talked about last time.

On the contrary, the other God – and we must render homage to Pascal for having seen that He has nothing to do with the philosophers' God – said "I am what I is." Whether He spoke truthfully or not, the fact that it was said had a number of consequences. I don't see why, even without glimpsing therein the slimmest chance of truth, we wouldn't inform ourselves about certain of these consequences in order to know the status of truth insofar as it says "I."

It is a bit interesting, for example, to note the following: since the truth says I and the response comes from our interpretation, it is an occasion for we analysts to notice something that I discussed a while back in my Seminar on *Desire and Its Interpretation* (Seminar VI). I remarked that by centering the question around "I," we must – if only to take it as a warning, or even umbrage – realize that interpretation must be better delineated, because it's exactly what prophets do. To say "I" in a certain wake, which is not that of our suffering, also constitutes interpretation.

The Other's fate is thus tied, not to *my* question, but to the question that psychoanalytic experience raises.

72   What is tragic is that, whatever fate this calling into question reserves for the Other, psychoanalytic experience demonstrates that it is owing to [*de*] the Other's desire that I follow [or: I am, *je suis*] – in the two senses of these marvelous French homonyms – that I follow [or: I am, *je suis*] the trail [*trace*].

This is, moreover, precisely why I am interested in the Other's fate.

3

We still have a quarter of an hour left, and [I want to discuss] a note I received [that] reads as follows: "Last Wednesday you made a connection, without providing any detail, between the ordered pair and 'a signifier represents the subject to another signifier.'"

That is quite true. It is no doubt why my correspondent drew a line underneath it, and below the line wrote the word "why" with a question mark. Under the word "why?" he drew another line, and then two big dots, or more precisely, two small blackened circles.

"When the ordered pair was introduced in mathematics, it took a *coup de force* [an extraordinary feat] to create it," [my correspondent continued].

This proves that the person who sent me this piece of paper knows what he's talking about – in other words, that he has a smattering of mathematical knowledge, and probably more than just a smattering. He is quite right – we begin by articulating the function of a set, and if we don't introduce the function of ordered pairs through a sort of *coup de force* known in logic as an axiom, there is nothing more to be done with it than what you initially defined as a set.

In parentheses he added, "whether direct or indirect, this set has two elements. The result of this *coup de force* is to create a signifier that takes the place of the coexistence of two signifiers." That is perfectly accurate.

[He then made] a second remark: "the ordered pair determines these two components, whereas in the formulation 'a signifier represents the subject to another signifier,' it would be surprising that a subject determines two signifiers."

I have only fifteen minutes left, but I hope nevertheless to have time to clarify what I said last week, for it is not difficult. I undoubtedly did not say it clearly enough, since, as you see, someone quite serious questioned me about it in this way.

I never, at any moment, subsumed the coexistence of two signifiers within a subject.

I placed on the board an ordered pair, which, as my interlocutor surely knows, can be written, for example, as follows: $<S_1, S_2>$. The two signs, $<$ and $>$, serendipitously turn out to be the two halves of my lozenge [◊], but in this case they merely serve to indicate that it is an ordered pair.

An ordered pair can be translated into [or: turned into, *traduite sous forme de*] a set, that is, articulated in the sense of the bonus expected from the *coup de force*. It is thus a set with two elements, which are themselves sets. The first is the set whose member is the first element of the pair. The members of the second set are the two elements of the ordered pair.

$$\{\{S_1\}, \{S_1, S_2\}\}$$

Far from it being the case here that the subject in any way subsumes the two signifiers in question, I assume you can see how easy it is to say that the S_1 in the first subset does not stop representing the subject, whereas the second subset renders present, most broadly, the form of relationship that we can call "knowledge" and that my correspondent called "coexistence."

The question I am raising about this is, in its most far-reaching form, the following: can we conceive of a kind of knowledge that brings together the conjunction of two subsets into a single set? Can it – going by the name of A, [for] Other with a capital O – be identical to the conjunction such as it is articulated here in a knowledge of the two signifiers in question?

This is why, after having designated with the signifier A a set made of Ss – I need no longer add 1, 2, etc., since I have substituted A for $\{S_1, S_2\}$ – I investigated what followed therefrom regarding the topology of the Other. I showed you, in a way that was no doubt overly figurative to be fully satisfying from a logical standpoint, but that nevertheless clearly brought it out, the necessity of this series of circles involuting dissymmetrically – that is, forever sustaining A, despite their ever greater apparent interiority. This figuration would suggest a topology in which the smallest of the circles joins up with the largest, with which I indexed this.

If we define A as possibly including itself – in other words, having become absolute knowledge – the odd consequence is that what represents the subject is only manifested therein in the form of an infinite repetition, the one you saw inscribed in the form of the Ss being endlessly written within the series of the circles' walls [see Figure 3.7].

To be inscribed only as the infinite repetition of himself, the subject is truly excluded, not from a relationship which is either inside or outside, but from what is initially posited as absolute knowledge.

I mean that, in logical structure, there is something that accounts for what Freud's theory fundamentally implies, which is that, at the outset, the subject, with respect to what ties him to some scrap of jouissance [or: drop in jouissance, *chute de la jouissance*], can only manifest himself as repetition, unconscious repetition.

This is thus one of the limits around which revolves the link between the reference to absolute knowledge – to the subject-supposed-to-know, as we call it in the transference – and the index of the repetitive necessity that stems therefrom, which is logically object *a*. Object *a* is indexed here by the concentric circles.

However, what I ended with last time is the other end of the question we must ask the Other with a capital *O*, inasmuch as we would impose on it the condition of not including itself. Capital A only includes S_1, S_2, and S_3, which are all distinct from what A represents qua signifier. Is it possible that, in this other form, the subject can be subsumed in such a way that, without joining back up with the set thus defined as the universe of discourse, he could be sure to remain included therein?

I perhaps glossed over this point a bit too quickly, which is why, in concluding, I am coming back to it today.

There is no more palpable way to depict the element as such than these points. These three points are the elements of the set that this fourth point [A] can depict once we define this set as an element.

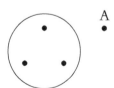

Figure 4.1: An Element Set

If, in A, there is no A qua element, but only S_1, S_2, and S_3, we say that A is not an element of itself.

Can I define the subject in an incredibly simple form by saying that he is precisely constituted – which seems to be exhaustive – by any signifier that is not an element of itself? In fact, neither S_1, S_2, nor S_3 are signifiers like capital A, the latter being Other to all of them.

By simply proffering, qua speaking subject [or: as the subject of a speech act, *comme sujet du dire*], the proposition that S_W – meaning any signifier whatsoever [*quelconque*] – is not an element of itself, will I be able, by means of speaking [or: through a speech act, *par un dire*], to assemble the signifiers thus defined in a set that brings them all together?

"By means of speaking" – in other words, through a proposition – is something that must be kept in mind in what follows, for it is something around which we must make, first of all, the function of this subject revolve in order to grasp his gap. Regardless of the use you then make of an enunciation, even assuming that it is used as a demand, it is because you have marked the gap that it demonstrates, as a simple saying, that you will be able to most correctly discern the status of desire as a gap [or: desire's gap (or the gap constituted by desire), *la faille du désir*] in the enunciation of demand.

Structuralism means that logic is everywhere, even at the level of desire. Lord knows there is more than one way to investigate desire. There are guys who bellow, there are guys who mouth off, and there are gals who dramatize. All of that is equivalent. But you will never know what it means for the simple reason that desire cannot be spoken. Desire is merely the inflection [or: suffix, *desinence*] of speaking, which is why the inflection must first be homed in on [or: gripped, *serrée*] in pure speaking where logic alone can demonstrate its gap.

We are going to form a subset of A. The subset B will include all the signifiers – *S alpha*, *S beta*, *S gamma*, *S delta* – that are not elements of themselves. This B is in fact the other signifier of my formula, S_2, the one to which all the others represent the subject – that is, the one that subsumes them qua subject.

In order for x, whatever it may be, to be an element of B, (1) it must not be an element of x, and (2) it must be an element of A.

What results from this? Is B an element of itself? If it were an element of itself, it would not correspond to the way in which we have constructed it as a set, because it brings together elements that are not elements of themselves. B is thus not an element of itself. If

B is not an element of itself, then it must belong to the subset made up of elements that are not elements of themselves. But this subset is B itself. We must therefore write that B is an element of B, which is what we rejected earlier. The conclusion we thus arrive at is that B doesn't correspond to the second condition – in other words, it is not an element of A.

For those of you who are not used to this sort of reasoning, which is nevertheless quite simple, I will illustrate it, even though my illustration here will be altogether childish. I posit B as the other signifier, namely S_2. On the left we have the two positions of B, which are equally unsatisfying, as it can neither be nor not be an element of itself. On the right, not being an element of A, B can only be situated outside.

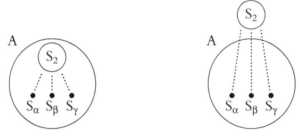

Figure 4.2: B's Place

How are we going to translate this exteriority? We will say that, in the final analysis, the subject – regardless of how he intends to be subsumed, whether on the basis of a first position of the Other with a capital O as including itself, or in the Other with a capital O as limited to the elements that are not elements of themselves – cannot be universalized. There is no all-encompassing definition with respect to the subject, even in the form of a proposition saying that the signifier is not an element of itself.

This also demonstrates, not that the subject is not included in the field of the Other, but that the point where he is signified qua subject is "outside" of the Other – in other words, "outside" of the universe of discourse.

To say – as I have heard people saying, supposedly repeating my words – that there's no such thing as a universe of discourse means that there's no such thing as discourse at all – well, it seems to me that if I had not provided a rigorous enough discourse here, you would know nothing about it.

Let this serve as an example for our own method, and as a resting place for what I hope next time we will be able to make headway with, in which you have an interest – not only since, as analysts, you are the live point [*point vivant*] of it, but also since, as analysands, you are searching for it.

December 4, 1968

V

"I AM WHAT I IS"

The *assujet*
"It's raining"
The Other's inconsistency

When alone, I sometimes jot down little notes for you. When assembling my papers today, I came across one that will serve me as an introduction here.

It is so unfortunate – I wrote, I no longer recall when – that God serves to exclude [*écarter*] owing to what I will call the proscribing of his name.

This took on the form of a prohibition precisely where people best knew the function of the term God – namely, among the Jews.

You know that for them there is an unpronounceable name. Well, this proscription serves precisely to exclude a certain number of references that are absolutely essential to maintaining the "I" in adequate light, enough light that it cannot be thrown to the dogs – in other words, to the professors.

1

Last time, you heard me, if not saw me, refer, almost in spite of myself, to "I" by means of the God in question.

Indeed, I translated what was one day proffered in the form of *'ehyeh 'ăšer 'ehyeh* as "I am what I is," and I justified, or believe I justified, that translation.

I told you that I myself was a bit overwhelmed when this enunciation slipped out. And then I said that Mount Sinai had emerged, in spite of myself, from the ground between my legs. I was expecting to receive a little note from someone pointing out that these words came out of the burning bush, but I didn't.

Can you imagine the effect it would have had if I had said that the   80
burning bush had emerged from between my legs? We can clearly
see here that a sentence gives itself orders retroactively. It is because
I wanted to end the sentence with "between my legs" that I put
Mount Sinai in the place of the burning bush.

It is, after all, the consequences of the thing that we see on Mount
Sinai. He who announced Himself as "I am what I is" – at least that
is the way I put it – merely enunciated the laws of "I am speaking,"
in the form that since that time has been transmitted in the imperative of the list of the Ten Commandments, said to be from God. I
already mentioned this in my Seminar on ethics [Seminar VII, *The
Ethics of Psychoanalysis*].

It is true, as I put it, that truth says "I." It seems quite self-evident
that "thou shalt love the one who said 'I am what I is,' and thou
shalt love only him."

By the same token, "thou shalt love," as it is put, "thy neighbor as
thyself." "Thyself" here is nothing other than that to which it is said,
that to which the commandments themselves are addressed as to a
"thou" – and even to a "thou art," whose truly magical ambiguity
in French I have been pointing out for a long time [*Tu es* (you are or
thou art) is pronounced exactly like *tuer*, the verb "to kill," and *tuez*,
the imperative "kill"; see Seminar III].

The prelude underlying these commandments is the "thou art"
that instates you as "I." In any invocation, we find that the same
penchant [or: opportunity, *pente*] is offered to this *Tu tuant* [lethal
Thou]. And we know that there is but a short step from the order
to responding to it. All of Hegel's work is designed to show what is
built upon that.

We could take up the commandments one by one, the one about
lying, and then the prohibition on "coveting thy neighbor's wife, his
ox or donkey," which is always the one that kills you. It is hard to
see what else we could covet, because that's precisely where desire
is located.

We should note that, owing to a self-evident connection, there
can be no speech, strictly speaking, except where the wall [or: fence,
clôture] around such a commandment preserves it. This explains
why, since the beginning of time, no one obeys these commandments very carefully, and it is also why speech, in the sense in which
truth says "I," remains profoundly hidden and emerges only by
showing the tip of its nose from time to time in the interstices in
discourse.

Inasmuch as there is a technique that places its trust in this
discourse in order to refind something therein, a path or way [*un
chemin, une voie*], as people say, and that assumes it is not totally

unrelated to truth and life, as people put it – but we must beware the flipside [*l'envers*] of discourse – it would perhaps make sense to question more closely what in this discourse can legitimately constitute a bridge toward the foundational and inaccessible term that the last of the philosophers, Hegel, rather audaciously believed he could eliminate with his dialectic.

Along the trail that I have begun to blaze, the "I" initially appears before the Other as allowing a logical gap to be discerned, as the locus of an original flaw borne in speech insofar as speech can respond.

The "I" appears first as subjugated [*assujetti*], as *assujet* [a neologism meaning something like "subjugated subject" or even "non-subject"]. I wrote this word somewhere to designate the subject insofar as he is only ever produced in discourse as divided [Seminar V, pp. 189–90]. If the animal who speaks can only at first embrace his partner qua subjugated, it is because he has always already been speaking, and in the very broaching of this embrace he can only formulate "Thou art" by killing himself in it. He others [*autrifie*] the partner; he makes him into the locus of the signifier.

Allow me to return for a moment to the "I is" mentioned last time, since I received the objection – from someone with a pretty good head on his shoulders – that by translating it in this way, I opened the door anew, as it were, to a reference to being. The "is" being, in accordance with the tradition's terminology, dependent upon being, it was thus heard, by at least one ear, as an appeal to being. Is it the case that I am thereby enunciating the supreme being that the tradition erects in order to answer for all the beings subsisting in nature in the earliest sense of the term, in some natural order? Does my "I is" designate that being around which everything changes and revolves, and which thus occupies a pivotal place in the universe, the place of the x thanks to which there is a universe?

Absolutely not. Nothing could be further from what I intended with my proposed translation. I am enunciating in the "I" of "I is" what truly gives the ground of truth [or: backdrop (or content) of truth, *le fond de la vérité*] solely insofar as it speaks. In order to convey this, I could amend the translation as "I am what the I is." Here the "is" can be read more clearly.

The commandments that undergird truth are, as I sufficiently indicated earlier, truly anti-physical. There is no way to speak the truth, to speak what we call by that name, without referring to them. Try it yourself. We can't manage to do so in the slightest. The commandments constitute an ideal point, and that is truly the word for it. No one even knows what that means.

Similarly, as soon as one begins discoursing, what arises are laws of logic – namely, a subtle coherence linked to the nature of what is known as signifying articulation. This is what makes it such that a discourse either holds up or it doesn't owing to the structure of what is known as the sign, which is related to what is commonly known as the letter, as opposed to the spirit.

What initially dominates discourse are the laws of this articulation.

82

2

In my classes here this year, I have begun to enunciate the Other's field, without incarnating it in any way, in order to test whether it can be conceptualized as the field of inscription of what is articulated in discourse.

It is on the basis of its structure that – this is the second stage – the possibility of "Thou" can be defined, which is going to reach us and appeal to something that will have to call itself "I" at the third stage.

What will appear, what we are expecting, and what we know full well, is that in every truth the "I" is unpronounceable. This is why everyone knows to what degree it is troublesome, and that it is preferable, as the laws of speech itself remind us, to never say "I swear."

So let us not presume anything about the Other, let us leave it an open question. Even if it is nothing but a blank page, it will already give us more than enough trouble, as I demonstrated on the board last time.

Let us assume that you have written the totality of signifiers on a blank piece of paper. This is conceivable, since you can choose a level at which the signifier is reduced to phonemes. On the condition that this piece of paper be a page – in other words, finite – it can be demonstrated that, if you assemble on the page anything about which you could claim "That is the subject," the term necessitated by this assemblage will have to be situated outside of the totality. S_2 – the other signifier that comes into the picture when I enunciate that the signifier is what represents the subject to another signifier – will be off the blank page. S_2 will not be found on the page.

What I will say in what follows about anything that is enunciated will have to begin from this phenomenon, which can be demonstrated to be internal to every specific enunciation. This is why we should dwell on it a bit longer.

Let us take the simplest enunciation. "It is raining" [*Il pleut*]. It can only be fully appreciated if we dwell on what emerges from the fact that it is said that there is some *pleut*.

83

This is the event brought about by discourse [or: discursive event, *l'événement du discours*], by which the very person who says it posits himself as secondary. The event consists in something being said [*un dit*], whose place is marked by *Il* [It].

But the grammatical subject is so difficult to clearly discern that we must proceed carefully. It can take on different morphologies in different languages, and it is not necessarily isolated. It is related to what I earlier called the *hors-champ* [outside of the field, off the page], more or less individualized, as I just reminded you, that can also be reduced to a suffix, for example, *pleut*. The little "t" at the end can be found traipsing all about in French. Why does it show up in places where it has no business being, where it is not part of the conjugation, as, for example, in *orne-t-il* [does it adorn (or decorate)]?

The grammatical subject is thus merely the place where something comes to be represented.

Let us return to S_1, insofar as it represents this something, and to S_2.

Last time, we had to extract S_2 from the Other's field, since it couldn't be included there, the S_2 that assembles S *alpha*, S *beta*, and S *gamma* in which we claim to grasp the subject insofar as these Ss satisfy a certain function, R, defined in the Other's field by "*x* is not an element of *x*."

$$R(x) = R : x \notin x$$

To write $R(x)$ transforms all of these elements – which happen to be signifiers here – into something that remains indeterminate since it is open, something that takes on the function of the variable (x). Once we specify that this variable must correspond to a proposition – which is not just any old proposition (it is not that the variable must be "good" or "red" or "blue," but that it must be a subject) – the necessity of this signifier [S_2] as Other arises because it cannot in any way be inscribed in the Other's field. In its earliest form, this signifier clearly defines the so-called function of knowledge, S_2.

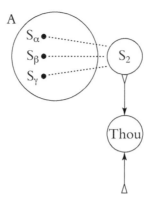

Figure 5.1: Knowledge outside of the Other's Field

I will have to come back to this, for this place has perhaps not yet been adequately emphasized in what has thus far been said about logical functions. Namely, the fact that qualifying the subject as such situates us [*nous met*] outside the Other. *Nous met* is perhaps a form of noumenon [*noumène*] that will lead us [*nous mènera*] further than we think.

When we consider the difficulties that are generated by the logical reduction of classical statements – by which I mean Aristotelian statements involving the universal and the particular – to the field of quantifiers, we should raise the question whether it wouldn't in fact be easier to realize that "all" [*tous*] and "some" [*quelques*] must be placed outside of the Other's field. Rather than say "All men are good," or "All men are bad," it doesn't matter which, wouldn't the proper formulation be to state that "men" – or whatever else, whatever you can adorn with a letter in logic – are "all [*tous*] good" or "are some [*quelques*] good"? In short, if we situate the universal and the particular as syntactic functions outside of the Other's field, doesn't it seem that we would then have less trouble reducing them to mathematics?

For, indeed, the field of mathematics involves desperately operating in such a way that the Other's field coheres – which is the best way to show that it doesn't, that it is not "consistent," to use the technical term – and testing it by making all the levels [*étages*] link up, for it is at many different levels that it does not cohere.

It is insofar as the Other's field is not consistent that enunciation takes on the form of demand, and it does so even before anything whatsoever that can carnally respond to it shows up there.

If we go as far as possible in questioning the Other's field, we can perceive its gap at a series of different levels. To test this, mathematics provides us an exemplary field of experience. For it can allow itself to limit the Other's field to well-defined functions like arithmetic.

What research in arithmetic in fact shows is not germane to us for the time being. You have heard enough about it to know that, in fields selected among the simplest, we are greatly surprised when we discover that completeness, for example, is missing – namely, that one cannot say that whatever is stated in that field must be either proved or disproved. Moreover, in one of the simplest fields, it can be called into question whether certain statements in it are provable. Yet another level appears at which it is provable that a statement is not provable in that field. And it becomes quite odd and strange in certain cases when the unprovable itself eludes us, in that it cannot even be asserted that it is not provable, and a distinct dimension appears which is known as the undecidable.

These scales, not of uncertainty, but of flaws in logical texture, can allow us to grasp the status of the subject as such, to find a prop for him, and – to go still further – to consider that he can be satisfied by adhering to the very gap that is situated at the level of enunciation.

Broaching the Other's field from outside of logic, nothing has ever stopped us, it seems, from creating a signifier with which to connote what is lacking in signifying articulation itself. If we are willing to summarize the Other's field as I have already done, and if my sizable audience here is willing to indulge me, I can perhaps convey and render necessary in a discursive statement, or even demonstrate in some logical construction, the following: that the signifier with which a subject is satisfied, in the end, identifying with it, cannot be situated as identical to the very flaw [*défaut*] in discourse – assuming you will allow me this condensed formulation. Here again I am articulating this as an aside.

Can those of you here who are analysts fail to realize that it is owing to the lack of exploration of this kind that the notion of castration – that you sensed in passing, I hope, to be analogous to what I am saying – remains so vague and uncertain, and is handled with the clumsiness and brutality that we see all around us?

In practice, it is, in fact, not handled at all. People substitute for it quite simply what the other cannot give. They talk about frustration where something else is clearly at work. They occasionally broach it by the pathway of deprivation, but as you see, deprivation is part and parcel of the flaw inherent in the subject that we must broach.

Before moving on today from what I am merely tracing the outlines of – without even being able to foresee what I will manage to get you to bear by the end of the year – I will give a brief indication to those of you who already have some knowledge of certain theorems that are enunciated in the field of logic.

S_2 clearly serves its function when, from outside of a certain arithmetical system, a well-defined capital A, it counts everything that can be turned into theorems within the system. Otherwise stated, a genius by the name of Gödel realized that "it counts" must be taken literally. If we give what is known as a Gödel number to each of the theorems that can be situated in a certain field, something can be broached that had never before been formulated concerning the functions I was able merely to mention earlier: completeness and decidability.

It is clear that everything is henceforth different from former times in which one could state that, in the end, mathematics is solely tautological, and that human discourse can thus remain what it is.

In the past, mathematics was supposed to be the field of tautology. Everything changes once it is most surely refuted that there is a capital A somewhere that remains identical to itself.

This result constitutes a true step forward.

3

To those who are confronted in psychoanalytic practice with what seems to be a transcendent aporia with respect to what is known as natural history, but who still do not see any reason to rely on logic to correctly situate what presents itself in the psychoanalytic field – it being the field of an entirely different kind of enunciation, the kind that allows for and also directs Freudian practice – I would point out that it is, first of all, insofar as the Other is not consistent that enunciation assumes the form of demand.

This is what provides the import of what is written as ($\mathcal{S} \lozenge D$), barred S lozenge capital D, in the complete graph that I have drawn here.

87

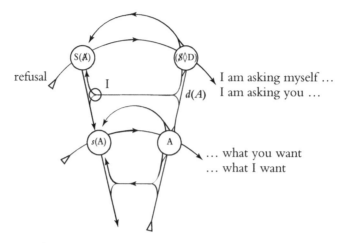

Figure 5.2: Converging and Diverging Vectorization

Every statement is distinguished by the fact that [the phrase] "I am saying that" is subtracted from it. The form in which the "I" – which is the "I" of grammar – is limited is thus spared all essential risk and subtracted from enunciation, thereby reducing enunciation to the enunciated. On the contrary, [the phrase] "I am saying that" is not subtracted from ($ ◊ D), and this leaves intact the fact that any enunciation whatsoever turns into a demand, owing solely to the Other's structure.

The question is twofold at this level: (1) it asks the Other what he is missing [*C'est la demande à l'Autre de ce qui lui manque*] – "I wonder [*Je me demande*] what you desire" – and (2), its double, which is the exact question I am pointing to today, namely: "I am asking you [*Je te demande*]," not what I am but rather, and this goes much further, "what I is."

The very knot that I formulated by proffering that man's desire is the Other's desire is instated at $d(A)$, the Other's desire [or: desire for the Other, *désir de l'Autre*]. If you take the two vectors defined by the graph – the one that begins from the Other and the one of the pure signifying chain that returns back to the intersection designated by ($ ◊ D) in order to complete the retroactive movement – they converge at $d(A)$, just as the two elements that I articulated converge there: (1) "I wonder what you desire" – in other words what you are lacking, which is linked to the fact that I am subjugated by you [or: I am subordinate to you (or I submit to you), *je te suis assujetti*], a question that is connected to the very level at which A is established – and (2), "I am asking you what I is," a question regarding the status of "I" as such, which is located here where I am indicating it with red chalk.

The convergence that constitutes the "I" is produced by any actual enunciation. If enunciating whatever comes to mind, which the fundamental rule of psychoanalysis posits as a principle, turns into demand, it is because it is, by its very function of enunciating being, a demand [or: question, *demande*] concerning "Thou" and "I."

Symmetrically, the demands or questions raised by the lack that is at the heart of the Other's field, insofar as it is structured by pure logic, converge on "Thou." This is what gives value and import to what we find, and which is just as vectorized, on the other side of the graph.

The subject's division is palpably rendered essential here, and this is what is instituted as "I."

Structure itself answers the question [*demande*] "Who is I?" with a refusal: S(Ⱥ), signifier of the barred Other, as I inscribed it in the functioning of the graph.

Similarly, "Thou" is instituted on the basis of a convergence between a request [or: question, *demande*] and a promise. [I am referring to] the most radical request, the one that is made to us, as analysts, the only one that, in the end, sustains the subject's discourse – namely, at the first stage, "I" am coming here to ask you "Who I am," which we respond to at the level of "Who is 'I'?", a perspective [*recul*] supplied here by logical necessity. [And I am referring to] the promise, the hope to assemble this "I" at S_2, which I designated in the transference with the term "subject-supposed-to-know." It is the knot or first conjunction, S_1 linked to S_2, that grounds knowledge in the ordered pair.

"I" is palpable only between two diverging poles: S(Ⱥ), which I articulate here as the no or refusal that gives form to the lack of response, and s(A), the Other's signified or what is signified to the Other. But what is this signification? For isn't it clear that the whole discourse that I am spinning, in order to provide a framework for the "I" of the question on which psychoanalytic practice is based – isn't it clear that I am spinning it while leaving no signification outside, thus far at least?

What does this mean, if not that – after having for many years trained you to ground our work in the linguistic distinction between the signifier as material and the signified as its effect – you may suspect that some mirage lies at the core of the field defined as linguistic, if only when we see the astonishing passion with which linguists articulate that what they are trying to grasp in language is pure form, not content?

I am going to return here to a point that I not unintentionally presented to you in my first lecture, one regarding pots. If I provided a digression there on mustard pots, it was no accident. Those of you who take notes should realize that none of what one might call my digressions upon first broaching a field are lacking in premeditation.

You may remember that I mentioned something that is truly worth pointing out in the first form of the appearance of pots, which is that their surfaces never fail to have signifying marks on them. Isn't the "I" somehow formulated there? If the potter's activity is the best image of human creation, it is because the properties of the utensil it produces give us the very precise sense that language – the language with which it is made, for where there is no language, there is no worker either – is a content. It is obvious, if we think about it for a moment, that pot making is the very thing that suggests the traditional philosophical opposition between form and content.

It was no accident that I pointed out, when I first discussed pots that, in places where they are destined to accompany the dead in their tombs, people do something more: they make holes in them. Indeed, the spiritual core of pots, their linguistic origin, is that there be a hole in them through which everything leaks out. When they are reunited with those who have passed over to the other side, pots also find anew their true origin, namely the hole that they were designed to mask in language. There is no signification that does not leak with respect to what is contained in a bowl.

It is truly odd that I made the following discovery after having talked with you about the function of pots. Looking up the status of the word where, good Lord, I usually look, namely in the Bloch and von Wartburg dictionary, I was surprised to see that the term is pre-Celtic, as is witnessed, it seems, by low German and Dutch, with which we share the term. Thus it comes to us from long ago, from no less than the Neolithic. But there is something even better. To get a handle on the idea, we rely on pots dating back to before the Roman invasion – or, more precisely, representing what was instituted prior to it – that were dug up in the area around Trèves [also known in English as Trier]. We find the written word *Pottus* on them which, according to Bloch and von Wartburg, amounts to what is known as a hypocoristic use of the name of the maker; they believe this suffices to indicate how old these pots are.

To me, the only thing that is important is that when pots appear, they are always marked on their surface by a signifier for which they serve as props. Pots provide a function here that is distinct from that of the subject, because the subject, in his relationship to the signifier, is not a prerequisite [*préalable*] but, rather, an anticipation. The subject is "presupposed," *hupokeimenon* – that is his essence, his logical definition. He is presupposed, almost induced, even certainly induced – he is not a prop. We are, on the contrary, justified

90

in giving the signifier a manufactured and even a utensil-based prop. The precise origin of utensils, insofar as it delineates the field of specifically human manufacturing, lies therein.

Signification as produced serves as a lure to veil from us the status of the essence of language, insofar as, by its very essence, it signifies nothing. What proves this is that, in its essential function, speaking [*le dire*] is not a signifying operation.

This is clearly how we analysts view it. What we are seeking is that which holds what is articulated about the Other in abeyance, and lies outside of the Other as such – S_2 as outside of the field. What is its subject? That is the question. And if this subject cannot in any way be grasped by discourse, what is the proper articulation of what can be substituted for it?

The meaning of castration is counterbalanced by that of jouissance. But it is not enough to perceive this relationship. In what became clear at a time that is not very distant, people simultaneously cried out for truth and jouissance [May 1968]. But it certainly does not suffice to aspire to jouissance without constraints, when it is clear that, for every being included in language and utensils, jouissance can only be articulated in the register inherent to both of them: the register of the remainder [or: leftover (or scrap), *reste*] that I defined as surplus jouissance.

We will pick it up there on January 8.

December 11, 1968

VI

TOWARD A PRACTICE OF LOGIC IN PSYCHOANALYSIS

Freud is watching me
From linguistics to logic
A [kind of] writing without equivocation
Form and content
From the pot to the wager

Happy New Year. 69 is a fine number. On such holidays, I always receive a little gift from somewhere. The latest one is a short article that came out in the January 1st issue of the *Nouvelle Revue Française* entitled "Quelques traits du style de Jacques Lacan" ["A few characteristics of Jacques Lacan's style"; Georges Mounin, *NRF*, 193, (January 1969): 84–92].

It's true that my style is a problem. I could have begun my *Écrits* with a very old article of mine on the problem of style, which I've never reread. Perhaps if I reread it, it would enlighten me. In the meantime, I am of course the last person to be able to account for mine, and good Lord, I don't see why someone else shouldn't take a stab at it.

That is what happened, and it was a professor of linguistics who did so. I need not personally assess the results of his efforts, but from what I have heard, people are rather inclined to think that it was perhaps not the best moment to publish it, given the suspicion in certain remote quarters about the general quality of teaching being dispensed by professors. In short, I have heard from certain people that they didn't find it terribly insightful.

I'll let you be the judge of that. For my part, I'm not complaining about it. I don't see how anyone can glean the slightest idea about my teaching from it.

But the author tosses in a barb. I apparently dared to write the words "Freud and I" somewhere. As you can see, he considers himself quite a hotshot. What I wrote may not have the exact meaning the author indignantly attributes to it, but it clearly shows the sort of reverence we find around us today, at least in certain fields. What could be scandalous – according to this professor who admits that he hasn't the slightest idea what Freud contributed – about someone, who has spent his life working with Freud's texts, saying "Freud and I"?

I will go further still. With this attack on my supposed lack of respect ringing in my ears, I could do no else than recall an anecdote that I have already told here.

It was back in the day when, along with P'tit Louis, I was engaged, with great difficulty, in one of those activities off of which coastal populations live. There were three great guys whose names are still dear to me, with whom I did quite a few things that I won't go into here, and there was one who went by the name of P'tit Louis. We had just eaten sardines from a tin and the tin was floating in the water near the boat. P'tit Louis spoke the following very simple words: "You see that tin over there because you are looking at it. Well, that tin has no need to see you to be looking at you [*te regarder*]."

The relationship between this anecdote and "Freud and I" leaves open the question where I situate myself in this couple. Well, rest assured, I still situate myself in the same place, in the place where I was and where I will be as long as I am alive and kicking. Freud has no need to see me in order to be looking at me.

In other words, as it is put in a text that I have already cited here, "a live dog is worth more than a dead man's discourse," especially when the latter has begun to rot on an international scale.

1

I endeavor to restore the functioning of Freud's terms, insofar as they involve no less than a reversal of the very principles of questioning.

Otherwise stated – which is not to say that this states the same thing – what is involved in this effort is the minimal requirement that conditions this renewed questioning.

This minimal requirement is as follows: to train psychoanalysts. This questioning cannot, in fact, be done without resituating the subject in his authentic position, which is why I recalled the position that is at issue at the beginning of this year. It is the one that, right from the outset, situates the subject as dependent on the signifier.

Everything worthwhile that was asserted in the early practice of analysis – where people assuredly took puns and word games into account, and for good reason – revolves around this fundamental condition. I simply took up that level and legalized it, as it were, by adopting what linguistics furnishes, and especially the basis it delineates known as phonology: the specific play of phonemes. It was truly necessary to realize that this quite simply confirmed – a bit late of course, but obviously less late than the general public, and thus less late than psychoanalysts – the trail Freud had blazed.

At the linguistic level, these coincide, for it is truly phonemic material itself that is involved in the games of the unconscious. But there's no reason to stop there, regardless, moreover, of the degree of competence I formerly showed in the use of what is, after all, merely one part of linguistics. You have since seen me do research – the kind that consists in grasping isomorphisms between the status of the subject and what has been promulgated by already constituted disciplines – wherever those disciplines provide us the opportunity to do so. Now we must investigate another discipline, one that allows us to note an isomorphism that seems immediate [*qui est de l'abord*], but whose fabric [*étoffe*] may turn out to be identical, as I have already claimed.

What is that discipline? I will call it the practice of logic [or: the logician's practice, *la pratique logicienne*].

This does not seem to me to be a bad term with which to precisely designate what is involved. Indeed, what necessitates this practice is the locus in which it currently operates, although it is not inconceivable that it will manage to explore other realms. What is this locus? After something happened that freed logic from the tradition to which it had been confined for centuries, the locus in which it now operates is the field of mathematics.

It is certainly no accident – it could have been foreseen, after the fact, unfortunately – that it is at the level of mathematical discourse that the practice of logic would manage to occur. What could be more tempting to logic than mathematics, where the discourse of demonstration seems to enjoy complete autonomy with respect to what is known as experience? It might have seemed, in fact, that this discourse obtained its certainty solely from itself – namely, the requirements of coherence that it imposed on itself.

94   What sort of image can we provide for the kind of logic that attached itself to the field of mathematics? Is it a mode of thought that is separate from mathematics, even if it sustains the scientific tide, which would be – with respect to a certain form of progress, where we have this and then that – *recessus* [a recess]?

Figure 6.1: The Recess

This image of a recess is worth exorcising, for we are going to see that logic involves nothing of the kind.

This gives me the opportunity to recall that it is always a mistake to resort to an image to explain a metaphor.

All attempts to subordinate metaphors to images must be considered suspect, for they are always propped up by the specular image of the body. This image is flawed in a way that can be illustrated very simply, even if it is no more than an illustration, merely by saying that the anthropomorphic image masks the function of the orifices. Hence the value as an apologue of my pot with a hole in it, with which I left you last year. The hole in the pot cannot be seen in a mirror unless we look through the said hole. Hence the inside-out value of pots as utensils that I only brought up in order to indicate the following: what human industry fashions in such elementary forms is designed, strictly speaking, to mask the true effects of structure.

This digression is designed to expressly introduce a distinction that should be kept in mind: form is not [the same thing as] formalism.

Even linguists – I'm not talking, of course, about those who don't know what they're talking about – can occasionally lapse into error on this score. For example, the author I mentioned earlier, who gives zero proof of his competence, says that I spoke about Hjelmslev, whereas I have never done so. On the contrary, Jakobson's name is remarkably absent from his article, at least I believe so – I [confess that I] merely "thumbed through it," an expression the author himself uses – which undoubtedly excuses him from having to gauge whether the use I made of the functions of metaphor and metonymy is relevant or not.

To return to the crucial point, which is the distinction between form and formalism, I will first try to illustrate it with several forms. Indeed, this is necessary for whoever is engaged, as the psychoanalyst is, in the cuts that, because they reach a field in which the body is

95

exposed, lead to the falling away of something that has some shape [*forme*].

To touch on one of the images that psychoanalytic practice brings out, and no one knows where it comes from, I will recall to mind the bowl that contains milk, the one that is evoked by being taken from the bottom, going by the name of "breast," the first of the various objects *a*. This bowl is not the structure by which the breast can be asserted to be homologous to the veneer-like connection of the placenta – it is its very physiological reality, without words being involved. However, in order to know that the breast is physiologically present before it is taken up in the dialectic of object *a*, in order for the breast to be visible, one must already have at one's disposal a rather advanced zoology, and that presupposes the express usage of a classification whose relations with logic we would be foolish to minimize.

We must, after all, be coherent. People were able to reproach Aristotle's logic, and its use of the terms "genus" and "species," for having simply been tacked on to a zoological practice – that is, to the existence of individuals that were zoologically defined. Although people make this somewhat reprimanding remark, we must nevertheless perceive, inversely, that this zoology itself entails a logic, and that it is a fact of structure, of logical structure, naturally.

As you see, there is a strict distinction to be made here between what is already implied by all exploratory experimentation [*expérience*] as such and what we are going to call into question regarding the emergence of the subject.

Formalism, in its function as a cut, can undoubtedly be better isolated in mathematics.

2

What is the status of the use of formalism in mathematics?

It has been said of mathematical discourse that it has no meaning, and that one never knows whether what one says in it is true. This is an extreme, paradoxical formulation, which was repeated by Kojève, but he was merely borrowing it from Bertrand Russell, about whom it is worth recalling that he was one of the founders of the logical formalization of this discourse – meaning that this formulation did not arise outside of the field.

Formalism in mathematics is the attempt to put mathematics to a test that we can define as follows: to ground what clearly seems to be the case, namely, that it functions without a subject.

To convey this to those who don't immediately grasp what I am designating here, ask yourself who would ever speak about the impact of the "observer" on mathematical constructions, the "observer" as he is isolated elsewhere? There is no conceivable trace in mathematics of what is known as "subjective error." Even if math is used to construct devices that allow people in other fields to give a measurable meaning to subjective error, it has nothing to do with mathematical discourse itself. Even when mathematicians discuss subjective error, there is no middle ground: either the terms of the discourse are exact and irrefutable or they are not. That is, at least, its requirement. Nothing is accepted therein that does not satisfy this requirement.

Then what about the mathematician? As I just said, formalizing this discourse consists in ensuring that it holds up all by itself, even without him. This implies the construction of the language known as "mathematical logic," but which would be better called the "practice of logic" or "logician's practice" [*pratique de la logique, ou pratique logicienne*] in the field of mathematics. The condition for carrying out the test [of grounding what functions without a subject] presents itself in a twofold form which may appear to be antinomic.

The first condition is that it be a language without equivocation. I just mentioned the fact that mathematical discourse is devoid of equivocation. Logical language seems to have no trouble reinforcing and refining this.

"Devoid of equivocation" concerns something that one can always call an "object," but it is not just any old object. To illustrate what I mean, consider how Quine, in his book *Word and Object*, while endeavoring to leave behind the field of mathematics in order to extend the new logician's practice to the study of everyday discourse, feels obliged to refer to what he calls an "object language." Which is tantamount to satisfying the condition of a language devoid of equivocation.

This gives me a perfect opportunity to bring out that it is, on the contrary, the nature of ordinary discourse [*discours fondamental*], not simply to be equivocal, but to consist essentially of the sliding of signification under any and all discourse. I emphasized this as soon as I began to refer to language.

Thus, the first condition of this language is that it be devoid of equivocation. This can refer only to a certain object targeted by mathematics, which is unlike any other object. This is clearly why Quine, once he applies logic to everyday discourse [*discours commun*], speaks of "ob language," prudently stopping after the first syllable [of "object"].

The second condition is that this language be pure writing. Nothing about it can constitute mere interpretation. The entire structure – I mean what can be attributed to the object – is what constitutes this writing. Thus nothing in this formalization is considered to be interpretation. The function of isomorphism – which constitutes a certain number of fields as being encompassed by one and the same written formula – is juxtaposed here to the fundamental equivocation of everyday discourse.

One can easily enter into the practice of what has been constructed in this way if one takes a bit of trouble – something I don't find beneath me, as opposed to what the article I mentioned earlier seems to suggest. Everyone can broach Gödel's theorem, for example – it suffices to buy a good book on the subject or go to the right classes. We are, after all, in a "multidisciplinary" era – which is, perhaps, a necessity that did not come from out of the blue, but rather from perceiving the trouble people have with what is improperly called "mental limitation." Gödel's theorems, for there are two of them, are, moreover, called "theorems of limitation."

They concern arithmetic, the discourse that seems to be the most well-founded. Two and two make four, after all. Nothing seems to be better founded than that. Naturally, people didn't stop there. Over time they noticed plenty of things, but all of them follow directly from two plus two equals four. In other words, we have here a discourse that, to all appearances, is what is known as "consistent."

The consistency of a system means that, when you enunciate a proposition therein, you can definitively say either that "it is acceptable as a theorem," as it is put, "of the system," or "it is not and its negation is" – if, that is, one believes it necessary to take the trouble to make a theorem out of everything that can be put negatively. This result is obtained by following a series of procedures about which there can be no doubt and which are known as demonstrations.

The progress of the logician's practice has allowed for the grounding of entirely new results, thanks solely to the use of formalization procedures. They involve making two columns, as it were. In one of them, we place what is stated in basic mathematical discourse, and in the other, we place the other discourse, the one that is subjected to the twofold condition of eliminating equivocation and being reduced to pure writing. The first discourse is the one in which mathematics boldly made so much headway, and, curiously enough, without having to revise it periodically in a way that destroyed what was taken for granted in prior eras. By way of contrast, the second discourse is called a "metalanguage," quite improperly in my opinion, for it is merely a closed field that is isolated by a specific practice in what it is quite simply language, the very language without which mathematical discourse could not be enunciated. It is no less improperly that people talk about a "formal language."

It is on the basis of the distinction between the first discourse and metalanguage that Gödel shows that the supposed consistency of the apparently surest area of mathematics, arithmetic, entails what limits it – namely, incompleteness. This means that, on the basis of the very hypothesis of consistency, a formula appears somewhere – and it's enough for there to be one for there to be plenty of others – about which we cannot say "it's true" or "it's false," if we follow the pathways of demonstration accepted as the law of the system. This is the first stage, the first theorem.

Second stage, second theorem. Here I will have to abbreviate. Not only can the system of arithmetic not ensure its own consistency except by constituting its own incompleteness, but as concerns the hypothesis, even if founded, of its consistency, it cannot demonstrate this consistency within itself.

99

I have taken a bit of time here to convey something that is not, strictly speaking, part of our field, if the psychoanalytic field is defined by some sort of olfactory apprehension [see *Écrits*, pp. 221, 280, 389, 407n.20, and 509].

When I said "is not, strictly speaking, part of . . .," the sentence implied that I would end it with "our subject." And you see what I encounter: the sore point that it is unthinkable to operate in the psychoanalytic field if we don't give the subject its correct status.

What do we find in the practice of mathematical logic if not the exact residue in which the presence of the subject is designated? At least this is what a mathematician, certainly one of the greatest, John von Neumann, seems to imply when he comments, undoubtedly a bit imprudently, that the limitations – I mean those that are logically tenable – are mere "mathematical residues."

Von Neumann is not aiming there at any sort of antinomy, or at some sort of classical brainteaser which involves learning, for example, that the term "obsolete" is an obsolete term, and speculating on that basis about the predicates that apply to themselves and those that don't, with all the paradoxes this can bring with it. That is not what is involved here, but rather the construction of a limit.

We undoubtedly discover nothing in logic that mathematical discourse didn't itself discover, since it is in this field of discoveries that the method is put to the test. Mathematical discourse is simply questioned regarding the following, which is nevertheless essential: up to what point can it account for itself? We could say "up to what point does it coincide with its own content?" if these terms had any meaning, if this were not in fact the very field from which the notion of content had just been, strictly speaking, eliminated. Something is presented here that has its own necessity or *Ananke*, its detour-related necessities, which von Neumann tells us are, in short, just fine. For they attest, after all, to the fact that mathematicians still serve some purpose, still have a role to play. In other words, it is because something is lacking in mathematical discourse that the mathematician's desire comes into play.

100   Well, I nevertheless believe that von Neumann goes a bit too far here. First of all, the term "residue" is improper. The impossibility – I have already discussed the "impossible" in several ways – that is revealed here has a different structure than the one we deal with in the falling away [*chute*] of object *a*. Moreover, and this is no less structural, the lack that is revealed here undoubtedly reveals the presence of the subject, but of no other subject than the one who made the cut, the one who separated the said metalanguage from a certain mathematical field – which is quite simply its discourse – from another isolated language, an artificial language, a formal language.

This cutting is no less fruitful, since it reveals properties that are clearly based on the very fabric of mathematical discourse. People haven't finished, and they won't for some time, elucidating the status of whole numbers, but the question of the place – whether ontological or not – of these numbers is totally foreign to the practice of mathematical discourse insofar as it operates with them and insofar as it can carry out the twofold process of constructing itself and formalizing itself.

3

At first blush, we are far from the center of our interest, and given the little time that remains, I don't know how to bring you back to that center today. Allow me, nevertheless, to quickly return to the point we arrived at at the end of the last class.

The truth says "I." What is the status of the "I"?

The "I" must be strictly distinguished from the subject qua reducible to the function of a cut [or: to the cut as a function, *la fonction de la coupure*], which is impossible to distinguish from that of the unary trait insofar as it isolates a function of the One [or: the One as a function, *une fonction de l'Un*] as simply unique, as simply a cut in numeration. Nonetheless, the "I" is in no way assured thereby, for we can say of it that it "is" and that it "is not," depending on whether it operates as a subject, and whether, by operating as a subject, it exiles itself from jouissance which is no less "I."

Here I must remind you what lies between the two lines, those of enunciation and the enunciated, in the graph constructed to respond to the constitutive questioning of analysis.

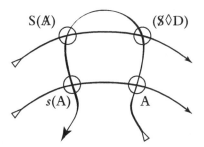

Figure 6.2: The Partial Graph of Desire

The intersection of these two [horizontal] lines by a third line, that of signifying materiality or the elementary differential chain of phonemes, allowed us to designate four points of intersection whose status is precisely given in written terms. Here we have (S ◊ D). Below that we have A, the field of the Other. To the left is s(A), lowercase s of capital A – namely, signification. And lastly, we have capital S(A̶), the signifier of barred A that I have broached many times, but never completely elucidated.

Homologous to the [right-to-left] imaginary return line i(a) → m [see Figure 3.3] that integrates the narcissistic relationship into the field of the enunciated, we have here, halfway [between the two main horizontal lines], what is required at the level of pure enunciation, incarnated in the written form (S ◊ D), which is pronounced barred S, lozenge, D.

Capital D stands for "demand" in this context, as it does wherever I write it, but it is not just any old demand here. "I wonder . . ." [*Je me demande . . .*], and let us write here [at A or d(A); see Figure 5.2] "what you want." The question [*demande*] concerns the Other's desire, in this total ambiguity that allows us to write "I wonder . . . what I want," because my desire is the Other's desire. There is no distinction between them here, if not induced by the very function of enunciation, insofar as it bears within itself its meaning as initially obscure.

As I already said, every enunciation, even the simplest, evokes its meaning as a mere consequence of its own emergence. "It is raining" is a discursive event [*un événement de discours*], regarding which it is but secondary to know what it means about rain. In certain contexts, anyone can say "It is raining." "It is raining" can have the most varied meanings. Need I mention, in this regard, that the exclamation "Leave!" [*Sortez!*] does not resonate everywhere as it does in [Jean Racine's tragedy] *Bajazet*?

If there is something to note about this graph that is more important than the commentary that accompanies it, it is the structural vectors. You will notice that they converge on the Other's desire, where "Thou" dominates "I" as Thou-ing/killing it [*le* tu-ant], as I put it. It is around the Other's desire that discourse, as we organize it in psychoanalysis under a fallaciously neutral appearance, leaves room for the hints of demand at its most acute point. Everything found at the source, as is indicated by the retroactive arrow, converges on the Other's desire.

What corresponds to the Other's desire as its imaginary prop is what I have always written in the form ($ \lozenge a$) – in other words, fantasy – wherein lies the "I" function, albeit under wraps. As opposed to the point of convergence known as the Other's desire, it is in a divergent fashion that the "I" hidden behind ($ \lozenge a$) moves – in a form that I initially called that of true questioning, radical questioning – toward the two points where the elements of the answer lie [see Figure 3.3].

On the upper line, [it moves toward] S(Ⱥ), signifying that A is barred. This is precisely what I took the trouble, and also gave you the trouble, of establishing as a prop for conceptualizing what I am enunciating here – namely, that the field of the Other nowhere and to no degree assures the consistency of the discourse that is articulated there. Never, even in cases that appear to be the surest.

On the lower line, [it moves toward] $s(A)$, a signification insofar as it is fundamentally alienated. And it is here that you must grasp why I began this year's Seminar by defining "surplus jouissance" and its relation with everything we can call the means of production, in the most radical sense of the term. It is the level of signification, assuming that pots are, as I pointed out, merely devices with which to mask the major consequences of discourse – namely, the exclusion of jouissance.

You see the *Entzweiung* – this is Hegel's term [sometimes translated by "diremption"] – the radical division between these two terms, which is the very one to which Freud's discourse at the end of his life led: the division of the "I" articulated as such [see "The Splitting of the Ego in the Process of Defense," SE XXIII, pp. 275–8].

There is, on the one hand, the field in which the Other – which was for a long time that of the philosophers – could in some sense, through some imagination, answer for truth. Yet this is ruled out by the mere examination of the functions of language. By which I mean that we know how to bring in the cut as a function that replies "No, no" to the God of the philosophers.

There is, on the other hand, in another register, the field in which jouissance apparently awaits the subject. It is precisely here that he is a slave, and in the very way in which people were heretofore able to reproach psychoanalysis for misrecognizing him – namely, he is subjected to "the social," as it is put. People don't realize that they are contradicting themselves, and that the materialism said to be historical has no meaning unless we perceive that it does not depend upon social structure, since Marx himself asserts that it is the means of production – in other words, that with which we make things that mislead [or: deceive, *trompent*] surplus jouissance, and which, far from being able to hope to fill up the field of jouissance, cannot even suffice for what is lost in it owing to the Other.

As usual, I couldn't proceed any faster, good Lord, than the beat of my own drummer. I can, nevertheless, indicate where I intend to pick things up next time.

I will tell you that it is not in vain that what I retained from what the God of the Jews says is "I am what I is." It is high time that something finally be dissipated there, something already clearly said by Pascal. If you are willing to read a short book published by Desclée De Brouwer [in Paris in 1956], entitled *Pari de Pascal* ["Pascal's Wager"], it may help you understand what I will tell you next time. The author, Georges Brunet, truly knows what he is talking about. As we saw earlier, that is not true of all professors. What he says doesn't go far, nevertheless, but at least he knows what he is talking about. His book will, in addition, be indispensable to you in unscrambling the little piece of paper folded in four found in Pascal's pocket when he died. I have already commented on that [see Seminar XIII].

I talk a lot about death, probably in order to deliver us from many other relations with others that I mentioned earlier. My relations with the dead Freud – that has an entirely different meaning.

But if you are willing to read this book by Georges Brunet, you will at least know what I am talking about when I speak about Pascal's text, which is barely a quarter of a text, as you will see. The text overlaps itself, is confused, crisscrossed, and annotated. It was turned into a text, of course, for the pleasure of professors. That pleasure doesn't go far, for they have never managed to glean absolutely anything from it.

There is something that is quite clear, however, and I will begin with it next time, which is that there is strictly nothing other than "I" that is at stake in it. People spend time wondering if God exists, as if that were even a question. God is – there is no doubt about that, yet it absolutely does not prove that He exists. The question does not arise. But we must know whether "I" exists.

Does "I" exist? I think I will be able to get you to sense that it is around this uncertainty that Pascal's wager revolves.

January 8, 1969

ON PASCAL'S WAGER

VII

INTRODUCTION TO PASCAL'S WAGER

Modern morality means giving up pleasures
Pleasure from Aristotle to Freud
Once it's wagered, it's lost
Does "I" exist?

I announced last time that I would speak about Pascal's wager. It's quite a responsibility. I even heard that certain people changed their schedules in order to find out what I would say about it, and that they are making an extra unplanned trip to Paris. All that to say that such a declaration is quite a burden.

As it is clear that I cannot provide an exhaustive account here, or summarize for you everything that has been said about Pascal's wager, I am forced to assume you have a basic knowledge of what it involves. I cannot restate Pascal's wager either, because, as I told you last time, it is not, strictly speaking, a coherent statement. Many are those who were surprised that someone who was clearly capable of some rigor could propose something so untenable.

In the last class, I think I introduced sufficiently, just barely sufficiently, what generally explains the use we are going to make of it. Let's not waste time repeating it today. You will clearly see the use I have in mind, especially since this is not the first time that I have talked about it. On a certain day in February 1966, I believe, I mentioned it specifically regarding object *a*. As you will see, we will continue to revolve around that object today. Those who recall what I said about it at the time – perhaps there are a few of you, I am even sure of it – already glimpse what is at stake.

It so happened that I was asked to speak on the same topic at Yale in October 1967. But I had my hands so full with those for whom I make the effort to teach – namely, psychoanalysts – that I failed to keep my promise at Yale. It was only much later that I heard this had been viewed as a bit scandalous. I admit that it was not terribly polite of me. I will try to say today what I could have said on that occasion, there being no need for any preparation to understand it.

Let us thus begin from the beginning, as if we were at Yale.

What is at issue?

1

You must have heard of something known as the wager, for it is mentioned several times in the collection entitled *Pensées*.

There was something as unseemly about the very text of Pascal's *Pensées*, right from the outset, as the use people made of what is known as the wager. Indeed, as you know, his *Pensées* consists of notes taken by Pascal for a grand opus he had in mind. But the book had not yet been assembled by the time he died. So it was assembled for him. What we have is an edition prepared by the men from Port-Royal [des Champs]. It was not at all badly cobbled together. They were friends of his, and one of them, by the name of Filleau de La Chaise – who was not the sharpest pencil in the box, but quite legible nevertheless – tells us that Pascal had very clearly explained to them what he wanted to do and that they did as they were told.

The fact remains that, in constructing the work, many things in the notes were left out, and other people have taken the risk of reconstructing his notes differently.

Still other people said to themselves that, as our culture progresses, we perceive, in short, that [his] discourse is not as simple as it seems, and that when you try to assemble it, something is inevitably lost. So they began to prepare what are known as "critical editions," but such editions take on a totally different import when it comes to a collection of notes. Here too, it was a bit tricky, for there are several different ways of grouping together the different "bundles" [of papers], as they put it, and we thus have several editions: those by Tourneur, Lafuma, X, and Z. This does not simplify things, but rest assured that it clarifies them.

109   As for the wager, it is totally separate.

It is a small piece of paper folded in four. What makes the book I recommended interesting is that you can see it for yourself, for it includes a reproduction of it.

There are also a number of different transcriptions of the wager. Indeed, its transcription poses a problem, given that we are talking about handwritten notes with various additions, deletions, entire paragraphs written between the lines of other paragraphs, sentences written in the margins with arrows, and so on. All of it is, moreover, quite precise, and provides ample material to examine and discuss.

But there is one thing we can be sure of, which is that Pascal never claimed that he had made his wager coherent.

This little paper must have been dear to him, since everything suggests that he had it in his pocket, in the very place where I currently have the thingamajig for the microphone, a gizmo that serves no purpose.

In short, you have heard tell of something that is part and parcel of the wager and that sounds like this: "giving up pleasures." Pascal said it and repeated it in the plural.

Everyone knows that the act of giving something up is supposed to be at the core of what is known as a Christian life. It is the background noise thereof. It sounds from afar like the sound of a bell ringing through everything Pascal tells us about ethics (others around him, too). We need to know if it is a death knell. In fact, it is not really a death knell, for every now and then it takes a more joyful turn. I would like to make it clear that it is the very foundation on which is built what one might qualify as modern morality.

To drive this point home, I will remind you of the status of what is known as enterprise insofar as it involves the reinvestment, as they say, of profits. The *capitalist* enterprise, to call a spade a spade, does not place the means of production in the service of pleasure. This is such a fundamental feature that certain thinkers, for example, who work in the margins, strive to rehabilitate expenditure – an effort that is certainly quite timid, that cannot imagine that it is sailing to success, but that tends rather to cast doubt on what might be called our lifestyle. Georges Bataille, a thinker in the margins of our field, cogitated and produced several highly legible works on this topic, which are nevertheless not likely to become influential.

110

When I say that modern morality means giving up pleasures, it is merely a first take on the question. By which I mean that, if we consider things historically, it corresponds to a turning point [or: breaking point, *cassure*]. Which doesn't mean that we need look no further, no more than when it comes to any other historical turning point, in order to grasp what is at issue, but there is no reason to minimize it. We would do well to take note of it.

There is never enough time for me to emphasize here what might have been meant by the search for "well-being" [*bien-être*] and what justified the use of the term. Nevertheless, those who pay attention to what I say, even just from time to time, even if only superficially, should remember what I have said about the Kantian distinction between *das Wohl*, feeling good, and *das Gute*, the good. This is clearly what I just referred to as a turning point. Whatever the justification given for Kant's claims – whether we should see the very soul of ethics in them or rather shed light on them through their relationship to Sade, as I have done – it is an undeniable fact that such thoughts were thought.

We have believed for some time that thought is underpinned by something that is perhaps related to what I have already mentioned – namely, structure, resulting from a certain use of the means of production. But there are perhaps other ways to broach it, as I am doing this year. In any case, what I mean by the term "well-being" is what is known in the philosophical tradition as *hedone*, pleasure.

Hedone, as it has been used, assumes that pleasure corresponds to a certain relationship that I will say sets "the right tone with nature," regarding which we men, or beings presumed to be such, are less masters than officiants. This is what oriented those who, in founding morality throughout Antiquity, took as their main landmark the idea that pleasure is what must guide us along this path, that it is in any case the first link. The question that arose next for them was to know why some pleasures do not set the right tone. The point then was to pleasure [*plaisirer*], as it were, pleasure itself, and to find the module of the right tone at the heart of pleasure; they went so far as to perceive that what lies at the margins, and seems to function perversely, is nevertheless justifiable with regard to what pleasure gives us a sense of.

111

It is for good reason that one can say that this aim led to asceticism. One can give it its watchword, which is the following: "not too much work."

Now, up to a certain point in time, this watchword was hardly extraordinary. I believe, however, that those of you who are here realize that this is no longer the case. We have to do a hell of a lot to reach this "not too much work." Going out on strike, for example, does not involve simply twiddling one's thumbs, but also dying of hunger in the meantime. Up until a certain era, people had no need to resort to such means. The fact that it requires so much effort to have "not too much work" clearly shows that something has changed.

Stated differently, the asceticism of pleasure barely needed to be emphasized, inasmuch as morality was founded on the idea that there is a good somewhere and that law resides in this good. In the series that I am designating, things seem to hang together. But we are no longer in a context that follows a natural progression.

Otium cum dignitate [dignified idleness] reigns supreme in Horace's work, as you may or may not know. Everyone knew it a century ago, because everyone read Horace, but thanks to the solid education you received in high school, you don't even know who Horace is. *Otium* is a life of leisure, naturally not our leisure activities, which are forced. You are given leisure time so that you will run out and buy a train ticket at the Gare de Lyon – first you have to pay for it, then dash off to the mountains where, for two weeks, your punitive homework assignment is to stand in line at the bottom of ski lifts. You don't go there to have a good time. Someone who doesn't go, who doesn't work at his leisure activities, is undignified. *Otium* is currently *cum indignitate* [idleness is currently undignified]. And it's only going to get worse, unless something drastic happens. In other words, in our times, to refuse to work is a challenge; it stands and can only stand as a challenge.

Excuse me for stressing this still further. Consider St. Thomas Aquinas. He might seem to be a rather gray-faced sort of guy. Nevertheless, insofar as he formally – I am only saying formally – reinjected Aristotle's thought into Christianity, he could only characterize the good as the Sovereign Good in terms that were, in the final analysis, hedonistic.

We mustn't view this monolithically, of course, if nothing else because all sorts of misunderstandings slip into such propositions, misunderstandings that were already obvious even when such propositions reigned supreme. To follow their trail and see how different spiritual guides worked this out would require a great deal of effort and discernment.

With these reminders I simply wanted to show you our orientation, owing to the fact that a radical shift has assuredly taken place with regard to pleasure. Our point of departure obviously can only be to question the ideology of pleasure on the basis of what renders somewhat obsolete for us everything that underpinned it. In order to do so, it makes sense to situate ourselves at the level of the means of production, because they are henceforth what really conditions the practice of pleasure.

[Following on what] I indicated earlier, we see that ski resorts can put advertisements on one page telling you how to spend your vacation properly – namely, hymns to the sun – and on the opposite page list ski lift requirements and conditions. It would suffice to add that all of that happens at the expense of the simple organization of everyday life, as is attested to by the sordid wasteland all around us, especially in big cities.

It was important to remind you of these points because they allow us to perceive how we make use of the pleasure principle in psychoanalysis.

2

In psychoanalysis, the pleasure principle is situated and reigns supreme in the unconscious. This means that, to us, pleasure – or rather, the very notion of pleasure – lies in the catacombs.

Freud's discovery serves in this regard as a secret late-night visitor. He is the one who returns from afar and finds that strange slippages have occurred during his absence. "You know where I found pleasure," he seems to say to us, "this flower of our age, this lightness? It is now overexerting itself in the underworld, *Acheronta*, working solely to ensure the whole thing doesn't blow up, to impose some moderation on all these madmen by interjecting some slip of the tongue, because if it worked out just fine, where would we be?"

Indeed, in Freud's pleasure principle there is something like a power of rectification, tempering, or "lowest tension," as he puts it. It is a sort of invisible weaver that oversees everything to ensure that the loom's gears don't get too hot. What possible relationship can there be between that and the sovereign pleasure of contemplative *farniente* that we find, for example, in Aristotle's work?

I am returning to this, not in order to go in circles, but because it is such as to make us suspect that there is, perhaps, some ambiguity in this contemplation – I mean, a fantasy. Maybe we shouldn't take it too literally, although the fact that it has come down to us after so many twists and turns makes it undoubtedly quite precarious to gauge what it involved at the time. I am saying this to correct what, at the point at which I have arrived in my discourse, might be thought to be some sort of reference to the good old days. I know this is hard to avoid, but it is not a reason to fail to point out that I don't lend it much credence.

Be that as it may, pleasure in Freud's work is stamped by an obvious ambiguity, which is the "beyond" of the pleasure principle, as he called it.

To say something about it here without going into detail, I will simply recall to mind that Freud wrote that jouissance is fundamentally masochistic. It is clear that this is but a metaphor, since masochism is also situated at a level that is organized differently than the foundational drive [*tendance radicale*] at stake here. When he tries to elaborate on what he at first articulated only metaphorically, Freud tells us that jouissance strives to lower the necessary threshold for the preservation of life, a threshold that the pleasure principle itself defines as an *infimum*, that is, the lowest of the highs, the lowest tension necessary for such preservation. But one can fall still lower, and it is there that pain begins and can but spread [or: express itself, *s'exhaler*]. Freud tells us that, in the end, this

113

movement tends toward death. Otherwise stated, behind the observation of a phenomenon that we can take to be linked to a certain context of practice – that is, linked to the unconscious – Freud opens up a strain of a totally different nature with his "beyond."

It seems clear that we have here a certain ambiguity – an ambiguity that what I just said didn't fail to preserve – between, on the one hand, the death drive, which is theoretical, and, on the other hand, masochism which is but a practice – a practice that is far more astute, but of what? A practice of jouissance, insofar as it cannot in any way be identified with the rule of pleasure. In other words, with psychoanalytic experience, jouissance *takes on color* [or: flushes, *se colore*], if you will allow me this condensed expression.

There is, of course, a whole backdrop to this reference. We would have to say that, with respect to space with its three dimensions, color could undoubtedly add one or two more, perhaps even three, if we knew how to do it. Stoics, Epicureans, and other doctrinaires of the reign of pleasure remain colorless regarding the investigation that we are conducting. Don't you see that based on my comment?

Since I introduced jouissance into our vocabulary, I have tried to indicate that its function is essentially a relationship to the body, but not just any old relationship. It is based on an exclusion that is at the same time an inclusion. Hence my attempt to create a topology that corrects the claims made in psychoanalysis heretofore. I'm not going to mention them all today, but it is clear that people talk about nothing else at every stage – the formation of the non-ego realm through "rejection" [*rejet*], the function of what is known as "incorporation" and that is translated as "introjection," as if it involved an inside-to-outside relationship and not a far more complex topology. As it has been expressed up until now, psychoanalytic ideology is, in short, remarkably awkward, and this is explained by analysts' failure to construct an adequate topology.

The topology of jouissance is the topology of the subject. It is the topology that "for oneselfs" [or: "for itselfs," *poursoit*] our existence as subjects.

Poursoir is a new verb that came to me. Since people have been talking about the in-itself [*en-soi*] and the for-itself [*pour-soi*] for some time, I don't see why we can't create variations. It's terribly amusing. We could, for example, write *en-soi* differently – as *anse-oie* [goose cove] or *en-soie* [in silk], and so on and so forth. When I am alone, I have a lot of fun. The interest of the verb *poursoir* is that it immediately gives rise to little friends, like *pourvoir* [in order to see] and *surseoir*. If *poursoir* is aligned with *surseoir*, we'd have to change the spelling, and write it as *pourseoir*.

This is of interest if it helps us think about things, especially the following dichotomy. Is the subject *poursu* against jouissance? In other words, does he recognize himself there [or: encounter himself there, *s'y éprouve-t-il*]? Does he play his little game in the matter? Does he, in the end, master it? Or is he rather *soursi* to jouissance? Is he dependent upon it, its slave? This is an interesting question, but in order to answer it, we must begin with the following: all of our access to jouissance is, in any case, commanded by the topology of the subject. This leads to several difficulties, I assure you, at the level of statements about jouissance.

Every now and then I talk with people who are not necessarily well known, but who are very intelligent, and who think that jouissance could be ensured on the basis of the impossible conjunction that I stated last time, between discourse and formal language. This way of thinking is obviously tied to a mirage that consists in believing that all problems related to jouissance are essentially linked to the subject's division. They conclude therefrom that if the subject were no longer divided, jouissance would be refound.

Yet we have to be very careful here. The subject determines the structure of jouissance, but all we can hope for from it, until things change radically, are recovery practices. This means that what the subject recovers has nothing to do with jouissance, but with its loss. A guy by the name of Hegel already addressed these problems, quite well I might add.

Hegel did not write *pour-soi* the way I do, and that is not unimportant. The way in which he constructed the adventure of jouissance is, of course, entirely dominated, as it should be, by the phenomenology of mind – that is, of the subject – but his mistake, so to speak, is one he makes right from the outset, and thus it cannot help but impact all of his work. Indeed, his dialectic, as it is known, begins from relations between master and slave, and the struggle to the death of pure prestige, as he says. What does this mean if not that the master has given up jouissance? As the slave accepts to be dominated only to preserve his body [*que pour le salut de son corps*], it is hard to see why, in such an explanatory perspective, he no longer has jouissance on his hands. You can't, after all, have your cake and eat it too. If the master initially takes the risk, it's clearly because he leaves jouissance to the other. It is quite odd that this is not absolutely clear.

Must I mention here what all of the literature of Antiquity attests to, namely, that it wasn't so bad to be a slave? It exempted you from a great deal of political bother, in any case. Let there be no misunderstanding here, for I am talking about a mythical slave, the one mentioned at the beginning of Hegel's *Phenomenology*. Yet this mythical slave has its historical correspondents.

Open up Terence's work, for example. It is no accident that in comedy, the young girl destined to be triumphantly married to the nice yet spoiled boy from a good family, is always a slave. In order for everything to work out properly, and in order to make fun of us, which is the function of comedy, she has to be a slave, even though she is actually from a very good family and became a slave by accident. In the end it all comes out, but the boy has gone so far that he cannot decently say at that moment, "Timeout, I don't want to play the game anymore. If I had known that she was the daughter of my father's best friend, I would never have taken the slightest interest in her." Ancient comedy is precisely designed to show us that the daughter of the master of the property next door is not the one we should pursue if we are interested in jouissance. She's a bit stiff, a bit too closely associated with her inheritance.

Please excuse me for having allowed myself to tell all these little tales, but it was in order to highlight the fact that what was at stake back then was quite different from what the tide of history recovered by freeing the slaves. They were freed from we know not what, but one thing is clear: at every stage this puts them in chains. At every stage of the recovery, it shackles them to surplus jouissance.

I believe I have made it amply clear, since the beginning of the year, that surplus jouissance is something other than jouissance. Surplus jouissance is what corresponds, not to jouissance, but rather to the loss of jouissance, insofar as, from the latter arises what becomes the cause that is conjugated with the desire for knowledge and with the activity I recently qualified as ferocious, which proceeds from surplus jouissance.

This is the authentic mechanism. It was important to remind you of this before taking up Pascal.

3

Pascal was, like all of us, a man of his times, and his wager obviously has to do with people's interest back then in how to split up the ante [or: pot, in a game of chance, which involves calculating probabilities, *la règle des partis*].

Lend me credence regarding such little historical points, for I have read everything that can be found. My friend Guilbaud has written a few short, very short articles – I only have reprints of them, but I will ask where you can find them – that are altogether decisive regarding the relationship between *la règle des partis* and the wager. He is not the only one, moreover, for this is also discussed in the book by Brunet.

117

I would have to explain *la règle des partis* at length to show you its importance in the development of mathematical theory. You should simply realize that there is nothing more cutting edge regarding what is at stake for us concerning the subject. Nothing more purely isolates the status of our relations with the signifier than what is known as gambling [or: craps or Seven-Eleven, *jeu*], insofar as it is a practice defined by the fact that it involves a certain number of rolls of the dice that take place in accordance with certain rules. It seems that nothing interests us here other than the most gratuitous manipulation of combinations, and nevertheless the question of the status of the decisions to be made is nowhere stronger and more necessary than in the field of the gratuitous. It is in relation to gambling that the wager takes on its import.

The wager satisfies none of the conditions that would be acceptable in a game [of chance, *jeu*]. Many authors have tried to rationalize it in some way with the respect to what, in fact, served Pascal as a reference point, but they only end up demonstrating that it doesn't work, and Pascal must have known it. This is precisely what makes the way in which he handles the wager interesting.

Adopting a shortsighted approach that is quite exemplary, writers – about whom we can at least say that they do us a favor by showing us how the impasse in which they get bogged down arises – highlight in Pascal's text how the different stakes are laid out [or: distributed, *rapports d'extension de l'enjeu*]. There is, on one side, a life the jouissance of which one gives up in order to wager it, just as the ante, once it is wagered, is lost, as Pascal indicates in his study of *la règle des partis*. On the other side, the partner's side, the ante consists of what Pascal calls "an infinity of infinitely happy lives."

The question arises here whether this infinity of *lives* should be understood in the singular or the plural [*vie* (life) and *vies* (lives) are pronounced identically in French; see *Pari de Pascal*, p. 135]. An infinity of *life*, in the singular, doesn't mean much, unless it involves changing the meaning the word "infinity" has in the context of *la règle des partis*. We are nevertheless delivered over here to the ambiguity of the little piece of paper. The word *heureuse* [happy] is unfinished [on the slip of paper], so why would we think that the word *vie* is complete? An *s* could also be attached to it, highlighting the numerical aspect of the comparison emphasized here between the antes. In any case, the stakes must be measured numerically.

The same is true of something that has no other name than "uncertainty." It, too, is taken up numerically. Pascal even writes that, compared to one chance of gain, we can assume an infinity of chances of loss, thus presenting numerically the element of chance,

118

which was completely excluded in what he said about *la règle des partis*, which assumes equal chances on both sides.

I am stressing the numerical aspect because on this little piece of paper – which is in no wise a written text or something worked out, but a mere succession of signs that were written – Pascal says (as he does elsewhere) that in wagering on the fundamental uncertainty – in other words, "Is there a partner or not?" – you have one chance out of two [of winning]. In other words, God either exists or He doesn't [p. 133].

We see how untenable this is, and we have no need to refute it. But do we clearly see where everything at stake at this level of uncertainty lies? Indeed, it is quite clear that nothing in this calculation is self-evident, and I can always object to the formulation of the wager that I'll hold on to what I have, for the life I have already keeps me busy enough. Pascal therefore ups the ante by telling us that this life is nothing. What does that mean? It can't be zero, for then there would be nothing to wager and no gamble. Pascal says that this life is *a* nothing, which is a horse of a different color.

This is precisely what is at stake in surplus jouissance. And it is because this is what is at stake that there is something that brings our fascination with this discourse to a head.

In taking such a gamble, aren't I wagering too much? The objection undoubtedly still holds, which is why Pascal includes it in the written argumentation of his supposed objector, the latter being nowhere but in himself, he being the only one who knows the contents of his little slip of paper. You can't avoid wagering, Pascal retorts, because you are already embarked [*engagé*; p. 133]. In what respect are you? You are not at all embarked, unless you have to make a decision.

What is a decision? In game theory, as we call it today, which follows directly from what Pascal inaugurated in *la règle des partis*, decision is a structure. It is because decision[-making] is reduced to a structure that we can deal with it in a thoroughly scientific manner. Yet, in the case of the wager, if you must decide between the two choices that are proposed, if you are embarked in any case, it is only from the moment that you are questioned in this way, and by Pascal himself – in other words, from the moment at which you authorize yourself to be "I" in this discourse.

The true dichotomy is not between God exists and God does not exist. Whether Pascal likes it or not, the problem becomes one of an entirely different nature once he asserts that we know, not whether God exists, but neither whether God is nor what He is [p. 133]. As his contemporaries understood and articulated perfectly clearly, this business regarding God is thus a business [or: matter, *affaire*]

119

of facts, which means a business of discourse, if you consider the definition I gave of facts when I told you that there is no such thing as a fact that is not stated [*il n'y a de fait qu'énoncé*]. This is why, when it comes to God, we are entirely dependent on the tradition of the Book.

But what is truly at stake in Pascal's wager is a different question, the one I already stated at the end of my last class: does "I" exist? Or what if "I" does not exist?

Whereas these premises are indispensable, it has taken me a while, and perhaps too long, as is my wont, to present the crux of what is at issue, which leads me to end today at a moment that is not especially opportune.

You should at least realize that if, as opposed to what people think, the wager does not concern the promise [of a future life], but the existence of "I," something can be deduced beyond Pascal's wager, on the condition that we properly situate the function of the cause as it is situated at the level of the subject – namely, object *a*. I will write it, not for the first time, as follows: "*a*–cause."

The essence of the wager is to reduce our life to something we can hold in the palm of our hand. Which is certainly not self-evident. We might well have an entirely different conception of life, an entirely different perspective – namely, that life includes us completely, that we are merely a transit point, a phenomenon. Why wouldn't people claim this? After all, it's been done. Isn't the idea that this life can be reduced to something that can be wagered a sign that what dominates, in the rise of certain relations to knowledge, is the *a*–cause?

In the next steps we will take, we will have to gauge, beyond this *a*–cause, what results from a choice between "I" and *a*. To say "I exists" [*Je existe*] has a whole series of consequences that are thoroughly and immediately formalizable, and I will calculate that series for you next time. Conversely, the very fact that we can calculate it in this way shows that the other position, the one which bets in order to search for the status of an "I" that perhaps does not exist, goes in the direction of the *a*–cause – namely, in the direction of what Pascal proceeds to do when he asks his interlocutor to give it up.

This is what gives the direction of our explicitly psychoanalytic research its meaning.

January 15, 1969

VIII

THE ONE AND LITTLE *a*

Desire and Grace
Marks and losses
How can we depict the effect of loss?
Measuring the Other's field
On masochistic jouissance

The One is the most difficult thing to conceptualize. People have been endeavoring to do so for a long time.

The modern approach to the One is based on writing, in accordance with what I extracted from Freud's work at one point, to the surprise, as I recall, of one of my seminar attendees who marveled, "How did you manage to find the *einziger Zug?*" That is the term Freud used to designate one of the forms of what he called identification. I translated it, in a way that has stuck, as "unary trait" [*trait unaire*].

At that time, I showed – and my demonstration was elaborate enough that I need not return to it today but simply recall it to mind – that the crux of the effect of what is known as repetition, in the field in which we analysts deal with the subject, lies in this unary trait.

I didn't invent that. Freud said it, assuming you pay attention to what he said. Repetition is linked in a determinant manner to a consequence that he designated as the lost object. In short, it concerns the fact that jouissance is aimed at in an attempt at refinding, and that it cannot be refound unless it is recognized by a mark. The branding from which loss results is introduced into jouissance by the mark itself.

It is essential to compare this fundamental mechanism with what was already present in Plato's work, which was moving in the same direction and concerned all essence. It arrived at the Idea, the pre-existence of every form, and simultaneously appealed to something that is not easy to conceptualize: recollection.

122 Having recalled these points, let us turn anew to Pascal's wager, whose relationship to repetition has not, I believe, escaped many of you who are here.

1

Why am I taking up Pascal's wager? It is certainly not to make a show of erudition, or to give some sort of philosophical reminder or philosophy of the history of philosophy.

Jansenism is part of the backdrop of Pascal's thought. What happened around Jansenism is of interest to us, if nothing else because historians are incapable of finding their bearings there, as they are regarding many other topics as well.

Owing to one of the surprising effects of silt buildup, which we must realize is also a dimension of history, the only thing that remains of the Jansenists is a sort of ghost – namely, that they were people who were known as "rigorists," in other words, as people who stopped you from living as you pleased. I happened to have direct contact with them a while back, but I won't say anything more about my personal relationship to Jansenism, because it would provide much too good an opportunity for you to undertake a precipitous examination of the historical or biographical determinants of my interests.

Have a look at the "Que sais-je?" [What do I know?] book on the topic. I apologize to its author for having forgotten his name, but I read his short book from cover to cover, not, of course, to learn about Jansenism, but to see an example of what one can say about it, when one takes things up simply, as the title of the collection indicates, at the level of *Que sais-je?*

The author knows [*sait*] many things. He begins with the origins, assuming there are any, of the question that is raised in it, and arrives at the point where Jansenism drowns in the riptide of the French Revolution. In the end, he admits quite kindly that, in the final analysis, we really don't know what Jansenism meant, which is a rather curious conclusion, all the same, but exemplary for a historical survey.

If we consider Jansenism at the level of the historical record, it begins as a debate among theologians. Cornelius Jansen happened to be one of the most representative of them. We can even say that he was eminently worthy of representing them, if only for the fact, which is exemplary, that – in everything going on at the time around Jansenism, the contradictions it brought out and the condemnations that followed in its wake – the fundamental objection, which virtually all of the participants in the debate proffered, was "well, first of all, you haven't read it."

What they hadn't read was the book by Jansen, Bishop of Ypres, entitled *Augustinus*, which came out posthumously, as you may know. It seems that the vast majority of those who were passionately for or against it not only hadn't read it but hadn't even opened it. There must have been a few who read it, two or three of the top brass like the great Arnauld, but in fact what need had one to read it? People had read plenty of other things that were fundamental. Long before *Augustinus* was published, there was, in particular, Saint Augustine, whose thought undeniably lies at the core of Christianity.

The question of Grace arises the minute we talk about Christianity. The interest we take in Christianity at a theoretical level corresponds precisely to the role granted to Grace. Who doesn't see that Grace is closely related to what – on the basis of theoretical functions that certainly have nothing to do with heartfelt outpourings – I designate as the Other's desire?

The Other's desire is man's desire, as I put it at a time when I had, in order to make myself understood, to take the risk of using certain improbable words, like "man" for example. I could have confined myself to saying that desire, insofar as it concerns you, is played out in the field of the Other – the Other understood as the locus of speech. In any case, you find on the graph of desire an oriented relationship whose vector begins from ($ ◊ D) and goes toward d(A), the Other's desire, and questions the latter by asking "I wonder what you [*tu*] want." This is balanced by "I am asking you what I want." If what is thereby stated is correct, how could one fail to see that it implies that any and every manifestation of desire tends toward "Thy [*Ta*] will be done"?

This is something worth mentioning at the outset in any appraisal of the nature of prayer. Prayer is not necessarily the privilege of spiritual people. Its knotting or inextricable entanglement with the functions of desire could be clarified thereby.

The *tutoiement* [use of the informal *tu* form of address instead of the formal *vous*] in the formulation does not have a simple point of departure, since, at the level of the subject, the question "who is speaking" remains intact, as I have said. It is nevertheless essential to realize that it is addressed to a faceless Other here. Indeed, there is no need for him to have a face, if we know how to distinguish the Other's field from one's relationship to one's semblable, which is precisely the definition of the Other in my theory.

It seems that, at the time we are talking about, the people legally in charge, namely the Church, were unable to handle disputes about

124

Grace in any other way for two full centuries than by prohibiting people from saying anything about it, whether for or against it. The result of the prohibition was, naturally, to merely fuel the fire and multiply the number of books and pamphlets on the subject.

This frenzy, that certain people would consider purely intellectual, was nevertheless closely associated with a movement whose impact on fervor was indisputable. The effects it occasionally generated at the time were labeled "convulsive" [*convulsionnaires*]. We need but recall what occurred on the grave of a certain deacon by the name of Pâris, which led to the closing of the [Saint-Médard] cemetery [in Paris], on the doors of which were written "By order of the King, God may not perform miracles here," which did not stop the so-called convulsions from taking place elsewhere. Even if we merely label its final consequence, we can see that the field in question is nevertheless quite close to our own.

As psychopathologists, we can variously gauge these things, but nothing obliges us to take them at face value or to restrict ourselves to asking if the interested parties should or should not have been committed. We nevertheless have the right to try to articulate something more far-reaching about this.

Why not do so at the most free, lucid, and playful [or: gambling-related, *joueur*] point, which is precisely Pascal's wager?

2

The plentiful funny business around Pascal's wager is quite fascinating. Perhaps the best way to leave it behind is to tell you right away that what we are dealing with here is the Name-of-the-Father.

125   In the wager, the Name-of-the-Father – let me emphasize once again that it is no accident that I could not formerly give the Seminar in which I was to speak to you about it – takes on a singular form that I beg you to take note of. It will be a nice change from the quibbling among authors who discuss the topic of whether it is worth our while to wager.

What is worth our while is to consider how the wager is formulated by Pascal. The singular form of the Name-of-the-Father is found in the statement at the top of this little piece of paper: "Heads or tails [*Croix ou pile*]."

Don't kid yourselves: it has nothing to do with the Cross [*Croix*]. It was the way people at the time said what we today call "heads or tails [*pile ou face*]." It is what I will call "the absolute real."

To help you grasp it, I would like you to realize that, in any science, in the modern sense of the term, when we measure something, nothing confirms for us that we are doing anything other than measuring our own measures. If it is conceivable that we arrive at the final stage of this science [someday], it will be at a point at which the only thing left to say will be "either that's it or it's not it." At that point, it is what it is. We would have to arrive at the point at which, heads or tails, the only thing involved is the real as an endpoint [*butée*].

At the outset, the wager contains something related to this end-point [*point-pôle*], the absolute real, all the more so in that – when the question is raised about the act of wagering – what is at stake is precisely something about which we can know "neither if it is, nor what it is," as Pascal expressly defines it. We might translate this by saying that what is at stake is to know whether the partner exists or not.

But it is not merely the partner who makes the wager interesting, there is also what has been staked. The fact that Pascal was able to raise the question of our measure [or: worth, *mesure*] with regard to the absolute real in the terms he uses means that he had taken a step forward. When historians who like to root around highlight the fact that people like Raymond Sebond, the father Sirmond, and Pierre Charron had already talked about something related to this risk, they misrecognize Pascal's innovation. It's no accident that the way in which he advanced had such a profound impact on the field in which it [*ça*] thinks. For he profoundly modified the approach to the "I" of the gambler, and he did so, the day he discovered *la règle des partis*, by performing what might be called an exorcism, as it were.

The problem at hand was to know how to fairly distribute the pot of money staked when people interrupted a game that was underway – whether they had to or by mutual consent – whose rules had already been spelled out. Pascal provides an answer on the basis of what is known as the mathematical triangle – which had already been discovered by someone by the name of Tartaglia, but Pascal didn't necessarily know his work – and he derives other series by returning to Archimedes and his laws of minimum and maximum, providing a new starting point for what will arise from integral calculus. But what is, strictly speaking, the crux [or: pivotal point, *pivot*] of what allows him to overcome the obstacles he encounters and find such a fruitful solution to the problem raised? It is the simple remark that what is wagered at the outset is lost.

This is the essence of gambling, insofar as it can be "logified," so to speak, because it is subject to rules. Where the appetite for winnings formerly deformed, refracted, and inflected theorists' articulations, this initial purification, all by itself, allowed him to

126

determine how to fairly divvy up the pot – the lost stakes – at the center [of the table] at any moment.

As analysts, this question interests us because we can link it to the essential explanation for the arising of a similar mode of series making [or: sequencing (or chaining), *d'enchaînement*]. If there is an activity whose point of departure involves dealing with loss [*l'assomption de la perte*], it is clearly ours, because every rule – in other words, every signifying concatenation – entails loss [or: an effect of loss, *un effet de perte*]. This is precisely what I have been trying to spell out since the beginning.

Psychoanalytic practice confronts us at every moment with the effects of loss. It attests to the fact that such effects are encountered at every step of the way. Analysts attest to this innocently – in other words, in the most harmful way possible – by chalking it up to an imaginary injury, by relating it to some narcissistic wound, in other words, by blaming it on our relationship to our semblable. Which has nothing to do with it. It's not because some bit [*parcelle*] that is supposed to be part of the body is detached therefrom that the wound in question functions, and any and every attempt at reparation is doomed to worsen the error. The wound at stake here is related to an effect that I initially qualified as symbolic, in order to distinguish it from the imaginary.

127　　This symbolic effect is inscribed in the gap that is produced between the body and its jouissance, inasmuch as the impact of the signifier or mark – in other words, of what I earlier called the unary trait – determines or worsens it. As we cannot know whether the gap was already there in the organism [see *Écrits*, pp. 78, 144, 149, 232, 346, 461, and 545], and all that concerns us is the worsening of it, let us say that the impact of the unary trait gives it its consistency.

What is traced out here is thus a relationship between the effect of loss – namely, the lost object insofar as we designate it as *a* – and the locus known as the Other, a locus that is still unknown and unmeasured, without which loss cannot occur.

To realize that loss is related to the way in which we function as desire, it suffices to have some experience with and perhaps even some passion for gambling.

How can we measure this relationship?

3

The fact is that there is something very strange here. A proportion [or: ratio, *proportion*] is already there in the numbers – that is, in the written signs with which we articulate the very idea of measure.

Regarding this point, let me emphasize that we know nothing of the nature of the loss. I can proceed as though we gave it no specific value [or: prop, *support*]. We simply plot points – I won't say where we can be struck [or: punished (or bail out), *écoper*], where we catch a few crumbs – without any need to know.

On the one side [see Figure 8.2], there is simply *a*, the function of loss – we know nothing more than that. On the other side, there is the One, and we certainly don't know its status, since it is simply the unary trait. All I want to retain here is this "we know nothing more than that."

Let us now write the ratio of the determinant [or: decisive, *déterminant*] 1 to the effect of loss. It suffices for us to do so in the following way:

$$\frac{1}{a}$$

If loss is involved, it seems clear that this ratio must be equal to the conjunction of 1 – via the *and* of addition – and the written sign of loss, *a*.   128

$$\frac{1}{a} = 1 + a$$

Figure 8.1: The Initial Formula

This is the inscription from which a certain proportion results. Its harmony, if it must be mentioned, is certainly not based on aesthetics. I will simply ask you to allow yourselves to be guided at the outset by the examination of its mathematical nature.

Indeed, the harmonies in question do not stem from a happy event or lucky encounter, as you will see, I believe, by comparing the series that results from the recurring function generated by this formula, and an entirely different series that is generated by something else but interests us just as much. You will see that we find therein the characteristic note: *a*.

This second series is the one that, taking things from another end, is generated by what we have called the *Spaltung*, the initial [or: earliest, *originelle*] splitting of the subject, and by the attempt to make two separate units come back together.

We must now explore this field step by step. In order to do so, it is necessary to clearly write out the status of the said series.

We write it in the following way, placing *a* on the left and 1 on the right, and we indicate a direction. This direction only exists, let me stress in passing, owing to our point of departure.

Below the 1 we put $1 + a$. Below the a, $1 - a$. A series is generated [on the right] by adding the two preceding terms to produce the subsequent term. We thus have on the right the following list, which is not unrelated to the list on the left.

129

a	1
$1 - a$	$1 + a$
$2a - 1$	$2 + a$
$2 - 3a$	$3 + 2a$
$5a - 3$	$5 + 3a$
$5 - 8a$	$8 + 5a$
Decreasing Series	Increasing Series

Figure 8.2: Decreasing and Increasing Series

I won't continue them any further because it is easy for you to check that the sequence of values in the series on the right preserves a constant ratio – namely, that $1 + a$ is to 1 as $2 + a$ is to $1 + a$. This is precisely what is written in the initial formula. This series of values can also be written as follows:

$$1 \quad \frac{1}{a} \quad \frac{1}{a^2} \quad \frac{1}{a^3} \quad \frac{1}{a^4} \quad \ldots \text{ etc.}$$

As a is smaller than 1, the [value of each successive] number will always increase.

On the left side, on the other hand, we write the following values: a^2, a^3, a^4, a^5, a^6. Since, let me repeat, a is smaller than 1, the [value of each successive] number will always decrease.

$$a$$
$$1 - a = a^2$$
$$2a - 1 = a^3$$
$$2 - 3a = a^4$$
$$5a - 3 = a^5$$
$$5 - 8a = a^6$$

Figure 8.3: Decreasing Series and Powers of a

Let us not leave behind Pascal, for what he does on this little piece of paper is provide an articulation, and there is no need for it to be addressed to some Other in order for the replies to take on a value which is not persuasive, but which can be logically formulated.

In our times, people have noticed that there is a way to resolve certain problems in which the number of throws of the dice counts. It is not of no importance to know at the end of how many throws of the dice a player has the last word. If he wins owing to the fact of what might be called, but in a purely retrospective manner, a mistake made by the other party, it is clear that the test will consist in proposing to the other party a luckier response [or: do-over (or rematch), *réponse*]. But if the result is the same, we can attribute it to a logical articulation – by which I mean an accepted logical articulation, which it suffices to define at the outset – by way of a demonstration, which would be articulated as follows on the board:

130

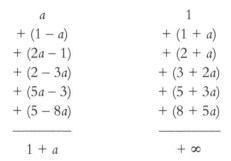

Figure 8.4: Sums of the Decreasing and Increasing Series

In our times, we know how to codify the laws of the function "yes or no," yet it is unfortunate that people forget that the refutable "yes or no" opens up more territory than what is purely and simply demonstrable. This is how Pascal's way of proceeding [*procès*], as I pointed out last time when I began to discuss the wager, leads him to initially question, with regard to a pure "heads or tails," what is rational about wagering an ante that involves life, but is not otherwise defined, against "an infinity of lives" that are qualified as "infinitely happy," without there being any indication of what that means either. We should perhaps reconsider the signs after him, in order to see if they can deliver us something that necessarily explains their meaning. This is precisely what we are in the process of doing by operating at the level of the signs *a* and 1.

We still don't know the value of the *a* that we are using. We simply see the series it generates in its relationship with the 1, and nothing more. We might even say that the question of the specific status of the *a* and the 1 has no meaning. They are merely terms that are mathematically juxtaposed in some way. They are not neutral elements, as when we define whole numbers and what can be done with them. The 1 in these series has nothing to do with the 1 in multiplication. Supplemental actions are necessary to make it serve there. The same is true for *a*. *a* and 1 are found wherever we find the relationship <1 over *a*>, in other words, in the whole series.

131   The interest in beginning with these two terms, and the only thing that forces us to begin with them, is that we need them to begin to write. They have no place in any reality [*réel*] that might seem to correspond to this ladder [the vertical list of symbols in Figure 8.2]. Yet we cannot write this ladder without them.

Beginning now with this ladder, I can allow myself to depict the ratio by writing it differently. This writing will also be the simplest, for we remain, it seems to me, within our limits, which are those of the unary trait, except that we are going to rotate it indefinitely, or at least try. On the left we have *a*, and on the right we have 1. We are not obliged to measure the segments for the terms to be correctly inscribed.

$$a \qquad 1$$
$$\vdash\!\!\!-\!\!\!+\!\!\!-\!\!\!\dashv \qquad a = 0.618$$

Figure 8.5: Another Way of Writing the Relationship <1 over *a*>

Please forgive me for condensing this by saying that we are going to rotate [180° the segment of length] *a* back toward the field of the Other designated here as [the segment of length] 1. What I just wrote, namely <1 − *a* = a^2>, indicates that what appears [on the right in Figure 8.6] is a^2. The rotating back of a^2 will give us a^3 here [more or less in the middle]. And the rotating of a^3 will give us a^4.

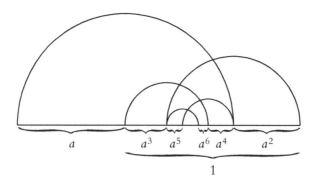

Figure 8.6: Successive Rotations

I hope you see that operations going in a certain direction will allow us to add up on the right all the even powers of *a*, namely a^2, a^4, a^6, whereas the same will happen on the left with all the odd powers, a^3, a^5, a^7.

$$
\begin{array}{ccc}
a^3 & & a^2 \\
a^5 & & a^4 \\
a^7 & & a^6 \\
\hline
a^2 & + & a \\
\hline
& 1 &
\end{array}
$$

Figure 8.7: Adding up the Odd and Even Powers of *a*

It is easy to see that by proceeding in this way, taking the sum first of all the even powers and then of all the odd powers, we arrive, on the right, at *a* as the total measure of all the even powers – *a* itself being excluded, of course – and on the left, at a^2 as the total measure of all the odd powers of *a*.

Adding a^2 to *a*, we get 1. In other words, by separately adding up the even powers and then the odd powers, we effectively arrive at the measure of the field of the Other qua 1, which is not the same as its pure and simple inscription qua unary trait.

I obtained this result by taking up the proportional basis of *a* in isolation. I can now take up its development in the increasing direction.

Namely by adding the increasing powers. What do we find, for example, when we add up the whole series of <1 over *a*> to the *n*th power until we reach a^{100}? It is a very well-known formula, but it is easy to carry out the calculation if you have a whole blank page in front of you. It takes no more than 10 minutes and you get the following result:

2,000,000,000,000,000,000,000,000,000,000

A series constituted in this way is known as a geometric or exponential progression.

There is nothing more striking than a series that includes an infinite increase in whole numbers. Yet, in the final analysis, it remains within the realm of the countable. Since I mentioned that the point where 1 and *a* lie is of interest to us only from a scriptural standpoint, I am not now going to neglect its impact. There are thus several points at which we see a difference between increase and decrease.

Decreasing infinity is generated in the same manner as increasing infinity, but it does not arrive at this infinity of whole numbers about which we nevertheless know a bit more, and which we have learned to reduce to its proper and distinct value. By beginning on the other side, as I showed you, you have a limit which the series approaches as closely as possible, in a way that is less than any value selected, however small, namely $1 + a$.

Pascal's point of departure in his notes is written quite simply: "infinite nothing" [*infini rien*; p. 132]. This is what attests to his sure-footedness, and it is also truly functional, determining everything that follows.

He very expressly specifies what he calls "nothing" in other of his notations; it is the simple fact that, beginning from any point whatsoever, as I told you, we obtain a limit in the decreasing direction. It is not because this series has a limit that it is less infinite, just as the fact that, on the other side, we obtain an increase which does not have a limit does not mean it is more specifically infinite.

Thus it is no accident that Pascal writes "nothing." He himself suspects that "nothing" is not nothing, that it is something that can be placed in the balance and especially at the level at which we must situate it in the wager.

But lo and behold, something appears that we must finally notice. A revelation is enunciated in the field of the Other that promises us "an infinity of infinitely happy lives." Pascal stays for a while at the level of this numerical statement, and then he begins to ponder. One life against two lives, is that already worthwhile? Of course it is, he says. What about three lives? Even more so. And naturally, the more there are, the more worthwhile it is. Except that as soon as we choose, we are – in every case, and even when we lose "nothing" – deprived of half an infinity [*demi-infini*].

This in fact corresponds to the way in which we can, by means of loss, measure the field of the Other qua One.

How is this Other generated? We can distinguish it from the One that is before the 1 – namely, jouissance. How can we measure it? If we have consolidated <$1 + a$> and have carried out our addition with infinite care, it is because it is on the basis of a and its relationship to 1 that we hope to analogously measure the status of the One of jouissance with respect to this supposedly realized sum.

The relationship between a, as the lack received from the Other, and 1, as the completed field of the Other that we can construct, can be depicted as follows:

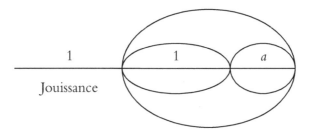

Figure 8.8: 1 over Jouissance

We analysts are familiar with this and we find it anew here. It is what is known as masochistic jouissance and it is the most characteristic and subtle form that I have provided of the cause of desire as a function.

Masochistic jouissance is an analogical jouissance. The subject analogically takes on the position of loss or waste represented by *a* at the level of surplus jouissance. In his attempt to constitute the Other as a field articulated solely in the form of a contract – the one that our friend Deleuze emphasized so well [in *Masochism: Coldness and Cruelty & Venus in Furs* (New York: Zone Books, 1989)], making up for the galloping imbecility that reigns in psychoanalysis – the subject employs the hidden ratio by approaching jouissance by the pathway of surplus jouissance.

You see that by approaching things as we did, we at least find here an entry point which explains psychoanalytic practice.

Masochism is undoubtedly not irrelevant to Pascal's work, given the way in which a certain renunciation functions there. But let us not jump the gun. To qualify everyone who has unwittingly debated this logic "masochists" falls under the kind of short-circuiting I have called unscrupulous [*canaillerie*], which, as I have said, turns into foolishness in this field.

Today I was only able to get you to enter into the field by the scriptural pathway alone. There we find a ratio that is already inscribed. We must, of course, crosscheck it.   135

As I said, *a* is what conditions the distinction between the "I" as sustaining the field of the Other and as able to be totalized as the field of knowledge, and the "I" of jouissance. What we need to realize is that in being totalized, the "I" of knowledge will never attain self-sufficiency, the kind that is articulated in Hegel's work as *Selbstbewußtsein* [self-consciousness]. Indeed, however perfect it may be, the "I" of jouissance remains entirely excluded. What you see on the board is nothing more than its image or illustration. If it is of interest to us, it is because it notably confirms that no addition of one [1] to the other [*a*] can ever totalize for us the divided "I" – in the form of any number, of any 2 resulting from an addition – finally joining back up with itself.

Far from being interminable, this field simply takes time to explore, and I will need time to articulate it to you. I will continue to do so next week. Those who take the trouble to learn what a Fibonacci series is between now and then, and I hope many of you will have no need to do so, will obviously be better prepared than the others for what I will do for the latter – namely, explain to them how such a series is constructed.

If its first term is 1, the second term is also 1. This latter 1 is added to what precedes it in order to generate the third term, namely 2, and so on and so forth, each term being generated by the addition of the two prior terms. We arrive at the following series: 1 1 2 3 5 8 13, etc. You will note in passing that these numbers are already written on the board [see the right-hand side of Figure 8.2], and that is no accident. The fact remains that the ratio of each of these numbers to the next is nevertheless not the ratio *a*.

It is interesting to note that all Fibonacci series are homologous. I will begin with that next time.

It doesn't matter what number you start with to generate your series. If you follow the law of adding the two preceding terms, it will be a Fibonacci series, and always essentially the same one. Whatever series it is, you will obtain between [two consecutive] numbers as you go to infinity, the written ratio – namely, the ratio between 1 and *a*. It is on the basis of *a*, in its relation to 1, that the series moves from one term to the next. In other words, whether you begin from the subject's division or from *a*, you find that they are reciprocal.

This approach, which I qualify as one of pure logical consistency, will allow us to better situate the status of a certain number of human activities. I am thinking in particular of mysticism.

I have mentioned mysticism before. In the early, dark years of my Seminar, I talked about Angelus Silesius – one of Pascal's contemporaries – to the three or four [of you] who were here. Just try to explain what his verses mean without having his distichs! I recommend you read *Le Pèlerin chérubinique* (*The Cherubinic Wanderer* [Mahwah, NJ: Paulist Press, 1986]). Aubier published it and it is not out of print.

In their own way, the mystics explored the relationship between jouissance and the One. Of course their pathway does not directly concern our pathway, but the place occupied there by the "I" or *Ich* is related, as you will see, to the question that is our true aim here, and that I am repeating at the end of today's class: "Does I exist? [or: Do I exist?, *Est-ce que j'existe?*]"

An apostrophe is enough to mess everything up. If I say "I exist [*j'existe*]," then you believe it, you believe that I am talking about myself, simply because of an apostrophe [as opposed to *Je existe*, I exists]. Well then, is it better to say, in speaking of the "I," "Does it exist? [*Est-ce qu'il existe?*]?" But yuck – who wants this "it"! It's the third person.

Of course I have said that we make an object of the "I." But we simply omit the third person. For we also use "it" to say "it is raining." In which case, we aren't talking about a third person: it is not your pal who is raining.

"It is raining." It is in this sense that I am saying "it exists." "Does any 'I' exist [*Est-ce qu'il existe du* Je]?"

January 22, 1969

IX

FROM FIBONACCI TO PASCAL

Fibonacci series
First matrix of the wager
Second matrix
The "getting-off-on-the-mother"
The Father has been dead all along

After taking you pretty far into the realm of Pascal's wager last time, I left you with a remark that punctuates what I just wrote on the board.

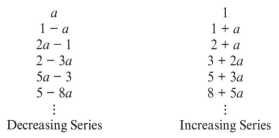

Decreasing Series	Increasing Series
a	1
$1 - a$	$1 + a$
$2a - 1$	$2 + a$
$2 - 3a$	$3 + 2a$
$5a - 3$	$5 + 3a$
$5 - 8a$	$8 + 5a$
$\vdots$	$\vdots$

Figure 9.1: Decreasing and Increasing Series

I highlighted the essential equivalence of two parallel series by telling you that, although we selected points of departure including a and 1, this was totally arbitrary.

"Arbitrary" takes on the same meaning here as Saussure gave it when he spoke about the arbitrary nature of the signifier. I mean that the cut [or: gap, *coupure*] between a decreasing series and an increasing series is located at a point that is situated solely on the basis of writing, since the 1 has no other function here than that of a trait – a unary trait – line, or notch [or: mark, *marque*]. Yet however arbitrary it may be, the fact remains that without this unary trait there would be no series at all.

This is the meaning that must be given to what we read in Saussure's work – which I constantly betray according to an author who is undoubtedly incredibly competent – namely, that without this arbitrariness, language would, strictly speaking, have no effect.

1

I invite you now to consider the increasing series that begins with 1 and is followed by $1 + a$.

Each subsequent term of the series is produced by adding together the two preceding terms [e.g., $1 + (1 + a) = 2 + a$]. This is equivalent to saying that each term, if we proceed in the opposite direction, results from the subtraction of the smaller from the larger of the two preceding terms [e.g., $3 + 2a$ results from the subtraction of $5 + 3a$ from $8 + 5a$]. 138

This series is, moreover, constructed on the principle that the ratio of every one of its terms to the next term is equal to the ratio of the latter to the sum of the two terms [e.g., 1 is to $1 + a$ as $1 + a$ is to $2 + a$ (i.e., the sum of 1 and $1 + a$)]. Now, to posit that a is equal to 1 over what follows it – that is, $1 + a$ – seems to add a second condition to the series, specifying it by a twofold condition.

$$a = \frac{1}{1 + a}$$

Figure 9.2: Variation on the Initial Formula

This is not the case, however, as is shown by the fact that the ratio of each of the terms [i.e., the whole numbers – 1, 1, 2, 3, 5, 8 – in the increasing series] to the next tends toward a, even if the second condition is not satisfied, once we have posited as a law that each of the terms is generated by the addition of the two preceding terms.

Addition as a function should no doubt be more rigorously specified here, but as we are not here to discuss group theory at length, we will stick with the operation commonly known as addition, which is already posited at the core of the first series.

In order to construct this series, we can simply write that U_0 is equal to 1, that U_1 is equal to 1, and that thereafter every U_n will be the sum of U_{n-1} and U_{n-2}.

Such a series is called a Fibonacci series. You can see that it is subject to one single condition.

If we perform any defined operation on it – whether we add one term to another, multiply one term by another, or perform some other operation – another Fibonacci series will result that will be essentially the same as the first one. You can confirm this and thus verify that the law of series formation is exactly the same – namely, that it suffices to add two of its consecutive terms in order to arrive at the next.

In the series with which I began, *a* seems to correspond to the golden ratio [or: golden or divine mean (or proportion, section, or even cut), *nombre d'or*]. Indeed, this ratio appears therein right from the outset in the form of the *a* that is manifested there owing to the core position of the initial formula I gave earlier [see Figures 8.1 and 9.2].

What becomes of this marvelous proportion in a Fibonacci series? Little *a* never fails to appear for the following reason. Consider the ratio of each of its terms to the following:

$$1/2 \quad 2/3 \quad 3/5 \quad 5/8 \quad 8/13 \quad 13/21 \text{ etc.}$$

I did not include 1/1 because it doesn't mean anything. [If we calculate the value of each successive fraction in the series,] we fairly quickly get the first two decimals, then the first three, then the first four, then the first five, and eventually the first six decimals of the number that corresponds to little *a*. It is very easy to verify that it is written:

$$a = 0.618 \ldots$$

It doesn't matter much that it is written in this way because we already knew that it was less than one. What is important is that very quickly, as soon as we get some distance from the beginning of the Fibonacci series, *a* appears as the ratio of any term of the series to the one that follows it.

What about the choice of *a*? We selected it because we were faced with a specific problem: how to depict what is lost owing to the fact of arbitrarily positing the inaugural 1, reduced to its function as a mark. On the other hand, what I just told you demonstrates that the choice of *a* is not at all arbitrary, insofar as it is the number on which the ratio of each term in a Fibonacci series to the one that follows it converges. It is like the loss that we are examining, which lies on the horizon of our discourse, the loss that constitutes surplus jouissance – it is but an effect of the establishment of the unary trait.

Moreover, if you need something to confirm this for you, it suffices to look at how the decreasing series that I wrote on the left is constructed:

$$a$$
$$1 - a$$
$$2a - 1$$
$$2 - 3a$$
$$5a - 3$$
$$5 - 8a$$
$$\vdots$$

Decreasing Series

The numbers in the Fibonacci series alternate from one side to the other here: a, $2a$, $3a$, $5a$, $8a$, $13a$, $21a$, etc. The coefficients of the a alternate from right to left and back again. The integers also alternate: 1, 2, 3, 5, 8, 13, etc.

As you can see, the as are always ahead of the integers. On the first line there is an a, whereas there will not be an integer, 1, until the next line. On the third line, there are two as, whereas we only find the integer 2 on the fourth line, and so on. If the as and the integers change places, it is so that each term remains positive. In other words, in order for each to come out positive, the whole numbers and the as must change places.

That's not all. Since a is less than 1 and since we know, moreover, that it is going to be expressed by a growing exponent [see Figure 8.3] owing to the first equation, the result of the subtraction is going to become smaller and smaller with respect to the series' limit [see Figure 8.4]. This is what is known as a converging series.

Toward what does it converge? Not 1. I showed this to you last time by rotating a back onto 1, and then the remainder, a^2, back on a, which produces a^3, and a^3 back as well, which produces a^4, all of which leads to a cut [*coupure*] that gives us $<a + a^2 = 1>$ [see Figure 8.6]. This is why the limit of this converging series is $<1 + a>$, which is itself equal to $<1/a>$ [see Figure 8.4].

What does this mean? What is depicted by what is operative here? We want to know how to correctly depict the possible conjunction of subjective division, which would result from a meeting up anew of the subject with . . . Let us put a question mark after "subject." What is the status of the absolute subject of jouissance with respect to the subject who is generated on the basis of this 1 that marks him, the point from which identification originates?

It is tempting to posit that the subject of knowledge knows himself. This is what Hegel terms *Selbstbewußtsein* [self-consciousness]. Namely, once the subject is posited by the inaugural 1, he need but join back up with his own depiction [*figure*] qua formalized. This is precisely where the error arises, because we fail to realize that this can be the case only by positing the known subject [*le sujet su*] such as we create him in the relationship [*rapport*] of one signifier to another signifier. Now, what is involved there is not a 1 to 1 ratio but a 1 to 2 ratio [or: relationship, *rapport*]. Thus at no time is the earliest division eliminated. The 1 to 1 ratio is simply imitated here. It is only on the horizon of an infinite repetition that we can envision something appearing that corresponds to the 1 to 1 ratio between the subject of jouissance [or: enjoying subject (or libidinal subject), *sujet de la jouissance*] and the subject instituted by [or: in, *dans*] the mark.

$$\text{False} \begin{cases} \text{the subject of jouissance} \\ \text{the divided subject of the mark} \end{cases}$$

The difference between these two subjects remains irremediable. No matter how far you take the operation that this [series of] subtractions generates [presumably the Decreasing Series in Figure 9.1], you will always find – from one term to the next, and written as the sum total of the losses – the ratio with which we began, even if it is not included in the original inscription, namely, the ratio known as little *a*.

This is all the more significant since what is involved is a ratio [or: fraction], and not a simple difference [or: remainder (or result of subtraction)] that becomes smaller and smaller by carrying out the operation ever further. This is easy to check.

The further you take the increasing series, the greater the difference between the integers – namely, what is inscribed under 1, the foundation of the earliest subjective identification – and the number of *a*s [e.g., the difference between 13 and 8 is greater than the difference between 8 and 5, etc.]. Indeed, in the series involving addition, what is involved is always the ratio of a number of *a*s corresponding to the smaller term, to an integer corresponding to the larger term. In other words, the greater the subject's coefficient, so to speak – that is, the larger the group [here the integers correspond to the number of subjects] – the greater the lack of units of *a*. There will not be enough *a* for everyone.

$$1$$
$$1 + a$$
$$2 + a$$
$$3 + 2a$$
$$5 + 3a$$
$$8 + 5a$$
$$\vdots$$

Increasing Series

That's the way it is [*Prenez cela*]. I may return to it at the level of an apologue in the form of a question.

What is surely of interest to us, and what is going to be of concern in our exploration of Pascal's wager, is what becomes of it in the sense in which *a* can be approached in a no less infinite way, which, once again, appears to us to be what provides, in an analogical form, the status of the relations between 1 and $<1 + a>$ – namely, the *a* in which alone can be grasped the status of jouissance with respect to what is created on the basis of the appearance of a loss.

Regarding the gap that exists between the Hegelian solution of *Selbstbewußtsein* (and all those that, in any way, proceed on the basis of a 1 to 1 ratio), on the one hand, and the solution provided by a rigorous examination of the function of the sign, on the other hand, let it suffice for me to indicate something that I will write in the following funny way. Ask yourself the question: what might provide an image for the figure of an ideal that could someday be complete [*clos*], the figure of absolute knowledge?

$$1-1$$

The H [1–1] in question that I just comically translated, is it man [*homme*], *homo*? Isn't it rather the hysteric? Why not? Let us not forget that Freud brought in the One in connection with neurotic identification.

Reread *Group Psychology and the Analysis of the Ego*, preferably in German (so as not to be obliged to resort to the atrocious French translation we owe to several zealous people, the only text – it doesn't even include a table of contents – we can refer to when we want to rely on French alone). If you turn to the chapter on identification, you will see that, of the three types of identification mentioned there by Freud, it is regarding the middle one, the one germane to the field of neurosis, that he mentioned the *einziger Zug*, the unary trait that I extracted from it.

143

I am reminding you of this because I will have to return to it later, for, strangely enough and as opposed to what you might imagine, the most ungraspable form of object *a* appears in neurosis where we analysts effectively begin. It is in order to prepare you for the surprise that I am announcing it here.

Let us now return to Pascal's wager and the way in which it can be written.

2

The trifling remarks that have been made by philosophers make us overlook most of the signification of Pascal's wager.

It isn't that they haven't made every effort to grasp it, including writing the premises of the wager in the kind of matrix currently used to display the results of what is known as game theory. In this form, the wager is called into question, as it were. You will see how strangely people claim to refute it.

Let us observe first that the wager is coherent with the following claim: we cannot know either whether God is nor what He is. What is one wagering about? About a discourse connected to God – namely, a promise that is attributed to Him, that of "an infinity of infinitely happy lives." Because I am speaking and not writing, and because I am speaking French, you cannot tell if life [*vie*] here is singular or plural, no more than you can tell, let me point out, by reading Pascal's little piece of paper, for it is stenographic in nature [i.e., full of abbreviations]. Yet everything that follows in Pascal's discourse clearly indicates that we must take it as a plural, because he begins to debate whether it is worth the trouble to wager simply in order to have a second or even a third life, and so on and so forth. He is thus clearly talking about a numerical infinity.

What is wagered is something we have at our disposal and that we stake in the game – namely, an ante [*mise*]. Let us try to depict this ante. It is legitimate to depict it since we ourselves have been able to grasp what is involved: that highly enigmatic plus that makes it such that we are all situated in the field of some discourse – namely, *a*. That is what is staked. Why write it in this particular square? I will justify it.

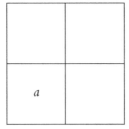

Figure 9.3: Matrix 1

There is, on the other hand, the "infinity of infinitely happy lives." How do we depict that? Must we imagine it as the proliferation of integers that provide a prop for the proliferation of objects *a*, the latter always being, moreover, one term behind the integers [see

Figure 9.1]? The question would be worth raising here if it didn't already bring with it several difficulties, as you have seen. Let us simply say that we are assuredly talking about the increasing series. In this square we put the sign for infinity, ∞.

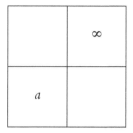

Figure 9.4: Matrix 2

The infinity in question here is the infinity of integers, which Pascal illustrates. Indeed, it is only in relation to this infinity that the element with which we began, the ante, becomes inconsequential [or: immaterial, *inefficient*], by which I mean neutral(ized). This is why the initial element [the ante] becomes equated with zero: it is identified with the addition of zero to infinity. The result of that addition can only be depicted on the basis of the sign that designates one of the two terms that are added together [i.e., ∞].

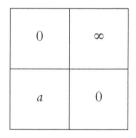

145

Figure 9.5: Matrix 3

This is how things can be depicted. I have constructed this matrix not because it strikes me as adequate but because it is what people ordinarily confine themselves to. These squares have no more importance than the matrices used to construct combinatories in game theory.

What I am calling A here is the field of a discourse [see Figure 9.6]. Depending on whether A exists or not, should be accepted or rejected, a division of cases results. If A is immediately accepted, *a* equals zero.

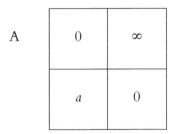

Figure 9.6: Matrix 4

This equating of *a* with zero means nothing other than the following: at the level of game theory, stakes that are risked must be considered to be lost. As soon as we try to formulate Pascal's wager as a game, it is no longer a sacrifice – it is the very law of the game.

Similarly, if A does not exist [this corresponds to the bottom row in Figure 9.6] – in other words, if the promise is not valid, if nothing that lies beyond death is tenable anymore – we have a zero here as well [in the lower right-hand corner]. But it means nothing other than the fact that the ante wagered by the other side [i.e., the other party], represented by ∞, is lost.

Subject

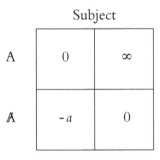

Figure 9.7: Matrix 5

As a matter of fact, in Pascal's wager, the [other party's] stakes are identical to the promise. It is because the promise is enunciated that we can construct a matrix. Once it is constructed and the subject's behavior is dictated solely by a signifying framework, there is no question. The dissymmetry of the stakes dictates one and only one behavior on his part.

The difficulty begins only when we perceive that the subject is hardly something we can frame on the basis of the combination [*conjunction*] of some number of signifiers, no more than on the basis of a 1 to 1 ratio, as I indicated earlier. A scrap [or: loss, *un effet de chute*] results from any and every signifying combination, and this gives our *a*, inscribed here in the lower left-hand square, a connection [or: connective (or operator), *liaison*] that is in no wise separable from the construction of the matrix itself.

This is precisely what is involved in the progress engendered by psychoanalysis. We must study the consequences of this connection which makes the subject a divided subject – in other words, [a subject who is] not tied to the simple establishment of this matrix. For then it appears altogether clear that one can construct, in other words write out, a matrix. For the zero that is situated at the bottom is the initial zero clearly marked by Peano's axiomatization as necessary to produce the infinite series of natural numbers [*Selected Works of Giuseppe Peano* (Toronto: University of Toronto Press, 1973)]. Without infinity, no zero comes into the picture. Because zero was essentially there in order to produce it [infinity].

It is also on the basis of such a fiction, as I reminded you earlier, that *a* is reduced to zero in Pascal's argument. You are losing no more than zero, he claims, it being clear that "the pleasures of life," as he puts it, don't amount to much, especially with regard to the infinity that is available to you. Pascal employs a mathematical notion [or: link, *liaison*] here, the one that expresses that any kind of unit added to infinity leaves the sign of infinity intact – except that, as I have shown you on a number of occasions, we cannot absolutely say that we don't know whether infinity is nor what it is, as Pascal argues, in order to render infinity opaque in the same way as he renders the divine Being opaque.

147

It is similarly impossible to add something to infinity to make it even or odd, since, as you have seen, all the even operations get added together in the decreasing series, and all the odd operations on the other side, to add up to the infinite sum [see Figures 8.4, 8.6, and 8.7]. As infinite as it may be, the series is nevertheless reducible to a 1 of a certain type, the 1 that combines with *a*.

As you can see, I am merely indicating here in passing all sorts of points that have been clarified by progress in mathematical theory and that in some sense help to lift the veil. What lies behind the veil is the articulation of discourse, whatever it may be, including that of the said Promise – namely, its scrap [or: loss, *effet de chute*] at the level of jouissance. If we neglect what the veil hides, we will misrecognize the true nature of object *a*.

Thus our practice, which is a discursive practice, shows us that we must delineate the wager differently if we wish to give it its true meaning.

Pascal himself indicates this meaning to us when he says: "you are [already] embarked." Now what could possibly embark [or: interest, *engage*] us less than such a matrix?

This is what makes the wager terribly confusing to those who seem singularly unprepared by their role as professors to master what is involved in a discourse.

"You are embarked" – what does that mean if not that, to proffer a play [*jeu*] on words, what is embarked [or: staked, *engagé*] is "I." This is where the "I" comes in.

If it is possible to wager [or: stake, *engager*] anything and everything [or: endlessly, *à perte*] in the game, it is because loss [*la perte*] is already present. This is because the ante [*la mise en jeu*] cannot be taken back.

What psychoanalysis teaches us is that there are effects that are masked by the pure and simple reduction of the "I" to what is enunciated. And when we are dealing with a game depicted by Pascal, how can we neglect for a single instant the function of Grace – in other words, the Other's desire? Don't you think that it perhaps also occurred to Pascal that even to understand his ridiculously portrayed wager, Grace was necessary? As I told you, the phrase "Thy will be done" is latent in any and every naïve portrayal of the subject's relationship to demand. It is what is called into question when this will falls short [or: is missing, *fait défaut*], a will which *is* precisely because it is not ours.

Otherwise stated, let us not dwell on this for too long, let us leave behind the God of the first matrix and move on to the only God who can possibly be at stake for Pascal.

Designating Him with the same letter, A, won't change anything. That letter will be sufficiently articulated in the new distribution of the matrix. We will see that this distribution is in no way different from Himself.

3

Figure 9.8: Matrix 6

Let us state things in a rough and ready way.

God exists [this refers to the row of the matrix with A on the left]. For a subject who is assumed to know this, we will now write the pair <0,∞> in one of the squares of the matrix. I am supposed to know it, but we must add something to that: I am "for" [or: I am in favor of it, *je suis pour*].

In the second case [to the right of the first], if, while being assumed to know that God exists, I am "against," then the choice I make is one between *a* and the infinity of infinitely happy lives that I deliberately lose. Here we have the pair <*a*,−∞>. This is clearly what is at work in all of Pascal's thinking.

Next we have the case in which I am assumed to know that God does not exist. Why not think then that I can wager the *a* all the same and simply lose it? In other words, <−*a*,0>. This is all the more possible in that loss is an integral part of *a*'s nature. In a game in which I hold on to little *a* only at the cost of <minus infinity>, I can legitimately wonder whether that is worthwhile [see the upper right-hand square of the matrix]. Should I work so hard to hold on to it? While there are people who hold on to it at the cost of <−∞>, think of the myriad people who have thrown *a* away without any concern for the immortality of their souls. They are generally the ones referred to as sages, *grandfatherly* guys [or: easygoing guys, *des gens pépères*], not just fathers [*pères*] but *grandfatherly*. This is closely linked to the father, as you will see.

Lastly we have those who, on the contrary, hold on to *a* and sleep like babies at night [*dorment sur leurs deux oreilles*]. As for the zero at the end, what strikes us in this distribution, <*a*,0>, is the coherence which is related to the subject-supposed-to-know. But isn't it a coherence that is constituted by a smidgeon of indifference?

"He exists" – I bet "for," but I know very well that He exists [see the upper left-hand corner]. "He does not exist" – of course I bet "against," but it can't be called a wager [see the lower right-hand corner]. None of that has anything to do with wagering. On the diagonal that runs from <0,∞> to <*a*,0> there are those who are so assured of their position that, for them, there is no wager at all. They simply follow the tide of what they know.

But what does it mean "to know" under such conditions? It means so little that those who know nothing can all be put in one square.

Allow me to point out in passing that I am not extrapolating in the slightest from Freud's views here, and that I am staying on my own turf. If you consult the volume that I mentioned earlier, you will see that Freud often remarks that, in the final analysis, the beliefs held by Christians do not lead them to behave very differently from non-Christians. It is as a purified subject, so to speak,

149

that what occurs in the diagonal starting from the [upper] left can be spelled out in our little matrix.

On the other hand, what clearly shows us something unexpected is the case of he who bets "against" even though he knows that He exists, and the case of he who bets "for," as if He existed, despite knowing full well that He doesn't.

This is where things get quite interesting. Consider that the minus infinity that you see in the upper right-hand square is translated in Pascal's little "scriptures" by the term "hell."

But that assumes we examine why the function of a has led to the highly debatable notion that there is something beyond death. It is undoubtedly due to the fact of its indefinite mathematical slippage beneath any kind of signifying chain. However far you carry out the final tightening of the chain, this function [a] always remains intact, as I already said at the beginning of the year in a certain schema of the relations between S and A. But this can lead us to wonder what is meant by the appearance of something in this matrix that takes the form of minus infinity. Shouldn't we translate this minus in a way that is more homologous to its function in arithmetic? Namely, that when it appears, the series of whole numbers doubles, which means splits in two [positive and negative]. It is the sign there of something that seemed to me worth recalling to mind only at the end of our last class – namely, if we equate what is brought into play in the renunciation proposed by Pascal with object a, and not with anything else, there is just as much infinity involved where the play of a encounters a limit as where it does not [see Figure 8.4]. In any case, it is a half-infinity that we wager, and that considerably balances out the chances in the first matrix.

Yet it is quite possible that we must view differently what is depicted in this myth, which Pascal reminds us is part of Christian dogma. It merely attests to the fact that God's mercy is greater than his justice, since he makes an exception for the chosen few, whereas we should all be in hell.

I am surprised that this proposition could have seemed scandalous, since it is so obvious that no one has ever imagined hell as anything but what happens to us every day. I mean that we are already in hell. This necessity, which encompasses us so thoroughly that we cannot realize the solidity of a – except on a horizon whose limit we should investigate, and this by an indefinitely repeated measure of the cut made by a [see Figure 8.6] – doesn't that suffice all by itself to discourage even the most courageous?

But there it is, we have no choice. Our desire is the Other's desire, and depending on whether Grace has failed us or not, which is something that is played out at the level of the Other – namely, everything that preceded us in discourse that determined our very conception – we are forced either to race to seal up [or: staunch (or quench or waterproof), *course d'étanchage*] object *a* or not to.

Let us not forget the fourth square, the one in the lower right-hand corner. It is no accident that I allowed myself to joke about those who are situated there. They are just as numerous and widespread as those in the upper right-hand square. I called them the grandfatherly type, but only provisionally, for we would be wrong to minimize the ease with which they move around.

In any case I would like to point out that it is there that, in analysis, we have situated the good ol' norm. Surplus jouissance is expressly modulated as not in the picture [*étranger à la question*], if what analysis can promise is a return to the norm. How can we fail to see that this norm is articulated in analysis as the Law, the one on which the Oedipus complex is based? However we look at the myth, it is quite clear that jouissance is absolutely distinguished from the Law there.

It is prohibited to get off on one's mother [*Jouir de la mère est interdit*], as they say, but that is not going far enough. What has consequences is that the "getting-off-on-the-mother" is interdicted [or: the "mother's jouissance" is prohibited, *le* jouir-de-la-mère *est interdit*]. Nothing is laid down if not on the basis of this first enunciated, as is clearly seen in the fable where the subject, Oedipus, never imagined he was enjoying his mother, owing to God only knows what sort of distractions. I mean owing to all the charms that Jocasta employed, and probably all the hassling [*harcèlement*] as well, such that it did not even come to mind, even when the evidence began to pour in.

What is prohibited is the "getting-off-on-the-mother," and that is confirmed by the different formulation of it found in *Totem and Taboo*. These formulations must be juxtaposed in order to grasp what Freud is articulating.

"Killing the father" blinds the young imbecilic bulls that I see gravitating around me from time to time in ridiculous arenas. "Killing the father" means that he cannot be dispatched. He has been dead all along. This is why something sensible gets alluded to [*il s'accroche quelque chose de sensé*], even in places where it is paradoxical to hear people wail that God is dead. It's obvious that by not thinking about it people risk missing a certain facet of things – namely, that the father is dead from the outset. But something remains: the Name-of-the-Father. And everything hinges on that.

That is where I began last time, and it is where I will end today.

I didn't invent the role [*vertu*] played by the Name-of-the-Father; I mean that it is not my own creation, it is found in Freud's work.

151

Indeed, he writes somewhere that its role founds the difference between the field of man and that of animals. This is the case every where, even when it appears in disguised forms – namely, when we talk about tribes that have no idea of the role played by the male in reproduction. And why not? The importance of the function of the Name-of-the-Father is demonstrated by the fact that even those who don't know about it invent spirits to serve it.

Freud articulates the nature of this function in a very precise place. I'm not going to spend my time telling you on which page or in which edition since there are now plenty of places where people read Freud's work and where there are people who are competent enough to inform those of you who are interested. The essence and function of the father qua Name, as the pivotal point [*pivot*] of discourse, is based precisely on the fact that one can never, after all, know who the father is. You can try to find out, but it is a matter of faith.

Progress having been made in science, people can now manage in certain cases to know who isn't the father, but in the end the father remains an unknown [*un inconnu*]. It is, moreover, quite clear that the initiation of biological research on paternity cannot but have an impact on the function of the Name-of-the-Father.

The Name-of-the-Father is the hinge [*pivot*] on which a whole field of subjectivity turns because it is solely sustained as symbolic. It is at this point that we must consider the other face – namely, its relation to jouissance.

This is, in short, what will allow us to make a bit of headway regarding the transmission of the Name-of-the-Father – namely, regarding the transmission of castration. That is our objective this year.

I will end today as usual at a point at which I have managed, none too early, to arrive and will say, see you next time.

January 29, 1969

X

THE THREE MATRICES

Two writings
Philosophy or repetition
The superego and *Durcharbeitung* according to Bergler

I am going to begin where I left off last time.

I talked about many things and, in particular, I managed to affect some of you with the obviousness of the mathematical genesis I provided of *a* starting solely from the One qua mark.

It relies on a record [*factum*] or fabrication that results from the simplest use of this One, insofar as, once repeated, it proliferates, since it is only established in order to endeavor to repeat jouissance, to find it anew insofar as it has already taken flight [see Freud's "Project for a Scientific Psychology" (1895) in SE I]. What was not marked at the outset is altered by the first One, which is inscribed in order to refind it, since at the outset it was not marked. The One is thus already posited in the founding of a difference that it does not constitute as such, but which it produces.

This earliest point makes repetition the key to a process about which we can wonder whether or not it can reach its endpoint [*terme*] once it has started.

We thus immediately arrive at the question of an endpoint. It is terminal only if we look at it solely in terms of Freud's career as a subject. He was also a man of action, a man who blazed a trail. How did he do so? I should perhaps recall this to mind given what I will talk with you about today. If we believe that the endpoint of the path traced out by Freud is the question he raised whether analysis is terminable or interminable, it can only be from the standpoint that a man's career finds its limit in death. This merely situates in time the question that I am revisiting by asking whether or not the process that begins for the subject owing to repetition, with repetition as its origin, has a limit.

This is the question I left in abeyance, but nevertheless raised by very clearly demonstrating on the board last time what I called the division or bipartition of two infinities. I indicated that it is what is ultimately involved in Pascal's wager.

The infinity on which his wager reposes is a numerical infinity. I took up this infinity and accelerated it, as it were, through the use of a Fibonacci series which is exponential, the numbers that it generates growing not arithmetically but geometrically. The further we get from its beginning, the more the series approximates the proportion known as a. As the numbers grow, a appears ever more exactly in an inverted form, $1/a$, which is all the more striking in that it ties 1 to a. The ratio of any number over the number that precedes it [in the series] asymptotically approaches the constant $1/a$.

I also wrote on the board the series that results from proceeding in the opposite direction. Owing to the fact that a is less than 1, the process of addition ends, not merely with a ratio, but a limit. Whether you proceed by addition or, on the other hand, by subtraction, in such a way that it is always true in this chain that, ascending, each term is the sum of the two preceding terms, you nevertheless arrive at a insofar as the sum of the series designates a limit this time. No matter how many terms you add up, you will never go beyond $1 + a$, which seems to indicate that by taking things in this direction, what is generated by repetition has an endpoint.

This is where I brought in the well-known table used by those who, in short, miss what is at issue when they attempt to cast Pascal's wager in the terms of game theory.

1

What we have here is a matrix constructed on the basis of four distinct cases.

Let us consider those in which God exists, A. In what we will see to be a rather astonishing impulse, people assign a zero [in the upper left-hand square of Figure 10.1] to what results from the observation of the divine commandments, confused here with the renunciation of something, whether we call it "pleasure" or something else. What believers are left with in this life is assigned a zero, owing to which their future life is qualified with the term "infinite," an infinity of infinitely happy promised lives.

If [on the other hand,] we assume that God does not exist, A̶, the subject of the game is written with an a, he being taken literally

– that's the word for it! – insofar as he is presumed to experience the limited, *and* problematic, happiness that is offered to him in this life. It is not unreasonable, some say, to choose it since, as God does not exist, it seems clear that there is nothing to be expected from the afterlife.

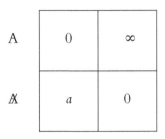

Figure 10.1: The First Matrix

I pointed out the fragile nature of this sort of matrix, because, according to game theory, the contents of the squares can only be established for a game involving two adversaries. If there were two adversaries here, the subject should be in this position [along the top of the matrix], whereas the enigmatic Other, the one who must either wager or not, should be found at the place indicated by A and Ā.

The problem is that God is not playing the game. In any case, nothing allows us to assert that He is. The result of this paradoxical fact is that the stakes here are conflated with the existence of the partner, whereas it is on the table, so to speak, that we find, not man, but the subject defined by the wager. This is why the signs included in this matrix must be re-interpreted.

There is a choice: "God exists or God does not exist." That is where the formulation of the wager begins. If we start with that and that alone, it is clear that there is no reason to hesitate, for what we risk winning by betting that God exists – namely, the infinite – is in no way comparable to what we will surely win if we bet the opposite, namely *a*. Still, our certainty [in the latter case] can easily be called into question, for what exactly will we win? The *a* is not precisely defined.

This formulation is of interest because it goes right to the root of the role played by the intervention of the signifier in any act of choice. It is nevertheless here that I raised a question and pointed out the inadequacy of the table. It is incomplete insofar as it does not involve a second story [or: floor, *étage*], which perhaps restores what such a matrix is supposed to involve when it is employed in game theory. I thus introduced the second story.

156

I

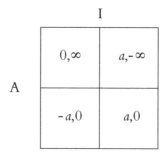

A

Figure 10.2: The Second Matrix

I distinguish the "I" who can envision betting against God, even if He exists – in other words, choosing *a* at his own expense – from the subject who is purely identical to the inscription of the stakes. The former chooses *a* knowing full well what his choice involves – namely, that he positively loses the infinite, the infinity of happy lives that is offered to him. I note this as follows: <*a*,−∞>.

The two squares that form a diagonal running from the [upper] left to the [lower] right reproduce what was found in the first matrix.

We still must fill in the fourth square, the one on the lower left. It is the case in which it is supposable that, even if God does not exist, the *a* – which is situated in that square [in the first matrix] – can be deliberately abandoned. It is thus negativized, subtracted: −*a*. It is coupled here with a zero that I will include without further commentary; even though it is a zero and seems self-evident, it nevertheless constitutes a problem.

Let us now extract the terms that our second composition added – namely, *a*, −∞, −*a*, 0. We are going to put them in a new matrix.

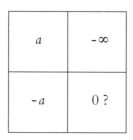

Figure 10.3: The Third Matrix

In sum, I will expressly emphasize what I just mentioned in passing: zero takes on the value of a question here. In order to grasp what it involves, let us begin by reconsidering the first matrix. The zeros that we find in it warrant our attention.

What did I say earlier? In the position of the player – that is, of the subject who alone exists – the only thing that in fact counts, the only thing that is weighed in the balance, is infinity against the finite character of *a*. The upshot being that the zeros merely designate the fact that, as Pascal highlighted by introducing the *règle des partis*, nothing can be accurately stated about a game having a beginning and an end established by rules, except on the basis of the following: what is placed on the table, what is known as the ante, is, right from the outset, lost. The game only exists on the basis of the fact that it is on the table, and, as it were, in the collective pot. This is implied by the very nature of the game.

It is thus owing to its very nature that the game can produce nothing but zero in the lower right-hand square. This zero merely indicates the fact that you are playing. Without the zero there is no game.

One could surely say the same thing of the other zero – namely, the one found in the upper left-hand square [of Figure 10.1], since it represents the loss of infinity to which the player resigns himself. But since what is at stake here is the existence of the other player, zero as the sign of a loss is already problematic.

Since nothing, after all, obliges us to rush to judgment, which is precisely when errors are made, we need not claim that this zero is symmetrical to the other one.

Indeed, when we look at philosophers' discussions of Pascal's montage, and his dialogue with Méré – who played a role in the way Pascal wrote, simultaneously throwing us off the scent (something that never occurs without our collaboration, naturally) about the status of this montage – it clearly appears that this zero does not so much represent the constitutive loss of the ante as the inscription of one of the choices that is offered, which is the choice not to sit down at the gambling table. This is clearly what was done by the person to whom the schema of the wager was addressed in a dialogue that was not simply imagined but actually took place. The zero thus does not represent the constitutive loss of the ante, but the "no ante" of he who decides not to sit down at the table.

We must now investigate what occurs in the second matrix in order to see how the wager is laid out there.

2

Last time I indicated how the text of our practice can be depicted.

If I was able to do so as quickly as I did, it was owing, in truth, to a certain graph that I had already constructed not with the hypothesis, but with the inscriptible – something that is thus tangible – which is responsible for the fact that *a* itself may merely be the effect of the inclusion of man's life in the game [or: gamble, *jeu*].

Pascal alerts us to this himself in terms that are not explicitly formulated, no doubt. "You are already embarked," he tells us, and it's true.

He bases this on the word [*la parole*], which for him is that of the Church. It is striking that it does not seem necessary to him to distinguish from Holy Scripture the more foundational [*radicale*] writing that resembles a watermark in his wager, and which nevertheless provides him with a great deal. The reason for this must certainly be sought in the long ineliminable nature of Scripture, which was the blind spot of centuries of thought which nevertheless cannot be characterized as obscurantist.

I am going to seek out the warp and woof [*trame*] of this foundational writing in mathematical logic. This leaves me in a position that is homological to his, except that I cannot avoid explicitly asking whether the very stakes of the wager do not depend on the function of writing itself.

The epigraph that I wrote on the board at the beginning of the year highlights where I differ from Pascal. It could simply be reformulated as follows: "What I prefer is a discourse without speech." This designates nothing other than a discourse based on writing.

Let us take a moment to consider the scope of what I am stating here, which is absolutely consistent with what I began to announce in the form of the triplicity of the symbolic, the imaginary, and the real. Here I must stress the difference that exists between philosophical discourse and what we are taught by a discipline that takes repetition as its starting point.

Every philosophical discourse ends up freeing itself [or: disengaging itself, *se déprendre*] from the very machinery [*appareil*] that acts on linguistic material. The entire philosophical tradition comes up against Kant's refutation of the ontological argument. In the name of what? In the name of the following: the forms of pure reason, the transcendental analytic, are suspected of being imaginary. This is also what constitutes the sole philosophical objection to Pascal's wager. Kant tells us that the God whose existence you may consider to be necessary is nevertheless conceptualized only within a framework of thought that relies on the prior bracketing [*suspens*] involved in aesthetics, qualified here as transcendental. Which means nothing other than the following: no speech can be proffered if not in time and space, and, following philosophical convention, we call their existence into question, insofar as it is supposed to be foundational.

The problem being that Pascal's God can in no way be called into question at the imaginary level, for he is not the God of the philosophers. Nor is he the God of any [field of] knowledge. We know, Pascal writes, neither what He is, of course, nor whether He is. He can in no way be bracketed by any philosophy, since it is not philosophy that grounds Him. Therein lies the value of Pascal's wager, and it is why I have selected it as an exemplary turning point, regardless of what people may think of resorting to something so antiquated.

Now, my discourse – when I take up Freud's, following the path he blazed – is essentially distinguished from philosophical discourse by not disengaging [*décolle*] from what we are caught up in and embarked by [*engagés*], as Pascal puts it. Rather than employing a discourse to lay down a law for the world and norms for history (or the other way around), my discourse is situated where the thinking subject initially perceives that he can only recognize himself as the effect of language.

160

Stated otherwise, and to put what I am in the process of saying in a nutshell, as soon as one sets up the gaming table – and Lord knows it is already set up! – prior to being a thinking subject, the subject is *a*. It is afterward that the question arises of relating that to thinking. He has no need to think in order to be established as *a*. It's already happened, which contradicts what one might imagine owing to the lamentable failure and the ever more shocking futility of all of philosophy – namely, that one can overturn the gaming table.

I can knock it over, of course, and tip over all the tables in Vincennes [where an Experimental University Center had just been created] and elsewhere, but that doesn't stop the true gaming table from still being there. The true table is not the university table, the one around which the boss gathers with his students in a nice little room, wherever it may be, whether it is his, warm and cozy, or one of our model classrooms for babies.

This is why I allowed myself to do a little scribbling yesterday – it is not really scribbling at all, I spent quite some time on it – which I am not sure you will see in print because it will either come out in one specific place, or it won't come out at all, and I am curious to see whether it will come out or not. In short, I went so far as to do something outrageous – I have been allowing myself to do such things for some time now when I am alone, and those things always come out at some point in one form or another – that involves saying (whether I'm deluded or not) that I would like people to realize that it is no longer possible to play the role suitable for the transmission of knowledge without being a psychoanalyst.

The transmission of knowledge is not the transmission of a value, even if values are now recorded on transcripts in the form of course credits. Well, precisely because something has happened to the value of knowledge, anyone who would, in the future, like to grasp the mainsprings of what one might call a "training effect" and occupy a relevant position in places where it is supposed to be produced – even if we are talking about mathematics, biochemistry, or anything else – would do well to be a psychoanalyst, if that is how we must define someone who takes seriously the question of the dependence of the subject on the discourse that has a hold on him [*qui le tient*], and not that he proffers [or: that he holds (in his hand), *qu'il tient*].

Let us turn back to the second matrix. As you are all products of academe, in other words, of philosophical teaching, I knew I could not broach it abruptly.

What does it mean that there is nothing but *a*s and zeros in the lower squares? First of all, as I just indicated, and as Pascal says, it was never *a* or 0. Since no one other than philosophers reads Pascal, everyone has remained deaf to it. When he says that *a* equals zero, that means *a* is the ante. This was clearly laid out in the *règle des partis*. But people remained deaf to it anyway, thinking zero had to be zero with respect to infinity, which was hogwash. What happens if we now place [in the matrix], not, as people futilely, imaginarily, said, *a* or zero, but rather *a* or −*a*?

If −*a* truly means what it seems to mean – namely, that a is negativized [*qu'on inverse* a] – what the heck is this thingamajig: $<-a,0>$?

And in this other case – whatever happens, it is at the expense of something which, because it is written $[-\infty]$, seems like it must be costly – what is this correlation $<a,-\infty>$, which perhaps allows us to perceive that our conjunction [i.e. plus and minus] signs change here?

We thus have, in any case, two pairs [*liaisons*: $<-a,0>$ and $<a,-\infty>$] that strike me as worth investigating. You see that they are not altogether classified like the ones before.

I am sorry that I have not gone further today than I already went, albeit too quickly, in the last few minutes last time, when I indicated that the link between *a* and ∞ is the one that goes by the name of "hell" in Pascal's scribblings.

I trumpeted that to people who were already heading out the door – we are all familiar with hell, it is everyday life. Curiously enough, we know it, we say it, we say nothing but that in fact, yet it remains limited to discourse, and to a few symptoms, of course. Thank God, because if there weren't symptoms people wouldn't even notice.

If neurotic symptoms didn't exist, there would have been no Freud. If hysterics hadn't already raised the question, there would've been no chance for the truth to have shown even the tip of its nose.

Now we must pause for a bit.

3

Someone – whom I thank, for one should always thank people who send gifts your way – reminded me, for unrelated reasons, about the existence of the chapter entitled "The Underestimated Super-ego" in *The Basic Neurosis* by Edmund Bergler, who explains everything.

Don't tell me that I, too, explain everything. For, as a matter of fact, I explain nothing. That is precisely what interests you. I try at various levels, and not simply here, to ensure that there are psychoanalysts who are not imbeciles. What I do is drum up interest, not to draw people into an out-of-the-way school [or: mislead them, *trou d'école*], but to try to provide the equivalent of what psychoanalysts should have to those who have no way to obtain it. It is a hopeless enterprise. But experience proves that the other enterprise, that of teaching it to psychoanalysts themselves, also seems doomed to failure, as I have already written.

I mentioned analysts who are imbeciles. I mean that they are imbeciles as subjects, for they are actually rather clever when it comes to managing their practice. Which is a specific consequence of what I am in the process of enunciating here – it fits perfectly with the theory. It proves not only that one has no need to be a philosopher, but that it is much better not to be one. Except that consequently one doesn't understand anything. Which explains why I spend my time enunciating that it's much better not to understand. The problem being that analysts understand little tiny things. Which then proliferate.

Let us take "The Underestimated Super-ego," for example. It's a fine chapter because, first of all, it brings together all the ways in which the superego is articulated in Freud's work. As Bergler is not a philosopher, he clearly does not see that they hang together. Moreover, he is charming for he tells us what he's up to. That's what's great about psychoanalysts, they tell all. He admits in a footnote [p. 118 n. 10] that he wrote to a certain H. H. Hart, who collected extracts from Freud's opus, asking him to send him a bunch of quotes regarding the superego. That can, after all, be done; that, too, fits with the theory. If writing is so important, one can do that: take a pair of scissors in hand and, everywhere you find the word "superego," snip, snip, you cut it out and compile a list of fifteen different citations.

163   I'm joking, naturally. But Bergler got me started. He read Freud's work, of course, at least I like to imagine he did. Nevertheless, he admits that to write this chapter he wrote to Dr. Hart to ask him for quotes about the superego. The result is that he can obviously point out to what degree they do not cohere. This is exactly the kind of thing you can find in every psychoanalytic journal, except mine, of course.

He starts with censorship in dreams. People think that the censor is innocuous, as if it were nothing to wield a pair of scissors with which you then formulate a theory. After that, the superego becomes something that titillates you. Later [in Freud's work], it becomes the big bad wolf. And still later, there is no longer any superego. And after that, he mentions Eros, Thanatos, the whole kit and caboodle. He still has to find a way to get Thanatos to fit in somewhere. He tells us that he works things out by bowing and scraping, bending and stretching. Oh, our dear little superego!

Fine. Thanks to this compilation, we end up with something that is quite laughable, it must be said. It is only in our times that no one laughs. Even philosophy professors can read this paper without laughing. It must be said that we have gone so far that we have checkmated this generation of them. There was a time when a not especially intelligent guy by the name of Charles Blondel yelled and screamed about Freud. At least he did something. Now, even those who haven't the slightest inkling what is involved in a psychoanalysis read just as preposterous things without balking. Everything is possible, everything is admissible. Intellectual segregation reigns supreme. In any case, we see the outlines of things elsewhere before they become real.

Bergler perceives a lot of things. When something is right there in front of his nose, he understands it. That's too bad, because he understands it at the level of his nose, which can't actually be like a nose – it must be pointed. So all he sees is a little tiny thing. He begins by perceiving – but only intuitively, at the level of sensibility – that what he finds in the quotes from Freud's work regarding the superego must bear some relationship to what he sees all the time [in his practice], which is something known as *Durcharbeitung* [rendered in English as "working through"].

People have spilled a lot of ink pointing out that it is untranslatable into French. As there is no word in French for work through or drill (or bore) [*travail à travers, forage*], it was translated by *élabora-*
164   *tion. Durcharbeitung* does not mean *élaboration*, that's for sure. As everyone knows, people in France elaborate. And it's mostly hot air.

Psychoanalytic working through has nothing to do with that. Analysands realize that it involves coming back to the same thing all the time, that at every turn of the way one is led back to the same thing, and that it has to go on for a long time if they are to arrive at what I have explained to you – namely, a limit or terminus, when they go in the right direction, that is. Bergler realizes that this is an effect of the superego – in other words, that the big bad thingama-bob supposedly extracted from the Oedipus complex, the devouring mother, or any of those vague phrases, nevertheless bears some relationship to the exhausting, badgering, necessary, and above all repeated facet of things by which in analysis you, in fact, sometimes arrive at an endpoint.

How can he fail to see that this has nothing in common with the stupid scenarios in which people, not having understood what is meant by an agency [*instance*, the French for Freud's *Instanz*], per-sonify the superego?

Bergler doesn't want any of that to occur on the other scene [*anderer Schauplatz*] that Freud talked about, the one that functions in dreams, but rather has it unfold like a skit [or: playlet (or sketch), *saynète*] on the stage where "analytic training" teaches you how to play with puppets. The superego is the policeman who beats up Punch who incarnates the ego. How is it possible that the connec-tion between the superego and working through that Bergler grasps so well clinically, does not suggest to him that one need not multiply agencies in the personality to find the superego?

He admits what he's up to at every step of the way. He tells us that people have noticed that it is related to the ego-ideal. It must be admitted that people understand absolutely nothing about that. No one has yet distilled it.

In order for his discourse to be something other than the memoirs of a psychoanalyst, Bergler mentions the case of a young woman in which it was clear that it was her guilt feelings that brought her into analysis. Let us hope that they were the same ones that led her to leave!

People could perhaps perceive that it would be of interest to provide a truly precise articulation that would allow us to realize that it is not a misuse of terms to relate, even in the name of a minimal intuition, the superego to *Durcharbeitung*, working through, in the treatment. This articulation might just so happen to involve a small maneuver allowing us to establish the measure of what cannot be measured because it is the initial ante. In certain cases, it may in fact be depicted with the greatest precision and written on the board. It is possible that it would be through a certain regular way of rotating from one side to another that we would manage to fill in something that, in certain cases, can be depicted as a 1 [see Figure 8.6].

165

A choice has to be made. You can't say that the superego is the big bad wolf and then wonder whether the severe superego isn't born of an identification with some person. That's not the way to raise questions. It's like when people tell you that so-and-so is religious because his grandfather was. To me that is inadequate. Even if you have a religious grandfather, you might conclude that it's bullshit, mightn't you?

It is important to specify identification's proper direction. We need to know whether identification is an aim or an obstacle in analysis. Perhaps we encourage identification, but it is in order that the identification simultaneously come undone. Something else may appear owing to the fact that it comes undone precisely because one has identified, something that in this case I will call a hole.

I will leave it there for today. I tried to show you here at the end that my discourse is of direct interest for aerating our practice.

Since Freud did not indulge in work based on his *sense of smell*, and didn't merely follow his nose [or: wing it; see, for example, *Écrits*, p. 221], one can in fact, if one follows the development of a term over the course of his thought, find therein the guiding lines that allow us to give it its coherence. If we want to make headway on the basis of something other than little vignettes, we must give the concept its consistency and solidity. This would perhaps allow us to see something other than simple analogical facts.

Bergler emphasizes the importance of details [pp. 128–31]. What I am saying in no wise detracts from that. Read his chapter to see that, even if it is relevant and well oriented, it is oriented like iron filings that are placed in a preexisting magnetic field. We find in it no true explanation for the power and importance of details. It's true that details are the only things that interest us, but we still must know in each case what is interesting. Without that, we end up relying on pure and simple resemblance and we connect up disparate details.

166

We will begin next time with the third figure.

February 5, 1969

TRUTH'S RETARDATION AND THE ADMINISTRATION OF KNOWLEDGE

Students write
The real qua abutment of knowledge
Lies as the secretion of truth
The Other identified with *a*

I am quite annoyed at everything that is going on. You too, I imagine. It's hard to ignore. I find myself wondering if I am here to do my usual thing, or to occupy the building.

Sympathetic ears were kind enough to grasp that certain of the things that I discussed in my second to last class bore some relation to a science. Who knows? Not a new science, but perhaps a clarification of the conditions of science.

Today I have the sense that I am going to gently inflect things. I have that sense for all sorts of reasons, if only because Mardi Gras is drawing nigh, so it seems fitting. I got that sense because of the tenor of what I thought about this morning before seeing you. I am going to inflect things a bit toward something that you can call as you like, but it involves something of a moral note.

How, moreover, could one avoid such a note given the aura, margin, and limits of my approach to Pascal's wager? We clearly cannot overlook this effect, even if what inspired me to talk to you about it is, of course, the fact that Pascal's wager is located at a certain turning point [*joint*].

Before coming to it, in order to lighten things up, however little – as I mentioned, Mardi Gras is approaching – I am going to read you a letter I received. I won't tell you who sent it to me or from which town it was mailed.

Dear Mr. Lacan,
We are students and we have read your *Écrits*, almost in their entirety. There is quite a lot in them. They are obviously

168   not always easy to read, but we nevertheless congratulate you
        for have written them.

It's not every day that I receive such congratulations! [They go on:]

    We would like to know how one goes about writing such
    difficult things –

I'm not mocking anyone, and certainly not these guys who I find
truly . . . Well, I'll tell you what I think of them. Two of them wrote
it together.

    – for that could help us pass our exams. We have bachelor's
    degrees in philosophy, but it is getting harder and harder to
    make the cut. We figure that we would do better to be cunning
    and astonish our professors rather than go on providing a form
    of flat, pedestrian discourse.

On top of that, they add:

    Could you offer us a few crafty tricks we could use in order to
    do so?

That struck me because I tell myself that, when you get right down
to it, that's what I am in the process of doing!

    We would like to ask one further favor, if it isn't too daring:
    could you send us one of your lovely bowties as a memento?
    We would really appreciate that.
            We thank you and hope to see you again, Mr. Lacan.
    All best wishes.

They are not very up-to-date. They don't realize that I have been
wearing turtlenecks for some time now.
    To me their letter echoes, confirms, and resonates with what gets
me when I hear simple souls claim, since the turmoil of May [1968]:
"Things will never be the same as before." Given where we're at, I'd
sooner say that "things will be more than ever as they were before."
Far be it from me, naturally, to confine the phenomenon to the little
glimpse provided by this letter. It is but one tiny facet of the business;
there are obviously plenty of other things at stake. Yet, from a certain
vantage point, this letter can serve as a summary of the way in which
my work has been received, in a radius that is not as great as that of
the city from which this letter was mailed, which is fairly far away.

As you heard, they are not very up-to-date. But in any case, their letter reflects one way in which my teaching is viewed. I don't see why I should hold the bowtie against them when a psychoanalyst – who played a pivotal role in a certain examining committee sent long ago by a certain British Society – considered it totally justifiable to weigh my bowtie in the balance against the rest of my teaching. There was all of my teaching in one scale, and in the other my bowtie – in other words, the accessory thanks to which those who presented themselves at the time as my students supposedly identified with me.

You see that these two fine, kind, naïve fellows are not the only ones interested in bowties. In any case, they are not as naïve as all that, because, as they say, they must perhaps learn to be cunning.

169

We will come back to that.

1

Let us now return to the way I laid things out.

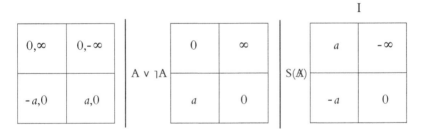

Figure 11.1: The Three Matrices of the Wager

The vertical lines here are designed to show where each of these schemas leaves off, so that they don't overlap, either in reality or in your minds.

The matrix on the left is the one with which I felt I could complete the one in the middle – that is, the one with which one can schematize, imitating what is done in game theory, what was actually done with Pascal's wager throughout the nineteenth century and even for a good bit of our own century, people demonstrating how Pascal tried in some sense to trick and cheat us.

I believe I convinced you that the zeros [in the middle matrix] do not really correspond to results of a wager made with a partner, because the wager concerns the *existence* of a partner, and it is regarding his existence that one must wager. Under such conditions,

the two lines of possibility that are offered to the wagerer do not intersect with any lines of possibility belonging to the Other, since we cannot even ensure the Other's existence. The choice here thus concerns the existence or non-existence of the Other, on the one
170 hand, and what his existence promises the wagerer and what his inexistence allows him, on the other. In this case, it is plausible – if one has a mathematical turn of mind, naturally – to wager and to wager as Pascal proposed.

Don't forget, however, that in order not to mislead you by making you believe that I am in any way endorsing his solution, I made a remark right from the outset, right from the moment at which I recalled the status of the wager as it is presented (not as we see it through the grid of the discussions that became classic on the subject). The remark I made is as follows:

At this level, one can just as well replace the choice to be made regarding the existence of God with another choice, which can serve the function just as well, but which totally changes its meaning. What may be involved is the radical formulation of the real, insofar as it is not conceivable – and we can truly sense it in this case – to imagine any other limit to knowledge than the road-block [or: abutment, *butée*] where what we have to deal with is the following and the following alone: something unspeakable which either is or is not. In other words, something involving a sort of heads or tails.

This was designed to remind you of something we must not lose sight of. Namely, that we are not fooling around here. We are trying to provide articulations such that the most important decisions that need to be made can be laid out. It just so happens that our era ever more clearly indicates that the most important decisions – insofar as they might be those made by a psychoanalyst – may also coincide with those that are necessary at a key point in the social body: the administration of knowledge.

Let it be clear that I am not providing a historical account here. Still I don't see why an apparatus as precise as Pascal's wager should prove any less generative for us than it was for its author, and that requires us to clearly conceptualize at what turning point it is situated. We are now going to re-clarify that situation.

2

It was not, as you will see right away, in order to provide a historical account that I reminded you last time that, in Pascal's era,
171 Revelation existed, and emphasized what the two stages – the word

of the Church and Holy Scripture – involved and the role that Holy Scripture played for Pascal.

Newton, who had plenty of other things on his plate, also wrote a long book – being a bibliophile, I happen to have it and it is superb – which is a commentary on the Apocalypse and on Daniel's prophecy. He put just as much care there into the calculation and manipulation of numbers, which are nevertheless highly problematic when it comes to situating the reign of Nebuchadnezzar, for example, as he did in his study of the laws of gravitation. A simple reminder, which is of no importance to us.

When Pascal proposed his wager – whatever the relevance of my remarks regarding the fact that it could not have been proposed except at the moment at which a form of knowledge, which is that of science, was born – it depended for him on what we can call the word of the Other, on the word of the Other understood as truth.

I am taking things up anew at this point because the way I articulated knowledge and truth – together and separately – in a dialectic that distinguished them, if not opposed them, is not unfamiliar to some of you here. I am hereby informing the others about it. They would already know about it if they had done like my charming correspondents did, if they had read almost all of my *Écrits*, for it is found in the last article collected there. Its title is "Science and Truth."

In another of the articles there, entitled "The Freudian Thing," I wrote something about truth that could be understood as follows: that its property is that it speaks. I would then be put in the box of obscurantism, why not, because it would bolster the notion that, following in Pascal's footsteps, I am supposedly trying to bring you back to religion.

"So," you will say, "truth speaks – sure, that's obvious." That is what you would say if you didn't understand any of what I say, which is quite possible. I never said that. I had truth say, "I, truth, speak" [*Écrits*, p. 340]. But I did not have truth say, for example, "I, truth, speak in order to say myself qua truth," or, "in order to tell you the truth." The fact that it speaks doesn't mean that it tells the truth. It's the truth and it speaks. As for what it says, you've got to work that out yourself.

That may mean, and it is what certain people do: "Talk all you like, it doesn't make any difference" ["Cause toujours, c'est tout ce que tu sais faire" is a well-known French expression implying that the listener doesn't believe a word of what the speaker is saying; *causer* means both to cause and to talk]. I dare say that I attributed a bit more to the truth. In the interim, I in fact attributed to truth the ability to cause/chat – and not simply in the sense implied by "cause

172

toujours" – to even cause/chat nonstop. In "Science and Truth," I
even recalled Lenin's quip about Marx's theory of the social order,
about which he says that it will triumph because it is true – but not
necessarily because it tells the truth [*Écrits*, p. 738]. That applies here
too.

I won't dwell on this, because people say that my name was
quoted in a complimentary way in the [communist] newspaper
L'Humanité – I wasn't able to go have a look see because I didn't
have time. According to that paper, I supposedly began to mediate
between Freud and Marx this year, sensing that it was a fashionable
thing to do. I heard about this when I had the flu last weekend and,
thank God, that suddenly inspired me to do what we call work – in
other words, turn everything upside down. I began looking through
the atrocious quantity of scribblings whose destruction I will have
to ensure before I disappear – because God only knows what people
will do with them otherwise – and I realized that my Italian translator, who I had praised when I decided to provide a sort of analogy
between surplus value and surplus jouissance, actually had no credit
when she told me that *a* is, in short, surplus value. For I had already
spoken so much about Marx – about use value, exchange value,
and surplus value with respect to a certain number of fundamental
articulations in psychoanalysis – that I have to wonder if I have
contributed anything new this year other than the name *Mehrlust*,
surplus jouissance, by way of analogy with *Mehrwert*. Freud's discourse and Marx's discourse absolutely do not unfold in the same
field, of course, even if they both discuss foundational matters.

Since I mentioned Lenin, it might not be bad to remind you that
Marxist theory, inasmuch as it concerns a truth, in fact states that
the truth of capitalism is the proletariat. That's true; it is a truth.
Yet – and this explains my remarks regarding the function of truth
– Marxist theory begins from the revolutionary consequence of this
truth. Naturally, it goes a tiny bit further, since it also constructs a
theory of capitalism.

What is meant by the proletariat? It means that work is reduced
to a pure and simple commodity, which means that the worker
173   himself is reduced to the same status [i.e., he is just another com-
modity]. But as soon as the worker learns that about himself, thanks
to the theory, we can say that, owing to this step, he finds pathways
to a status – call it as you will – qua savant. He is no longer part of
the proletariat *an sich* [in itself], as it were; he is no longer a pure
and simple truth; he is *für sich* [for himself], he is what is known as
"class consciousness." And he may even simultaneously become the
class consciousness of a party in which no one ever speaks the truth
again.

I am not being satirical here. I am in the process of recalling to mind obvious things, which is why it is relieving. These obvious things are not the scandals people try to make them out to be when they understand nothing whatsoever. If we have at our disposal a correct theory of the status of knowledge and truth, it is hard to see why we should be surprised, in particular, that it is from the most "Lenin-ially" defined relationship to truth that the whole "lenient-ification" in which the apparatus is immersed stems. If you can get it into your head that there is nothing more lenient-ifying than those who are hard-core [les durs], you will have grasped a truth that has long since been recognized.

Hasn't it, in fact, been recognized for a long time, if not forever? If people hadn't been persuaded that Christianity is not the truth for so long now, and I will tell you why, they might have realized that – for a while, and not a short while – it was the truth. It proved that around any and every truth that claims to speak as such, prospers a clergy that obligatorily lies. Which truly makes me wonder why people are so flabbergasted by the functioning of socialist governments!

Will I go so far as to say that truth secretes pearls of untruth [or: real gems of lies, la perle du mensonge]? That would clear the air a bit, an air that exists, moreover, only owing to a certain form of cre-tinization whose name I must immediately provide since, at the end of what we will get through today, I will have to situate it in one of these little squares – it is what is known as "progressivism."

I will try to give you a better definition of it than the one that comes from referring to the effect of scandals – I mean the fact that progressivism produces scandalized souls. Reading Hegel on "the law of the heart" and the "frenzy of self-conceit" should have long since made such things apparent. Yet when things get a bit nasty, no one thinks of recalling Hegel's notions at the opportune time. That is why I placed as an epigraph to my discourse this year something that means that what I prefer is a discourse without speech.

174

What is thus at stake – what could be in question here if we wanted, as they say, to lick the bowl to the point at which we can truly enjoy it by pointing it out – is to perceive that such things don't really have such bad effects. Since I say that, in serving the field of truth, that service as such – a service no one is asked to provide, it must simply be one's vocation – necessarily leads to lying, I also want to point out, because one must be fair, that it forces one to work awfully hard. Personally I adore that – when it is others who do the work, naturally. I love reading books by the many ecclesias-tical authors whose patience and erudition I admire – they collect myriad quotes that perfectly suit my purposes at times. The same is true of authors of the communist Church. They are also excellent workers. I may not be able to bear some of them in everyday life, any more than I can stand personal contact with priests. But that doesn't stop them from being able to write very fine works, and I enjoy reading a certain number of them, for example, the one entitled *Le Dieu caché* [*The Hidden God*]. That doesn't make me any more willing to rub shoulders with its author.

The fruit knowledge can glean from this should not be entirely neglected, because when you concern yourself a bit too much with truth, you become so bogged down in it that you end up lying. The only true question – since I said that I would go all the way here – is not at all whether it has consequences, since, after all, it is a way of selecting elites, and this is why it scoops up so many retards, regardless of the field. That's going all the way.

Don't think that I'm saying this just for fun, just to take a swipe at groups that have no reason to be any freer of retards than others. I'm doing so because we analysts may be able to offer something very important on this point.

Consider the key discreetly provided by our dear friend Maud, Maud Mannoni, for those who do not know her. I am talking about the relationship between those who are mentally retarded and the configuration that interests us, which obviously fascinates us when it comes to truth. This is even why we know better than others how to keep our noses clean. Even our lies – those we are forced to tell – are less impudent than other people's; less impudent but more cowardly, it must be said. There are some, however, that retain some vivacity in this arena, and this leads to certain texts I am mentioning that suddenly begin to pour down on the topic of mental retardation.

I myself got quite used to all that in the early years of my practice. I admired the armfuls of flowers, flowers of truth, I received when I inadvertently took into analysis the kind of person Freud – he was so wrong! – seemed to feel he had to turn away: someone who was mentally retarded. I must say that there is no analysis that works better, if by that we mean one that brings the analyst joy. It is perhaps not the only thing one can hope for from a psychoanalysis, but it is clear that, since they harbor within themselves truths that they bring out in the guise of pearls, unique pearls – a term that I have heretofore reserved for lies – the mentally retarded [*débile mental*] can't be altogether stupid [*débile*]. What if they are a bit cunning?

You will understand what I am saying better if you read the right authors, in other words, Maud Mannoni. It's an idea that some people have already had. Dostoyevsky called one of those people who behave most marvelously, regardless of the social field they encounter and regardless of the awkward situations they get themselves into, *The Idiot*.

I sometimes mention Hegel, but that is no reason not to do so again. He talks about "the ruse [or: cunning] of reason." I must say that I have always mistrusted that notion. In my experience, reason is very frequently misled. Indeed, I have never seen even a single one of its ruses succeed in my lifetime. Perhaps Hegel did. He spent his time in the minor courts of Germany where there were plenty of retards, and, in truth, that is perhaps the source upon which he drew. As for the ruse that may be at work among those who are "poor in spirit" [or: simpleminded, *simples d'esprit*], the ones that someone who knew what he was saying called "blessed" [Matthew 5:3], I will leave the question open.

I'm now done with my simple reminder, which was highly necessary and salubrious given the current context.

3

176

I would now like to take things up again where I left them last time – namely, in the matrix that is distinguished by the following, that it is no longer important to know what one is staking.

After all, what Pascal's wager means is that you cannot play this particular game correctly unless you are indifferent – that is, unless you are convinced that the infinite, insofar as it is located to the right [presumably in the middle matrix in Figure 11.1] in the row that corresponds to God's existence, is a stake that is far more interesting than the thingamajig about which we don't even know very well what it is [*a*], and which is represented how? When you read Pascal, this thingamajig amounts to all the dishonest things you'll refrain from doing when you follow God's commandments [*Pari de Pascal*, p. 136], and a few additional inconveniences – namely, in your dealings with the holy water font and a few other accessories – when you follow the Church's commandments.

It requires, in short, a stance of indifference with regard to its status. And this is attained all the more easily in the wager such as Pascal presents it in that, after all, we know neither what He is nor if He is – as Pascal emphasizes and we are lucky to have it straight from his pen.

We have here an absolutely fabulous negation. Let's not forget that, for centuries prior to that, the ontological argument had a certain weight for all sensible thinkers. I won't fly off on this particular tangent, but we would do well to learn from it. The ontological argument boiled down to saying nothing other than what I am in the process of teaching you – namely, that there is a hole in discourse, that there is a place where we are not capable of situating the signifier that is necessary for everything else to hold together. They believed that the signifier "God" could do the trick. Indeed, it does the trick at the level of something that may well be a form of mental retardation – namely, philosophy.

It is generally agreed, among atheists, I mean, that the Supreme Being has a meaning. Voltaire, who generally passes for a cunning little rascal [*petit malin*], clung to it with all his might. Diderot was way ahead of him, a full length ahead, as can be seen in everything he wrote. Which is probably also why almost everything he wrote that was truly important only came out posthumously, and in all it didn't amount to nearly as much as in Voltaire's case. Diderot had already glimpsed the fact that there is a lack somewhere and that naming it is tantamount to simply sticking a cork in it.

With Pascal, we find ourselves at a turning point, a jumping off point where someone dares to say something that has been there all along – like when I said earlier "things will be more than ever as they were before" – except that there is a moment at which there is a parting of the ways. It must be realized that Pascal says that "the God of Abraham, Isaac, and Jacob" has nothing to do with "the God of the philosophers," for the former is a God who speaks, I beg you to take notice of this, but there is something quite original about Him: His name is unpronounceable. A question thus arises.

This is why it is, curiously enough, owing to a son of Israel, a guy by the name of Freud, that for the first time we perceive the true center of the field, not only of knowledge, but the reason why knowledge hits us in the gut, and even grabs us, as it were, by the balls. He mentions the Names-of-the-Father, along with the whole slew of myths that it brings with it. If I had been able to give my Seminar on *The Names-of-the-Father*, I would have shared the results of my statistical research with you. It's amazing how little the Father is mentioned even by the Church Fathers. I am not talking about the Hebraic tradition where it is constantly in the background. Of course, if it is in the background, it is because it is highly veiled. That is why in the first lecture – the one after which I closed up shop that year [1963/64] – I began by speaking about the sacrifice of Isaac. Such things are worth discussing, but there is little chance that I will ever be able to return to it, owing to changes in configuration, context, and even audience.

I will, however, allow myself one little comment. Now and then, I raise questions like this one: "Does God believe in God?" Here's another one for you: "Had God not stopped Abraham's arm at the last moment, in other words, if Abraham had been in too much of a hurry and had slit Isaac's throat, would that have constituted what is known as a genocide?" People talk quite a bit about genocide at present – the word is very trendy. Pinning the locus of a truth onto genocide, especially concerning the origin of the Jews, is a noteworthy milestone. In any case, as I pointed out in that first lecture, slitting the throat of a certain ram who was clearly there as a totemic ancestor was what corresponded to the suspension of the genocide.

This brings us to the second stage, the one that appears when there is no longer any indifference – in other words, when one considers the initial action taken in the game.

As Pascal declares, I must accept that what I stake in the game is already lost, otherwise I don't play at all. That is what is meant by the two zeros in the middle matrix. The upper one indicates the ante, and the lower one "no ante." Except that it only hangs together if the ante is considered to be worth nothing. And Pascal says as much. It is true in a certain sense. Object *a* has no use value. It doesn't have any exchange value either, as I already said.

Yet there is the following, which was already at issue in the ante, once people perceived how it functioned, and now that psychoanalysis has allowed us to take a step forward regarding the structure of desire:

It is because *a* is what drives [or: animates, *anime*] everything that is at stake in the relationship between man and speech, that a player (although not the one Pascal spoke about) named Hegel – he sensed something, even if his system is defective, appearances to the contrary notwithstanding – understood that there is no other game than that of risking everything [*le tout pour le tout*], which is even what is known as "taking action" as such. He called that "the struggle to the death for pure prestige."

This is precisely what psychoanalysis allows us to rectify. Far more than life is at stake. We don't, after all, know that much about what life is. We know so little about it that we don't even cling to it all that tightly, as you see every day if you are a psychiatrist or simply 20 years old. Something else is at stake – which has never been designated and still isn't despite my calling it *a* – and it has no meaning except when it is juxtaposed to the idea of measure. In its very essence, measure has nothing to do with God, yet it is in some sense the very precondition of thought. As soon as I think of something, no matter what I name it, it boils down to calling it the universe – in other words, One.

Thank God, thought had enough room to wander about within the bounds of this precondition to realize that the One is not self-created and that we must discern the relationship it has with the "I." This is what is described by the fact that in the middle matrix

178

there is an *a* which is no longer the ante – that is, the *a* that is abandoned to the fate of the game – but the *a* insofar as it is me representing myself [or: it is me imagining myself, *c'est moi qui me représente*], insofar as I wager against, specifically against the closure of the universe that will be One if it wants to be, but as for me, I am *a* as well.

When we look at this ineradicable God closely, He has no other basis than that of being the faith we have in the universe of discourse, which certainly isn't nothing. If you think that I am doing philosophy here, I will have to tell you a tale. One has to put the heavyweights aside to get people to understand what one means.

As you know, like other eras, the modern era had a beginning. Which is why it deserves to be called modern, because otherwise we could say, as Alphonse Allais does, that people were awfully modern in the middle ages! If the modern era has a meaning, it is because of certain advances, one of which is the myth of the desert island. I could just as well have started with that as with Pascal's wager. It continues to bother us. What books would you take with you to a desert island? Oh what fun it would be, amid the seafood, to have a pile of classics published by Pléiade, with nothing to do but read! But this myth nevertheless has a meaning. And to illustrate it, I am going to give you my answer. Quake in your boots for a minute. What book would I bring with me to a desert island? Go ahead, answer.

[A voice from the audience:] The Bible.

Of course, [someone had to say] the Bible! I couldn't care less about the Bible! What the hell would I do with it on a desert island? To a desert island, I would bring the Bloch and von Wartburg dictionary. I hope you all know what it is, for this is certainly not the first time that I've mentioned it. It is entitled, in a way that naturally allows for confusion, *Dictionnaire étymologique de la langue française* ["The Etymological Dictionary of the French Language" by Oscar Bloch and Walther von Wartburg (Paris: Presses Universitaires de France, 1932)].

The title doesn't mean that they give you the meaning of words on the basis of the thought that led to their creation. It means that they give you an idea of the dates of the forms and usages of each word over the course of time. It is so enlightening and so prolific that one can, in effect, do without people. We see to what degree language provides company all by itself.

Baltasar Gracián, who invented the desert island, was of a different class than Daniel Defoe. He was a Jesuit and, moreover, he was no liar. It is in the *Criticón* [*The Critick*] that the hero, returning from somewhere in the Atlantic, spends some time on a desert island, which for him at least has the advantage of keeping him safe from women. As for Daniel Defoe, it is extraordinarily curious that he didn't realize that Robinson had no need to wait for Friday. The sole fact that he was a speaking being and knew his language – English – perfectly well was an element that was as essential to his survival on the island as his relation to a few little natural trifles with which he managed to craft a hut and feed himself.

180

Whatever may be at issue in this world, which is a world of signifiers, I can do no better today, since it is getting late, than sketch out once again what I provided here in the first terms I proposed – namely, those we can define somewhat rigorously thanks to the current stage of mathematical logic, and by beginning from the definition of the signifier as what represents a subject to another signifier. The latter is, I say, other, which simply means that it is a signifier [or: is signifying, *il est signifiant*]:

$$S \to A$$

What characterizes and founds the signifier is absolutely not something that is attached to it by way of meaning, but rather its difference – in other words, not something that is stuck to it and would allow us to identify it, but the fact that all the other signifiers are different from it. Its difference resides in the others. This is why it constitutes an inaugural step to ask whether one can make a class, a bag, or, in short, a One, that famous One, out of this Other.

As I have drawn it here [see Figure 11.2], if A equals 1, it must include S insofar as it represents the subject to what? To A. And this A, being the same A you just saw here, turns out to be what it is: a predicate, insofar as the 1 in question is no longer the unary trait but the unifying 1 that defines the field of the Other.

Stated differently, we see the following get reproduced indefinitely, with, here, something that never finds its name, unless we arbitrarily give it one. It is precisely in order to say that there is no name that names it that I designate it with the most discreet letter, the letter *a*.

181

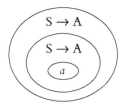

Figure 11.2: A as Unifying One

What does this mean? Where and when does this process, which is a selection process, occur?

The game [*jeu*] in question, insofar as it is truly played, is not *jocus*, a play on words, but *ludus*, in the original Latin (as we too easily forget), about which a great deal could be said. It certainly involves the lethal game I spoke about earlier [Hegel's "struggle to the death"], and it runs the gamut from the ritual games the Romans inherited from the Etruscans – the word itself is very likely of Etruscan origin – right up to no more nor less than the Circus games [or Roman Games, *Ludi Romani*], and something further that I will mention when the time comes. Well, there is in this game something that questions the 1 regarding what it becomes when it is missing me, *a*. And if I once again posit myself qua "I" at the place where it is missing me, it will be in order to question it regarding what results from the fact that I posited this lack.

Consider once again the decreasing series [see Figures 8.3 and 8.4] that I have already written on the board, which goes toward a limit:

$$1 - a = a^2$$
$$2a - 1 = a^3$$
$$\vdots$$
$$\overline{\qquad}$$
$$1$$

Figure 11.3: Decreasing Series

I do not know how to characterize this series otherwise than by saying that it boils down to the following twofold condition, which is merely one condition, in fact: to be a Fibonacci series, on the one hand, and impose on itself as a uniform law what results from any Fibonacci series – namely, the ratio between 1 and *a*.

On the [left-hand vertical] line that I drew, which continues to infinity, I have already written the total we arrive at by adding up the different terms of the series, which continue to decrease in magnitude the further we go. Assuming we have begun from the subtraction of *a* from something [e.g., $1 - a$], the [summation] process arrives at a limit.

Adding the even powers and the odd powers of *a* easily gives us 1 as their sum. The fact remains that what defines the ratio of each of these terms to the next – in other words, its true difference – is always, right up to the very end and in a way that does not decrease but remains strictly equal, *a*.

The formulated statement of the decreasing chain demonstrates that, despite its appearance linked to schematization, it is always the same circle that is at stake [see Figure 11.2]. It is through an action [*acte*] that we posit this circle or Other qua field of discourse, taking care to exclude any divine existence here; it is through a purely arbitrary, schematic, and signifying act that we define it as One. This act is an act of faith, but faith in what? Faith in our thought, whereas we know full well that this thought subsists only on the basis of signifying articulation, insofar as it is given already in the indefinite world of language.

What do we do in the logical realm with this shrinking [*resserrement*, the closing in of the circles in Figure 11.2], whereby we try to make *a* appear as a remainder in the whole? Having lost it, having unwittingly played some sort of game of "loser wins," we manage to do nothing but identify the Other itself with *a* – namely, find in *a* the essence of the supposed One of thought, in other words, determine thought itself to be the effect, and I would go further still, the shadow of object *a*.

At the point at which it appears to us here, *a* deserves to be called the "cause," certainly, but it must be specified in its essence as a privileged cause. The play of language in its material form plays on an admirable meaning here. Let us call it the "*a*-cause" as I have already dubbed it more than once.

It will not sound too cacophonous in French, because the expression *à cause de* [because of] exists. But have we always clearly grasped its resonances? Is this to avow that *à cause de* is merely an *a*-cause? When it comes to that, each language has its value. Spanish says *por amor*. One could easily derive the same effect from it.

I must stop here because we have run out of time. I will confine myself to announcing that the converse proof confirms it, and by confirming it, completes it.

The converse proof is based on the trajectory that the relationship to knowledge has started us out on. The point is not to investigate the One insofar as at the outset I situate a lack in it, and then find that the One is identical to [*s'identifie à*] that very lack. The point is to investigate this 1 insofar as I add *a* to it. 1 + *a* is the first form, that of the upper line in the right-hand matrix [see Figure 11.1].

What does 1 + *a* yield when the radical questioning of knowledge takes place in its field? It is knowledge added to the world insofar as, armed with this formula, this prefatory banner, it can transform the world.

What is its logical series, investigated in the way in which I did it at the level of progressive differences? Its correlate is $<-\infty>$, which will perhaps allow us to better clarify *a*'s function. It is easy to glimpse plenty of things in this minus infinity, and one thing in particular that deluded writers for a long time and not in just any

183

old era, but at the time at which the ontological argument had a meaning – namely, that what desire is missing is the infinite, strictly speaking. Perhaps we will be able to say something about it that gives it a different status.

Consider the fourth square of the matrix on the right [Figure 11.1], where we find a zero. In the way in which I articulated it using the schema of the relationship between S and A, it is radically distinguished from what it is in the first schema – namely, the ante or, on the contrary, indifference. Here it clearly represents a hole.

At a third stage we will have to demonstrate what it corresponds to in psychoanalysis, and you will see what originates in this very hole.

February 12, 1969

JOUISSANCE: ITS FIELD

XII

"THE FREUD EVENT"

Michel Foucault is perfectly well informed
Ethics revisited
Pleasure, hallucinations, and dreams
Intuition and formalization
The truth about knowledge

You have been kind enough to follow me thus far along the narrow paths into which my discourse has ventured this year.

The trail it is blazing seems to be raising questions about its origin and direction in certain of your minds. In other words, it is possible that you no longer know very well where we are at.

This is why it strikes me as an opportune moment to comment on the title I gave this discourse, *From an Other to the other*. Indeed, it is altogether conceivable that nothing could have been elucidated about an endpoint [or: end, *fin*] at the beginning [of this Seminar], whether in a preface or even a program. We must go pretty far along a path for the point of departure to be clarified retroactively.

This is true not merely for you, but for me too. I must thus take my bearings from the stages we have gone through in the course of this drilling operation, as it were, which is clearly what interests you, what makes you stay, what keeps you here, at least for some, if not all, of you.

I thus happened to take another look at the [typed-up] text – who knows, perhaps with a view to publishing it – of what I enunciated ten years, a dog's age, ago now, at my 1959/60 Seminar, having entitled it *The Ethics of Psychoanalysis*. It was deeply satisfying to me to revisit it. If I in fact publish something that strives to reproduce as faithfully as possible the path I followed at that time, it could not, naturally, fail to be retroactively affected by what I have enunciated since that time, especially here. It is thus a delicate operation, which is the only reason I can't content myself with the excellent

188   summary that was made of that Seminar, two years later, by one of
the participants, namely Safouan. I will have to tell you why I didn't
publish his summary back then, but I will do so in the preface to
what comes out.

The satisfaction I felt – that you can share in if you trust that I
will faithfully represent the path traced out there – stemmed from
the fact that nothing forces me to revise what I offered at the time,
yet I can insert into it, as into a sort of crucible [*coupelle*], things
I enunciate presently that are, let us say, more rigorous regarding
psychoanalytic ethics.

Having endeavored to write out what I felt I had to select as my
point of departure when I raised the question – something that had
never been done before – of what psychoanalysis brings with it by
way of ethics, I stated, quite rigorously it seems to me, what was new
in what was contributed by what I call, using an unexampled term,
"the Freud event" [or: the major event constituted by Freud's work,
l'événement Freud; see *Ornicar?* 28 (January 1984): 7–18].

I am happy to see that a very broadminded Society is currently
able to appreciate the originality of an author like Freud.

Michel Foucault demonstrated this last Saturday to a dodgy
group known as the French Society of Philosophy, where he raised
the question "What is an author?" [see *Textual Strategies* (Ithaca,
NY: Cornell University Press, 1979), pp. 141–60]. This led him to
highlight a number of notions that deserve to be mentioned regarding such a question, for example: what is the function of an author's
name? He managed to highlight the originality of this function at
the level of a semantic investigation, confining himself to its situation closely tied to discourse and then showing that it leads to a
calling into question, splitting, or ripping apart of the relation to
discourse that prevails in what is known as the Society of Minds or
the Republic of Letters.

Freud played a major role in that. Indeed, the author in question,
Michel Foucault, not only emphasized, but stressed throughout his
talk the function of the "return to." In the little announcement he
circulated before his talk, the expression "return to" was included at
the end, followed by an ellipsis. I considered myself summoned to
his lecture because of that, no one in our times having given more
weight to the "return to" Freud than yours truly.

The lecturer did, moreover, bring this out very clearly, and demonstrated that he was well informed about the special meaning and
189   key point constituted by this return to Freud with respect to the
current slippage, shifting, or profound revising of the function of
the author, especially of the literary author. This is what gave rise,
in short, to a circle that [literary] critics believed they could qualify

with a term that assuredly none of those who are at the forefront would gladly adopt, but that we find ourselves assigned, like a bizarre label that has been stuck to our backs without our consent: "structuralism."

There is no reason for us to be surprised that these critics are, in our era, just as in others, behind the times regarding what is being done.

1

I thus began, ten years ago, to raise a question that had never before been raised regarding the ethics of psychoanalysis.

It is quite odd that it had not been raised before that, but what is certainly stranger still is the remark with which I felt I had to illustrate it: that the ethics of the psychoanalyst, such as it is constituted by a code of moral behavior, did not provide even the slightest sketch, outline, or beginning of an ethics of psychoanalysis.

I didn't immediately make that remark, and I don't even know if I emphasized it very strenuously, for my audience at the time consisted of psychoanalysts, and I thought I could, in some sense, directly address what must – when morality is at issue – be called by the name "conscience," and let us add to that "moral."

On the other hand, I immediately announced that the Freud event brought to light the fact that the key point or center of ethics is no other than what I emphasized at that time with the last of the three dimensions or categories that served as the point of departure of my entire discourse: the symbolic, the imaginary, and the real.

As you know, I designated the real as the crux of psychoanalytic ethics. I assume, of course, this real to be subjected to the very severe interposition, if I may express myself thusly, of the joint functioning of the symbolic and the imaginary. It is because the real is not easy to access, so to speak, that it serves us as the reference point around which the revising of ethics must revolve. 190

In order to broach it, I thus began from a text that has remained in the shadows for the most part and which, as fate would have it, re-emerged only thanks to the work of people who are not the best oriented as regards our field: the neopositivists. They believe they must investigate language from the angle of what they exemplarily express as the "meaning of meaning," investigating the status of meaning, the fact that things have signification. I noted at the time how futile this attempt must be, and that theirs is a path that is diametrically opposed to ours. But it is no accident that it was the neopositivists, and especially Ogden, who prepared for publication the book by Jeremy Bentham entitled *Bentham's Theory of Fictions* [London: Kegan Paul, Trench, Trubner & Co., 1932].

It is quite simply the most important text that was written from the perspective known as utilitarianism. As you know, people tried at the beginning of the nineteenth century to solve a problem that is, let us say, ideological, and that was of burning interest at the time and for good reason: the distribution of goods. *The Theory of Fictions* is, regarding that, an exceptionally lucid calling into question of all human institutions.

If we view things from the sociological vantage point, there is nothing that better isolates the category of the symbolic; the latter is the very one that reactualizes, but in an entirely different manner, the Freud event and what stemmed therefrom. We must not take the term "fictions" here as referring to something illusory or deceptive – for it qualifies what falls under its dominion and what it takes up with no characteristic of this kind – but as covering precisely what I highlighted aphoristically by emphasizing that truth, because its locus can only be the locus in which speech is produced, that truth, by its very essence [*par essence*] – excuse this "by its very essence," I'm only saying it to convey something, don't attribute to it everything philosophy imbues it with – that truth, let us say, in and of itself, has a fictional structure [see *Écrits*, pp. 376, 625, and 684].

This is the essential point of departure that allows us to examine ethics as such, for we must be able to accommodate all cultural diversity. We situate it here in brackets or quote marks around the term "fictional structure." This presupposes a stance taken with regard to this fictional character, insofar as it affects every foundational articulation of discourse in what one may, roughly speaking, call social relations. This point can only be reached on the basis of a certain limit.

Our dear Pascal just suddenly came to mind – who before him would have dared to note, quite simply, "Truth on this side of the Pyrenees, error on the other side"? The formulation was to have been included in the discourse he left uncompleted and that was quite legitimately, quite ambiguously as well, collected under the heading of *Pensées*. Well, it is on the basis of a certain degree of relativism, and of the most radical kind, relativism with regard, not only to mores and institutions, but to truth itself, that ethics can begin to be explored.

It is in this respect that the Freud event proves so exemplary. In the fall term of my Seminar on *The Ethics of Psychoanalysis*, I highlighted and stressed the radical change that resulted from the event that his discovery constituted – namely, the function of the unconscious. Correlatively, Freud brought into play the so-called pleasure principle in a way that was radically different from everything that had been done hitherto. We shall see why, and in a way which, I think, will strike you by its elegance.

There are enough of you who have proven open to my discourse, or at least affected by it, that I need not gloss the pleasure principle in any but the briefest of manners.

The pleasure principle is characterized, first of all, by the paradoxical fact that its surest result is, not hallucination – although that's what it says in Freud's text – but the *possibility* of hallucination. Let us say that hallucination is, in Freud's text, the specific possibility of the pleasure principle.

To account for the effects of the unconscious, Freud constructed a whole apparatus that is found in Chapter 7 of the *Traumdeutung* [*The Interpretation of Dreams*], regarding the clarification of the dream-processes, the *Traumvorgänge*. Yet we had the good fortune to have its underpinnings fall into our laps and under our scrutiny, for they are found in a certain *Entwurf*, a "Project [for a Scientific Psychology]," which was written during the years in which, guided by hysterics – who were and still are admirable theoreticians – he familiarized himself with the unconscious economy. Correlatively, he wrote this *Entwurf* to Fliess, a project that was highly elaborate and infinitely richer and more carefully constructed than what he summarized later in Chapter 7, which he surely relied on as he did so.

What Freud constructed at that time, which he called the "Ψ system," regulates the function of what he calls the pleasure principle in an organism [see Seminar VII]. To crudely sketch it out, it is not a simple relay in the organism but a true closed circle with its own laws, an autonomous system that intervenes in the cycle (that is classically defined by the general physiology of the organism) of the stimulus–motricity [reflex] arc – not to say "stimulus–response," for this would be to abuse the term "response," which for us implies a far more complex structure. This system interrupts the basal [reflex] arc and is defined not simply as the effect of the thwarting that occurs but, strictly speaking, as obstructing the function itself.

A living animal is endowed with a motricity that is assumed to be free, allowing it to escape overly intense, ravaging stimuli that may threaten its bodily integrity. The economy of the so-called Ψ system certainly does not operate so as to perfectly adapt this motor response [to circumstances] – its adaptation is, moreover, far from always being adequate, as we know. The apparatus articulated by Freud is found in certain living beings, and not just any old which ones; it certainly doesn't suffice to say that it is present in all the higher vertebrates or beings endowed with a nervous system. Freud

192

is concerned with what occurs in human beings, even if he takes the risk now and then of interpreting what occurs in related species. He only does so to provide a comparison with what occurs in humans, and everything in Freud's text indicates that the latter are defined as speaking beings.

It is at this level that homeostatic regulation develops, and it is defined by the return to an identity of perception. In other words, in the course of the research – in the broadest sense of the term – that this system carries out, through the detours it takes to maintain its own homeostasis, its specific functioning leads to the refinding of an identical perception. Inasmuch as it is regulated by repetition, this perception is distinguished by the fact that it does not bear within itself any "index of reality" [*critère de la réalité*]. The system can, in some sense, only be affected by such indices from the outside, by the simple conjunction of a little sign or qualifier.

193

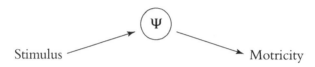

Figure 12.1: Stimulus–Motricity

In this schema, you see two circles, the reflex circle constituting the φ system, and the central circle constituting the Ψ system, which defines a closed zone, with its own form of equilibrium.

Freud clearly distinguishes the function of afference with regard to the energetics attributable to each of the two systems. The Ψ system only intervenes on the basis of signs, with a specific periodicity, which come from each of the sensory organs, and that perhaps come to assign to certain of the *percepta* introduced into the system a *Wahrnehmungszeichen*, an index that they are clearly perceptions that are acceptable from the standpoint of reality.

What does this mean? Certainly not that we approve of Freud's use of the term "hallucination" here, which for us has clinical connotations. It certainly did for Freud as well. Since hallucination, strictly speaking, necessitates entirely different coordinates, we must assume that he wanted to specifically emphasize the paradox of the functioning of the system that develops around the pleasure principle. We thus have in this text the major instance of his use of the term. Freud exemplifies it by the function of dreams, and that suffices to orient us. It essentially concerns the possibility of dreams.

This is the adventurous path Freud takes in order to explain the functioning of the apparatus that regulates the unconscious insofar as it governs a foundational economy that allows us to evaluate not only all of our behavior but all our thoughts, too. As opposed to what philosophers traditionally base themselves on when they broach what is meant by the good for man, here we see that the whole world depends on the dream of the world [or: the world as a dream, *est suspendu au rêve du monde*].

This step is what I am calling "the Freud event." It consists of nothing less than a halt to the celestial rotation, which was traditionally assumed to be the foundation of all reflection, and which was clearly designated in Aristotle's work as the focal point to which every conceivable good must be linked. It is the radical calling into question of all effects of representation, and the disappearance of any and every correspondence between representation and what is represented as such.

194

Let us not too quickly say the "subject," for if the term *hypokeimenon* [substratum or the underlying thing] is used by Aristotle with reference to logic, it is in no sense isolated as such. It took a long time, and all the progress of the philosophical tradition, for knowledge to come to fully revolve, in Kant's work, around the foundation of a relationship between the subject and something that remains entirely dependent on what appears, on the *phainomenon* [phenomenon], while excluding the *noumenon* – in other words, what lies behind it. This is the meaning of idealism. And yet this representation is comfortable, whereas, from the standpoint of idealism, thinking beings never deal with anything but their own measure, posited as *the* reference point, on the basis of which they believe they can, at least in theory, state the fundamental laws of representation.

From Freud's standpoint, nothing about representation is tenable except what, at a point that profoundly explains behavior, is linked to a structure that is made up of frameworks and networks located altogether outside of the circuit of the subject in whom representation is supposedly unified. This is the true meaning of the little schemas that neuronal links (just recently discovered at his time) allowed Freud to construct. It suffices to consult the *Entwurf* to perceive the decisive importance of these lattices [or: grids, *treillis*] in the articulation of what is at work.

It has been clear to us for a long time already that we can no longer identify what is at work with the movements, displacements, or transfers of energy that occur along the neuronal chain, which we have located by other than physical means. It is obvious that Freud already suspected as much. It is not in this way, which in experience turns out to be altogether distinct, that we can find the appropriate use of the schemas that I just characterized as networks. In order to grasp what they allowed Freud to intuitively prop up and depict, we need but look at what is laid out in them. At each of the intersections [in his figures], a word is written, a word that designates a specific memory, a specific word that was spoken in response, a specific word qualifying relationships, a specific word that branded, marked, or so to speak "engramified" [*engrammatisant*] the symptom.

Buy *The Origins of Psychoanalysis*, which includes the *Entwurf* along with Freud's letters to Fliess, and you will see the following: what Freud found an easy prop for in these neuronal links – which he had at his fingertips at the time owing to the fact that they had just been discovered – is nothing other than the signifying chain [*l'articulation signifiante*] in its most elementary form.

Pick up the latest book to come out, or rather pick up [Jean-Louis] Krivine's *Théorie axiomatique des ensembles* [(Paris, PUF, 1969); in English, *Introduction to Axiomatic Set Theory* (Dordrecht: D. Reidel, 1971)], and you will see the exact same schemas as those used by Freud, except that they are oriented more or less as follows and are used to illustrate set theory:

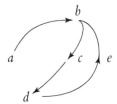

Figure 12.2: Freud's Model

Let me indicate in passing that each point connected here to another point by an arrow is considered, in set theory, to be an element of the other set.

What is involved is nothing less than what is necessary to correctly articulate and provide mathematical set theory with its most formal foundations. Read the first few lines of this book and you will already see the true necessities involved in each axiomatic step that is taken, when one takes things up from a formal standpoint, at the most foundational level of signifying articulation.

Let me highlight in particular the notion of parts, which is especially exemplary. The way in which people say that one of the elements of a set, elements that are always themselves sets, is included in [or: belongs to] another set, is based on formal definitions that absolutely cannot be identified with the intuitive signification of the term "to be included within" [or: to belong to]. Indeed, let us assume that I draw a figure that is a bit more complicated than the one above, and that I write on the board a note saying "identification of each of these set theory terms." It does not at all suffice to have one of them written and apparently constitute a part of the universe that I am instituting here in order for us to be able to say that it is included in [or: belongs to] any of the other terms – namely, that it is an element thereof.

In other words, to articulate a configuration of signifiers in no wise signifies that the whole configuration – that is, the universe thus constituted – can be totalized. On the contrary, this universe leaves a specific set outside of its field, unable to be situated as one of its parts, but simply articulated as an element with respect to other sets thus articulated. There may thus be a lack of coincidence between the intuitive assertion that a specific element is part of [or: belongs to] this universe and the formal articulation of this assertion. That is an entirely essential principle by which mathematical logic can instruct us, I mean allow us to situate certain questions in their rightful place – you will see which questions I mean.

196

The mechanisms of the unconscious define a minimal logical structure that I have long been summarizing with the terms "difference" and "repetition."

On the one hand, nothing grounds the functioning of the signifier apart from the fact that it is absolute difference. A signifier holds its own only insofar as the other signifiers differ from it. On the other hand, signifiers function in a repetitive articulation. This is what allows for the institution of a first logic, whose functions are displacement and substitution. Indeed, a reference point that is pinned down with signifiers [*épinglage signifiant*] is destined, by this very pinning down, to slide [i.e., displace, metonymically slip]. As for the other function, it has to do with the fact that the nature of the signifier, qua pinning something down, allows for the substitution of one signifier for another, a substitution from which we may expect meaning effects.

But what must be stressed here in order to grasp the true nature of psychoanalysis is the importance of dreams. From Freud's standpoint, the functioning of the reality principle is precarious right from the outset. It is certainly not annulled for all that, but it is essentially dependent on the radical precariousness to which the pleasure principle subjects it, insofar as it implies the possibility of dreams. It is through dreams that, for the most part, we can initially broach the functioning of the signifier and the minimal logical structure whose terms I just re-articulated. We must thus take what this perspective implies all the way.

Our whole way of working with dreams indicates that what is involved is sentences. Let us leave aside for the time being the nature of their syntax; they at least have an elementary syntax involving the two mechanisms that I just recalled to mind [displacement and substitution (i.e., condensation)]. What is important is that dreams appear to us as hallucinatory, with the specific accent that Freud gives this term. What does this mean, if not that dreams are already in themselves interpretations, wild interpretations, of course, but interpretations nevertheless.

Now, as Freud quite calmly wrote, dreams present themselves as rebuses. Although I highlighted this, I certainly am not the one who invented it, nor discovered it in the text. What does that mean if not that dreams, owing to their pleasurable function, provide a pictorial translation of each of the terms – that are signifiers from a diachronic point of view, given the progression in which their articulation is instituted – a pictorial translation that does not in itself subsist except insofar as it is articulable in signifiers. What are we thus doing when we substitute our reasoned interpretations for these wild interpretations?

We need but mention here the practice of each of those who are analysts. For the others, let them reread in this light the dreams included in the *Traumdeutung*, and they will realize that these reasoned interpretations involve nothing other than reconstituted sentences; and they will perceive the cracks [or: fissures, *point de faille*] where, qua sentences, and not qua meanings, they allow us to see where things go wrong [or: what messes up, *ce qui cloche*]. Desire is where things go wrong.

Consider the truly exemplary dream described by Freud at the very beginning of the chapter [VII] in which he investigates the dream-processes, the *Traumvorgänge*, and in which he tries to provide what he calls their "psychology." We find there a dream that was dreamt by a father whose fatigue forced him to leave the body of his dead son in the next room, where it was to be watched over by an old man. The father [fell asleep and] dreamt that his son was alive and standing before him; the child approached the bed he was lying on, seized him by the arm, and told him in a reproachful voice, *Vater, siehst du denn nicht, daß ich verbrenne?* "Father, don't you see I'm burning?"

What could be more moving, more pathos-inducing, than what happened next? The father woke up, went into the next room, and saw that the candle had fallen over, lit the sheets on fire, and was already burning the cadaver while the watchman slept. Freud then tells us that the dream was produced merely to prolong the man's sleep despite the first signs he had perceived of a horrible reality [the glow from the next room, he having left the door between the rooms open].

Yet mustn't we go further, and grasp that the fact that reality coincided with [or: covered over, *recouvre*] the dream proved that the father was still sleeping? How can we fail to hear the tenor of the words spoken here, when Freud tells us, moreover, that all speech in dreams was heard somewhere before, that it was in fact pronounced at some point by someone. How can we not see that this child was burning with desire, but in the field of the Other, in the field of him who is addressed, the father in this case? What was at stake, if not some failure [*faille*] on the father's part, insofar as he was a desiring being, with regard to this cherished object, his child? This is what is not analyzed, albeit quite sufficiently indicated, in what Freud tells us. It is from this that reality itself, in its coincidence [with the dream], protects the father. In any case, Freud agrees, the interpretation of this dream is not the reality [the glow coming from the next room] that caused him to have it.

What thus guides us when we interpret dreams is certainly not, "What does it mean?" or "What does it want by saying that?" but rather, "What, by speaking, does it want?" It apparently does not know what it wants.

That is truly where the question lies, and where we must bring in our formulas.

2

Our formulas establish a basic ratio that is linked, in some sense, to the simplest function of numbers.

This ratio is generated by what is known in mathematics as a subgroup, in which additions take place – namely, the Fibonacci series, in which the sum of the two preceding terms provides the third term. It is on that very basis, as I told you, that something is generated that is not related to what is known in mathematics as the rational – namely, the unary trait – but which, right at the outset, provides this first proportion, the earliest of them all, that is known to all mathematicians:

$$a = \frac{\sqrt{5} - 1}{2}$$

via this simple proportion:

$$\frac{a}{1-a} = \frac{1}{a} = 1 + a$$

Figure 12.3: Formulas

198

199   Let us now substitute the word "knowledge" for *a* in the formula. We don't yet know what it is, since that is what we are investigating. If 1 is the field of the Other – that is, the field of truth insofar as it is not known – we can write:

$$\frac{\text{knowledge}}{\text{truth} - \text{knowledge}} = \frac{\text{truth}}{\text{knowledge}} = \text{truth with knowledge in addition}$$

Figure 12.4: Knowledge and Truth

Let us try to decipher these ratios. The first means knowledge about [or: over, *sur*] the unconscious. In other words, there is a knowledge that says, "There is a truth somewhere that is not known," and that is the truth that is articulated in the unconscious. That is where we must find the truth about [or: over, *sur*] knowledge.

Isn't that what we said earlier about dreams? I am isolating them from the other unconscious formations for the sake of clarity, which doesn't mean I can't also apply this to them. We are mistaken, regarding dreams, when we wonder, "What do they mean?" For that is not what is important. What is important is, "Where is the crack [or: fault line, *faille*] in what is said?" and it is found at the level at which what is said in them is distinct from their presenting themselves as wanting to say something [or: meaning something, *voulant dire quelque chose*]. Nevertheless, they say something without knowing what they are saying, since we are obliged to help them with our reasoned interpretations.

It remains to be known whether dreams are possible. That they are – in other words, the unconscious *was* discovered – is indicated by the singular ratio that we can write with the help of the term *a* qua the earliest effect of inscription, assuming we give it a little extra nudge so that it can repeat [perhaps in the formulas in Figure 12.3] in bringing together repetition and difference in this minimal operation known as addition.

There is a knowledge that lies over the truth from which knowledge is subtracted ["truth – knowledge" in Figure 12.4]. It is here that we must take up truth – in other words, speech that is asserted – about [or: over, *sur*] knowledge as a function. But we must be able even, at times, to juxtapose them on the same line, and investigate the combination of them that is written as follows: truth plus knowledge.

Since we are running out of time, I can merely recall to mind now an economic analogy, which is also quite palpable in our experience, that I presented here regarding truth as work. The work of truth is
200   quite evident in analytic discourse at least, because it is painful. We

have to blaze a trail, without veering either to the right or to the left into some sort of intuitive identification that would short-circuit the meaning of what is at stake by referring to something wholly irrelevant – need, for example.

On the other hand, I associated knowledge with the functioning of prices. Prices are certainly not established at random, no more than in any other effect of exchange. But it is clear that prices do not in and of themselves constitute work; that is the important point, for knowledge does not either, regardless of what people say.

Knowledge is something that was invented by pedagogues. People will soon tell us that it is acquired by the sweat of one's brow, as if it were necessarily correlated with burning the midnight oil. Good electrical lighting allows us to do without that. But I am asking you a question. I am not asking, "Have you never learned anything?" – because to learn is a horrible thing, for one has to slog through all the idiocy of those who explain things to you, and it is painful to remind you of that – but rather, "Coming to know something, doesn't that always occur in a flash?"

[Learning how to] do something with your hands – for example, stay on your horse or on your skis – none of what people say about the so-called learning process [*apprentissage*] has anything to do with knowledge. Knowledge is the following: people present you with signifiers, and owing to the way they are presented to you, they mean nothing to you, and then there is a moment at which the fog clears, they suddenly mean something – that's the way it's always been. We can see, in the way a child handles its first letters of the alphabet, that there is no learning process, but instead a big uppercase letter collapses into the shape of an animal whose name is said to begin with that letter [like S for snake]. The child either makes the connection or he doesn't. In the majority of cases – in other words, in the cases in which he is not given too much pedagogical attention – he does.

Whenever knowledge is produced, it is not useless, of course, that the subject has taken this step in order to grasp what occurs by way of knowledge effects [or: what occurs without knowledge effects, *ce qui se passera d'effets de savoir*] in these little schemas. I am sorry that I did not bring this out more completely earlier, but I was running out of time and we will come back to set theory if necessary.

What does it mean to know? We must take things further and investigate this fundamental analogy. Knowledge still remains perfectly opaque here, since in the numerator of the first ratio it is a singular knowledge, whereas in the denominator we find truth, which is perfectly well articulated, which knowledge fails qua knowledge. Yet, it is from this very ratio that we expect the truth about knowledge.

201

I am not leaving you here at the level of a pure and simple enigma, since I introduced knowledge with the term *a*. This is to say that any possible manipulation of knowledge must in fact consist in the articulation of object *a*, which I have already sufficiently spelled out.

Will I have the audacity to end with that today? I will have to give a plausible meaning to what would be written on the basis of a crossed conjunction [*conjonction croisée*] of the type used in arithmetic, between knowledge concerning the unconscious and knowledge investigated as a foundational function, insofar as it, in short, constitutes the very object toward which all desire tends insofar as it is produced at the level of articulation.

In our meetings to come, we will have to consider how knowledge, qua lost knowledge, is at the origin of the desire that appears in any possible articulation of discourse.

February 26, 1969

JOUISSANCE
POSITED AS AN ABSOLUTE

"Hot seat" civilization
Knowledge on the sexual horizon
The torpor of sexuality
The logical structure of jouissance
The One lies

$$\frac{knowledge}{truth - knowledge} = \frac{truth}{knowledge}$$

I left you last time with an equation based on the ratio known as harmonic [see the lower formula of Figure 12.3], that I was easily able to translate, owing to things I've said before, by what I just wrote on the board.

Such an a priori formula bears within itself a certain degree of obviousness, the kind that corroborates what psychoanalysis is most commonly recognized as having contributed, which is as follows: we know that somewhere, in the part of us that we call unconscious, a truth is enunciated that is such that we can know nothing about it.

This very fact constitutes a bit of knowledge.

1

I thus wrote that "knowledge" over [or: about] the function of "truth-minus-knowledge" must yield "truth" over [or: about] "knowledge."

On this topic, and to tell you about something that happened to me this week, I heard a formulation – I apologize in advance to its author if I distort it a bit – which was proposed as one of the premises of research carried out along the lines of my teaching, and which aimed at situating psychoanalysis, not at any cost as a science, but as something epistemologically prescribed, research regarding the function of science being a hot topic today. The formulation is as follows: psychoanalysis is supposedly something like "a science without knowledge."

My interlocutor went that far, encouraged no doubt by a certain current trend, inasmuch as, at a level that is clearly also based on experience, the transmission of knowledge is being accused of being a mode of social domination.

I took him to task, proffering that it is not true that nothing in psychoanalytic experience can be articulated by teaching, that nothing in psychoanalysis can assume the form of a knowledge-based doctrine, and that owing to this – since what is at stake is what is presently being called into question – nothing can be skillfully [*magistrale*] enunciated in terms that are the very ones with which I enunciate that knowledge here.

Nevertheless, from a certain vantage point and in a certain sense, what my interlocutor said is true.

It is true that analytic knowledge is not knowledge with respect to what it appears to be, with respect to what people are inclined to take it for. Because psychoanalysis enunciated the earliest, deepest connection between knowledge and sexuality, people all too quickly rushed – I realize this is a pleonasm – to conclude that it is knowledge about sexuality.

It is nothing of the kind. Psychoanalysis is not knowledge about sexuality.

"Has anyone ever learned from psychoanalysis how to treat [or: handle, *traiter*] his wife well?" Women are important, after all. There is a proper way of broaching them, you must hold them [*tient en main*] in a certain way, a way that is unmistakable to them. They may tell you: "You don't hold [or: handle, *tenez*] me the way you're supposed to hold a woman."

We like to think that, by the end of an analysis, the obstacles that stop men – the men to whom women say such things – from doing so properly can be cleared away. As for technique, if you will allow me to express myself thusly, the result depends on the man's natural knowledge, to the skill [*l'adresse*] – if you will allow me to employ this latter word with all the ambiguity that, given language's ordinary resources, the French term possesses, designating the faculty designated by this term as well as the person to whom it is addressed – to the supposed skill that would be granted him at the end of such a clearing away.

It is plain that psychoanalysis has nothing in common with the register I just called "technique." We know the magnitude of the latter. Marcel Mauss, for example, incidentally pointed out this domain and indicated the cultural characteristics of the very extensive function that he called "bodily techniques" [*Techniques, Technology and Civilization* (New York and Oxford: Durkheim Press/Berghahn Books, 2006), pp. 77–96]. It is no accident that, in our civilization, they are, not strictly speaking eluded, but repressed into the corners.

I need but allude here to the dimension of the truly erotic techniques that are highlighted in certain cultures that one certainly cannot characterize as primitive, Hindu culture, for example. Nothing that is stated in a book like the *Kama Sutra* can strike you as anything other than amusing little pornographic stories, whereas the text can be understood at a very different level. It can also have an import which – with respect to the complete confusion surrounding the word that I will employ – is designated, not improperly but only approximatively, as metaphysical.

Let us once again consider what is immediately obvious. The angle from which knowledge of sexuality is broached in psychoanalysis is that of the prohibitions that may weigh on this knowledge, and this is why knowledge takes on its import from the way I write it on the board: *a* [see Figure 12.3]. This angle is new in the sense that it had never before been explored. I will not say that we broach sexual knowledge from this angle, but that we are confronted with it. We approach sexual knowledge from the spot where this prohibition weighs, and this is why Freud's first statements about the unconscious emphasize the specific function of censorship.

This prohibition affects a certain "there," the place where it speaks, where it makes avowals, where it admits that it is preoccupied by such knowledge.

We should admire once again in passing how rich language is. Isn't "preoccupied" a better translation for *Besetzung* [usually rendered as "cathexis" in English], Freud's *besetzt*, than "investissement" [investment] or this "investi" [invested] that French translations constantly use? It is "pre-occupied," occupied in advance, by something whose position then becomes more ambiguous.

This is clearly what requires us to always return to the function of the unconscious. What can be meant by knowledge that preoccupies us when its defining characteristic, at a certain level that is articulated on the basis of truth, is that it is what we know the least about?

To begin to clarify things, we might say that, from a certain standpoint, in our culture, in our civilization, in the bubbling stew in which we find ourselves – which is, in any case, the only term that justifies your gathering here – we might go so far as to claim that psychoanalysis fosters a sort of hypnotic trance, one that is such

206

that sexuality is, after all, it's quite true, kept in an unprecedented state of torpor among us.

None of which constitutes a reason why psychoanalysis could in any way serve to contest – since that is what is at issue – the well-foundedness of the transmission of any knowledge whatsoever, even of its own.

Psychoanalysis does, after all, constitute [a field of] knowledge. It clearly discovered something, however mythically it has been formulated. It discovered what is known in other registers as "the means of production" – production of what? Of a satisfaction. It discovered that there was something articulable and articulated – something that I designated as "montages" [see Seminar XI], and it literally cannot be conceptualized otherwise – something psycho-analysis calls drives.

This has meaning – which means that psychoanalysis does not present the drives as such – only because they are sometimes sat-isfying. Which implies that, when we see the drives function, they bring their own satisfaction with them. When, from a theoretical perspective, psychoanalysis points to the operation of the oral, anal, scoptophilic, or sadomasochistic drive in a behavior, it is truly in order to say that something is satisfied by it. It is self-evident that what is satisfied cannot be designated otherwise than as what lies below – a subject, a *hypokeimenon* – regardless of the division that must necessarily stem therefrom for him, in the name of the follow-ing: that he is merely the subject of a functioning instrument, the subject of an *organon*.

I am using the term here less in its anatomical sense – as an exten-sion of the body, a natural appendix that is more or less animate – than in its earliest sense as a device or instrument, which is the sense in which Aristotle uses it in the context of logic. The two realms overlap, of course, and, owing to this, some of the body's organs – which are moreover ambiguous and hard to discern, since it is all too obvious that certain of them are mere holdovers [or: scraps or remnants, *déchets*] – find themselves thrust into the role of instrumental supports.

A question thus arises: how do we define this satisfaction? There must, all the same, be something fishy here, since what we do when faced with these montages is dismantle [*démonter*] them.

207   Does the fact that we dismantle them imply, in and of itself and right off the bat, that dismantling them is curative? If it were so, it would seem that it should happen more quickly, and that we would have long since gotten to the bottom of it. If we foreground the essential nature of fixation, it is because the matter is not as simple as all that. What we have to keep in mind in the psychoanalytic

field is perhaps that something is indeed inscribed at its horizon, and that is sexuality. It is as a function of this specifically maintained horizon that the drives are inserted into their instrumental function.

You see how carefully I am asserting things here. I have spoken about horizons and fields, but not about sexual acts. Those of you who were already here two years ago will recall that I provided other premises to the notion of action [or: the act, *l'acte*] than those of taking for granted that there is such a thing as a sexual act. I thus also concluded at that time that, if we take "action" in the structural sense – which is the only one in which it subsists – we can enunciate that *there's no such thing as a sexual act*. We will return to this, and you obviously suspect that it is in order to return to it from a different angle – this year's angle, which runs from one Other to the other – that we find ourselves anew on a path along which it is nevertheless worth recalling what we concluded when approaching it from a different angle.

As for the satisfaction that is essential to the drive, this, too, we are forced to leave in abeyance if only in order to choose the path by which we can manage to define it.

For the time being, we can jump straight to the heart of the matter that is located somewhere at the level of the equals-sign of the equation I wrote on the board. It is at the center of today's investigation. To what satisfaction can knowledge itself (cor)respond?

2

I am deliberately discussing knowledge here as notionally approachable, as the kind of knowledge that is supposed to be [or: would like to be, *serait*] identical to the field such as I just delimited it, that is supposed to be "knowing how to make it happen" [or: "knowing how to get around" or "knowing how to do something," *savoir-y-faire*] in this field.

Is that sufficient? "Knowing how to make it happen" sounds a bit too much like know-how [*savoir-faire*], regarding which there was perhaps a misunderstanding earlier, which I encouraged, moreover, in order to hit you in the right spot – that is, in the gut. It is rather "knowing how to be there" [*savoir-y-être*].

This leads us back to the angle we are taking here. It brings us back to the bases, as is fitting, of our endeavor. Indeed, what Freud's discovery proposes is that we can be there without knowing we are there, and also that when we most firmly believe we are taking pains not to "be there" [*se garder de cet* y-être], when we are sure we are

208

elsewhere, in another [field of] knowledge, we are smack dab in the middle of it. That is what psychoanalysis says: we are there without knowing it. We are there in every field of knowledge. This is why psychoanalysis is of interest to those who call knowledge into question. It is not because of any truth, or any ontology. Regardless of our field of inquiry, sexuality lies at the horizon, owing to the function of knowledge.

You can, I hope, admit that this is worth examining more closely.

We are there without knowing it. Do we lose something there? There seems to be no doubt about it, since it is our point of departure. We are utterly and completely conned. Consciousness [or: conscience, *conscience*] is duped owing to the following: it serves a purpose that it does not think it serves. I said "dupery" not "trickery" [or: deception, *tromperie*]. Psychoanalysis does not question the truth of the thing. Psychoanalysis can never be made to proffer a discourse on the veil of Maya or the fundamental illusion of the *Wille*. "Dupery" implies something, but here it is not as easy to resolve as elsewhere. A dupe is someone that someone else exploits. Who does the exploiting here?

Emphasizing dupery, the question nevertheless proliferates. This is what makes it such that, in an area which is that of the consequences [or: aftermath, *suites*] of Marxist theory, people get a bit excited, thinking that psychoanalysis, which is so awesome, might serve as a guarantor there. I heard this said in an interview I gave. As I told you, I prefer a discourse without speech, but when I go to see people it is in order to talk, so they talk, they talk more than I do, and this leads them to say things like: "After all, psychoanalysis could serve to corroborate the theory of social exploitation." They are not wrong. However, the exploiter is less easy to grasp here; so is the mode of revolution. It is a dupery that benefits no one, at least on the face of it.

Does this imply that knowledge of analytic experience is knowledge that simply prevents us from being duped by the most popular strains? What good would that do us if it were not accompanied by "knowing how to get out of it" [*savoir-en-sortir*]? – or, more precisely, an intuitive [*introïtif* contains intro-, *intuitif* (intuitive), and *trou* (hole)] knowledge, a "knowing how to enter" [*savoir-entrer*] into what is at issue regarding the lightning flash that may result therefrom regarding the necessary failure of something that is perhaps not confined to the sexual act alone.

With regard to this question, [most] psychoanalysts have in fact remained on the fence [or: threshold, *seuil*]. Why have they done so? The fact that they have remained on the fence in their practice can only be justified theoretically, and that is what they strive to do. But

209

the fact that they have remained on the fence at the theoretical level as well is, I would say, their problem – let them find their own way out of it. That doesn't stop those of us who are here, insofar as we are in the hot seat, to try to do like others and go further.

We find ourselves here at a crossroads where, as opposed to what I said earlier, we must perhaps learn from other disciplines, with respect to a certain text about which it turns out, in time, that it is not so different from ours, since the function of the sign and even that of the signifier take on their full import there. I am referring to Marxist criticism. It would perhaps suffice to have a little less progressivism on both sides for us to arrive at fruitful theoretical intersections.

As everyone knows, I contribute something on the topic that is also an *organon*, one that might serve to cross that border. Some call it "the logic of the signifier." I have, it is true, managed to make a few statements on the topic. Nothing prepared those trained in psychoanalysis for it, but others, coming from other fields, found it quite stimulating.

"From other fields" – it's not so easy to say exactly from which ones, for it is not simply a question of their political allegiance but also of a certain number of current fashions. Well after I first began to enunciate the logic of the signifier, all sorts of questions began to arise regarding the handling of the signifier, regarding what a discourse is, regarding what a novel is, and even regarding the appropriate usage of formalization in mathematics.

There as elsewhere, people were in a bit of a hurry. Haste has its function, and I long ago stated what it is in logic [see "Logical Time and the Assertion of Anticipated Certainty" in *Écrits*]. Still, I only enunciated it to point out the mental traps – I would go so far as to qualify them thusly – into which it precipitates us. In wishing to stress to what degree what I proffer qua logic of the signifier remains marginal – owing to the fact that certain people's frenetic adherence to pure formalization is designed, so they say, to ensure that it is not metaphysical – they will end up realizing that, even in the realm of purely mathematical exercises, the use of formalization exhausts nothing, leaving, as it does, the question of the status of the desire for knowledge unanswered.

Who knows? Perhaps, in spite of myself, in mathematics there will someday be something known as "Lacan's theorem." Someone in my entourage suggested it a few days ago. I certainly haven't sought that out, for I have other fish to fry, but that's typically the way things work. The more people want to consider an unfinished discourse as finished – and that is truly a characteristic of something that should normally lead elsewhere – the more garbage they produce. We can leave the statement of the theorem to some obscure future moment.

Let us return for the time being to knowledge, and take as our point of departure the other end of what is stated on the board. It is not the same to state a formula by beginning with one end of it or the other.

As opposed to our experience, we might say that knowledge is what truth is missing [or: lacks].

This is clearly what destabilizes the debate about a certain logic, and that one alone, Frege's logic, because it sets out on the crutches of two values, truth and error, which can be written as 1 and 0. Note the difficulty Frege has finding a proposition he can qualify as veridical. He has to go so far as to invoke the number of moons Jupiter or some other planet has, in other words, things that are quite round and altogether isolable, without realizing that he is resorting to the oldest prestige [or: illusion, *prestige*] by which the real appeared as what always returns to the same place. If he can resort to nothing other than astronomical entities, it is because he does not have many other formulas that can be stated as truths. There is no question for a mathematician, of course, of enunciating 2 and 2 make 4 as a formula that bears its truth within itself, for it is not true. If in each of the 2s there happens to be one that is the same, 2 and 2 only make 3.

The fact that truth is the desire to know, and nothing else, is obviously designed merely to make us raise the following question: What if there were a prior truth? As everyone knows, that is the meaning of Heidegger's "letting be" [*laisser-être*, *Gelassenheit*]. Is there something to let be? It is here that psychoanalysis contributes something.

211

Psychoanalysis says that there is, indeed, something that we can let be. Yet psychoanalysis intervenes in it. And it intervenes in it in a way that interests us, beyond the fence on which psychoanalysts remain, because it makes us wonder about the desire to know.

This is why we return to the drive.

3

The drive is undoubtedly mythological, as Freud himself wrote. But what is not mythological is the supposition that a subject is satisfied by it. Now, this is unthinkable without already implying the existence in the drive of a certain knowledge of its characteristic qua sexual placeholder [or: substitute, *tenant-lieu*].

But what does it mean to say that "this is unthinkable"? Things can go so far as to lead us to consider thought to be suspect. Perhaps we know absolutely nothing about what it means "to hold the place of sexuality" [or: "to be a stand-in for sexuality," *tenir-lieu du sexuel*]. The very idea of sexuality may be an effect of the passage of what is at the heart of the drive – namely, object *a*.

As you know, that is what happened a long time ago. Our dear Eve handed Adam the fatal apple. This, too, is a myth, all the same. It was from that point on that he viewed her as a woman. He realized all the things I mentioned earlier. Prior to that, he hadn't realized that she was something extracted from his ribcage. He had found it all very nice and pleasant – they were in paradise. It was probably at that very moment – indeed, there's no doubt about it when you read the text – that he not only discovered that she was Woman, but that the dear little guy first began to think. That's why saying it "is unthinkable" that the drive already involves or implies a certain knowledge doesn't take us very far.

The proof of this is, moreover, that this is where it connects up with idealism. There was a guy named Simmel who spoke about sublimation before Freud did. As his point of departure, [he chose] the function of values. He explained very clearly how the feminine object comes to take on a privileged value therein. It's a choice like any other. There are values, people think in values, then they think in accordance with values, and then they construct values.

If I told you that psychoanalysis and Freud don't concern themselves with illusion or the veil of Maya, it is because both practice and theory are realist(ic). Jouissance is what cannot be perceived unless we note the constancy in Freud's statements. But we can also perceive it in experience, by which I mean psychoanalytic experience. Jouissance is an absolute therein; it is the real, which I defined as what always returns to the same place.

We know that because of women. This specific jouissance is such that at the outset only the hysteric situates it logically. Indeed, she is the one who posits it as an absolute. It is in this respect that she reveals the logical structure of the function of jouissance. For if she posits it in this way, in which respect she is a fine theoretician, it is at her own expense. It is precisely because she posits jouissance as an absolute that the hysteric is rejected, not being able to respond to it except by means of an unsatisfied desire with respect to herself.

This position in the logical unveiling begins from an experience whose correlation is perfectly palpable at every level of psychoanalytic experience. I mean that it is always in a place beyond where jouissance is an absolute that all the articulated determinations of desire logically fall into place.

This reaches a degree of coherence when we refute claims that it is invalid [*caducité*] owing to the accidental nature of its origin. It's not

212

because hysterics were there at the outset [of psychoanalysis] owing to a historical accident that the whole story was able to unfold. It is because they were at the exact point at which the impact of speech could expose the hollow that results from the fact that here jouissance serves the function of being outside of the game's limits. As Freud said, the enigma is to know what a woman wants, which is, in this case, a displaced way of labeling the status of its place here. It is from that point onward that knowing what a man wants takes on its value.

The fact that the entire theory of psychoanalysis, as people sometimes say, develops androcentrically is certainly not men's fault, as people think it is. In particular, it is not because men dominate. It is because they have gone off the deep end. From that moment on, only women, especially hysterical women, understand anything about it.

213                    $1 - a$ truth – knowledge

The statement of the unconscious, such as I just wrote it on the board, bears the mark of a at the level where knowledge is missing. This is so to the extent that we know nothing about this absolute. Which is the very thing that constitutes it as an absolute. It is not connected [*lié*] in the statement [of the unconscious]. But the unconscious part of the enunciation asserts that this is desire qua what the 1 is missing [or: the 1's lack, *manque du 1*]. Which does not in any way guarantee that this is the case. It does not guarantee that what the 1 is missing is truth. Nothing guarantees that it isn't a lie. This is even why Freud designates in the *Entwurf* the unconscious concatenation as always taking as its point of departure a *proton pseudos* [SE I, pp. 352–6], which cannot be correctly translated, when you know how to read, except by a "sovereign lie." If it applies to the hysteric, it is only insofar as she takes the place of man.

What is at stake is the function of this One insofar as it dominates everything about the field that people rightly term metaphysical. It is the One that is called into question, far more than being, by the intrusion of psychoanalysis. It is the One that obliges us to shift our emphasis from the sign to the signifier.

Were there a conceivable field in which sexual union functions, where it seems to work out, as in the case of animals, only the sign would be involved. "Turn me into a swan" [*cygne* means swan but is pronounced exactly like *signe*, sign], as Leda [Queen of Sparta] said to one of them. After that, all goes well. Each of them passes half the dessert to the other, they are joined, and become One. Yet if psychoanalysis proposes something, it is precisely that this One does not stick, and this is why psychoanalysis introduces something new, in the sole light of which, moreover, even the exploits of the eroticism I mentioned earlier can take on meaning.

Indeed, if sexual union brought satisfaction at its end, we could expect no subjective process from any experience, by which I do not mean from those experiences which, in analysis, provide the configurations of desire, but from those which, far beyond it, in the area already explored and practiced, are considered to be the pathways of ascesis, in which something like being manages to be realized.

Don't we know that nature – in order to provide for the necessities of reproduction in the thousands and tens of thousands of extant species – does not always seem to need to resort to the jouissance that is highlighted here only on the basis of the exclusion, in some sense, of something that represents feminine nature?

214

There are plenty of non-tumescent organs that operate at the level of certain arthropods and arachnids. Jouissance is in no way reducible here to some form of naturalism. What is naturalistic in psychoanalysis is simply the nativism of the apparatuses known as drives, and this nativism is conditioned by the fact that man is immersed in a sea of signifiers right from birth.

There is no reason whatsoever to link that up in any way with naturism.

The question that we are going to turn to, and that I will take up at our next meeting, will, I hope, be clarified by the premises I have articulated today.

Sublimation is the point where Freud himself indicated what I earlier called the stopping of psychoanalysts at a threshold [*seuil*].

Regarding sublimation, he tells us only two things, the first of which is that it has a certain relationship *am Objekt. Am, an.* You have already heard of *an sich* [in itself]. The German *an* is not at all the same as *en* [in] in French. When people translate *an sich* by *en-soi* [in itself], that isn't it at all. Which is why my *en-Je* [literally "in I" but a homonym of *enjeu*, stake or ante], with which I qualify *a*, is also ambiguous. I would like to call it, by adding an apostrophe, *l'a-je* [*a*-I or I-*a*, a homonym in French of *l'âge*, age]. You would thereby immediately see what we are sliding toward, which is the proper use of languages as they are actually used.

Secondly, when Freud discusses sublimation, he highlights that if it has a relationship with the object, it is by means of something he takes advantage of at the level at which he introduces it, and that he calls idealization, but that, in its essence, is *mit dem Trieb*, with the drive. You can find this in his *Einführung zur Narzissmus* ["On Narcissism: An Introduction" (see SE XIV, p. 94)].

Have a look at the other texts, of which there are a certain number – I feel I don't need to enumerate them for you – from the *Three Essays on the Theory of Sexuality* right up to *Massenpsychologie* [*Group Psychology and the Analysis of the Ego*]. The emphasis is always placed in them on the fact that – as opposed to the censoring interference characteristic of *Verdrängung* [repression] and, in short, as opposed to the principle that thwarts the emergence of work – sublimation is, strictly speaking and as such, a way of satisfying the drive.

Sublimation is with the drive, but a drive that he qualifies as *zielgehemmt*, "aim-inhibited" [or "diverted from its aim"], as it is translated.

215   I have already tried to articulate the status of this aim. Perhaps we must, in fact, associate the path of the target [or: goal, *cible*] with the level of the aim in order to see more clearly here. But do we really need to quibble after what I have told you today? There's nothing easier than to see the drive find satisfaction elsewhere than in its sexual aim. However this aim is defined, it is outside of the field of what is essentially defined as the apparatus of the drive.

In concluding, I will only ask you one thing, which is to see what this leads to wherever something is organized around the sexual function, something that is not instinct – which we would find it very hard to situate somewhere starting today – but a social structure.

People might be surprised that those who have striven to show us the societies of bees or ants have spoken only about their groups, communications, games, and marvelous intelligence, and that none of them have emphasized the fact that anthills, like beehives, revolve entirely around the realization of a sexual relationship. It is precisely to the degree to which these societies take on a fixed form in which the non-presence of the signifier is revealed that they differ from ours.

This is why Plato, who believed in the eternal nature of the ideas, creates an ideal politeia in which children belong to everyone. From that moment on, you can be sure that what his society revolves around is, strictly speaking, sexual production. Plato's horizon, no matter how much of an idealist you imagine him to be, was no other – except, of course, for a series of logical consequences, and it is out of the question that they bear fruit, as they would cancel out all the effects of his dialogues in society.

I will leave it there today. Next time we will take up the topic of sublimation.

March 5, 1969

XIV

THE TWO SIDES OF SUBLIMATION

Gilles Deleuze's elegance
Logic and biology
The Other as a terrain scrubbed clean of jouissance
There's no such thing as a sexual relationship
The logistics of defense
Woman qua sexual Thing
A love beyond narcissism
The anatomy of the vacuole
Tickling the Thing from the inside

Woman?	The (feminine) Other [*LA utre*]?	The thing?
X	Locus of speech to (or: with) which one makes love	Vacuole of jouissance

Sublimation to accede to Woman
(courtly love, idealization of the object)
Sublimation to accede to jouissance with the drive
The representative of representation

On the board

I put some words on the board to help you situate a few of the remarks I will make here today.

They should, in fact, suffice, given how long I've been talking about this. I mean that on the basis of the terms found on the first line in the form of questions, I should be able to give the floor to at least a few of you so that, in my stead, you will do this weekly discursive work that consists in ploughing ahead.

Indeed, it would be nice if someone would relieve me, as happened

in certain of the preceding years [of this Seminar], and if a few of you
would be willing to assume the task of taking a certain number of
existing objects a bit further, things that have already been published, refining which could prove worthwhile owing to the passage
of time [since their publication].

It is clear, in effect, that there are stages and levels in what I enunciate, if you think about the point from which I had to begin. At the
outset I had to drive home the point that the unconscious – I mean
the unconscious Freud talks about – is structured like a language.
This was visible to the naked eye without my getting involved,
without there being any need for people to put on my glasses, yet it
had to be done all the same.

Someone who is kindly disposed toward me told me recently that
reading Freud is, in short, too easy – one can read his work and
see nothing therein. Maybe he was right, since it has, overall, been
proven by the facts. The first giant thing that I had to pry us out
of had never even been perceived, thanks to a series of operations
designed to popularize Freud's work. Still, it took me some time to
get across the idea of the unconscious structured like a language,
even in the circle of those who, in this regard, were the best prepared
to realize it.

Because of all of these delays, things happened which are far from
discouraging to me. It happened, for example, that Gilles Deleuze,
pursuing his work, published, in the form of his theses, two capital
books, the first of which is of great interest to us. If we consider
but its title, *Difference and Repetition*, we can see that it must have
some connection with my discourse, with which the author is quite
familiar. And then, just like that, immediately thereafter, I had the
pleasant surprise to see appear on my desk another book he brought
out entitled *The Logic of Sense*. This was, moreover, a true surprise,
for he had told me nothing about it the last time I saw him, after he
successfully defended his two theses.

It would be worthwhile if someone, one of you, for example,
would study a part of this book. I don't mean the whole book,
because it is a long one, but still it is designed the way a book
should be designed: each of the chapters is well integrated into the
whole, such that one gets a sense of the whole book by selecting a
well-chosen chunk. You would do well to realize that he was lucky
enough to have the time to bring together in a single text, not only
what is at the heart of what I have stated – and there is no question
but that my discourse is at the heart of his books, since he admits
as much in them, and that my "Seminar on 'The Purloined Letter'"
forms the point of entry into and the threshold to the book – but
also all the things that have assisted and nourished my discourse,

219

supplying it at times with its framework, Stoic logic for example. With the supreme elegance peculiar to him, he shows the essential undergirding it provides, taking advantage of the work of all those who have shed light on this aspect of Stoic doctrine. This is difficult, because only snippets of it have been bequeathed to us by outsiders, and we are forced to reconstruct that doctrine by looking at it from an oblique angle, in some sense, in order to glimpse what its true outlines were – the outlines of a thought that was not only a philosophy but a practice and an ethics, and even a stance toward the world.

In this book [*The Logic of Sense*], in which I am often mentioned, the only point where the author indicates that he differs from a doctrine that is said to be mine is found on page 289 [p. 360 in the English translation] – at least, he says, if we are to believe a certain paper which, at a turning point in my teaching, presented the essentials of my doctrine regarding the unconscious to the whole psychiatric community. Deleuze supplies this proviso, but, given the serious relevance which that report has in general, owing to its two excellent authors – Laplanche and Leclaire – he doesn't hesitate, of course, to impute to me what he terms the multivocal nature of signifying elements at the level of the unconscious.

When I reread the paper in question, since Deleuze drew my attention to it with his remark, I found formulated therein that the possibility of all meanings is produced on the basis of the true identity of the signifier and of the signified that results from a certain way of manipulating metaphor – in a way that goes a bit beyond what I had done. The authors make the S, which is pushed down below the bar owing to the metaphorical effect of substitution, function – conjoined to itself – in such a way as to represent the essence of the relation in question, and play out as such at the level of the unconscious. I shall all the more willingly leave this point to the authors who represented me in this fine paper, since it in fact results from a certain manipulation on their part of what I had hitherto stated.

I hope someone will be willing to take on the task of examining it in detail, something I certainly cannot do owing to the excessive number of tasks my path involves, a path that is destined by its very nature not to be able to stop, given that it must go on for a long time still. That person would have to connect what Deleuze states in the whole of his book with what is stated in that paper, which is not absolutely irrelevant, but which is mistaken [*faille*]. It would be necessary to establish why it is mistaken and make perfectly clear what exactly is erroneous. He would also have to show in what sense this mistake is coherent with what, in that paper, hinges on the necessity,

220

as I have emphasized several times in prior years, of furnishing an accurate translation, which comes down to saying a proper unpacking, of the function known as *Vorstellungsrepräsentanz* and its impact in the unconscious. If someone were willing to volunteer to publicly examine this question, I think it would be of great interest to those who rely on my teaching and who, of course, feed it, accompany it, and complete it, sometimes in a clarifying way. It is, in effect, always necessary to explain what, in this or that work by one's students, did not adequately convey, not the trajectory of what I was stating at that moment, but what everything that followed showed its true trajectory to be.

Until someone is willing to do so, I will mention that the paper in question, "The Unconscious: A Psychoanalytic Study," was published – it's hard to know exactly why – in *Les Temps Modernes* in July 1961, in other words, quite a while after it had been given at a conference in Bonneval. I myself gave a talk in Bonneval, the text of which, written up quite a bit later too, is included in my *Écrits*: "Position of the Unconscious."

I will turn now to what is on the agenda today, picking up where I left off last time regarding the topic I announced: sublimation.

1

Last time, I pointed out and highlighted two things about sublimation.

In Freud's work, there are, of course, many passages we could cite, but one that is of capital importance is found in "On Narcissism: An Introduction." It mentions the relationship of idealization *am Objekt*, with the object.

221   Secondly, sublimation is essentially connected to the fate, transformation [*avatar*], or *Schicksal* [destiny or vicissitude] of the drives. Sublimation is the fourth avatar mentioned by Freud in his article entitled "Triebe und Triebschicksale" ["Drives and Their Vicissitudes," SE XIV, p. 126]. It is characterized by the fact that it occurs *mit dem Trieb*, with the drive. At least those of you who have heard me emphasize the word "with" on a number of occasions in the past – specifically when taking up Aristotle's formulation, "One must not say that the soul thinks, but rather that man thinks with his soul" [*On the Soul*, 408b, 13–14] – may find it fascinating to note this in Freud's work. Something is satisfied "with" the drive.

How could the drive find satisfaction in sublimation [*Qu'est-ce que la pulsion trouverait donc à y satisfaire*], when Freud situates the drive for us as a montage – something that I have always stressed as essential to the drive – of the following four terms: the *Quelle* or source, the *Drang* or pressure [or: impetus, *poussée*], the *Objekt* or object, and the *Ziel* or aim [*but*]. The aim is what is at issue today, insofar as in sublimation the drive is inhibited as regards its aim, sublimation eliding the sexual aim as it does.

This is ordinarily translated by imagining that the works that we appreciate, those that take on "social value," a term Freud stresses, are produced by their authors at the expense of their sexual satisfaction, and that some sort of obscure substitution takes place there. It does not at all suffice to confine ourselves to that if we are to give what Freud enunciated its full import.

I prepared you for this topic step by step and indicated its premises in our last two meetings. I explicitly articulated that sexuality, with regard to what interests us in the psychoanalytic field, certainly constitutes a horizon, but that its essence is still much further off. Neither the knowledge nor practice of sexuality is clarified or modified for all that.

This is what I would like to draw your attention to, at a point at which, of course, advances are being made in biology. Things we discover at the level of regulating structures often strangely resemble my statements regarding the functioning of language, but it is assuredly more than prudent not to content ourselves with crude schemas when it comes to sex.

If you carefully read work done by someone like François Jacob regarding what is known as a bacteriophage and regarding everything that rigorous experimental technique allows us to begin to perceive in the operation of living matter, it will perhaps occur to you that even before there can be any question of sex, there is an awful lot of copulating going on. Which is why it is perhaps not irrelevant that at another end of the field, our end, which certainly has nothing to say on the topic of biology, we also perceive that talking about sex is a bit more complicated than that.

We shouldn't, for example, confuse the status of relationships [*rapport*] – this term being taken in the logical sense – with the relations [*relation*] that establish the conjoint function of the two sexes. It seems self-evident that there are only two, but why wouldn't there be three or more sexes? I am in no wise alluding here to the rollicking uses that have been made of the term "the third sex," for example – a book that is especially remarkable, I might add as an aside, for the irresponsibility it evinces. Biologically speaking, why wouldn't there in fact be three?

The fact that there are two certainly constitutes one of the fundamental bases of reality, but we should note how far the logical consequences of this go. Indeed, by a curious reversal, whenever the

222

number 2 arises, sex appears, at least in our minds, and it slips in through a back door all the more easily because we know nothing about sex.

I am going to offhandedly mention a strange fact. There is an extra chromosome somewhere, about which it is quite curious, moreover, that one can never say in advance in which sex it will be found in a specific species. It is excessive, out of joint, and dissymmetrical.

Thus, prior to stating something about sexual relationships, we would do well to pay attention to the fact that they have nothing to do with what completely replaces them, especially in psychoanalysis – namely, identifications with what we call, in this case, male or female models [or: stereotypes or standards, *types*].

That said, and appearances notwithstanding, what psychoanalysis demonstrates is precisely that even this identification with a model is not as simple as all that. On the whole, it is only very awkwardly that people manage to say something about it. They talk about "masculine positions" or "feminine positions." And they very quickly slide toward "homosexual positions." The least we can do is be somewhat struck that every time Freud wishes to provide a precise statement, he himself admits that it is altogether impossible to rely on the male/female opposition, and he replaces it with that of active and passive.

223   It would be interesting to raise the question whether any of these terms, "masculinity" or "femininity," or "maleness" or "femaleness," can legitimately serve as a predicate. Can one say "all males"? Can that be stated, even in a naïve use of qualifiers? Why couldn't an Aristotelian proposition take, for example, the following form: "all males in creation"? The investigation would also involve the following question: does "all non-males" mean "all females"? The abyss that opens up by relying on the principle of non-contradiction might also be taken in the opposite direction. That would make us wonder about something I mentioned earlier: what sexual content the principle of non-contradiction itself contains.

In fantasies that have stemmed from the improbable broaching of sexual relationships, other modes than that of yes or no come into play. Consider, for example, that of the polarity of the sexual couple, as we see it under the microscope. Once an egg has been fertilized, filaments are produced and some sort of field is established between the two nuclei, which we must conceptualize less as a field of gradations than as a field involving an increasing and decreasing "bi-directionality" [*bi-vectorialité*] depending on the proximity to each of the poles. Must this image of a field – which is so fundamental in other domains, that of electromagnetism, for example – suffice for us to think that sex and its fundamental relationship are of that order, namely two poles, and that some sort of spherical framework gets established between them?

If we begin to raise this question, we realize that the foundations of this conception are perhaps not as obvious as all that. Whereas certain [biological] forms support such a picture, plenty of other questions can be raised. There are effects of dominance, influence, repulsion, and even of rupture, which are perhaps of a kind to incite us to call back into question where this schema leads. It is, of course, impossible to do so except from the moment at which we realize the role it plays, which is never discussed and even naïve, as they say.

People speak, for example, of *Fortpflanzung*, reproduction, as the supposed purpose of sex. The image of sex provided is that, when two people sleep together, a baby is sometimes born. I began with the effects of sexual copulation at the cellular level in order to indicate that, in sexual union, it is less a question of the third party produced than of the reactivation of a fundamental production, which is that of the cellular form itself, which, stimulated by this, becomes capable of reproducing something that lies deep within itself – namely, its configuration.

Let us thus pay attention to the contaminations that make it so easy for us to make a function, the essential nature of which perhaps escapes us, coincide with the notion of plus or minus in mathematics or even that of one or zero in logic. Let us pay all the more attention to it in that Freudian logic, so to speak, clearly indicates to us that it cannot function in binary terms. Everything Freud introduced by way of a logic of sex is based on a single term, which is truly its original term: a lack known as castration. This essential "minus" is of a logical nature, and nothing can function without it. All normativity is, for both men and women, organized around the transmission [or: transferring or transposition, *passation*] of a lack.

That is logical structure as it stems from Freudian experience.

2

I must now remind you of what I developed at length in the Seminar that I mentioned at one of our recent meetings, entitled *The Ethics of Psychoanalysis*.

I explained in it that the very dialectic of pleasure – which involves a level of stimulation that is both sought after and avoided, a suitable [*juste*] limit or threshold – implies the centrality of a zone that is, let us say, prohibited because the pleasure would be too intense there.

I designate this centrality as the field of jouissance, jouissance itself being defined as everything related to the distribution of pleasure in the body.

It is this distribution and its internal limit that conditions what – at that time, and with more words and illustrations than I can provide here, naturally – I designated as a "vacuole" [Seminar VII, pp. 150 and 152]: a prohibition at the center that constitutes, in short, what is closest to us even as it is outside of us. One would have to use the word "extimate" to designate it.

I had, at the time, noted in Freud's texts – I don't have time today to remind you which ones – the appearance of a term that was all the more striking as it differs from the one he uses elsewhere. In his work, the word he uses for "things" [les choses] is always Sachen. Here, however, he uses das Ding.

I won't repeat today the emphasis I placed on das Ding, as I don't have time to do that either. The only thing I can remind you of is that Freud introduces this term by means of the Nebenmensch [neighbor or fellowman], the man who is the closest [plus proche], the man who is oh so very ambiguous because we don't know how to situate him. Who is this neighbor [prochain] who resounds in the formulation found in Scripture, "Love thy neighbor as thyself"? Where can we find him? Where, outside of the center of myself that I cannot love, is there something that is closer [plus prochain] to me? Freud can only characterize it – forced as he is, in some sense, by his deductive argument – as something that is absolutely primal, something he calls a scream [cri]. It is in an ejaculatory exteriority that this thing can be identified, by which what is most intimate is precisely what I can recognize only outside of myself. This is why I need not actually scream for there to be a scream.

I mentioned, in this context, the magnificent engraving by Edvard Munch entitled *The Scream*, and demonstrated that nothing is better suited to the expressive value of a scream than the fact that it is situated in a calm environment with, not far off, on the road, two people who are walking away and don't even turn around. It is essential that nothing but absolute silence come out of the twisted mouth of the female in the foreground representing the scream. It is from the very silence that the scream centers that the neighbor arises – the presence of the closest being, the expected being, all the more so in that it is always already there – the neighbor who never appears, who has no *Erscheinung* [appearance, manifestation, or occurrence] except in the actions of the saints.

Is this neighbor what I called the Other, which allows me to make the presence of signifying articulation in the unconscious function? Certainly not. The neighbor is the intolerable imminence of jouissance. The Other is merely the terrain scrubbed clean [or: median strip (or central reserve) wiped clean, *terre-plein nettoyé*] thereof.

Given how long I have been laying out the definition of the Other for you, I can say these things quite rapidly. The Other is quite precisely a terrain [*terrain*] scrubbed clean of jouissance. It is at the level of the Other that those who take the trouble can situate what is articulated in Deleuze's book with admirable rigor and accuracy as both distinct from and in agreement with everything that modern logic allows us to define regarding what are known as events, staging [*la mise en scène*], and the whole nine yards linked to the existence of language. It is in the Other that we find the unconscious structured like a language.

226

Our question for the time being is not how this sweeping clean occurred or who did it. We have to begin by acknowledging it. Perhaps we can say something sensible afterward. Still, it is very important to define it thusly, because it is only by doing so that we can even conceptualize what is perfectly well expressed in Freud's work, which I formulated using two terms that I believe must be stressed: the formalization and the impassibility – of what? Of desire.

This is what Freud states in the last sentence of the *Traumdeutung* [*The Interpretation of Dreams*, SE V, p. 621]. The desire in question, unconscious desire, remains impassible in its stability, transmitting the exigencies of what Freud rightly or wrongly calls the past. It is not because there is *Vergänglichkeit* [transience, impermanence] that this must immediately make us think of good or bad impressions, the traumatic neurosis of the little child that lasts forever in each of us, or other commonplace notions. They are certainly not unserviceable, but what is essential is the permanence, constancy, and impassibility of desire, which is completely reducible to something formal.

At what level, then, is a sexual relationship situated, as regards what we can formulate about it? At the level of Woman? Of the Other qua locus of desire that slides under all speech, intact and impassible? Or rather of the Thing, the locus of jouissance? That is the meaning of the questions I wrote on the first line on the board.

As I told you, there is no such thing as a sexual relationship. And if there is a point where that is asserted, and quite calmly, in psychoanalysis, it is in the fact that we don't know what Woman is. She is an unknown in a [black] box – except, thank God, through representations. She has never been known in any other way since time immemorial. If psychoanalysis highlights anything, it is that we only know her through one or more representatives of representation. This is truly the place to highlight the term Freud introduces [*Vorstellungsrepräsentanz*] regarding repression. We are not talking for the time being about whether women are repressed, but rather about whether Woman is, as such and, why not, in herself too.

227   This discourse is not androcentric. If Woman in her essence is something, and we don't know whether or not she is, she is just as repressed for women as for men. And doubly so. First of all, we don't know what Woman is because the representative of her representation is lost. Secondly, even if we recover this representative, it is subject to *Verneinung* [negation]. What could it be but a negation to attribute to her the characteristic of not having what it is out of the question she could ever have? It is nevertheless from this angle alone that Woman appears in Freud's logic – an inadequate representative, next to it the phallus, and then the denial [*négation*] that she has it, in other words, the reaffirmation that this thing is integral to her, is perhaps her true representative, but has no relationship to her. That, in and of itself, should give us a little lesson in logic and allow us to see that what is missing in the whole of this logic is precisely the sexual signifier.

When you read Deleuze's work – perhaps a few of you will take the trouble to do so – you will become familiar with things that your weekly attendance at my seminar apparently has not sufficed to familiarize you with, for otherwise there would be more such books for me to read. You will see that he says somewhere that what is essential to structuralism, if the word has any meaning – as a meaning was given to it in a public forum, I can't claim credit for it [or (possibly): why should I be the only one not to use it, *je ne vois pas pourquoi je m'en ferais le privilège*] – is both a blank [*blanc*] or lack in the signifying chain, and what results therefrom by way of errant objects in the signified chain.

The errant object is, for example, a pretty little blown-up balloon [or: bubble, *baudruche*], a little balloon, with eyes and a little mustache painted on it [Lacan is, presumably, pointing to some image]. Don't believe that it is a man. It is indicated that it is a woman, since it's, all the same, in this form that we see this ungraspable woman going about every day. It is even what allows us to relativize and realize that it could be otherwise.

When we go back in prehistory to a less logical time, when there perhaps wasn't yet an Oedipus complex, we find little statuettes of women which must have been precious – otherwise we wouldn't have discovered them. They must have been tucked away in corners. They look like this:

Figure 14.1: Prehistoric Venus

We no longer have a little balloon here with eyes and a mustache, but a formidable backside. This is what a prehistoric Venus looks like. I didn't draw it very well on the board, but it hopefully conveys something. It was less andromorphic. It does not at all mean what paleontologists think it means – that women looked like that. The representative of representation was different for them than it is for us. It was not a balloon or two – you recall [Thérèse's] invocation in *The Mammaries of Tiresias* [in Guillaume Apollinaire, *Three Pre-surrealist Plays* (Oxford: Oxford Paperbacks, 1997), p. 49], "Take flight, birds of my weakness . . ." For them, the representative of representation was assuredly like that. Which proves that the representative of representation can change depending on the era.

With these premises laid out, we can now make a little headway regarding sublimation.

3

I have already told you enough about how Freud articulates sublimation that I shouldn't have to repeat it now: it is *zielgehemmt* [aim-inhibited], involves idealization of the object, and operates with the drive.

Freud explored a certain number of paths by which sublimation can occur. The simpler ones are obviously the *Reaktionsbildungen*, the reaction formations. If we know where the barrier is – namely, on the verge of jouissance – it is clear that one can imagine and classify sublimation as a reaction formation to imminent jouissance, even if that does not clarify it. But that does still does not suffice to explain how it succeeds [or: fails (or stalls, falls away, or wins out), *décroche*].

Now, in a sentence at the end of a short footnote, Freud indicates that, apart from all the possible ways he lists of broaching sublimation, there are others which are quite simple [SE VII, p. 178]. Yet he quite simply doesn't tell us what they are. Perhaps he had some trouble thinking them through himself. Although he gave us, on the basis of our logical material, the elements known in mathematical logic as "intuitive" or – much less appropriately, "naïve" – that doesn't mean he himself completely perceived that it could be formalized.

We sublimate, he tells us, with the drives. But what do we actually know about the drives? Where do they come from? From the horizon of sexuality, which has not in the least been clarified heretofore by the fact that the drives bring sexual satisfaction with them. But we are told that their jouissance is related to sexuality. It's not half-bad that we began here by initially positing that we know nothing about sexuality. On the other hand, what I articulated is that what is known in topology as a rim structure [or: edge structure, *structure de bord*] is involved in the drive.

This is the only way to explain certain of the drive's features. We can roughly say that a drive is always characterized by orifices with a rim structure. Only rim structures, taken in the mathematical sense, allow us to begin to understand what Freud articulates about *Drang*, pressure – namely, that the flux conditioned by the rim is constant. In my *Écrits* I added a little note, which I improved in the latest edition, in which I referred to what is known as "curl flux" in vectorial theory [see *Écrits*, p. 721 n. 3, 843 n. 847, fn1].

In sum, the drive designates, all by itself, the conjunction of logic and corporeality. The enigma bears on the following: how did rim jouissance manage to get equated with sexual jouissance?

If you have a little imagination – I mean the possibility of linking up what you think somewhere in that grey matter of yours with your experience, which is obviously accessory and always takes place too quickly – you may nevertheless object that when it comes to sexual jouissance, what is at issue is tumescence, for example, and then orgasm. What do they have to do with rim functions?

Well, were there no vacuole configuration, no hole that is characteristic of jouissance – which is something unbearable to what is regulated as tempered tension – we would see nothing in sexuality that is analogous to what I call the drive's rim structure. The rim is constituted here by a sort of logistics of defense.

This logistics of defense is, after all, encountered at every turn of the way, and even in sexual practice, precisely to the degree to

230

which the latter differs from something that happens very quickly. If people did not confine themselves, regarding women's jouissance, to vague little scraps left over from Freud's vocabulary, perhaps something would begin to interest you, in a closer, more direct and compelling way, regarding – not sexual relationships, about which we can't say much – but the handling [or: orchestrating, *maniement*] of sexual jouissance. The enigma, in the eyes of some, of the vaginal wall's sensitivity, the character – which I will not call unsituable, but in some sense neighboring [or: frontier (or adjacent), *limitrophe*] – of feminine jouissance, and all the enigmas that appear, we know not why, when we study feminine sexuality, turn out to far more easily fit in with the topology that we are trying to broach here.

It is not my goal to take up the topic here in detail. What is important is what I am proposing, which is that something here resembles the Thing, that Thing that I made speak long ago in a text entitled "The Freudian Thing." This is why we give it feminine features when we call it Truth in the myth. But what we mustn't forget – and this is the meaning of the lines on the board – is that the Thing is assuredly not sex(uat)ed [*sexué*]. This is probably what allows us to make love to it, without having the slightest inkling what Woman is qua sex(uat)ed Thing.

What I have just stated will perhaps allow me to [merely] introduce, given the time, the two directions from which sublimation can be studied.

If I took the trouble to dwell at some length on courtly love in my Seminar on ethics, it is because it allowed me to assert that sublimation concerns women in love relationships, at the cost of constituting them qua Thing. As I will not, alas, go into all of that again this year, you will have to read the long study I provided at that time of courtly love, in order to give this its proper import. I will strive to get you the text of it rather quickly. It is very enlightening and you will reread it to advantage in light of the definitive formulations that I can now finally provide.

When we study foreplay rituals, and the various stages [or: bases, *stades de gradus*], as it were, leading up to a gentle [or: orchestrated, *ménagée*] jouissance, but one which is also virtually sacralized, it is rather amusing to see the awkwardness – which I can't call touching for it is simply repulsive – with which this is broached by people in places where we find a concentration of jumbled texts, which no longer interest anyone, naturally. I am referring to those who are irreducibly professors. Such people live in conditions that we all know when we go see them, and whose major symbol was very prettily provided by Anatole France in his book entitled *Le Mannequin d'osier* [*The Wicker Work Woman: A Chronicle of Our Own Times*,

231

Vol. II]. (I would have had to provide you with a very different sketch for the wicker-work woman – the inverse of the one I drew (Figure 14.1).) A kind of stupor and stupefaction comes over them. "My God," they say, "how could those people who were so unrefined back then in the Dark Ages" – you can just guess how much less refined they were than the professor in question and his old lady – "have imagined such exalted homage to all those women whose praises are sung by the poets, and who all have the same characteristics, every single one of them?"

Of course they all have the same characteristics. We are talking about a representative of representation. They are like the prehistoric Venuses that all have the same characteristics. Which doesn't mean such women did not exist or that the poets did not make love to them in accordance with their merits.

There are many other things as well that flabbergast the professors, including the emphasis placed on testing men, cruelty, and a thousand other such things.

I enjoyed talking about courtly love for two-and-a-half months [in that Seminar], and I hope that those who attended enjoyed it too. I will try to write it up in a way that can be transmitted.

In any case, courtly love, or at least what remains of it for us, is an homage rendered by poetry to its principle – namely, sexual desire. Otherwise stated – and despite Freud's claim that, unless special techniques are employed, love is only accessible on condition that it always remain narrowly narcissistic – courtly love is the attempt to go beyond that.

But there is the other direction [from which sublimation can be studied], which is the relationship between sublimation and what are known as works of art.

Freud tells us that sublimation provides the very satisfaction of the drive, and it does so in a product that is granted social esteem. Yet, this esteem remains altogether unexplained, except by the hypothesis of diversion: we take pleasure in some of the things that are turned out en masse and rendered affordable to us in the form of novels, paintings, poems, and novellas because we don't want to deal with our own problems, which are far more important! To look at it from that angle leaves us no way out.

I will not sketch the way out today, so as not to provide an overly quick introduction to what I will say next time. I will simply say that the relationship between sublimation and jouissance – insofar as it is sexual jouissance, since that is what is at issue – can only be explained by what I will literally call the anatomy of the vacuole.

This is why I drew on the right something enclosed that represents the vacuole [see Figure 14.2].

232

Imagine for a moment this vacuole as akin to the auditory apparatus possessed by animalcules – known, I know not why, as "primitive," whereas nothing is more primitive than anything else. Consider a daphnia. It looks like a tiny shrimp, but is far simpler. It is found in every waterway. In a doohickey that serves it as an auditory, but at the same time vestibular, organ – in other words, for balance – the daphnia has what is called an otolith.

Figure 14.2: Object *a* in the Vacuole of Jouissance

I know that because I read about it after an article by a psychoanalyst – I'll tell you which one next time – brought it to my attention. It becomes very amusing if you replace the otolith with a little piece of iron and then deploy magnets around it. That makes the daphnia come – we can but presume so, given the extraordinary postures it assumes. Just like men do in their moral lives.

233

Object *a* plays the same role with regard to the vacuole. It is, in other words, what tickles *das Ding* from the inside. *Voilà.* That is what constitutes the essential merit of everything known as a work of art.

That is what I wanted to say to introduce what I will talk about next time.

The thing is worth looking at in detail, for object *a* assumes more than one form, as Freud explicitly states in his analysis of the drive when he says that the object may be highly variable and shifting. Nevertheless, we have managed to enumerate four forms of the object: oral, anal, scoptophilic, if you will, and sadomasochistic.

What is that one? I will have a few surprises in store for you regarding it next time.

March 12, 1969

XV

HIGH FEVER

I'll lay my cards directly on the table: I won't be giving my Seminar – call it as you like, my lesson, my thingamabob – today.

[After a likely problem with the sound system:] I'll start again. It's no accident you didn't hear me at first, as I'm not inclined to talk at all. Moreover, that is what I'm going to do or, more precisely, not do. I intend not to speak to you today. There's something relieving about that. I can get exhausted sometimes.

Yet it is not relieving because, as you can see, I am quite tired – for very simple reasons. Imagine whatever you like, a little Hong Kong flu over the weekend, because naturally a psychoanalyst cannot allow himself to fall ill during the week. In any case, the result is that I won't speak to you today.

Furthermore, I resolved to tell you, "Listen, I am calling in sick; the Seminar, as you call it, won't take place today," and then take off. But that would be too simple.

*

I mentioned last time what a pleasure it would be for me if someone would respond, if one of you would speak up and give me a sense of what you make of what I am trying to sketch out this year.

It is obvious that plenty of things incline me to want that. First of all, a certain feeling about what this thing I am doing – what I am pursuing here by way of what is known as a teaching, although we don't, in fact, really know why – could, in the end, be. Does it truly fit the framework of a teaching, apart from the fact that it takes place at the École Normale? That's not clear.

Secondly, my God, that's the right word for it today, why are there so many people here? It's truly a problem. I am forced to con-clude that it must, all the same, be of some interest. The fact remains that, given the speed at which things are moving, I have no reason to believe that the interest in what occurs here will last very long.

It just so happened this week – which obviously wasn't very stimulating as I rarely have such a high fever – that I began to wonder what is going on. Surely because there must be something not very stimulating in such a state, which is still dragging on, it took me two days to come up with a working hypothesis, that's the word for it! I told myself that what I am doing here, whether you know it or not, truly falls under the heading of work.

Certain things that I have said this year will perhaps allow you to glimpse this.

The way I usually talk to you, when I have my little papers with me, might shock you. I sometimes look at them. There are a lot of them, surely too many, but in any case what I do closely resembles what happens on a workbench or even on an assembly line. The papers obviously come from somewhere, and will end up being transmitted to others. And because of that, in effect, something happens about which, when I leave, I am always perplexed enough to question, a bit anxiously at times, those who I know can tell me something pertinent. It is clear that I am doing something that truly resembles work, [insofar as it is] carried out with certain tools, [and gives rise to] something constructed, a product(ion).

It is obviously interesting to watch it being done. It's not that common to have the opportunity to watch someone at work. I have the sense that what my work aims at, what it is intended to do, can but completely escape most of you here. That makes it all the more interesting.

Nonetheless, to watch someone work without knowing where that work is headed or what it's for adds a somewhat obscene dimension to it. That isn't the case for all of you here: some of you know quite well what it's for – at least what it's for in the short run. Since I am using this worker metaphor, I will say that my bosses know what it is for. Or, conversely, if you like, that those who know what it is for are my bosses. Some of you here are among them. I am working for you.

There are others among you who lie between the two camps and who also have an inkling what it is for. They in some sense insert the work that I'm doing here into another text or context, which is that of something that is occurring, for the time being, in what is known as the university system. I am very interested in that [or: It directly involves me, *J'y suis très intéressé*]. By which I mean that there is something happening once again at universities that is closely related to what I am doing by way of work.

Owing to my temperature and the break it gave me, I had some leisure time. You can't imagine how happy I was to take advantage of my 39°C [102°F] – for once I could lie down. It was very pleasant.

237

And when the fever abated a bit, I could open up some amusing newspapers. There is one, as you know, the one that is run by Jean Daniel, known as *Le Nouvel Observateur*. They undoubtedly gave it that name in order to make people believe that there is something new in what is observed. We would be foolish to expect that to be true, and the proof lies in what I read while lying down – a whatsit that, if I recall correctly, is entitled "Trapped Youth." I don't know why – perhaps it had something to do with my fever – but that infuriated me.

The title first of all, naturally. Anyone who uses the word "trapped" [*piégé*] should know that its use is repugnant to me, for it is a crude way of arousing castration anxiety, especially when it is addressed to young people, [as it is] for the time being. That strikes me as being in very bad taste.

Secondly, I have to admit that the article makes nothing but very astute, relevant points. There is perhaps not a single one of them which, if you take it as a sentence, as a justification or legitimation of whatever you like, not a single sentence to which I can seriously raise an objection. Everything is just fine. But what is annoying is that the article completely misses the point.

For, naturally, I am not against any of the forms, even the most extreme ones, of what, for the time being, likens the student protest [*contestation*], as it is put, to the most revolutionary conjunctions. But I think that none of that manages to escape the trajectory of something that has occurred as a consequence of certain facts which are as follows.

[French] universities were inadequate to serve their function, and suddenly that was so glaringly obvious, people believe, that it gave rise, let us say, to *May* [the student uprisings in May 1968]. This is a very important point regarding its interpretation. Universities were no doubt inadequate compared to their glory days, the ones they may have had, and compared to their traditional function, which involved the employment of various functions related to the transmission of knowledge, which had a variety of impacts depending on the era.

If we consider things from the standpoint of quality, splendor, or historical influence, it is clear that universities had not been especially brilliant for some time, but there were nevertheless pockets here and there that had held up quite nicely. Universities proved inadequate at a certain level because they were no longer up to snuff owing to certain social exigencies. We should wonder whether their not being up to snuff, not in all areas, but in certain ones, was not, in the final analysis, intentional – I mean, if we look at it from the vantage point of power, whether it was not something that was

238

deliberately done so as not to put the powers that be in a pickle [*embarras*].

It is clear that a certain evolution, which is that of science, risks creating problems that are entirely new and unexpected for those in power. They have been coming for some time. It would truly be a retroactive meaning effect to realize that this was perhaps why the word "revolution" took on another meaning, a different emphasis than the one it has had throughout history, in which revolutions, by definition, are nothing new. Only revolutions have ever put an end to their power. The Revolution, with a capital *R*, perhaps didn't realize early enough on that it is linked to something new that is appearing in a certain function of knowledge – a function that renders it, in truth, difficult to handle in the traditional manner.

To clarify a bit what I mean by that, I will relate it to what I indicated earlier: to people's fascination with work whose meaning and goal escapes them. The relationship between the worker and the boss that I used to exemplify what might motivate your presence here is one that can be extended. The boss knows what the worker is doing in the sense that the latter is going to provide him with profit, but he's not sure that he knows the meaning of what he's doing any more clearly than the worker does.

Consider, for example, Fiat's assembly line or any other assembly line. I am mentioning Fiat because I already mentioned it, here or elsewhere, and I visited it. I had, in fact, the distinct impression of seeing people working without me having any idea what they were doing. I was ashamed of myself. It doesn't make you ashamed, so much the better. But I was very bothered by it. I was with the boss, Johnny, as he is known and as I call him. Johnny was manifestly ashamed of himself as well. This seemed clear in the questions he asked me afterward which seemed blatantly designed, in order to hide his embarrassment [*embarras*], to get me to say that the workers at his factory appeared to be happier than at Renault's.

I didn't take his question seriously, having interpreted it, as you see, merely as a displacement, or perhaps a way of avoiding the question I had asked him: "What is all of that for?" Not that I'm saying that capitalism serves no purpose. No. Capitalism serves a purpose and we mustn't forget it. It is the things that it produces that serve no purpose. But that is an entirely different matter. And that is precisely its problem. In any case, what it is underpinned by, and this is its strongpoint, should become clear thereby.

This strength is much the same as the one I mentioned earlier which runs counter to power. It is of another kind and poses a great many problems to those in power. Here, too, it obviously happens *nachträglich*, after the fact; the meaning of what is happening must

239

be seen retroactively. Capitalism has completely transformed the habits of power. The latter have perhaps become more abusive, but in any case they have changed. Capitalism introduced something that had never before been seen, which is known as liberal power.

There are very simple things that I can, after all, only speak about on the basis of highly personal experience. Consider the following. No historian has ever heard tell of a government agency that people leave by tendering their resignation. Where authentic, serious, subsisting powers exist, people never tender their resignation because the consequences of doing so are very grave. Unless it is simply a figure of speech: they tender their resignation, but they are killed on the way out the door. Those are the places where power is taken seriously. How can people view as liberal and constituting progress institutions in which, when someone has sabotaged everything he was supposed to do for three to six months and turned out to be totally inept, he can tender his resignation and nothing happens to him? Institutions in which, on the contrary, he is told to wait so he can run again [in the next elections]. What does that mean? No one ever saw such a thing in Rome, in places where power was serious. No one ever saw a consul or a tribune of the plebs tender his resignation. It was unimaginable, strictly speaking. Which simply means that power now resides elsewhere.

It is obvious, and the whole of the nineteenth century clarifies this, that if things unfold via resigning, it is because power is in other hands – I'm talking about positive power. The only benefit of the communist revolution, I am referring to the Russian revolution, is that it restored [political] power's functions. However, we see that it is not easy to hold on to, especially in times in which capitalism reigns supreme.

Capitalism reigns supreme because it is closely linked to the rise of science. Yet even this power, this camouflaged, secret, and, it must also be said, anarchic power – I mean that it is divided against itself and this is undoubtedly so owing to its connection with the rise of science – is now just as encumbered as a fish would be with a bicycle, for something is happening in science that it cannot control. There would have to be a certain number of mediocre thinkers that don't forget the following: that a certain permanent association is useless between protest and uncontrolled initiatives that take the form of revolution, for that is still what best serves the capitalist system.

I am not in the process of telling you that we must undertake reforms. Reforms, which are an indisputable consequence of the May stirrings [émoi], will merely make its effects still worse. If we had inadequate teachers, we will be given a whole slew of them and they will be even more inadequate, you can be sure of that. Owing to reforms, things will get worse and worse. The question is to know what to do about this phenomenon.

It is clear that no answer can be provided by a watchword, but that a process – that tends to eliminate the best teachers, in the long run, owing to protest, which in fact the best teachers feel compelled to engage in – would have exactly the desired effect, which would be to block the best teachers from taking the most interesting route, from having access to a turning, sticking, or updated point concerning the function of knowledge in its most subversive form. For it is obviously not at the level of agitating clamor that a decisive turning point regarding something can be refined, handled, and produced.

I am not saying what that thing is, and for good reason, because it can't be said. Yet it is there and there alone that a new one [knowledge] can present itself, the only new one in the name of which what justifies calling into question what has presented itself up until now as one philosophy or another – namely, as a function tending to establish a universal or unitary order – can appear. It would be a new one regarding the way of relating to ourselves that is called knowledge.

The trap that consists in refusing and in doing nothing further, for the time being, is, strictly speaking, the one with the greatest disadvantages. It guarantees that everything that exists and subsists will go on subsisting, and in the worst way possible.

To anyone who may have illusions about what is known as "progress," I would like to state the following.

Since it was an interview that served as the basis for the article that, going by the title of "Trapped Youth," incited me to say what I just said, I can but confer on the interviewee [Sartre] the epithet I have always felt he deserved: he's an entertainer [*amuseur*]. Objectively speaking, his thinking goes no further than that.

This is rather serious. It is the testimony, after all, of a man who has lived long enough to have experienced two interwar periods. I lived through the one between the two world wars with Giraudoux, Picasso, and others, surrealists, and the only original one in the bunch was Giraudoux. Which is to say that I didn't have much fun.

Picasso had already been around for some time at that point. Whatever you may think of it, surrealism was a remake. Its entire core existed before 1914, and this projected an irreducibly unsatisfying *je ne sais quoi* onto the presence of the surrealists between 1918 and 1939. You might note that I was their friend but never signed anything they published. That did not stop a schmuck by the name of L* [Camille Laurin], who is Canadian, from observing this, and from making a big deal out of my surrealist roots, I don't know why – to initiate people in Saskatchewan [to my work], no doubt. There

was also [G.] Parcheminey, a narrowminded lout on the first team
with which I was associated, who really wanted that to come out. I
explicitly told him that there was no reason to take it into account
since I had myself been especially careful to never indicate any links
I had with them. That didn't stop him from writing "Lacan and the
Surrealists." It would be impossible to more accurately propagate
error.

Now we are in a new interwar period, a defective one because it
has no endpoint. That is what troubles them, because it is clearly
overdue. Capitalist power, that singular power the scope of whose
originality I beg you to consider, needs a war every 20 years. I'm not
the one who first noticed that; others have said it before me. A war
can't be waged right now, but it will obviously happen in the end.
A war can't be waged right now and, because of that, capitalism is
quite stymied.

In any case, during the interwar period, there was Sartre. He was
no more fun than the others. That didn't faze me. I never said anything about it, but it is curious, isn't it, that people feel the need to
encourage young people to run up against obstacles that are placed
before them, to go to the front lines, in short, and rather mediocre
front lines at that.

It's all well and good, isn't it, to be able to confront muscle-bound
[university] safety officers, because I approve of something known
as courage. [Physical] courage is not very meritorious. It has never
seemed problematic to me. It just happens to be of no interest. In
such a case, to run straight at the obstacles placed before you is to
behave just like a bull. The point is to find a different path than the
one where the obstacles lie – or, in any case, not to be especially
interested in obstacles.

In all of that, we find a true tradition of aberration. People begin
by saying, for example, that philosophies, over the course of the centuries, have never been anything but ideologies – that is, reflections
of the superstructure and thus of the ruling classes. They believe
that settles the question: philosophies are of no interest and we must
look elsewhere. Which is completely wrong. We continue to fight
ideologies qua ideologies. That is precisely why they exist. It is quite
true that there have always, naturally, been classes that ruled, or
enjoyed, or both, and they have had their philosophers. The latter
were there to get yelled at instead of them. And people did so; they
followed orders. But that is not at all accurate, now is it?

Kant was not a representative of the ruling class of his time.
Kant still is, not only perfectly acceptable, but you would do well
to learn from him, if only to try to understand some of what I am
in the process of telling you about object a, and more specifically

about what is going to be situated on top of it [or: added to it, *venir là-dessus*].

*

Last time, I spoke about sublimation. We obviously must not stop   243
there. It's no accident, all the same, that a little suspension or suspense, as you like, is occurring at this point.

Try to describe the relationships of our copresence – seen from
your point of view? from mine? The question arises. Let us chalk
that up to sublimation.

It would be better, in any case, to chalk it up to that today,
because that situates you at the feminine end. There's nothing dishonorable about that, especially at the level at which I placed it, the
highest elevation of the object.

There are things that I did not highlight last time – but I hope
that there are good listeners among you – the idea, for example, that
sublimation is the effort made to allow love to occur with a woman
[or: allow one to make love to (a) woman, *permettre que l'amour se
réalise avec la femme*], and not only . . . well, to make believe that it
occurs with a woman [or: that one makes love to (a) woman, *que ça
se passe avec la femme*].

Nor did I highlight the fact that in the institution known as
courtly love, the woman does not love, at least in theory, for no one
knows anything about it. Can you imagine what a relief that would
be? Yet it sometimes happens, nevertheless, in novels, that the
woman gets swept away. We see what happens afterward. At least
in such novels, we know where we are headed.

Thus, sublimation perhaps occurs there. I am saying so because
it is high time we said so before we broach another phase, which I
sketched out last week and which concerns sublimation at the level
of the drive. That form of sublimation, alas, perhaps concerns us far
more. I provided a first prototype of it in the form of a jingle bell,
something round with a little thing, object *a*, that bounces around
a great deal inside. Before it makes its entrance, let us rely on nicer
shapes.

As regards relationships between men and women, I thus need
not fear acts of folly on the part of my audience. Nevertheless, I
would be grateful if someone would now be willing to provide a sign
of having heard something by asking a question, either about what
I just said, or, something I would like even more, about what I have
been saying since the beginning of the year. I would like a question
or two regarding this pleasant topic regarding which, as you see, I
myself am making the courtly effort to be up to the task, even on a
day when I am exhausted.

Who would like to pose a question or two? [Lacan is met with silence.]

244   Now don't discourage me. Because, after all, I, too, might be tempted to tender my resignation.

Those whom I called my bosses – namely, the people for whom I work – don't threaten to resign. But suppose that were to happen. It could happen someday. Well, I would simply do my work in front of them. Those of you here who are not, in short, psychoanalysts in my eyes – at least from my perspective – serve primarily to give analysts the sense that they cannot stop me from continuing to do my work. Even if no one responds to me, I see very interesting faces over there among the non-analysts. I know my audience, all the same.

If none of the non-analysts ever respond, ever provide a response – one that amuses me a bit – imagine that one day I manage, all the same, to shake up [*décrocher*] the psychoanalysts, and rebuke them for thinking that work is only for analysands. What is totally wrong in my way of working for them [or: to their way of thinking, *pour eux*] is that I do, in short, what analysands do. They have definitively relegated work to their analysands. They confine themselves to listening. Last I heard, one of them went so far as to say, "Come listen to me listening. I invite you to come hear me listen."

Now I will perhaps manage to shift things related to that strange ground, which is closely linked at its exposed points to the subversive nature of knowledge's function. But it will not be an open seminar. I don't find that very serious.

I wonder about the word "handling" [when it comes to] knowledge, because it is beginning to be extended in a worrisome way. One guy, a good egg by the way, came to see me, and he will do quite well. Naturally, things happen when people first meet with me. He came back a second time, because you have to see someone at least twice. He told me that the time before "there was manipulated" [or: "he had manipulated there," *il y avait manipulé*]. I racked my brains trying to figure out what he meant. I got him to explain himself, and he meant that I had manipulated him.

It is always interesting to note the slippage in how people use words. The word "manipulate" has now entered into our permanent vocabulary through a form of fascination that is based on the following: people think that no one can have any real effect on a group without "manipulating" it and that this is now generally

245   acknowledged and recognized. After all, we can't be sure – as they say, the worst-case scenario is perhaps the surest to happen [*le pire est peut-être sûr*] – that it is not, in fact, true. It may in fact be true. But the fact that being manipulated can take on an active value is a

shift that I am pointing out to you. Let me know if it spreads, if it keeps going like that.

Well, these are obviously not the best conditions under which to explore questions regarding knowledge as they manifest themselves in psychoanalysis, or to the extent to which psychoanalysis can contribute something here.

*

Last time, I drew your attention to the book by my friend Deleuze, *The Logic of Sense*, and I asked Jacques Nassif to speak to you about it this time; for in truth I am not astonished, but I am, as they say, quite embittered by the total lack of response from my audience after inciting you so directly.

It was not manipulation. There are other ways to maneuver. But the total silence, the total lack of response to my desperate appeals for someone to attest to having heard something . . . I will allow you a makeup exam: you can write to me. The written exam comes after the oral exam. Well, if at the end of the academic year I decide to hold two or three classes by invitation only, you might want to know that, apart from the people who I already know, those who will have written to me will be permitted to attend.

Nassif, do you still have the strength – after this exhausting session, exhausting to me at least – to take the floor? Well, it is awfully nice of you.

[An exposé by Jacques Nassif followed.]

March 19, 1969

XVI

STRUCTURES OF PERVERSION

Capturing jouissance
The object is extimate
From the barred Other to little *a*
The pervert as a defender of the faith
Exhibitionism and voyeurism,
sadism and masochism

Today I am going to lay out some first truths.

It appears not to be pointless to return to this ground, and it seems, moreover, difficult to organize the complementary fields that might allow us to get in tune with everything that is currently being produced, which is profoundly interested in what psychoanalysis has to say at this point in time.

At our second to last meeting, I indicated that sublimation had to be investigated with regard to the role played in it by object *a*. It was this topic that showed me that it was, if not necessary, at least certainly not pointless for me to return to what specifies its function, and to do so with regard to the experience it grew out of, psychoanalysis such as it has been practiced since Freud's time.

In that class, I was led to return to the texts by Freud that progressively established what is known as the second topography. It is certainly an indispensable echelon for understanding all the "finds," as I would call them, I myself have proposed at the point at which Freud's search left off. I have already emphasized what the word *circare* means in my speech: revolving around a central point as long as something remains unresolved.

Today I will try to indicate the distance at which psychoanalysis has remained, up until my teaching, from a certain exposed point [*point vif*] that was formulated everywhere in the experience that preceded it – namely, the function of object *a*.

It was sketched out in certain statements but was never totally
purified, resolved, or developed. I won't say that I need to correct it,
but that I can now at least justify taking some further steps.

1

What I wish to say about sublimation today explicitly concerns
works of art.

Freud broaches them with awkward prudence, not allowing
himself to view them in any other way than as having commercial value. They are things that are pricey, and whose prices are
undoubtedly incomparable [*à part*], but not that different from any
other prices once they are put on the market.

What must be stressed is that their price is given to them by a
special jouissance value, a value related to what I isolate and distinguish in my discourse as jouissance – jouissance being a term that
is only established by being evacuated from the Other's field, and
thereby from the position of the Other's field qua locus of speech.

It is clear that the function of object *a* interests us in relation to
sublimation. If object *a* can function as equivalent to jouissance, it
is owing to a topological structure.

To realize this, it suffices to consider the function by which the
subject is founded and introduced only as a signifying effect, and to
refer back to the schema that I have drawn on the board for you a
hundred times since the beginning of the year – that of the signifier
as the representative of the subject before another signifier which, by
its very nature, is other [i.e., different from the first signifier]. Owing
to this, what represents the first signifier can only be posited to be
prior to the second signifier – hence the need to repeat the relationship of S to A qua locus of the other signifiers.

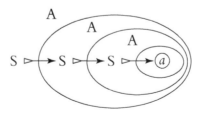

Figure 16.1: Variation on Figure 3.7

This relationship leaves intact the locus in which I have written
a. It should not be understood as a part. Everything that is stated
[in works on set theory] about how sets function, their elements

potentially being sets in their own right [or: being under the authority of sets, *en puissance d'ensemble*], justifies us in equating this
residue, although distinct owing to the function of *a*, to the weight
of the Other as a whole [*dans son ensemble*].

Object *a* is located in a place here that we can characterize with
the term extimate, combining the intimate with radical exteriority.
It is insofar as object *a* is extimate, and purely in the relationship
instated by the establishment of the subject as a signifying effect,
[that it] gives rise to a rim structure in the field of the Other.

We can easily discern a variety of rim structures. Such structures
can choose, as it were, to join up [1] in the form of a sphere, which
is apparently the simplest of topological structures, in which the rim
thus sketched out joins up at a point, the most problematic point
there; [2] in the form of a torus where the opposite edges join, each
point in one vector joining up with the corresponding point in the
opposite vector; [3] in the form of a cross-cap; or [4] in the form
known as a Klein bottle by combination of the two possibilities [of
joining opposite vectors with the same orientation point to point, or
joining opposite vectors with different orientations].

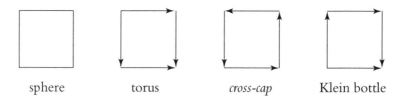

sphere   torus   *cross-cap*   Klein bottle

Figure 16.2: Two-Dimensional Representations of
Three-Dimensional Shapes

It is easy to perceive the kinship between these four topological
structures and the various objects *a*, of which there are also four.
Such as they in fact function in the relationships between the subject
and the Other generated in the real, each of the four objects reflects
one of the four structures.

I am simply pointing this out here, and I will return to it later, but
I wish first to remind you of the concrete function object *a* plays in
clinical work [or: differential diagnosis, *la clinique*].

Before object *a* can possibly exist – thanks to the methods
involved in its production – in the form that I qualified earlier as
commercial, it is in a position to function as a locus in which jouissance is captured, at levels precisely exemplified in clinical work.

250   I am going to skip straight to the nub of the subject to which my
first remarks, in coming to talk to you today, perhaps provided
more detours.

2

In Freud's theoretical work, the relationship between neurosis and perversion was very quickly spelled out. How did it, in some sense, force Freud to take notice of it?

Freud worked at the outset with neurotic patients who had all sorts of problems, and their narratives tended to lead him to examine what initially struck him as traumatic experiences. Nevertheless, the way in which these experiences were received, so to speak, by apparently traumatized subjects created a problem, and the question of fantasy arose, which is clearly at the crux [or: knot (or nucleus), *noeud*] of everything related to the economy for which Freud selected the term "libido."

Yet, must we still truly believe that neurotics' fantasies allow us to reclassify perversion, to handle it anew from the outside, on the basis of experiences that did not derive from perverts? In the same era, people were descriptively presenting the so-called field of sexual perversions – need I remind you of the names of Krafft-Ebing and Havelock Ellis?

Let us note that Freud's first take was already topological in nature. Since he opined that perversion was the flipside of neurosis [SE VII, p. 165, and SE IX, pp. 189 and 191], he already sensed something that gestured toward the surfaces that interest us so deeply, owing to what happens when they are cut.

Neurosis was perhaps a bit too quickly presented as a function with different stages compared to perversion, and as partly repressing perversion, at the very least, as a defense against perversion. But very quickly it appeared that simplifying things in this way did not resolve the problem in the slightest.

Isn't it clear, and wasn't it immediately clear, that no resolution could be found by simply locating a perverse desire in a neurotic's narrative [*texte*]? If that is part and parcel of the spelling out and deciphering of the neurotic's narrative, the fact remains that the neurotic never finds his satisfaction in the treatment at that level. Similarly, in broaching perversion itself, it very soon appeared that it presents no fewer problems or defenses with respect to structure than neurosis does.

251

In hindsight, it seems that all of this is related to an approach to technique whose impasses seem, after all, to have arisen merely because analytic theory was mistaken regarding the very ground we must stick to, whether in neurotics or perverts. If we, instead, consider things starting from the level that allowed us to articulate the return to our terra firma – that nothing happens in analysis unless it is related to the status of language and the function of speech

– we obtain the mapping that I provided in my Seminar entitled *Formations of the Unconscious.*

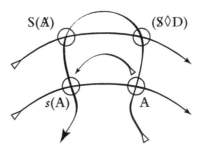

Figure 16.3: The Graph of Desire

It was no accident that I began from what is apparently the furthest, regarding these formations, from what concerns us in clinical work – namely, witticisms. It is on the basis of witticisms that I constructed this graph which, although it has not yet revealed all its obvious features to everyone, nevertheless remains fundamental here.

As you all know and can see, it is made up of a network of three chains, two of which are already marked, if not elucidated, by formulas, some of which I have amply commented on. Specifically, the formula ($ \lozenge$ D) indicates the subject's fundamental dependence on something that is utterly distinct from need – namely, demand. The signifying form or "defiles of the signifier," as I put it [*Écrits*, pp. 517, 525, and 687], specify demand, distinguish it, and do not in any way allow its effect to be reduced to the simple terms of physiological appetite. This is already necessitated – but turns out to be clarified by this medium – by the simple fact that needs concern us in our analytic work only because they come to be equated with sexual demands.

I have labeled the other points of intersection [see the small circles in Figure 16.3], those involving A qua treasure trove of signifiers, as a simple reminder here.

I want to make a point now, since no one else has ever highlighted it.

It's obvious that these three chains cannot be supposed, established, or fixed except inasmuch as there are signifiers in the world, that discourse exists, and that a certain type of being is caught up in that discourse – a being known as man or speaking being – only owing to the existence of a possible concatenation that constitutes the very essence of signifiers. Nevertheless, it is the lower floor [of the graph] that we can specify with the category that I called the symbolic. You see the symbolic function here, with the possibility of a short-cut back [*retour court*; see the right-to-left arrow between the two main left-to-right lines in Figure 16.3], that occurs on the basis of a statement in the simplest discourse. It is at this fundamental level that we can assert that there is no such thing as a metalanguage, and that nothing symbolic can be constructed except on the basis of normal discourse. In the upper chain, on the other hand, we can perceive that what is at stake is the effects of the symbolic in the real. Thus the subject, who is the first and major effect of the symbolic, only appears at the level of the second [i.e., upper] chain.

If something has not yet taken on its full weight, even though it is always brought out in my discourse, and especially this year – since it is the object and it is on the basis of the object that I am making headway – it is the status of S(A). It is the signifier that reveals the fundamental incompleteness of what is produced qua locus of the Other, or more precisely, of what, in this locus, sketches out the pathway of a certain type of entirely fundamental lure. The Other as a locus from which jouissance has been evacuated is not simply a scrubbed clean place, burnt circle, or place open to the play of roles, but something which, in and of itself, is structured by signifying impact. This is precisely what introduces therein the lack, bar, gap, or hole that can be termed object *a*.

This is what I intend to convey now with examples taken from the experience to which Freud himself resorts when he articulates the drive.

3

Freud strongly stressed the importance of the oral and anal drives in psychoanalysis, considering them to be first sketches, called pregenital, of something that, upon maturation, would fulfill some sort of myth of completeness prefigured by orality, and some sort of myth of a gift or discharge of a present prefigured by anality.

Isn't it strange that after having so strongly stressed these two fundamental drives, he leaves them far behind, at least apparently so, and that it is with the help of the scoptophilic and sadomasochistic drives that he articulates the montage that involves the source, pressure, object, and aim?

I am going to suggest right off the bat that what the pervert does is not based on some sort of scorn for the other or partner, as people said for a long time, and as no one has dared to say for a while now, primarily because of what I have said about it. His conduct must be gauged in a far richer fashion. To convey it, at least to an audience like the one I have before me today, which is quite heterogeneous,

I will say that the pervert is he who devotes himself to plugging up the hole in the Other. In order to flesh that out, I will say that he is, up to a certain point, in favor of the Other existing. He is a defender of the faith.

Moreover, if we look, in this light, a bit more closely at the case histories that make the pervert an odd auxiliary of God, we can shed light on bizarre comments that are made by writers whom I will term morons [*innocents*]. We read, for example, in a treatise on psychiatry which is, by my faith, very well constructed with respect to the cases it compiles, that exhibitionists do not engage in their antics only in front of little girls. They also sometimes do so in front of tabernacles.

It is certainly not such details that clarify things for us. We have to first locate – something I already did a long time ago here – the isolable function of the gaze in the entire field of vision, as it arises in connection with works of art [see Seminar XI].

It isn't easy to define what a gaze is. It is even a question that can very easily sustain an existence and ravage it. At one point I saw a young woman for whom this question, combined with a structure that I need not go into here, turned out to go so far as to lead to a retinal hemorrhage with long-lasting consequences.

People wonder about the effects of exhibiting – for example, whether or not it frightens the witness who seems to provoke it. People ask themselves whether the exhibitionist truly intends to provoke shame, fright, or [some sort of] echo – something that is either ferocious or consenting – in her. But that is not what is essential to the scoptophilic drive, which you can describe as you like, as active or passive, I'll leave you the choice – it appears to be passive, since it allows something to be seen. What is essential is above all to make the gaze appear in the field of the Other.

But why? If not to evoke the flight of the gaze [or: vanishing point, *fuite*] or what is ungraspable in the gaze in its topological relationship to the limits imposed on jouissance by the pleasure principle.

The exhibitionist watches out for [or: watches over, *veille à*] the Other's jouissance.

What is it that creates the mirage or illusion here that the exhibitionist has scorn for his partner? It is that we forget that, beyond the fact that the partner serves as a specific prop for the other, there is the fundamental function of the Other who is always there, clearly present, whenever speech functions: the locus of speech in which any partner is merely included, the point of reference where speech is posited as true.

It is with regard to the field of the Other qua deserted by jouissance that an exhibitionistic act is carried out in order to make the gaze emerge therein. It is in this respect that we see that it is not symmetrical to what happens in voyeurism.

Indeed, what is important to the voyeur – and very often owing to the fact that everything that can be seen was, in some sense, profaned in front of him – is precisely to interrogate what cannot be seen in the Other.

What constitutes the object of the voyeur's desire in a little girl's thin body is quite precisely what can be seen there only insofar as she props it up on the basis of what is ungraspable, on the basis of a simple line where the phallus is missing. The fact that the voyeur, as a little boy, was so mistreated that nothing that might grab him about this mystery seems to hold the attention of an indifferent eye – this is what propels him all the more to restore to the Other the thing that was neglected in him, to supplement the field of the Other with it, unbeknownst even to what props it up. Here, giving jouissance to the Other – which is the very aim [*fin*] of perversion – seems in some sense to escape owing to this unknowing.

This demonstrates, first of all, that no drive is simply the converse of another – drives are not symmetrical. It also demonstrates that what is essential here is the functioning of a supplement: something that, as regards the Other, interrogates what is lacking in the Other as such and makes up for it [or: fends it off, *y pare*].

Certain analyses are exemplary here, and they are always the most naïve [*innocentes*] ones.

After having cast doubt last time on a certain philosopher [Sartre] for his lack of seriousness, it is impossible for me not to recall his extraordinary analysis of the voyeur who endeavors to see through a keyhole what truly cannot be seen. Nothing can make him come crashing down more surely than being discovered while being captivated by this slit [*fente*]. It is no accident that a slit is also known [in French] as *un regard*, "a gaze," and even *un jour*, "a day" [as in something that lets in the light of day]. Being put in a humiliating and even ridiculous position is not at all linked to the fact that he is beyond the slit, but to the fact that he can be detected by another person in the posture of someone who, because he is so sure of himself, sees nothing, a posture that is demeaning compared to the standing position solely from the standpoint of narcissism. You can easily find this analysis on a page in *Being and Nothingness*, an analysis that has something imperishable about it, despite the bias included in what is deduced therefrom as to the status of existence [see Part Three, Chapter 1, Section IV].

The following step is of no less interest. What, then, is object *a* in the sadomasochistic drive?

255

People believe they have found the key to sadomasochism in the game played with pain, but then they immediately retract that and say that it is, after all, only amusing if the pain does not go too far. This sort of blindness, lure, false fright, and vague groping regarding the topic reflects, in some sense, the level at which every such analysis remains. Isn't it, in fact, the mask thanks to which sadomasochistic perversion escapes our grasp? Doesn't it seem to you that highlighting the prohibition characteristic of this jouissance must, here too, allow us to locate what is at issue?

This may strike you as overly daring, or even as speculation that is hardly likely to lead to *Einfühlung* [empathy or sympathetic understanding], and for good reason, because perversion, true perversion, escapes the majority of you, regardless of what you may believe. It's not because you dream about perverse acts that you are perverts. To dream about perverse acts can serve an entirely different purpose – that of sustaining desire, above all, something one truly needs when one is neurotic. That does not authorize us in the slightest to believe we understand perverts.

It suffices to have worked with an exhibitionist to realize that we do not understand anything about what, apparently, I will not say gets him off [*le fait jouir*], because he does not get off, but he gets off all the same, on the sole condition that we see what I just mentioned – namely, that the jouissance at issue is the Other's.

There is a gap here, of course. You are not crusaders. You don't devote yourselves to making the Other – that is, something blind and perhaps dead – come. But that interests the exhibitionist. That's the way it is: he is a defender of the faith.

In order to give you a handle on exhibitionism, I allowed myself to talk about crusaders [*croisé*], about believing in the Other [*croire à l'Autre*], and about the cross [*croix*]. French words link up like that – each language has its echoes and its coincidences. *Croa-croa*, too, as Jacques Prévert said ["Tentative de déscription d'un dîner de têtes à Paris-France" in *Paroles* (Paris: Gallimard, 1949, p. 7)].

The crusades existed. They, too, were waged for the life of a dead God. That signified something just as interesting as it would be to know what has constituted the game between communism and Gaullism since 1945. It has had enormous effects. When the knights were crusading, love was able to become civilized in the places they left, while, when they were elsewhere, they encountered civilization – in other words, what they were seeking, a high degree of perversion – and at the same time reduced everything to rubble. Byzantium never rose from the ashes of the crusades. We must pay attention to such games, for they can be played again, even now, in the name of other crusades.

But let us turn to our sadomasochists who are quite different.

When it comes to the scoptophilic drive, as I said earlier, there is one [the exhibitionist] who succeeds at what he must do – namely, bring the Other jouissance – and another [the voyeur] who is there only to plug up the hole with his own gaze, without letting the person he looks at see what she [or: he] is to even the tiniest degree more. We find something similar when we consider sadists and masochists, on the sole condition that we perceive where object *a* is located.

It is strange that people don't perceive an essential function here, whereas we live at a time in which we have, in short, very clearly resuscitated all sorts of interrogation practices [*la question*]. There was a time when interrogation played a role in judicial mores at a high level; now we leave that to agents who practice it in the name of some sort of madness – in the supposed interest of the nation or troops, for example. Already after the last war, the one in which so many things occurred, people prolonged the pleasure on the stage [*sur les planches*] for a while by showing us simulacra, little staged scenarios. In short, it is strange that people don't perceive the essential function played by speech in an interrogation: the confession.

Sadistic games are not only interesting in neurotics' dreams; we can see what is at issue where they are played out. Sadists may well have reasons for doing this or that, but we know that we must be wary of reasons: they are secondary compared to what takes place in practice. The latter in fact always involves peeling something away from a subject – what? What constitutes him in his fidelity – in other words, his speech.

People could perhaps realize, nevertheless, that speech has something to do with it. I will indicate right away that it is not speech that is object *a* here, but it is a first sketch, designed to set you on the right path. Nevertheless, broaching the question from this angle is likely to give rise to misunderstanding, for it suggests the very thing I am refusing – namely, a symmetry between masochism and sadism.

It is clear that the florid, real, true masochist, Sacher-Masoch himself, organizes everything in such a way as to no longer be able to speak. Why is that so interesting to him? Let us take a close look. What is at stake is the voice.

What is essential here is that the masochist turn the Other's voice, and it alone, into something he can provide a guarantee for [or: prop up or serve as guarantor for, *donner le garant*] by responding to it like a dog would. This is clarified by the following: he seeks out a type of Other who can be called into question regarding the voice – his dear mother, for example, as Deleuze illustrates, whose

257

icy voice was permeated by every form of arbitrariness. A [kind of] voice that he perhaps heard all too often elsewhere, addressing his father [or: from his father, *du côté de son père*], also completes and plugs up the hole.

Yet, there is something in the voice that is more topologically specific, for this particular object *a* is what makes the subject most interested in the Other. Which is why the topological comparison that is illustrated here [see Figure 16.2], that of the hole in a sphere, must be rectified because this specific sphere is not really a sphere, since it is precisely at the hole that it folds in upon itself.

A close examination of what we find in certain organic structures – for example, the apparatus of the vestibule or semicircular canals [of the ear] – shows us radical forms that I already gave you a glimpse of a couple of weeks ago when I mentioned one of the most primitive animals: the daphnia. Let us add to it the crustacean known as *Palaemon* [a kind of pink shrimp], a very pretty name full of mythical echoes. But we mustn't let this distract us from the fact that this animal, when stripped of its exoskeleton, as it is whenever it molts, has to bring a few grains of sand back into its outer open cavity which, despite its lowly level on the scale of animals, is nevertheless a true ear, in order to tickle it on the inside. It does so for good reason, for otherwise it could not move around in any way whatsoever.

It is strictly impossible to conceptualize the function of the superego if we don't understand – and it's not the whole story, but it's one of its mainsprings – the function of object *a* realized by the voice qua support of signifying articulation, the pure voice insofar as it is or isn't instated in the locus of the Other in a way that is perverse or not.

A certain form of moral masochism can only be based on this point: the impact of the Other's voice, not in the subject's ear but at the level of the Other that he establishes qua completed by the voice. Like the exhibitionist, whose way of getting off we saw earlier, the masochist's gravitational center is located at the level of the Other and involves handing the voice over to him as a supplement, not without a certain possible derision that appears in the margins of masochistic functioning.

It suffices, I must say, to have lived in our times to realize that there is jouissance in handing the function of the voice over to the Other, and this is all the more true in that this Other is less able to be imbued with value [*moins valorisable*], having less authority. Of all the imaginable perverse jouissances, this method of purloining or stealing jouissance may, in a sense, be the only one that is ever fully successful.

258

The same is certainly not true for sadists. They, too, try to complete the Other, but in the opposite way, by taking speech away from him and imposing their own voice on him, even if that generally fails. It suffices, in this regard, to look at Sade's work, where it is truly impossible to eliminate the dimension of the voice, speech, discussion, and debate.

Sade tells us about the most extraordinary excesses perpetrated on victims whose incredible survival may surprise us. But every single one of these excesses is not merely commented on, but instigated on the basis of a [spoken] order. What is most astonishing is that the order gives rise to no revolt. Yet we, too, have been able to observe historical examples in which such things happened. Among the flocks of those who were shoved toward crematoria [in concentration camps], no one apparently ever saw anyone even so much as bite a guard's wrist.

The play of the voice finds its full register in sadism. Yet there is a hitch: jouissance escapes here, exactly as in voyeurism. Its place is masked by the astonishing domination of object *a*, but the jouissance is nowhere to be found. It is clear that the sadist here is merely the instrument of the supplement given to the Other, but which the Other does not want in this case. He does not want it, but he obeys all the same.

That is the structure of these drives, inasmuch as they reveal that a topological hole can establish, all by itself, an entire subjective conduct. You can see that every analysis that revolves around supposed sympathetic understandings [*Einfühlungen*] really deserves to be relativized.

4

As all of this had to be rather carefully stated, I ended up spending quite a bit of time on it and we have only a few minutes left. I will thus confine myself to indicating what the neurotic's problem is.

Have a look at my article entitled "Remarks on Daniel Lagache's Presentation" [in *Écrits*], which is indispensable for finding one's way about in what is out of joint [*égaré*] in everything Freud says about identification.

Vacillation is manifest across his works, and his statements about what he calls "the reservoir of libido" clearly contradict each other. He makes it into the *Ich* [ego] at times, namely narcissism, and into the *Es* [id] at others. The ego, obviously being inseparable from narcissism, finds itself in a problematic position. Is it by offering up an object to the id that the ego becomes an effective agency, from which interest in objects would then arise [*rejaillirait*]? Or is it, on the contrary, on the basis of an object forged in the id that the ego manages to become imbued with value secondarily, qua semblable, just like certain other objects supposedly do?

This is what requires us to reformulate the whole question of identification.

The neurotic finds himself confronted with narcissistic problems because he wants to be the One in the field of the Other. Idealization plays a primordial logical role here. But simply by making this remark, I am suggesting at the same time that we investigate the nature of primary narcissism. Isn't it just a figment of Freud's imagination? Aren't we, along with him, undergoing a retroactive effect that is image-based and even unspeakably skewed? Aren't we overdoing things a little bit, just enough to fall into the neurotic's trap?

Next time, I will try to convey that it is at the level of secondary narcissism, in its characteristic form of imaginary capture, that the problem of object *a* arises for neurotics, in a way that is altogether different from the way it arises for perverts.

We believe we can assume that the neurotic must have had some relation, not of supplementation, but of complementation to the One, and we attribute this to the oral drive. Nevertheless – and in a way that is quite apparent on condition that we get over our fascination with neurosis – the oral drive also happens to be centered around a third object that slips away and is just as hard to get a handle on as the gaze or voice.

The breast, that famous object, is, with the help of a play on words, turned into the mother's womb [*sein*, breast, also means "womb"]. But behind the breast, and just as plastered [like a veneer, *plaqué*] onto the wall that separates the child from the mother as it is, we find the placenta.

It is there to remind us that a child in the womb does not constitute a single body with its mother, for the child is not even enclosed in her uterine envelopes; the child is not a normal egg, but is broken, broken in the envelopes by the aforementioned plastering [or: plating, *placage*]. Moreover, as we now know, it is owing to the latter that all sorts of conflicts can occur that arise from a mixing of blood [between mother and fetus] and from the incompatibility of blood types.

261   It thus appears that, when it comes to the drive, something cannot be eliminated: a third object that I called a veneer, or pendant [*pendeloque*], I would also say, for we shall see it again in eminent forms in every cultural product, in the thing that is attached to the wall and that lures us.

Isn't this, in fact, what appears in the neurotic's experience? To try to cover it up [*combler*] with a myth of primal unity, a lost paradise, supposedly put an end to by the trauma of birth – isn't that to fall precisely into what is at work in the neurotic's case? Indeed, what is at stake for him is the impossibility of making object *a* return to the imaginary level, in conjunction with the narcissistic image.

The first lines of this are already sketched out quite clearly in the article I mentioned, and I will return to it to articulate this point in detail.

No representation props up the presence of what is known as "the representative of representation." We see only too clearly here the distance implied by this term. A representative is not at all the same as representation.

This is what allows me to indicate that all of this is re-ordered on the third line of the graph, the one that crosses the other two. It is, strictly speaking, what, based on a symbolic concatenation, is related to the imaginary, where it finds its ballast. It is along that line that, in the complete graph, you find the ego, desire, fantasy, and lastly the specular image, before we find, at the lower left, the tip of the arrow, which can only be grasped on the basis of a retroactive effect. It is there that the retroactive illusion of primary narcissism is inscribed.

We will have to recenter the problem of the neurotic around that. It also manifests the fact that sublimation is doomed to fail in the subject qua neurotic.

Thus, if my formula ($ ◊ *a*) – barred S, lozenge, little *a* – qua formula of fantasy, must be foregrounded with regard to sublimation, I must first critique a whole series of side implications that were unjustifiably derived from this, owing to the fact that analysts' experience of the signifier's impact on the subject involved work with neurotics.

The fact remains that this experience could not have taken place otherwise.

March 26, 1969

JOUISSANCE: ITS REAL

XVII

THOUGHT (AS) CENSORSHIP

Terrorism and freedom of thought
"How can we replace that?"
From Hegel to Freud
"I don't know – what I think"
The effects of our science

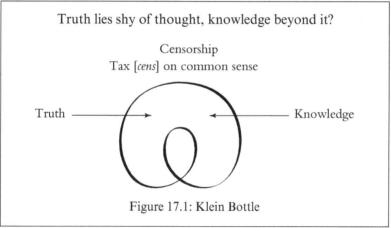

Truth lies shy of thought, knowledge beyond it?

Censorship
Tax [*cens*] on common sense

Truth ⟶   ⟵ Knowledge

Figure 17.1: Klein Bottle

[On the board]

Vacation has interrupted our work here. And as you can see, I, too, have taken some time to get restarted.

Having begun to explore the topic of sublimation, which I will link up again with certain points, I left off discussing the structure of perversion. I mentioned that in perversion, the subject takes it upon himself to make up for the defect [or: lack (or shortcoming), *faille*] in the Other.

This is not the most accessible of notions. My schemas, or my notions, if you will, render its definition quite accessible, but they require a certain grasp of psychoanalytic experience. It is thus only for those who are familiar with my terms that such a formulation can be seen to constitute a step forward. This is certainly a disadvantage, but one that is not unique to my teaching, as it is a factor common to every science from the moment that it begins to develop.

I am not saying that this suffices to authenticate my teaching as scientific, insofar as it endeavors to make up for the lackadaisical attitude which, in the name of its supposed reliance on clinical work, always ends up banking, to account for this experience, on some sort of flair – which could not, of course, be put to use if it had not already received cardinal points that were the fruit of a construction, a very learned one at that, the one Freud bequeathed us. The question is whether it suffices to assimilate that orientation and then allow yourself to be guided by it regarding what you take to be a more or less lived apprehension of clinical work, for the latter is quite simply a place where you tend to slip back into the worst biases.

People take this [assimilating and being guided] to be sheer common sense. I believe we must levy a poll tax on this common sense [or: charge it rent, *exigence censitaire*], as you see on the board. I mean that those who brag about it should be required to prove their mettle in another realm. I will try today to explain why such proof should be provided elsewhere than in the field in which most of them have done nothing – either to authenticate what they have received from Freud concerning what constitutes the structure of our field, or to attempt to account for or extend it, which is certainly the least we should expect.

I was one of the first to hear about a text that just came out.

Its mere title is so shameful that I will not pronounce it here. The two [pseudonymous] authors, who declare, right from the very first lines, that they are psychoanalysts, claim their intent to expose the atrocious toll of what they sweepingly designate as the protest movement. That gives you an idea where it is heading. The psychical regression, infirmity, and sordid infantilism manifested by all those who, for whatever reason, engage in demonstrations – Lord knows, their forms can be quite nuanced – lead the authors to the level of what people are capable of thinking in a certain current of psychoanalytic work. They don't go beyond it.

I won't comment on it any further. I will merely mention that it was not written by anyone whose face we have ever seen here.

I confirmed that by questioning some of my most authentic students regarding who could even be vaguely suspected of having participated in such a project. I must admit that I may have offended a few people simply by asking them this question, but in the end, given my position, I have to be able to respond to it. I can thus assert quite confidently that none of those who have, at any time, participated here, asked questions, or to any degree attended this Seminar, have failed to repudiate in horror this extravagant initiative, which is a true debasement [*déculottage*] of psychoanalysis to its lowest imaginable point.

So the dirty laundry has now been aired in public. This does not mean that some of those I just mentioned won't ever go the slightest bit in that direction in the end. I can boast that the fact that they don't do so – and that, regarding protesters, not all French psychoanalysts line up behind these two authors (whose names I happen to know through certain channels, and they are hardly small fry, belonging as they do to an eminent Institute that everyone knows) – owes to my teaching, about which I nevertheless cannot say that it has had great success in psychoanalysis.

One of the people who I thought I should ask about his possible participation in this book – although my suspicions did not go so far as to believe he wouldn't repudiate it – is the same person who, at a certain turning point in my adventures in teaching, qualified what I say as terrorism, nothing less than that. We must thus believe that it is the terrorism unleashed by my teaching that makes it such that – while, apart from a few rare exceptions, French psychoanalysts have (we might as well say so) distinguished themselves neither by great originality, nor by especially effective opposition to or application of my teaching – certain assertions are now impossible in French psychoanalytic circles and that, in order to make such claims, one must truly reside in a milieu, and they do exist, where it is prohibited to so much as thumb through the few pages of my work that I have allowed to come out.

You will soon hear about the [two authors]. I am talking about them because a computer-produced weekly magazine has already showcased, on an important page, the narcissism imputed to protesters in this book, completely overlooking, naturally, my revamping of the term ["narcissism"].

Well, since there is terrorism, and since, after all, I am not the only terrorist, the authors' attention might well have been drawn to the fact that terrorism is far from absent from their own field. That field is not simply governed by research based on comfort [or: convenience, *bien-aise*] and mutual mirage, but – in a certainly rather varied way – something occurs there that cuts and excludes, and that even excludes one after another [*voire qui s'exclut de l'un à l'autre*].

268

Observing this typical effect of certain functions in our times, and especially of those that can, in some way, be justified on the basis of a specific way of thinking, makes me propose to communicate to you today a few reflections that are not too distantly related to the common term, which is used and abused by many: "freedom of thought."

1

What must we understand by "freedom of thought"? What the hell could allow us to consider that those three words convey anything whatsoever?

Let us, first of all, spell out the question. Does thought – considered from an objective standpoint, let me abbreviate it like that – have anything to do with freedom? Naturally there isn't the slightest freedom there.

Nevertheless, objectively speaking, the idea of freedom originates somewhere – from the function, or more precisely stated, the *notion* of norms. From the moment that this notion comes to the fore, the correlated notion of exceptions to the norm – or even transgressions of it – arises. It is here that thought can somewhat justifiably introduce the notion of freedom.

In short, it is in conceptualizing utopia – which, as its name implies, is a place that is nowhere, *no place* – that thought is free to envision a possible revision of norms. This is how things presented themselves in the history of thought, from Plato to Thomas Moore. With regard to the real locus in which norms are established, it is only in the field of utopia that freedom of thought can occur. This is what we see in the works of Thomas Moore – the very creator of the term "utopia" – and in returning to Plato, who subsumed the term "norm" under the Ideas. He, too, constructed a utopian society for us, the Republic, in which the freedom of his thought from the political norms of the time was expressed.

Even the slightest use of what I have proposed as distinguishing the imaginary from the real allows us to clearly discern what is centering and formative about referring to the image of the body. The very idea of a macrocosm, as I have already indicated, has always been accompanied by a reference to a microcosm that gives it its weight, meaning, top, bottom, right, and left, and which is, in the final analysis, based on a mode of apprehension – said to be a mode of knowledge – from which a whole current, that is rightfully inscribed in the history of thought, proceeds.

269

On my graph, which I drew on the board again last time, the two horizontal lines are crossed by a fishhook-shaped line that rises and falls in such a way as to cut the other two, mapping out four essential intersections. In the intervals between the two lines, which are those of enunciation [upper line] and the enunciated [lower line], we find, along the fishhook-shaped line, the imaginary formations – namely, the relationship between desire and fantasy, and that between the ego and the specular image. This implies that the symbolic registers, inasmuch as they are inscribed on the two horizontal lines, have imaginary props. But what is legitimate about them, I mean rationally assimilable, must remain limited.

It is in this respect that Freud's doctrine is a rationalist doctrine. It is solely in terms of what can be articulated, in defensible propositions, in the name of a certain logical reduction, that anything whatsoever can be admitted or, on the contrary, excluded.

At the point we are at in science, where is the imaginary function insofar as it is taken to ground scientific investigation? It is clear that it is totally foreign to scientific investigation. Never, in anything we broach – even in the most concrete sciences, the biological sciences, for example – do we ever wonder what an ideal case would look like. Consider our embarrassment when people raise questions about such things – for example, "What is health?" Scientific advancement has nothing to do with some sort of ideality. What is of interest regarding everything that exists that we must investigate is how it can be replaced.

I believe this is amply illustrated by the way we investigate the functions of the body's organs. It is no accident, excess, acrobatic act, or exercise if what appears most clearly in the analysis of such functions is the fact that one can replace an organ with something that doesn't resemble it in the slightest.

If I am choosing such a timely example, it is certainly not for the sake of sensationalism, for what is at stake is of a very different nature. If this is the case, it is because science did not develop on the basis of Plato's Ideas [or: Forms] but on the basis of a process linked to mathematics, and to a kind of mathematics that is not found in its Pythagorean origins, for example – let's say, to give you a sense of it, those that link a number to a Platonic type of ideality. In Pythagoras' work, One has an essence, Two has an essence, and even Three does; when we reach Twelve we stop, out of breath. That has absolutely nothing to do with the way in which we currently investigate the nature of numbers. Peano's formulas have absolutely nothing in common with this sort of Pythagorean exercise.

The concept of functions, in the mathematical sense of the term – it is no accident that it is a homonym of the organic functions, which

270

we investigate in the way I mentioned a moment ago – is always, in the final analysis, based on a concatenation between two signifying chains. $x = function\ of\ y$ [$x = f(y)$]: such is the point of departure or solid ground on which mathematics converges, for it was not nearly that pure at the outset. Given the way the symbolic chain works, strictly speaking, it is the point at which one arrives that gives meaning to what preceded.

I won't say that set theory is the culmination of mathematical theory, for people are already edging forward, but as it is in fact accepted by many, at least in our times, let us stick with it. We can observe that what is essential in the order of numbers is reduced there to its articulatory possibilities. Everything is constructed therein in such a way as to strip numerical order of all the ideal or idealizable and imaginary privileges that I just mentioned when I discussed the One, Two, and other numbers, in the tradition we can globally characterize as gnostic. There is no trace of oneness [or: a unit (or unity), *unité*] in Peano's definitions. A number is defined in relation to zero and the successor function, without oneness having any privilege, whether the oneness of corporeality, essentiality, or even totality.

271   It must be emphasized that a set can in no way be confused with a class, and that to speak of a "part" is profoundly contrary to the functioning of the theory, whereas the term "subset" is precisely designed to show that set theory is incompatible with the notion that the whole is made up of the sum of its parts. As you know, the union of a set's subsets constitutes something that is in no way identifiable with the set.

In the end, sets are even stripped of recourse to spatiality itself. It is here that we must find the meaning of set theory.

2

I apologize for this introduction. It was designed to indicate the terms of an opposition that is as profound as it is necessary. What is defined in this opposition? A revolution in – or subversion, if you will, of – the movement of a form of knowledge.

I said "knowledge," for it is clear that I have for some time now left behind the functioning – which is merely inaugural here, or even presumed – of thought. I spoke about thought because I took Plato as my point of departure.

It is not at all on the basis of an objective orientation that we must investigate freedom. From that perspective, thought is only free in utopia, which has no locus in reality [*réel*]. Yet, one of the

interesting things about the process I have taken up here is assuredly
to show that this discourse has something to do with thought, which
is truly obvious in the subjective field.

What can we call, for example, the perspective gained [*recul pris*]
regarding the two faces of knowledge [*connaissance*]? A reflection? A
debate? A dialectic? You see the variety of possibilities here. I could
undoubtedly bring in plenty of others if, against all odds, you were
to provide me with some sort of response here.

In the foreground we thus find the notion of "all" [or: every, *tous*].
Is there anything in what I have just said that can be accepted by one
and all? Does "all" have a meaning?

We come upon the same opposition here as earlier. We will have
to realize the change that has occurred in logical necessity, and we
will be led to promote the function of axioms – namely, a certain
number of logical prefigurations considered to found a series, and,
moreover, to make that series depend on whether or not it agrees
with the axiom. The uncertainty of "all" will be called into question,
not simply because the unanimity of "all" is the most difficult thing
to obtain in practice, but because the logical translation of "all"
turns out to be quite precarious – assuming we are as demanding as
the theory of quantifiers in logic is.

272

Without going further into these points, which would take us far
afield with regard to what we need to investigate, I will ask how the
status of freedom of thought is expressed in the register of knowledge. Hegel's work constitutes a landmark here that is not simply
convenient but essential.

In the realm that interests us, Hegel extends the inaugural cogito.
Thought is revealed if we investigate the center of gravity of what is
qualified as *Selbstbewußtsein* [self-consciousness], which is nothing
other than "I know that I am thinking." But what Hegel adds to
Descartes is that something varies in "I know that I am thinking."
What varies is the point where I am. [According to Hegel], *that*
I don't know – I almost said "by definition." The illusion is that
"I am where I am thinking." Now, freedom of thought is nothing
other than that here. Forbidding me to think that "I am where I
want [something]," Hegel reveals that there isn't even the slightest
freedom of thought. It will take time, in the course of history, for
me, in the end, to think in the right place, in the place where I will
have become knowledge. But at that moment, there will be absolutely no further need to think.

I am giving myself over to a rather mad exercise here, for it is
obvious that none of this can mean much to those of you who have
never opened Hegel's work. Still I hope that there are enough of you
who are sufficiently familiar with the master/slave dialectic to recall

what happens to the master who has freedom – at least this is how Hegel defines the mythical master – when he formulates his mastery in language, which is something foreign to it. He perhaps then enters the world of thought, but it is assuredly also the moment at which he loses his freedom. It is the slave, qua base consciousness, who makes history. As he works, his thought is, in every era, subservient to the step forward he has to make in order to accede to the kind of state where what is realized? The domination of knowledge.

People's fascination with Hegel is almost impossible to undo. It is only people of bad faith who say that I have promoted Hegelianism within the Freudian debate. But don't imagine that I think we can be done with Hegel just like that. The notion that the truth of thought lies elsewhere than within itself, that it is at every moment necessitated by the subject's relation to knowledge, and that this knowledge itself is conditioned by a certain number of necessary stages, constitutes a grid whose applicability we cannot help but sense at every point in our experience. It takes on value as an exercise; it has exemplary value for training. We must truly make an effort of "dis-ordination" or true awakening if we are to wonder how there can be a delay that is such that I have to think in order to know, regardless of how little I know.

If we look more closely, we have to wonder. What does the articulation of actual knowledge have to do with the way in which I think about my freedom – in other words, "I am where I want [something]"?

Hegel clearly demonstrates that I cannot think that "I am where I want" [or: "I am wherever I want (to be)," *je suis là où je veux*], but it is no less obvious, if we look closely, that what is known as thought is that and that alone, such that "I am where I want" – which is the essence of freedom of thought as regards enunciation – is what no one can, strictly speaking, enunciate.

At that moment you see something – not in the *Encyclopedia*, but in the *Phenomenology of Spirit*, where the dialectic characteristic of thought is most vividly portrayed – which is that anything can happen in the absence of a history of knowledge. Throughout the *Phenomenology*, it is truth that allows us to point to what thought does not know about its function. Henceforth it is clear. From what point does Hegel detect it, if not from his knowledge, by which I mean the knowledge of his time, scientific knowledge such as Kant summarized it, on the basis of Newtonian knowledge? I will use a word for it for those in the know: he detects it on the basis of this ultimate-knowledge [*savoir-limite*] that marks the apogee and the end of theology.

The difference between Hegel and Freud is as follows:

273

Thought is no longer solely a question raised regarding the truth of [or: about, *du*] knowledge, which is already quite a lot, and the essential component of Hegel's step forward, but it also, Freud says, bars access to a certain knowledge. Need I recall what is at stake in the unconscious? Or how Freud conceptualized our first access to this knowledge? Hegel's *Selbstbewußtsein* is an "I know that I am thinking," whereas Freudian trauma is an "I don't know," which is itself unthinkable, since it presupposes an "I am thinking" that is stripped of all thought. The point of origin, not developmentally, but structurally, when it comes to understanding the unconscious, is the nodal point of a faltering knowledge. It is the point from which desire is born, in the form of what can thus be called the desire to know – on condition that we bracket the last two words, since we are talking about the structure of unconscious desire *tout court*.

274

Regarding the famous "He did not know he was dead" dream, I long ago indicated on the upper line of my graph "he did not know" as the calling into question of the enunciation made by the subject who is divided from the outset. This is what makes the dimension of desire into that of the Other's desire. It is because the Other's desire cannot be formulated in the traumatic fantasy that desire takes root in what can be called the desire to know, with "to know" in brackets.

We immediately come anew here upon the fundamental themes I have already emphasized. If the Other's desire is such that it is closed, it is because it is expressed in the fact, which is characteristic of the traumatic scene, that the body is perceived there as separate from jouissance. The function of the Other is incarnated here: the body qua perceived as separate from jouissance.

Freud's step forward concerning the function of thought with regard to *Selbstbewußtsein* is the following: he shows that the essence of "I know that I am thinking" is merely the overemphasis placed on "I know" in order to forget "I don't know," which is its real origin. The statement "I don't know" is already put in abeyance, so to say – yet I am not saying it – by the division it implies owing to the sole fact of the presence of negation. "I know that I am thinking" is designed to definitively veil "I don't know."

In Hegel's work, truth is the place where "that I am thinking" is really located. In Freud's work, truth designates the place from which "that I am thinking" is explained.

Let us note that, if we must take this quite rigorously, nothing can be said about this place that has any meaning. It is created by "this means nothing." It is the place where "this means nothing" orders [or: commands, *commande*] a replacement for "this means."

275   **3**

I'm not sure for how many of you this reminder of first truths can serve a purpose. For the others, I put a few keywords on the board [see Figure 17.1], which recall what I have already elucidated at length in a topology.

The little circle – drawn on the neck toward the bottom where the surface is supposed to loop back on itself [*rebrousser*] – is a reference to the Klein bottle because it gives us the possibility of a division in a surface topology. We can situate truth on one side and knowledge on the other. Note that, somewhere in this schema, there must be something that brings them together, which takes the form of a Möbius strip.

Truth here is the truth we investigate in the unconscious as knowledge's creative failing [*défaillance*] and the point of origin of the desire to know. This knowledge is doomed, in a sense, to never be anything but the correlate of this failing. That at least is what gives rise to the schema. But don't we need to investigate this further?

How can we define thought, not just the spontaneous thought of whoever tries to orient himself in the realities of life, but thought as such – in other words, as questioning itself regarding where a certain way of knowing really situates the subject, as Hegel asked? We might wonder whether all thought must not be essentially defined as censorship.

That, indeed, is what is implied by Freud's work. Owing to the fact that "I don't know" is radically forgotten, it is impossible to return to its place. "Thought [as] censorship" [*Pensée censure*], call it as you like. Play with the syllables and it becomes "censorible thoughtship" [*Censée pensure*].

Don't you get the sense that we see here one of the essential correlates of what is declared in our times to be the end of philosophy?

There is a structural objection to be made to this supposed end, which is that philosophy – or, better put, metaphysics – has never done anything but consider itself to be at its endpoint. You mustn't believe that to trot out Kierkegaard, Marx, or Nietzsche, as they say, suffices to take us very far beyond the limits of this frame. It is of interest only for continuing to investigate what is, in our times, let us note it all the same, most contested – even if people invoke [*s'arme*] it all the time – namely, freedom of thought.

276   Wherever people strive to accomplish something that truly seems to be to make knowledge dominate – I mean, where people work seriously, not where it is a free-for-all [*la foire*] – they don't have freedom of thought. The fact remains that students in Prague are striking to get it. What does this mean?

My whole discourse is devoted to getting psychoanalysis to perhaps contribute a first sketch of a reflection here.

In analysis we proceed by getting the subject to speak in a way defined by free association, which means without a link to the Other. When you speak in analysis, it means that you have been freed from all rules. What can that lead to, good God?

Such an exercise cannot even give rise to an aesthetically pleasing text. When the surrealists wanted to proceed on the basis of free association ["automatic writing"], you can bet they nevertheless ended up relying heavily on scissors in order to create something that we will talk about again later: works of art. The fact that people can manage to make them in that way is already highly indicative, but altogether impermeable to anyone who has no idea of object a. But we are not talking about object a today.

Such an exercise [free association] usually can only arrive at something profoundly inadequate from a logical vantage point. This is, in reality, what Freud means when he says that the unconscious knows nothing about the principle of non-contradiction. The principle of non-contradiction is, in logic, something that is incredibly elaborate and that can be done without even in logic, because a whole type of formal logic in the field of knowledge can be constructed that makes no use of negation.

Nevertheless, if we can employ a discourse that is free of logic, it is certainly not, for all that, free of grammar. Which means that there must be something in grammar that is replete with properties and consequences. A fantasy is expressed in nothing better than a sentence whose sole meaning is grammatical, which, at least in the play and formation of the fantasy, is only activated grammatically – for example, "A child is being beaten." If something can occur around this sentence, it is insofar as something is not censored there and cannot be censored there except on the basis of [or: from, *de la*] grammatical structure – the agent, for example.

The neuroses therefore reveal the distinction between grammar and logic. We should take a further step to discover, as I am endeavoring to do, a homology [between them].

This homology is not obvious, the neuroses not revealing it immediately. It is only by having studied a bit of logic that we can know, for example, that the consistency of one of the most well-assured systems – namely, arithmetic – depends on localizing something undecidable. It took a proper logic, which is no more than a century old, to demonstrate this, and it brought out a certain number of flaws [or: gaps] therein.

There is a homology between the flaws in logic and those in the structure of desire – namely, [1] that desire, in the final analysis,

277

connotes knowledge of relations between men and women via
something that is very surprising: the lack or non-lack of an *organon*
or instrument, in other words, the phallus; [2] that jouissance of
the instrument blocks the jouissance that is the Other's jouissance
insofar as that Other is represented by a body; and [3], in short (as I
think I have said forcefully enough), that there is nothing that takes
the form of a sexual act that can, strictly speaking, be structured. If
all of that is correctly demonstrated, it is conceivable that the circle
[in the schema of the Klein bottle] closes and that this something
joins truth back up with knowledge from behind.

Thought is, in fact, the *Vorstellungsrepräsentanz* that represents
the fact that there is something unrepresentable, because it is barred
[*barré*] by the prohibition of jouissance. At what level? At the simplest level: the organic level. The pleasure principle is nothing but
this barrier to jouissance. The fact that this barrier is metaphorized
in the prohibition of [access to] the mother is, after all, merely a
historical contingency, and the Oedipus complex itself is simply
appended to that.

But the question runs deeper. Castration – namely, the hole
in apprehension or the "I don't know" regarding the Other's
jouissance – must be reconceptualized from the perspective of its
relationship to the widespread, omnipresent effects of our science.

There is clearly a relationship between these two points that seem
to be very far apart. It is, on the one hand, this barring [or: barrier,
barrage] which makes it such that something we talk about all the
time, sex – far from solving anything whatsoever in the erotic field –
gets ever more obscure and signals ever more the inadequacy of our
signposts. At issue, on the other hand, are the widespread effects
of our knowledge – in other words, the prodigious eruption of the
relationship to object *a*, our mass media merely turning it back on
itself [or: being the twist (or the fallout) thereof, *le retour*], rendering
it present.

Doesn't this, in and of itself, indicate the status of freedom of
thought?

278   Let us assume that its structure is in fact that of a Klein bottle,
and that its limit is in fact the locus of the twist [*retournement*] where
the front side becomes the backside and vice versa. It suffices to
think that the limit that apparently separates truth from knowledge
is not fixed and that, by its very nature, it is everywhere, for a question to arise: how to act in such a way that the division between
truth and knowledge is not attached, in a purely imaginary way, to
a fixed point?

By not having even begun to raise the problem, psychoanalysts
demonstrate that they are absolutely unable to leave behind a

certain stasis regarding this limit. No treatment of neurosis that is limited to the exhaustion of the subject's identifications – in other words, that by which he has reduced himself to the Other – can promise to resolve what constitutes a knot for the neurotic.

I won't say what constitutes a knot for the neurotic today because I would be obliged to lay it out too quickly. But I will say that, owing to the nature of the neurotic, which is quite profoundly the fact that we ask [*demande*] him where he is at with regard to his desire, we can wonder whether analysts are not unwittingly complicit here in sustaining the very foundation of the neurotic's structure – in other words, the fact that his desire can only be sustained by [this] question [or: questioning, *demande*].

If we can say that psychoanalysis consists in the break with hypnosis, it is perhaps for a very surprising reason if we consider it, which is that in psychoanalysis, at least in the form in which it is currently stagnating, it is the analyst who is hypnotized. In the end, the analyst ends up becoming the gaze and voice of his patient. That is very different from what is presented – owing to an illusion at the level of thought – as reliance on clinical experience. Endeavoring to ensure that this switch does not occur perhaps does not constitute an attempt to free oneself from clinical experience.

I am merely indicating pathways that we will explore in future classes.

I would like to make a final remark before stopping today. If I have limited myself in my life to commenting on my experience and to questioning it in relation to Freud's doctrine, it is precisely with the aim of not being a thinker, but of questioning an already constituted thought, Freud's, while taking into account what determines it – namely, what, to speak like Hegel, does or does not constitute its truth.

April 23, 1969

XVIII

INSIDE OUTSIDE

Analysis of idealism
Optics and representation
Spot, lack, and camera obscura
The object restored to the Other
Hommelle and *famil*

Those of you who happen to be philosophers perhaps glimpse that I have been returning here to a topic that is a bit out of date owing to weariness, rather than because it has received an actual solution. I am referring to the terms "idealism" and "realism."

1

Idealism can easily be gauged [*cuber*]. We need but look at what has been written about it by those who have expounded it.

I will rely on the fact that, up to a certain point, it has not been refuted. It has not been refuted philosophically, but rather by common sense, which is realist, of course, realist in relation to the terms with which idealism raises the question – namely, if we listen to it carefully, that we can only know reality [*réel*] through our representations of it. The idealist position – which, if we begin from a certain schema, is irrefutable – can nevertheless be refuted assuming we do not take representation to be a pure and simple reflection of reality.

It is noteworthy that idealism has been decisively critiqued by philosophers themselves. What was initially promoted in the mythology of representation was displaced onto another mythology, one that calls into question, not representation, but the function of thought qua ideology. Idealism only holds up insofar as it confuses the intellectual order with that of representation. As you can see, this can be very simply articulated.

One can believe oneself to be a realist when one takes thought to be something that is dependent on what, in this case, is called reality [*réel*]. But does that suffice? Even within the mythology – that's what I call it – of ideology as depending on a certain number of conditions (namely, the social conditions of production), is it a realist position to refer to a reality that cannot be fully apprehended as such, owing to the fact that thought is always dependent on it – all the more so in that we believe that we are equal to the task of transforming this reality?

These are sweeping reflections. What I would like to point out is that this reality – about which we must consider our knowledge to be progressing, since this is the meaning of the so-called critique of ideology – is part and parcel of a subversion that we bring to reality. The question then is whether this knowledge that is progressing is already located somewhere or not. This is the question I raised with the term "subject-supposed-to-know."

Science's step forward consisted in excluding what is mystical in the idea of knowledge [*connaissance*] – that is, in giving up on experiential knowledge [*connaissance*] – and constituting instead a formulated knowledge [*savoir*]. The latter is an apparatus that develops on the basis of the radical presupposition that what we are dealing with are nothing other than apparatuses used by the subject. Science's step forward involves, moreover, the notion that the subject can be purified as such, to the point of no longer being anything but the prop of what is articulated as knowledge [*savoir*] organized in a certain discourse, a discourse that has nothing to do with *opinion* [i.e., *doxa*] and that is distinguished therefrom as being scientific. Even when this step is taken and understood, a presupposition and even a bias remains that is all the less critiqued as it is not perceived, and no serious question has been raised about its implications which, in spite of ourselves, persist.

This bias is as follows. In discovering knowledge, we conceptualize it – whether we like it or not, for it is endemic to thought – as already organized somewhere. Must we believe this is the case? As long as the consequences of a radical bracketing of the subject-supposed-to-know are not tested, we remain mired in idealism, and in its most backward form, the one that is, in the final analysis, unshakable in a certain structure known, in a word, as theology.

The subject-supposed-to-know is God, and that's the end of the story. One can be a genius – and yet not an obscurantist, to the best of my knowledge – in short, one can be Einstein and explicitly resort to God. God must be supposed to already know, since Einstein – arguing against a restructuring of science on the basis of probability theory – claims that the knowledge presupposed by what he articulates in his theory is corroborated by something that is consistent with what is clearly a presupposition regarding the subject he, employing the traditional term, calls God. This good old God is perhaps difficult to fathom with regard to the world order he sustains, but he is not a liar or disloyal, nor does he change the rules in the middle of the game. The rules of the game already exist somewhere; they are instituted owing to the simple fact that knowledge already exists in God. He is the one who presides over the deciphering known as knowledge [*savoir*].

True atheism – the only atheism that deserves the name – is the atheism that results from calling the subject-supposed-to-know into question. It is not clear that it is possible for thought to face this question, or even if formulating it constitutes any sort of step in this direction.

This is certainly not to say that it isn't a step that preoccupies me essentially, because what I have to articulate – namely, psychoanalysis – is of a piece with it. Yet I can but convey first what I must require of analysts – namely, that they at least have a discourse that is up-to-date regarding what they actually provide: analytic treatment or experience – call it as you like – it's all the same. Indeed, their thinking is so far behind the times in this regard that it is easy to get them to realize that they account for what subjects do in treatment in terms that involve such elementary biases that they constitute a true degradation of what critical thought has been able to reach at certain turning points.

Don't think for a minute that this is harmless. It has multiple consequences that run the gamut from, first, reinforcing in analysts everything that Freud says constitutes intellectual resistance, to distorting their modes of intervention which, in the end, merely reinforce the same biases in the subject – more or less rightly said to be (a) patient, for he is braided [*tressé*] in the very act of psychoanalytic experience.

To indicate what is at stake – and it is truly blatant – I will center it around the terms inside and outside.

The fact that these terms are present right from the outset in Freud's work doesn't mean that we shouldn't investigate them as stringently as possible [see SE XIV, p. 119]. For if we don't, we risk producing the kinds of deviations that stop us from perceiving what in analytic experience feeds the belief in the subject-supposed-to-know, or at least converges on it. As long as the "subject-supposed-to-know-before-we-know" is not seriously called into question, we can say that our entire approach will remain bogged down in a form of resistance, in a mindset that does not detach from it, since a flawed conception of the ground on which we raise questions inevitably induces distortion at the theoretical level.

When we consider the use analysts make all the time – not simply day after day, but every minute – of the terms "projection" and "introjection," how can these terms not have, if they are not correctly critiqued, an inhibiting effect on analysts' own thinking, and, worse still, a suggestive effect in their interpretations, in a way which – it is not excessive to say so – can only be cretinizing.

An inside and an outside seem self-evident if we consider an organism – namely, an individual that, in fact, truly exists. The inside is what is within its skin. The outside is everything else. To conclude that what he imagines [se représente] about the outside must also be inside his skin seems, at first glance, to be a modest, self-evident step to take. This is precisely what Bishop Berkeley bases his claims on. Regarding what is outside, you know, after all, only what is in your own head. Consequently, it will, in any case, always be a representation. Whatever you say about the world, I can always comment that it is based on how you picture it [vous vous le représenter]. It is truly odd that, at a certain moment in history, such an image was able to prevail to so great an extent that a discourse – that could not in fact be refuted, at least in a certain context – could rely on it: that of a representation designed to sustain this idea of representation. The secret core of what is known as idealism consists, in the final analysis, in the representation that gives such an advantage to representation.

It is certainly striking that by simply broaching it as I am, the veil, so to speak, begins to quiver. If it is so simple, people say to themselves, how could people have even dwelt on it? To foster this quivering, we must now show how this mirage-like representation is constructed, and I will do so – in other words, I will imagine it for you. Nothing could be simpler.   283

We need not even resort to Aristotle's little treatise On Sense [and the Sensible], which is a rather striking text, all the same, to perceive that – given the way in which he approaches the eye and the way he intends to account for vision – he does not have at his disposal something that is second nature to us, namely, the most elementary optical apparatus, the camera obscura.

Let me take the opportunity to say how advantageous it would be if someone would do a study on optics in Ancient science. That science went very far, much further than people think, in all sorts of areas related to mechanics, but it seems clear that, as regards optics strictly speaking, it had a remarkable blind spot. The model that marked the era of representation in which the core of idealism crystallized is as simple as anything. It is that of the camera obscura

– namely, a closed unlit space, in which a little hole opens out onto the world outside. If there is light in the outside world, its image appears and moves on the inside wall of the camera obscura as a function of what happens outside.

It is extremely striking to see what was articulated at a certain moment in science by the finest of minds, that of Isaac Newton, who, as you know, broke as much ground in optics as in gravitation. It is no accident that, at the time, he was, let me remind you, said by his contemporaries to be equal to God's designs, which he was able to decipher. I am saying this to confirm the remark that I made earlier regarding the theological envelope surrounding the first steps of our science.

Optics is essential to imagining the subject as something that is on the inside. One might even claim that the function of the subject is modeled on the camera obscura.

It is quite astonishing that it seemed to be accepted that it is of no importance where we locate the little hole on which the site of the image depends. Wherever it is placed, an image will be produced across from it in the camera obscura. It is only from the side in which the little hole is located that we see the world – that is, what is outside, and what is no longer anything but an image since it is translated as a mere image inside. This apparatus seems to imply that anything outside, in a space that nothing limits, can in theory come to occupy a place inside the room. It is nevertheless clear that, if we make multiple holes, there will no longer be any image at all.

I won't dwell on this topic for very long, for that is not what is most germane for us. I will confine myself to remarking that it is there and there alone that a notion – the notion that what concerns the psyche must be situated on the inside of something that is limited by a surface – finds support.

A surface? Of course, we are told, Freud already talked about a surface turned toward the outside, and we thus localize the subject on that surface. The subject is, as they say, defenseless against what is inside. As representations cannot be placed elsewhere, we put them there, and we put everything else there, too – namely, what are known, variously and confusedly, as affects, instincts, and drives. All of that is situated on the inside.

But why are we so concerned with knowing the relationship between a reality and its locus, whether inside or outside? We would do well to first investigate what it becomes qua reality.

We should perhaps begin to detach ourselves from the fascinating fact that we cannot imagine a living being's representation [or: thinking] being anywhere except inside its body.

2

Let us leave that fascination behind for a moment and ask ourselves what happens regarding the inside and the outside when what is at issue is, for example, a commodity.

We have heard often enough about the nature of commodities to know that we must distinguish between their use value and their exchange value. We tell ourselves that exchange value is obviously what happens outside. But let us put our commodity in a warehouse. The latter, too, must exist. A warehouse is an inside – it is where we keep and store the commodity. When casks of oil are outside of the warehouse, they are exchanged and then they are consumed: use value. It is rather odd that it is when they are inside that they are reduced to their exchange value. In a warehouse, by definition, we don't destroy or consume them, but rather preserve them. Use value is prohibited on the inside, where we would expect it, and the only thing that subsists there is exchange value.

What is most enigmatic is when we are no longer talking about commodities but rather about the fetish of fetishes: money. In that case, what value does this thing – which has no use value, but only exchange value – have when it is in a safe? It is quite obvious that people put it there and keep it there. What is this inside that seems to render completely enigmatic what is locked away there? Isn't it – in its own way, with respect to what constitutes the essence of money – an inside that is altogether outside, outside of what constitutes the essence of money?

I am making these remarks merely in order to broach the status of thought.

Thought, too, has some connection with exchange value. In other words, it circulates. To those who have not yet understood that a thought can only be conceptualized, strictly speaking, by being articulated, by being inscribed in language, and by being able to be sustained under conditions of what is known as the dialectic – which means a certain play of logic, with rules – these simple remarks should suffice to raise a question, like the one I raised a moment ago regarding money placed in a safe: What does it mean when we keep a thought to ourselves? If we do not know what it is when we keep it to ourselves, its essence must thus lie elsewhere – in other words, already outside, without us having to engage in projection to say that the thought wanders about out there.

Otherwise stated, we should realize something which was not immediately apparent to everyone. However convincing Berkeley's argument may be, it is certainly possible that what constitutes its strength is an intuition based on a model that suggests that representations can only be on the inside. But the fact that we allow ourselves to be duped by yet another image – and especially an image that depends on a certain state of technology – is not what is important here. What is important is that the argument in question is in fact irrefutable. In order for idealism to hold up, there must be, not only Bishop Berkeley, but a few other people with whom he can have a debate about whether we have an apprehension of the world that merely defines the philosophical limits of idealism. It is to the degree to which, in discourse, we can't get out of it, we have nothing to retort, that it is irrefutable.

Regarding the topic of idealism/realism, there are obviously those who are right and those who are wrong. Those who are right are in reality [*dans le réel*]; I am speaking from the standpoint of realists [see R in Figure 18.1]. Where are those who are wrong? They, too, have to be located on the schema. What is important is that – at the level of the debate, of the articulable discussion, at the point at which the philosophical discussion had arrived at that time – Berkeley was right, even though it is obvious that he is wrong.

Figure 18.1: From Berkeley to Object *a*

This is what I will refer to as Berkeley's schema. It is based on the principle of the camera obscura, represented by the circle. Inside I have placed the subject of representation [S_r]. Reality [*réel*] is distinguished from it by simply being outside, as if it were self-evident that everything that is outside of it is real. This demonstrates that this first sketch of the field of objectivity is false. If this is true, must we then provide a different sketch of it? And how can we do so? What happens to the inside and the outside?

We are clearly forced to redraw the schema, for we find ourselves at the limit or midpoint [*médium*] between the symbolic and the imaginary, and because our cogitations require at least some intuitive prop. But doesn't that mean that we must radically abandon the terms projection and introjection in psychoanalytic intervention, terms that we use constantly without providing the slightest critique of Berkeley's schema?

Another probably very unfortunate apprehension of things involves failing to distinguish, in everything that is constructed outside, different orders of reality. To realize this it suffices to raise

286

the question of what this edifice owes to an order that is not necessarily reality at all, since it is our own fabrication. This is what we
should investigate, since we must intervene in the field of something
that is known as the unconscious, which is not at all – as opposed
to what people say – a field of elemental, organic, carnal facts or
biological stirrings, but which is articulable, since it is intellectual in
nature, even if it is inescapably articulated in words.

The radical nature of what is at the basis, not of what I am teaching, but of what I need but recognize in our everyday practice and in
Freud's work, raises a question about the status of the inside and the
outside, and about the way we should conceptualize what must correspond to those facts that are always so awkwardly handled using
the terms introjection and projection.

Things go so far that, when Freud initially defines the ego, he
himself dares to articulate things by saying that, starting from a
certain state of confusion with the world, the psyche separates into
an inside and outside. Yet nothing in his discourse indicates whether
this outside is identifiable with the indeterminate space that it is identified with in the everyday view of it, or whether this inside is the same
as something that we now consider to establish a requirement of the
organism, all of whose components we are going to look for inside.

3

We can already take an additional step forward by demonstrating
what is unthinkable about the schema of the camera obscura.

We need but return to Aristotle to realize that, owing to the fact
that he does not refer to a camera obscura, the questions that arise
for him are completely different from those that arise for us, and
that his conception renders unthinkable, strictly speaking, any conception of the nervous system, for example.

Read the first few chapters of the little treatise entitled *On Sense
[and the Sensible]*, for the text is quite provocative. It already touches
on the question, which led to so many subsequent discussions,
whether there is something in vision that opens out onto reflection. Paul Valéry's "seeing oneself see oneself" [*Monsieur Teste*, in
Œuvres (Paris: Gallimard, 1960 [1896]); and *La jeune Parque* (Paris:
Gallimard, 1917)] is broached by Aristotle, and in the funniest way
imaginable, via the fact that, when you push on an eye, phosphenes
result – in other words, something that resembles light [437a–b]. It
is for that reason alone that he feels we can state that the eye that
sees also sees itself, in some sense, since it produces light when we
press on it.

Many other things in his treatise are provocative – for example, the formulations he arrives at that make the translucent dimension of things essential when accounting for the fact that the eye sees, on the basis of one thing and one thing alone: it represents an especially well-suited apparatus in the translucent realm. It is not the case that what we have here is something that in any way resembles an inside and an outside, but rather that the eye sees because it shares in a quality that I would call visionary. Which is not all that dumb. We have here a certain way of thrusting the subject into the world. The question has undoubtedly become a bit different for us.

The thousand other theories stated at his time, which Aristotle had to argue against, all in some way involved something that we have no trouble finding anew in our images, including that of projection. For, I ask you, what does the term projection presuppose when it involves, no longer what is seen [or: what sees itself, *ce qui se voit*] but the imaginary, a certain affective configuration with which we assume that our patients modify the world at certain moments? What is this type of projection if not the assumption that the light beam that illuminates the world comes from inside – just as, in Antiquity, certain people imagined rays that radiated out from the eye to light up the world and objects, however enigmatic this shining vision was? Our metaphors suggest that we might still be at that point.

What is not the least marvelous about this text by Aristotle is the fact that it allows us to put our finger on, not so much what he himself establishes, as on all those he refers to – Empedocles, for example, who claims that eyes have something in common with fire, to which Aristotle retorts by appealing to a different element, water [438a–b]. Let me incidentally indicate that it bothers him that there are only four elements. As he explicitly says, there are five senses and it thus seems hard to correlate them. He finesses things by unifying taste and touch, since they are both related to earth [438b–439a]. But enough joking.

289 There is nothing especially funny about these things in and of themselves. Yet, they are exemplary. If we read the texts, which, however superficial they may seem to us, were not written by stupid people, to simply immerse ourselves, as it were, in what animates them, we see something that localizes the field of vision for us, assuming we have reanimated it, so to speak, owing to what we have placed in it by inserting it into desire via perversion. Otherwise stated, the mainspring of the function of object *a* in the visual field is suggested to us there, assuming we have already practiced using it to some degree.

Figure 18.2: Object *a* between Outside (Other) and Inside (Subject)

In the visual field, object *a* is related, with respect to objective structure, to the function of a third term, and it is striking that Ancient thinkers literally did not know what to do with it. They miss it, and yet it is the biggest thing going. They, too, find themselves caught between two things: sensation – in other words, the subject – and the world that is sensed. They have to rouse themselves, as it were, in order to introduce light as a third term – the light source, quite simply – insofar as its rays reflect off objects and form an image for us inside the camera obscura.

Then what? After that we have this marvelous nonsense about the synthesis carried out by consciousness, which is located somewhere, and, it seems, particularly conceivable, owing solely to the fact that we can situate it in folds of the brain. Why would an image suddenly become synthetic because it is in a brain rather than on a retina? The concept of object *a* is sufficiently suggested by the hesitant steps that were taken throughout the tradition, which show that Ancient thinkers quite clearly realized that the solution to the problem of vision was not simply light. Light is a precondition, of course. In order for us to see something, it must be light out. But how does that explain the fact that we see?

Object *a* in the scoptophilic field, if we try to translate it at the level of esthesia [sensitiveness], is quite precisely a blank or black spot, as you like, something that is missing behind the image, so to speak, and which, by a purely logomachic effect of synthesis, we situate so easily somewhere in a brain. It is quite precisely insofar as something is missing in what presents itself as an image that we find the mainspring for which there is only one solution: object *a* – in other words, precisely qua lack and, if you will, qua spot [*tache*].

By definition, a spot is something that presents itself in the field as a hole or absence. We know from zoology that, in lamellar beings, the little optical apparatus – which is so well constructed and fills us with such wonder – known as an eye first takes the form of a spot [*tache*]. Do we consider it to be purely and simply an effect? Light produces spots, that's clear enough. But we are no longer at that stage. Ancient thinkers could not do otherwise than situate spots as essential and structuring in all vision, than situate them as the place of lack, as the place of the third term in the field rendered objective, or in the place of light, and that was their blunder. But it is not a blunder if we realize that this metaphorical effect – the effect of the metaphor of a point negated in the field of vision – must not be chalked up to a deployment that is more or less illusory. It is, instead, something that ties a subject to this field, a subject whose knowledge is entirely determined by a more radical and essential lack that concerns him qua sexual being. This is what shows how the field of vision is inserted into desire.

Why, after all, can't we admit the following: that all of what makes it such that there is viewing or contemplation, visual relations that interest speaking beings, is connected to and finds its root solely at the level of what, because it is a spot in the field, can serve to plug up lack, completely articulated lack, lack that is articulated qua lack – namely, the only term thanks to which speaking beings can situate themselves as belonging to one sex or another.

It is at the level of object *a* that we can conceptualize the articulable division of the subject into a subject who is wrong because he is right – that's Bishop Berkeley for you – and another subject who, doubting that thought is worth anything, in reality proves that thought is in and of itself censorship. It is important to situate the gaze qua subjective, because it does not see. This is what renders thinkable the fact that thought itself is based on the following and on the following alone: that it is censorship. We can thereby metaphorically articulate thought itself as constituting a spot in logical discourse.

291

4

After this rather long discussion, there is still something that I want to say today. At least I will try to broach it.

I arrived at the point of talking about perversion as based on another way of inscribing the outside. This outside is not an infinitely open space [or: space opening onto infinity, *espace ouvert à l'infini*] to us where we situate just any old thing called reality. The outside we deal with is the Other and it has its own status.

It is certainly not owing to the effort of psychoanalysts alone that we can currently explore its status on the basis of a purely logical investigation and articulate it as lacking [*marqué d'une faille*]. On the graph of desire, the sign S(Ⱥ) – which represents the response given by the Other with a capital *O* at the end of what is posited in desiring enunciation – is quite precisely the gap [or: defect or flaw, *faille*] represented by desire.

It is no accident that the terms here are manifested by little letters – that is, by an algebra. The very nature of an algebra is to allow for multiple interpretations. S(Ⱥ) can mean all sorts of things, even the death of the father. But at a radical level, that of the logicization of our experience, S(Ⱥ) is precisely what is known as structure, assuming that it is located somewhere and fully articulable.

If my discourse can be characterized as structuralist – despite the reservations you know I have about such philosophical labels – it is because it demonstrates the relationship that exists between what permits us to establish a rigorous logic and, on the other hand, certain irreducible defects [*défauts*] in articulation we see in the unconscious, from which the very effort attested to by the desire to know proceeds.

As I told you, what I define as perversion is the returning, in some primary sense, or restoring of *a* to the field of A. This is rendered possible by the fact that *a* is an effect of seizing [*prise*] something primitive or primordial. Why wouldn't we admit it, on the condition that we not turn it into a subject? It is to the degree to which the animal being I mentioned earlier, with regard to its skin, is caught up [*pris*] in language that something in him is turned into *a*, the *a* that is returned to the Other, as it were. This is why, when I mentioned perverts the other day, I ironically compared them to men of faith, and even to crusaders. Perverts give God his true plenitude.

292

Perversion is the structure of the subject in whom the reference to castration – namely, the fact that women are distinguished by the fact that they do not have phalluses – is plugged up, masked, or filled in by the mysterious operation of object *a*. Perversion is a way of warding off the radical gap in the signifying order that castration represents. The basis and principle of perverse structure is to ward it off by supplying this Other, insofar as it is asexual, with something that plugs up its lack of a phallus. If you will allow me to end today with a couple of plays on words, I will return to a formulation I proffered here once before. Didn't I already designate the pervert's Other with the term *hommelle* [*homme* means man and *elle* means she; hence "she-man"]?

It sounds picturesque, but it merely sounds that way, and it will help you get your bearings regarding the outside with respect to the play of the unconscious.

As usual, I was not able to go as far as I had hoped, but before leaving you today, I nevertheless want to point to a path that leads from perversion to phobia, where I see the intermediary step that will finally allow us to authentically situate neurotics and the status of the inside and the outside for them.

Why not write *hommelle* by modifying S(Ⱥ), in the sense that here it is on the basis of an A without any gap [or: without any failing or flaw, *non défaillant*] that we have the signifier capital S? S(A) provides the key to perversion. Isn't it, conversely, at the level of the signified of the gap that the division of A is found in neurotics? Namely $s(Å)$, the signified of the barred Other.

This is of great topological interest and it also shows that it is at the level of the enunciated that the text of the neurotic symptom is articulated. This explains why it is between the field of the ego – such as it is specularly organized – and that of desire, insofar as it is articulated with respect to the field dominated by object a, that the neurotic's fate is played out.

293

We will see this better next time. Using the old graph of desire, I will be able to show you the place that $s(Å)$ occupies in the neurotic's game. I will take it up as regards phobia first, returning to something I already articulated regarding little Hans [Seminar IV] but which was, I noticed, insufficiently conveyed in the accounts of that seminar.

To posit that the signified of A qua barred, marked by its logical failing [*défaillance*], comes to be fully signified in the neurotic, clarifies for us what is inaugural in the neurotic's experience. The neurotic does not mask the conflictual articulation at the level of logic itself. The fact that thought fails [*défaille*] in its very locus as a game with rules, gives its true import to the distance that the neurotic himself takes from this in his experience.

In order to end on another of my plays on words, which the current state of our language allows, why not play with the word *hommelle*, and transform it at the lower level [of the graph] into *famil* [*fam* sounds like *femme*, woman, and *il* means he; hence "he-woman"]? Doesn't this *famil* seem to make the metaphorical function of the family itself flash before our eyes?

If what the pervert needs is an uncastrated woman – or more exactly, he makes her uncastrated and *homme-elle* – can't the *fam-il* be seen at the horizon of the neurotic's field: this something which is a "He" somewhere, but whose "I" is truly the stakes of what is at issue in the family drama?

It is object a qua liberated. The neurotic is the one who poses all the problems of identification. He is the one we must, at the level of neurosis, deal with in order for the structure of what we must resolve to be revealed – namely, the signifier of barred A, structure *tout court*.

April 30, 1969

XIX

KNOWLEDGE AND POWER

The disjunction between knowledge and power
From One to 1
Object *a* appears when we count
A takes the form of *a*
Anacliticism revisited
Phobia as a central hub

Anxiety, as I said once upon a time, is *not without* an object. What did "not without" mean in that formulation?

It simply meant that, corresponding to anxiety, there is something that is analogous to what is said to be objective on the basis of a certain conception of the subject. "Not without" does not designate a specific thing that is analogous to the object, which anxiety, according to psychoanalysis, signals in the subject; it simply reveals that the thing is not lacking. It thus presupposes the fact of lack [or: lack as a fact].

Now, as I highlighted at the time, as soon as we mention lack, we presume that a symbolic order has already been established.

1

What is a symbolic order? It is more than just a law, it is also an accumulation [of things that are], moreover, numbered. It entails things being in their place [or: It is an order(ing), *C'est un rangement*].

If we define the real as the abolition at the level of thought [or: thought-out abolition, *l'abolition pensée*] of symbolic material, it can never lack for anything. An animal that dies owing to a whole series of perfectly adaptive physiological effects – that we cannot in any way call hunger, for example, [even if] it spells the end of the organism qua soma – is lacking in nothing. It has enough resources in its territory to measure [or: pace (or defer), *mesurer*] its so-called mortal decline. A cadaver is also something real.

What forces us to conceptualize the imaginary is the effects by which an organism subsists, since something must indicate to it that such and such an element outside of itself – in the environment, in the *Umwelt* as they say – can be absorbed by it, or, more generally, help it stay alive. This means that the *Umwelt* is no more than a sort of halo or double of the organism. That's what we call the imaginary.

A whole facet of the *Umwelt* can, of course, be described in terms of correspondence [between the organism and its environment], without which the organism could not survive for even an instant. The category of the imaginary undoubtedly implies, in and of itself, that the *Umwelt* can fail, but its failure still does not imply that anything is lacking. It is the beginning of a series of effects by which the organism wastes away, as I said earlier, taking its *Umwelt* with it. It dies along with its mirage, which may very well be what we call – although we don't know why we do so – the epiphenomenon of the aforementioned hunger.

Up until that point, everything thus boils down to various levels of the structuring of reality. In order for lack to appear, it must be said that "something is missing" [*il n'y a pas le compte*]. In order for something to be missing, there must be things that are counted [*compté*]. From the moment that there are things that are counted, what is counted has effects on the order of images. These are the first steps of *épistémé* or science. The first "copulations" of the act of counting with images is the recognition of a certain number of harmonies, musical harmonies, for example, which serve as a model for all harmonies.

It is here that we can observe lacks that have nothing to do with what, in harmony, are simply considered to be intervals. There are places where something is missing. All of so-called Ancient science consisted in betting that the places where something was missing would be reduced someday, in the eyes of the sage, to constitutive intervals of a kind of musical harmony. We must establish an order of the Other thanks to which reality acquires the status of a world or cosmos that implies this harmony.

This was done as soon as there were in the world – in this world of adventures and concrete events said to be historical – emporiums and storehouses where everything has its place [*rangé*]. Emporiums and empires – which have existed for quite some time, we are not the ones who invented them – are the same thing. And they run parallel to and prop up the conception of Ancient science that is, in short, based on the following, which was accepted for a long time, that knowledge and power are the same thing.

He who knows how to count can divide up and distribute; and he who distributes is, by definition, fair. All empires are fair.

If doubt has been raised about this recently, there must be some reason for it. Our times attest to the horizon of what has occurred, owing to something the sages of old didn't want to admit is no longer a prodrome at all, but a blatant rip – namely, that discordance has broken out between knowledge and power.

What excuses the fact that I continue to open these lectures to the general public, despite the fact that they are addressed in theory to psychoanalysts alone, is quite simply the following. In order that things not drag on discordantly for too long, with everything discordance brings with it by way of strange mumblings, repetitions, and absurd collisions, we must name this disjunction, define in what respect it operates, and not think we are going to fend it off with some sort of momentary power inversion – by saying, for example, that everything will work out because those who were oppressed up until now will start exercising power themselves. I don't, of course, personally rule out the possibility of it happening, but it seems clear to me that such an inversion will not make any sense either unless it is inscribed in what I just called the essential turning point, the only one that changed the meaning of everything that was organized qua supposed empire, even if it was that of knowledge itself – namely, the disjunction between knowledge and power.

This formulation is somewhat crude. It does not lead to any *Weltanschauung*, strictly speaking, or to any presumption, whether utopian or not, regarding a change brought on by we know not what. But it must be articulated, and it can be articulated, on the basis of Freud's work. Freud obviously doesn't provide an updated take on things in the form of a system that could, in any way at all, be compared to that of those who wanted to make the myth of the conjunction of knowledge and power last. Freud himself appears here, far more, as a patient. Through his speech, which is that of a patient, he attests to what I am calling the disjunction between knowledge and power.

He was not the only one who attested to it; others attested to it as well, each in his own way. But he read it and noted its effects in symptoms that are produced at a certain subjective level, and tried to treat them. This is precisely where we see that he himself was the patient of this effort, work, and discourse.

I myself am nothing but the consequence of his discourse. In my discourse, I attest to what experience of this disjunction leads to – in other words, to nothing that, according to all appearances, fills it in or allows us to hope to ever reduce it to a norm or cosmos. That is the meaning of what I am endeavoring to do here in a discourse that Freud inaugurated.

This is why I began with a close reading of what is attested to by his discourse, and not only insofar as it demonstrates mastery, for its inadequacies are what are most instructive.

In looking back at the Seminar I gave in 1956/57, I was able to gauge something about the distance covered in the thirteen intervening years – by whom, by what? By my discourse, on the one hand, and also by the obvious manifestations of the laceration that this discourse designates.

Naturally, this growing obviousness owes nothing to my discourse, but it attests to the fact that there is a discourse, which is certainly not up-to-date, but not too far, we might say, behind the times.

That said, this discourse is obliged, not merely to lag behind, but to continually make fundamental adjustments *nachträglich*, after the fact, *après coup*. This is because, given the failure of the laws that regulate the status of the University, nothing includes it in an updating of the forms of transmission whereby what is at stake in the major advances in knowledge made in recent years can subsist, such that it shows itself to be intrinsically distinct from any effect of power.

We will thus return to fundamentals.

2

The term that I highlighted in my 1956/57 Seminar, when I was focusing on the case of little Hans and trying to decipher it, could not have been that of object *a*.

Were that Seminar now to be published in extenso – going beyond the summary of it that came out in the *Bulletin de psychologie* entitled "The Object Relation and Freudian Structures," which wasn't all that bad, by the way – the reader could check what I said, for more than a trimester, in Freud's work. His text ["Analysis of a Phobia in a Five-Year-Old Boy," SE X, pp. 5–149] is incredibly confusing owing to its labyrinthine appearance, and we see in it a sort of bumbling attempt on his part to spell something out. Freud goes around in circles. And, in truth, what is the outcome, apart from the fact that little Hans is no longer afraid of horses? So what? Was the whole point of such a study to ensure that one boy, or even a thousand little boys, be freed from something embarrassing known as a phobia? Experience proves that phobias don't take much longer to heal spontaneously than through an investigation of the kind that was carried out in this case by Hans' father, who was a student of Freud's, and by Freud himself.

At the time, 13 years ago, I thus had to emphasize, spell out, and study the true stakes, which went well beyond the case – namely, what was being played out at every moment at the edge or border between the imaginary and the symbolic.

It is there that everything got, in fact, played out, and I will offer a few comments about it in my remarks today. But let us begin anew from the point at which we must explicate the play of the three orders, the real, the symbolic, and the imaginary, as regards what was truly involved. It concerned the turning point that makes it such that we are all patients – whatever misadventures and symptoms we each have – [the turning point] I designate as a certain disjunction between knowledge and power.

Let us be crude and sweeping by positing somewhere what I earlier called reality [*réel*]. The way I described it, it is obviously of interest.

I have not yet been to see it, but there is, apparently, a film by Louis Malle about Calcutta. In it you see a large number of people who die of hunger. That's reality. Where people die of hunger, they die of hunger. Nothing is missing. Why do we begin to talk about lack? Because they were part of an empire. Without the necessities of that empire, there would not even be a Calcutta, there would not have been a concentration of people in that area. I am not enough of a historian to know that for a fact, but I accept it because people say so.

Modern empires let their lack show precisely insofar as knowledge has grown in them to a degree that is undoubtedly incommensurate with power. Modern empire is such that, wherever it spreads its wings, this disjunction comes too, in the name of which we are given a motive – famine in India – that incites us to subvert or overhaul something the world over, *to finally do something real* [*faire kékchoz de réel, quoi*]!

In order for there to be a symbolic, we have to count to at least 1. For a long time, people thought that counting could be limited to One, to the One of God – there is only one God – the One of empire, the One of Proclus, or the One of Plotinus. Which is why there is nothing wrong with symbolizing the field of the symbolic here by this 1.

The One is not simple, of course, and progress was made when it was realized that it functions as a numerical 1 – in other words, that it engenders an infinite number of successors, on condition that there be a zero. I am sticking here to the exemplification of the symbolic by one of the best established current systems.

300

At whatever level of structure we situate this counting in the symbolic, it has effects in the imaginary, which I defined earlier as the register in which the reality of an organism – in other words, a reality that is entirely situated – is completed by an *Umwelt*. What my discourse proposes – and it is up to those who rely on it to put this formulation to the test – is that counting has the effect of making what I call object *a* appear at the level of the imaginary.

Figure 19.1: The Appearance of *a* owing to Counting

Now one image plays a special role in human beings: the specular image, which is at the core of the dimension we call narcissism. We know, moreover, that this does not make man into such an exception in the realm of living beings, for in many other animals we find, at certain levels of their behavior – that is, of what is known as ethology, animal mores – images of an apparently equivalent structure that are similarly special and that play a decisive role in their development as organisms.

The crux of what is at stake here is the relation between the specular image, $i(a)$, and object *a*, about which all the moments observed and articulated in psychoanalysis are of capital interest to us for gauging what that image, in its value as a model, yields by way of symptoms – specifically as regards the effects, which are blatant in our times, of the disjunction between knowledge and power.

301

$$\frac{i(a)}{a}$$

I thus first defined object *a* as essentially based on the malicious [or: mischievous, *malicieux*] effects in the field of the imaginary of what happens in the field of the Other, in the field of the symbolic, in the field where everything has its place, in the field of order [or: in the field where everything is put away, *rangement*], in the field of the dream of unity.

Let us observe that the very structure of the field of the Other is thus actually implied here, such as I tried to get you to sense it thanks to a schema I put on the board in more than one of my earlier classes this year. What can be located as *a*-effects in the field of the imaginary imply nothing but the following: the field of the

Other itself takes, as it were, the form of *a* [*est . . . en forme de* a]. This "takes the form" [*en-forme*] is inscribed in a topology where it appears in this field as making a hole in it. This is, of course, but an intuitive image.

I took a further step by showing that returning these little *a*-effects in the imaginary to the Other – namely, to the field from which they come – constitutes perversion. It's quite simple, a slightly apologetic way of presenting things, like "render unto Caesar what is Caesar's" [see, for example, Mark 12:17], as was once said by a guy who was rather clever – for the bugger was clever.

To return *a* to the one [*celui*] from whom it comes – that is, to the Other with a capital *O* – is the essence of perversion. I find it striking, nevertheless, that in saying things like that, what I say is accepted, as though I were cutting into butter with a chainsaw. This obviously proves that analysts don't know what they can be sure of in such a field. We have to see what we can draw out of this formulation.

What constitutes an effect of the symbolic on the field of the imaginary? This is still problematic, yet we cannot doubt but that it concerns the subject, since we make the subject into something that is inscribed only on the basis of an articulation of [or: that derives from, *du*] the Other's field, with one foot out and the other foot in.

Let us try to recognize the face of the subject at stake here.

3

302

Freud began, long before I did, to measure the dimensions of a certain room, the darkness of which is far less easy to ascertain than the darkness of the room I mentioned last time, the one that served for over two centuries as an optical model.

Freud explored this room several times. We need not be surprised that he gave different names to the same things he found there during his various excursions. But what we need to recognize here is the precise value of one of the terms he proposed.

Freud talked a great deal about love, and took nothing about it for granted. It's not because it went to the heads of those who followed that we needn't resituate things at the level from which he began.

As regards love, he distinguished between anaclitic and narcissistic relationships. Since in other realms he juxtaposed object cathexis to cathexis of one's own body (the latter being referred to as narcissistic cathexis), people thought they could erect on that basis some sort of wild speculation – of the communicating vases type – according to which object cathexis in and of itself proves that we

have left ourselves behind [*qu'on est sorti de soi*], and that we have
invested our libidinal substance properly. Object relations theory
is based on such wild speculations, and I discussed it 13 years ago
when it was still topical, along with the whole myth of the supposed
"oblative" stage, also characterized as "genital."

What Freud says about anaclitic love as being propped up on [or:
leaning against, *un appui pris*] the Other gave rise to the development
of a sort of mythology of dependency, as though that were what it
was about. It seems to me that we can better grasp anaclitism by
correctly defining what I situate at the level of the fundamental
structure of perversion – namely, a certain play (said to be perverse)
of *a*, by which the Other's status is ensured by being covered over,
filled in, or masked, and which is found in all sorts of effects that
interest us.

If we wish to provide a logical approximation of it, we can obviously turn it into a stage, assuming we take that discursively. The
anaclitic relationship is primary here and the only true foundation
of a whole series of supposedly significant mists blown our way in
order to explain why the child misses the paradise it supposedly
enjoyed in some sort of maternal physiological environment, the
ideal form of which never existed.

What is essentially involved here is merely the play of the definable object as the effect of the symbolic in the imaginary, the play
of the imaginary with regard to anything that can claim to represent
the Other for a while, and the mother may play this role as well as
anyone or anything else – the father, an institution, or even a desert
island. Object *a* serves here to mask the structure of the Other that
I called "taking the form" of *a*, insofar as that structure is the same
thing as *a*.

This formulation is the only one that allows us to grasp what we
might call the masking or blinding by which any sort of anaclitic
relationship is established. Yet we don't get very far by expressing things thusly. That's because, as you can imagine, what is at
stake here is not easy to get at, especially as regards what is known
as imagination. Lively imagination, the imagination by which we
receive what we avidly call significations – which are sometimes
funny, sometimes not – in fact concerns an entirely different sort of
image, which is far less obscure: the specular image.

The specular image has, moreover, become far less obscure since
our mirrors became clear. We will never know what we owe to
the appearance of clear mirrors unless we reflect about it a bit. In
Antiquity, and this continued into the times of the Church Fathers,
whenever something was likened to being seen in a mirror it meant
the exact opposite of what it means to us. Since their mirrors were

made of polished metal, they created quite obscure effects. This is perhaps what allowed a specular vision of the world to last for so long. The world must have seemed obscure to them, as it does to us, but that pretty much coincided with what they saw in the mirror. That may have allowed the idea of the cosmos to last quite some time. If things appear to be less simple to us, it is merely because we have perfected mirrors and have simultaneously done other things related to elucidating the symbolic.

Since we are talking about knowledge, let us note that psychoanalytic experience provided something new here. It brought out the fact that ever since the Other began to function – whoever he may be, whoever may find himself in the position of functioning qua Other with a capital *O* – he has never known anything about what happens to the realm of satisfactions rendered to the Other by including *a* [in it].

This is what inspires me when I allow myself to raise insidious questions to theologians here and there, questions like "Are we sure that God believes in God?" But even if it is thinkable, that is not what is interesting. What is of ever more concern to us, as the impasses that constrain our knowledge multiply, is to know *not* what the Other knows but what he wants. That is the fundamental question in all psychoanalytic work, and I believe I have formulated it in accordance with an investigation which, like all prodromes, began to be sketched out at a certain philosophical turning point. It concerns the advancing of knowledge with its form of "taking the form" of *a*, the form that is sketched out altogether differently than in a mirror, whose topology is sketched out by an exploration – which has thus far barely begun – of perversion, but which comes into focus at many other levels than that of pathological experiences. What does this knowledge that advances want? And what does it lead to? Note that these are not altogether the same question.

This remains to be elucidated. We would be wrong to imagine that psychoanalysis closes the circle or has found the last word regarding the perversions, even if it makes use of the relationship to object *a* in order to apply it more broadly than I can right now.

In the years lost – the extent of which I don't know if anyone will ever attempt to gauge – while I strove to bring this discourse to light and develop it, however precariously, I took up certain topics. Not the same ones at every stage, but those topics could, were we to return to them here as symptoms, enlighten us regarding the relations between the subject and the Other.

I can't make room here for Angelus Silesius, even though his *Cherubinic Wanderer*, which I often made use of in the past, could be taken up anew in light of the anaclitic relationship as I define it.

304

His famous couplets or scanned distichs, including four metrical feet – in which the proper identity of what, in him, seems to him to be the most essential is depicted – are now impossible to grasp if not in terms of God and object *a*.

Since I won't go into that here, let it suffice to note that all the functions that can be placed under the heading of order, hierarchy, and dividing up as well, and, owing to this, everything that is related to exchange, transitivism, and identification itself – all of that is part and parcel of the specular relationship, which is very different from the preceding one.

305 All of that is related to the status of the body image, insofar as, at a certain theoretical turning point, it is related to an essential property in the libidinal economy under consideration: the body's motor mastery. It is no accident that some of the same consonants are found in "mastery" and "motor" [*maîtrise* and *motrice*] – that says it all. Thanks to this motor mastery, the organism that can be characterized by its relations to the symbolic – man, as he is known – moves around without ever leaving a well-defined area, because it prohibits him from entering a central region which is strictly speaking that of jouissance. It allows him to behave like a good man, as they say, on any occasion. The body image thereby takes on its importance such as I spell it out in the narcissistic relationship.

If you refer back to the schema that I provided in my paper entitled "Remarks [on Daniel Lagache's Presentation: 'Psychoanalysis and Personality Structure'" in *Écrits*] – on several propositions made by a guy whose name will be remembered thanks to me – you will see that, in order to designate the relationship that is established between the subject and the Other's field, I made that field function like a mirror – and why not, since the Other is not subtracted from the imaginary, and because, in an image, I can't provide anything that doesn't coincide with ordinary space? I did so only in order to be able to bring out the second term: the other signifier to which the subject is represented by a signifier. This is no other than what is indicated here by the enigmatic capital I, the place from which the conjunction of *a* and the body image [*i(a)*] is presented to him in another mirror. This is what occurs in phobia.

What do we see when we examine any case of phobia, assuming it was written up somewhat seriously – which is often the case, for analysts generally don't indulge in publishing cases without providing a rather complete anamnesis – when we examine, for example, the chapters on phobia in Helene Deutsch's book on neurosis, when we examine, for example, the case of someone she was asked to see because he had a phobia of hens at a certain point?

It is perfectly well spelled out, but does not become fully unraveled, naturally, until a second stage of the exploration. For we see that, in the period before the symptom arose, hens were already of considerable significance to him. They were animals that he took care of in the company of his mother, and he and his mother gathered the eggs together. Deutsch provides details about the practices of those who work with such fowl, including the fact that they touch the hen's cloaca to check if the egg is there, ready to come out, after which they simply have to wait.

306

This was, indeed, what greatly interested the little boy in this case ["A Case of Hen Phobia" in *Neuroses and Character Types: Clinical Psychoanalytic Studies* (New York: International Universities Press, 1965)]. When he was bathed by his mother, he asked her to do the same on his own perineum. How can we fail to see here that he aspired to supply her with an object that was undoubtedly of extraordinary interest to his mother – for reasons that are not otherwise explored but which are palpable? The first stage is obviously, "Since you are interested in eggs, I must lay some for you." It's thus no accident that eggs took on such importance to him. If it is possible that object *a* can be involved in this manner, it is clearly in the sense that there is a demographic facet, so to speak, to the relations between the subjects, which implies rather naturally that what is born is situated in the place of an egg.

I am mentioning this stage first in order to indicate the meaning of what happened when the phobia arose. His brother – who was quite a bit older [ten years] and stronger than him, and who was perfectly well aware of everything that went on in the poultry yard – grabbed him from behind one day, saying, "I'm the cock and you're the hen" [p. 86]. The younger boy defended himself and fought back immediately, declaring, "But I won't be a hen" [p. 86]. (Note that the *n* in "hen" in English is pronounced exactly like, and with the same gruffness as, the *n* in *l'Un* [the One] which I spoke about earlier.) He doesn't want to be the hen. He says no.

A guy named Alain thought he'd made a great discovery when he said that "to think is to say no." But why did this boy say no – when, at the prior stage, he was so happy to be able to be one more hen for his mother, a deluxe hen, as it were, one that was not in the farmyard – if not because narcissism was involved, namely, rivalry with his brother and activation of a power relation? This is clearly borne out, because his brother grabbed him by the waist and hips, immobilized him, and held him in that position for as long as he wanted to.

That is when a transfer [*virement*] occurred – I am not saying a shift [or: turning point (in sexual orientation or clinical structure), *virage*] – regarding what was invested in a certain signification, a transfer from one register to another, from the imaginary to the symbolic. The preceding function, which was imaginary, broke down. The hen henceforth took on for him a perfectly signifying function – namely, it frightened him.

307   The field of anxiety is certainly not without an object, as I reminded you at the beginning of class today, provided we clearly see that this object is what is at stake for the subject in the field of narcissism. It is the one that reveals the true function of phobia: to replace the object of anxiety with a signifier that frightens us, for a danger that is signaled is reassuring compared to the enigma of anxiety. Experience thus shows that, assuming a shift [*passage*] to the field of the Other occurs, the signifier presents itself as what it is with regard to narcissism – namely, devouring. This is clearly what gave rise to the primacy of the oral drive in classical psychoanalytic theory.

Phobia must not be viewed as a clinical entity, but rather as a central hub [*plaque tournante*]. That is what I wanted to broach today. Phobia usually veers [*vire*] toward one of the other two neuroses, hysteria or obsession, and it also intersects with the structure of perversion. It enlightens us, in short, about all sorts of consequences that it has, and which don't in any way need to be limited to a specific subject to be perfectly perceptible. It is far less an isolable clinical entity than a figure that is clinically illustrated – strikingly so, no doubt – but in infinitely varied contexts.

On the basis of phobia, we will investigate further what we began with today: the disjunction between knowledge and power.

May 7, 1969

XX

KNOWLEDGE AND
JOUISSANCE

The conjunction of knowledge and jouissance
The Other and its "taking the form of"
The four effacings of the subject
Person and subject
The foreclosure of jouissance

In psychoanalytic practice, it is impossible not to consider the impact of the subject to be primordial.

It is constantly at the forefront of psychoanalysts' minds, assuming we believe what is said in case studies. Analysts write, for example, that the subject acts on or manifests a certain intention based on what they call an identification. They account for something paradoxical in his behavior by saying, for example, that he turns his original aggression against himself, or simply that he turns against himself (and from what position if not that of another position he came to occupy?) his aggression toward someone with whom he identifies.

In short, the subject is presented at every moment by such analysts as endowed with what at least seems to be an odd autonomy, and above all a matchless mobility, since there is hardly any position in the world of his partners – whether or not they be considered his semblables – that he cannot occupy. This is the case, at least, let me repeat, in the kind of thinking that attempts to account for such paradoxical behavior.

The status of this subject is never critiqued, since odd statements also go so far as to talk about the "choice of neurosis," as if his having shifted toward one neurosis or another at a certain moment were reserved for some sort of special position of this will-o'-the-wisp subject [*sujet en poudre*].

There is no reason to dispute in any way the legitimacy of the term "subject" with which I am referring to this literature. One can,

of course, admit that at the outset psychoanalytic research did not
provide any logical articulation whatsoever of what presents itself
as altogether determinant, apparently, in a certain way of reacting
to trauma. It would nevertheless suffice to realize that the moment
in the anamnesis that people consider to be the earliest and orienting, was obviously retroactively produced by the sum total of the
analyst's interpretations. Not only the interpretations he thought of
in his head, as they say, or when he wrote up the case history, but
also those where he intervened in what connected him to the patient,
a connection which – in the register in which it is inscribed, that of
the questioning or putting in abeyance [or: bracketing, *suspension*]
of the subject – can hardly be described as involving equal partners,
even if the analyst is subjected to every transference that can be
imagined there.

You thus see why, in psychoanalysis, when the subject is involved,
it is always essential to return to the question of structure. It is this
return that constitutes true progress, for it alone can help advance
what is improperly known as clinical work [or: clinical diagnosis, *la
clinique*].

I hope that everyone here grasps this. If you were pleased that
my remarks became clearer at the end of the last class when I discussed a case, keep in mind that it is not specifically the mention of
a case that constitutes the clinical character of what is said in this
teaching.

1

Let us thus return to the point at which we can formulate things,
after having already indicated several times how the subject forms
on the basis of a first and very simple definition.

This definition begins from the signifier, because the signifier is,
after all, the only element about which analysis provides certainty,
and I must say that it shines the spotlight on the signifier and gives
it its full weight.

"A signifier is what represents a subject to another signifier."
This is the formulation, the embryonic formulation, as it were, that
allows us to situate a subject that we do not, in any case, know how
to handle in a way that would apparently accord with common
sense, the latter being based on the notion that something constitutes the identity that differentiates one guy from the guy sitting next
to him. Were we to confine ourselves to this, any descriptive statement about what happens in the analytic relationship would be like
the description of a puppet show, in which the subject is as mobile as

speech itself, the speech of the puppet master, who, when he speaks for the puppet in his right hand, cannot speak at the same time for the one in his left hand – which doesn't stop him from being able to shift very quickly from one to the other.

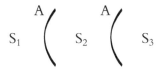

Figure 20.1: Simplified Schema of the Signifying Relationship

I have written this out for you often enough here that I don't need to reconstruct it or comment on it for you. We have here the first relationship, which gives rise to all the others, of S_1 to S_2, of the signifier that represents the subject to another signifier.

I have already attempted to isolate what is at stake in the second signifier, S_2, the other of these two signifiers, the one to which the subject will be represented by a signifier. I have discussed the field in which A as a locus is inscribed, a locus that is the Other with a capital O – in other words, the body. You recall, I think, that by inscribing in this way everything that constitutes a second signifier, we can merely, at the level of the very inscription of S_2, repeat – for everything that can be written after that – the mark of A qua locus of inscription. In short, we thus see it being hollowed out by what last time I called "taking the form of" A [or: A's "form-taking," *l'en-forme de A*] – namely, the *a* that makes a hole in it.

For our purposes, I am going to give it a new name today, "*l'*enforme *du A*."

I believe that I can take this for granted, having heard that some of you were struck by this *enforme du A*, and that they found it rather easy to use – clinically, I mean.

Let us dwell on this for a moment. The formulation is designed to show the true status of *a* – namely, the true status of the topological structure of A itself, of what makes it such that A is not complete, that A is identifiable neither with a 1 nor a whole of any kind. In short, it absolutely must be taken and represented as the kind of set we encounter in the paradox of the set of all sets that do not contain themselves, a paradox which, not surprisingly, was developed by logicians.

312

I think you are already quite familiar with this paradox. We can say one of two things about the set of all sets that do not contain themselves. Either it contains itself and we thus have a contradiction. Or it does not contain itself and it therefore does contain itself, which leads to a second contradiction.

This is quite simple to resolve if we posit that the set of all sets that do not contain themselves cannot, in effect, be written as a function except in the following form: the set E has the property <*x* qua different from *x*> –

$$E(x \neq x)$$

This is where it intersects the problematic status of the Other with a capital *O*.

If the Other with a capital *O* has the topological characteristic that I say it has, which is such that its *enforme* is *a*, we will be able to put our finger very directly on what this signifies regarding the status of the signifier. It suffices to posit that, regardless of the conventional use made of it in mathematics, the signifier cannot in any way be understood to be able to designate itself. In and of themselves, S_1 and S_2 cannot in any way be representatives of themselves if not by distinguishing themselves from themselves.

This alterity of the signifier from itself is what is, strictly speaking, designated by the term Other with a capital *O*, designated as A. If we write the Other with a capital *O* as A, thereby turning it into a signifier, what it designates is the signifier qua Other. The first Other that comes into being, the first Other encountered in the field of the signifier, is radically Other – in other words, Other than itself [or: different from itself]. That is, it introduces Otherness as such into its inscription, qua separate from this very inscription.

This A, insofar as it is outside of S_2, inscribes the *enforme* of A – in other words, the same thing as *a*. Now this *a* is, as we know, the subject himself, insofar as he can only be represented by a representative, which is S_1 here. The first alterity, which is that of the signifier, cannot express the subject except in the form of what we have learned in psychoanalytic practice to discern on the basis of a specific strangeness [*étrangeté*].

313   I need not go back into that here, since I laid the foundations for it in the Seminar I gave back in 1961/62 on identification [Seminar IX]. If I am reminding you of those foundations today and summarizing them for you, it's in order to get you to realize something which isn't brought home to us by anything other than psychoanalytic experience – namely, the status of the little *a* that is essential to the subject and marked by the strangeness with which every analyst is familiar.

I have, moreover, already enumerated the various little *a*s for long enough that people know – from the breast to excrement, from the

voice to the gaze – what the word "strangeness" ambiguously signifies, between its affective charge and its suggestion of something that
is marginal, topologically speaking.

I will strive to convey to those who aren't forced to take *a* as an
experiential given a *je ne sais quoi* that can evoke its logical [*rai-
sonnée*] place with respect to the landmarks of what we take to be
practical experience – wrongly so, for it is no more practical than
psychoanalytic experience.

Let's get right to it.

2

Since *a* is supposed to be what is most foreign [*étranger*] to representing the subject, let us try to take something that is apparently
less foreign as our point of departure.

At the outset, you can take the subject to be as indeterminate as
you like, as what distinguishes this guy from the one who is sitting
next to him, and you can take what represents him to be a type of
materiality that is quite common: a trace.

This is what I did when I spoke about identification. What I
mean by a trace is the trace of a hand or foot, a hand- or footprint
[*empreinte*].

Note that a trace is distinguished from a signifier differently at
this level than a sign is. A sign is, as I said, what represents something to someone. Here [on the other hand] there is no need for
someone: a trace suffices unto itself. Can we situate on that basis
the status of what I called the meaning [or: orienting, *sens*] of the
subject earlier?

We can already raise the question of what becomes of what signifies a subject when, as opposed to a natural trace or footprint, a
trace no longer has any other prop than the *enforme* of A.

What does that mean? A trace becomes the *enforme* of A [or: A's   314
enforme] depending on the varied ways in which it is effaced. The
subject consists in the very ways in which a trace, like a [foot- or
finger]print, happens to be effaced. I already highlighted this with a
play on words by referring to the "four effacings [or: four ways of
effacing, *effaçons* (which combines *façons*, ways, and the first person
plural of *effacer*, to efface, *effaçons*)] of the subject." The subject
is he who effaces the trace by transforming it into a gaze, gaze [or:
opening (like a manhole), *regard*] to be understood here in the sense
of slit or glimpse (between things) [*fente, entre'aperçu*]. This is the
way in which the subject broaches the other who left the trace, who
passed that way and has moved on.

It is not enough to say that the subject leaves no trace behind. What defines him and betrays him at the same time – what effectively distinguishes the animal who speaks from every other living organism – is the fact that he can efface his traces. And he can efface them as such: as being *his* traces. This suffices for him to be able to make them into something other than traces, to make them, for example, into appointments he makes with himself. The white pebbles that Tom Thumb drops along the way are something other than traces.

Consider what we see already in a pack of hounds which, in following something, conducts (that's the word for it!) itself in a certain way, but this conduct is inscribed within the realm of smell or flair [*flair* also refers to smell in French], as they say. This is not necessarily altogether foreign to the human animal. But at the level of the pack, this conduct is one thing whereas scansion, based on the voice, of a trace that has been located is something else. Does barking correspond to [*recouvre*] traces? Who would dare say so? We are approaching a limit here, for barking is already what we might call a first sketch of speech. But, where language exists, the medium of the voice is distinct from the pregiven of the voice. The medium of the voice autonomously characterizes a certain type of trace there.

A being that can read its own trace can reinscribe it somewhere other than where he first left it. This reinscription is the bond that makes him dependent henceforth on an Other whose structure does not depend on him.

All of this opens up onto the register of the subject defined as "he who effaces his own traces." In order to better convey to you the original dimension of what is at stake here, I will go so far as to call him "he who replaces his traces with his signature."

You know that we don't ask for much to constitute someone as a subject. Down at City Hall, an illiterate person need but sign papers with an X, a symbol of the barred bar or of an effaced trace. This is the clearest form of what is involved. When one initially makes a sign, and then something that cancels it out, that is enough to constitute a signature. The fact that it is identical for all illiterates who are asked to sign doesn't stop it from being accepted as authenticating the certificate in question, for it attests to the presence of someone who is legally considered to be a subject – no more and no less.

To confine our attention to that would be to make the subject, whose level I am trying to define, into an absolute, whereas I intend, on the contrary, to point to his dependency. My comment begins here.

The signifier is born of effaced traces. What, then, is the consequence thereof? It is that these effaced traces have no value except owing to the system of other traces, except owing to the other traces established as a system, whether the traces are similar or the same. It is there and there alone that the typical import of language begins. The other effaced traces are the only ones recognized – recognized by whom?

Well, the answer is: by the other traces.

Mystery solved. The traces are recognized by other traces in the same way that, in the definition of the subject, a signifier represents him to another signifier. A *pâ-âté*, as Don Gusman Brid'oison [who stutters] says in Beaumarchais' *The Marriage of Figaro* [*pâté* in Act III, Scene 15, refers to an ink stain obscuring a word on a marriage contract], doesn't count. This is why he is so interested in it: to him, someone who takes traces so seriously, it might have counted. It is a hasty step [*pas hâté*; *pâ-âté* sounds just like *pas hâté*].

Let us turn here to what we know. These traces – which are effaced merely by being forced below the surface [(as with a nail set) or: merely as a foil, *que d'être en repoussoir effacées*] – have another prop which is clearly the *enforme* of A, necessitated by the following: that it produces an *a* that functions at the level of the subject. We must therefore consider these *a*s at the level of their substance.

Consider, for example, the gaze. Its importance in eroticism raises the question of the relationship between what is inscribed at the level of the gaze and the trace. Does an erotic gaze leave traces where it becomes inscribed in someone else? This is where the dimension of modesty comes in, a dimension that is characteristic of the subject as such alone.

I am going to briefly lay out the relationship between the signifier and the *enforme* here in a slightly different way than usual.

It is no accident that writing has come to the fore in our times. The only thing that can give a grammatology its correct status is the relationship between writing and the gaze qua object, the gaze in all its ambiguity, which I mentioned earlier regarding the relationship to the trace, that which is glimpsed [*l'entrevu*], and in short, the cut in what is seen [or: the carving up of what is seen, *la coupure dans le vu*], the thing that opens up beyond what is seen.

The emphasis placed on writing is surely crucial if we are to correctly gauge the status of language. The fact that writing must be considered primary with respect to speech can, after all, be considered, not merely licit, but obvious owing to the very existence of a form of writing like Chinese writing, where it is clear that what the gaze apprehends bears a relation to what gets translated into the

316

voice – namely, that there are phonetic elements, but there are also many that are not phonetic.

This is all the more striking in that, from the vantage point of the strict structure of a language, no language [*langue*] holds up in a purer way than Chinese, where each morphological element is reduced to a phoneme. This is obviously where it would have been simpler, so to speak, if writing were merely the transcription of what is enunciated in words, whereas, on the contrary, far from being a transcription of speech, Chinese writing is a separate system – a system to which what is carved up [*découpé*] in another medium, that of the voice, may be attached.

The cut is certainly what predestines these media, materially definable as the gaze and the voice, to be what institutes the kind of set, replacing the trace, on the basis of which a topology can be constructed – a topology which, in the end, defines the Other.

As you see, these are merely substructural considerations. They are hardly the earliest ones, for they don't tell us how the Other arose, but simply how the Other holds together once it arises. Where it came from has, up until now, clearly been bracketed.

That was a tangential remark, for after this 1 and 2 concerning the gaze and the voice, I will go on to say what could come after them in this vein.

As you can see, what comes to the fore in the form of demand does not immediately arise in the relationship between the subject and the Other qua structured. We are obliged to assume here that the gaze and the voice are already constructed before broaching what will constitute an element in demand. This is odd, because the most common way of handling what is at stake in analytic regression gives such primacy, as regards object *a*, to breasts and waste products [*déchet*] that it largely overlooks the gaze and the voice.

317   When we find an object *a* in demand, it gives us the opportunity to point out that what is demanded is never anything but a place. It is no accident that "place" evokes *placage* in French [plastering or plating], which is the meaning that allows us to suggest that the breast is analogous to the placenta.

The breast defines the subjective relationship as it must be established in the mother–child relationship. Its role as an amboceptor between the two is in reality its primary role. It is as object *a*, as a being that is laminated onto her ribcage [or: side, *paroi*], that the subject-child formulates himself [or: links up, *s'articule*], that his message is received by the mother, and that he is responded to. What is demanded with signifiers – namely, the breast – is our third term, and you see its connection here with the other *a* element, the voice.

Now, by articulating things in this way, what is generated by the play of signifiers – meaning, that is, strictly speaking, the signified – must be situated here as the effect of what this play sloughs off [*effet de chute de ce jeu*].

Meaning is not simply an effect, but an effect that is rejected, gets swept away [*s'emporte*], and accumulates, too. From this perspective, culture is related to something that stems from an economy based on the structure of object *a* – namely, from waste products [or: scraps, *déchet*]. We should describe what constitutes the material of dictionaries – which are said to be the mass of meanings that have revolved around a signifier in the course of a certain recordable practice in order to become commonplace – as waste products, the excrement of subjective relationships. This is related to the register of the anal object.

Such are the four effacings [*effaçons*] by which the subject can be inscribed, the subject who naturally remains ungraspable because he can only be represented by a representative, for he subsists only insofar as he is inscribed in the field of the Other.

This is what we have to reckon with if we wish to correctly account for what is at stake in a psychoanalysis.

3

The gap that separates the subject from the person, as they can be defined, is very wide indeed. This means that we must distinguish between them very carefully.

Every form of personalism in psychoanalysis gives rise to all sorts of confusions and deviations. What is designated as the person in other, so-called moral, registers cannot, from a psychoanalytic perspective, be situated at any other level than that of the symptom. The person begins where the subject is anchored differently than I define it for you, where it is situated far more broadly, in a way that brings into play what is undoubtedly situated at the origin of the subject – namely, jouissance.

Psychoanalytic experience teaches us to trace out here, differently than had been done before, the atlas – in the cartographic sense – of the play [*jeux*] of the signifier in relation to the subject. In doing so, it does not claim to reconstitute some sort of new whole, but simply to inaugurate a method. But the fact remains that, in doing so, it overturns old systems of projection, each of which constituted a whole.

As an aside, I could highlight here all sorts of prescriptions [*indications*], which are suggestions, that are made, index finger wagging. Note that the signification of the index [finger pointing] is entirely

318

different in a discovery in progress than what is distinctive about a certain sort of signifier that we can turn it into in language.

I am thus proposing to some of you who are here – and who, I believe, have a penchant for returning to what Freud said about the leader as a key element of identification in *Group Psychology and the Analysis of the Ego* – to verify how all of this becomes clearer in the perspective that I am tracing out.

Indeed, the latter shows the solution that renders possible how the subject, strictly identifying with *a*, becomes what he truly is – in other words, a subject who is himself barred. What we have seen in our times, and which can thus obviously recur, is, as it were, the reduction of an entire mass to the function of a unidirectional [or: unequivocal, *univoque*] gaze. The only thing that can account for this is the perception of the possibilities offered up in this register to a signifier that is special because it is the most elementary, and reduced to the signifier Freud designates as being purely and simply the mark or unique function of the 1.

We thus have here the system to which thought is wholly subject. Note carefully that there is no question that what can be articulated, and specifically what can be articulated by way of knowledge, can stem from it.

The fact that a living being is enveloped in language, in a system of signifiers, entails that images are always more or less marked in that being, as they are taken on qua signifying in the system. This is rendered obligatory by the function of types and of what is known as the universal. Now, since images are taken up in the play of signifiers, something is lost, as all of psychoanalytic experience attests – namely, the imaginary function insofar as it answers for [or: corresponds to, *répond de*] the harmony between male and female.

319

How can this not be palpable, obvious to everyone, and incorporated into some effective way of revamping institutions?

If there is something that psychoanalysis demonstrates it is clearly that, owing to the taking up of the subject in language, everything that can be designated as "male" is ambiguous, or even revocable upon closer scrutiny, the same being true for "female"; and, moreover, that there is absolutely no recognition as such of male by female or of female by male at the level of the subject.

This is corroborated in reality by very precise data. Any in-depth exploration of the history of a couple demonstrates that their identifications are multiple, overlap, and always, in the end, form a composite whole. Psychoanalytic experience allows us to observe that, at its level, there is no signifying coupling [or: pairing, *couplage*]. This goes so far that, although there are several pairs of oppositions proposed in the theory – like active/passive, voyeur/

what is seen, and so on – no opposition that would designate the male/female couple is ever considered to be fundamental.

The ambiguity that remains surrounding any aspect of this relationship that could be written at the signifying level contrasts, moreover, with what we know radically distinguishes the sexes at the biological level – assuming, of course, that we omit the so-called secondary sex characteristics found in mammals, as well as the possible tissular distinction between the sexes with regard to phanerogamic sex. But let us leave that aside as the crux lies elsewhere.

The crux is, in some sense, prior to the question that I have raised here. We need to know the status, in the signifying system, of the so-called function of the phallus.

In the way it effectively intervenes in what we may call the sex(uat)ed relationship [*rapport sexué*], it is clear that the phallus cannot, in any case, serve anything other than a tertiary function. It represents either what is initially defined as what is missing, in other words, grounding the type of castration characteristic of women, or, on the contrary, what in males indicates, in a highly problematic way, what we might call the enigma of absolute jouissance. In any case these are not correlative or distinctive landmarks. One and only one landmark dominates the entire register of relations between the sexes.

320

I intend to justify here why – in a long structural discussion, built on detailed analyses of written accounts of our work with neurotics – I have characterized this special signifier as the "missing signifier."

The question concerns the articulation of the function of the subject, and it is important because, no matter how far the articulation of knowledge is taken, the subject demonstrates the gap therein. At the point at which I was able to enunciate that the phallus is the missing signifier, at the point in my discourse when I risked, let us say, proposing it for the first time [Seminar VI, pp. 23, 336, and 349 (see also Seminar VIII, p. 237)], the context was not yet, I suspect, well enough articulated for me to say what I am saying today.

The trace, which I referred to earlier, provides us with the necessary foundation upon which to build. Let us return to our point of departure, and let us recall the Arab proverb that I long ago quoted in my *Écrits* [p. 157].

"There are four things" – I forget the fourth one, or else I am not really trying to remember it right now – "that leave no trace, a gazelle's hoof on a rock, a fish in water, and" – this is the one that interests us most – "man in woman." What one might object to the latter can be stated in the following form, the importance of which we are familiar with from neurotics' fantasies: "Actually, a slight illness from time to time."

But that is precisely what is instructive. The role of venereal diseases is no accident from the standpoint of structure. We cannot begin from any trace whatsoever to forge the signifier of sexual relationships. Everything is reduced to the phallus, the signifier that is not, in fact, part of the subject's system, since it is not the subject that it represents but, as it were, sexual jouissance qua outside of the system – in other words, qua absolute.

Sexual jouissance is distinguished from all other forms of jouissance by the fact that something in the pleasure principle, which we know constitutes a barrier to jouissance, nevertheless allows access to it. Sexual jouissance is jouissance *par excellence*, it is true, but we can admit that when we read that in the work of Freud – and if anyone truly deserved to be called a scholar, he did – it nevertheless fills us with wonder [*faire rêver*]. But sexual jouissance is not part of the subject as a system [or: the subject's system, *le système du sujet*]. There is no subject of sexual jouissance.

321

The sole point of these remarks is to allow us to zero in on the meaning of the phallus qua missing signifier.

The phallus is the signifier that is outside of the system and, in short, the one that is conventionally used to designate what is radically foreclosed in sexual jouissance. If I have spoken, for good reason, about foreclosure in order to designate certain effects of the symbolic relationship, it is here that we must designate the point where it is not subject to revision [*révisable*]. I added that everything that is foreclosed in the symbolic reappears in the real, and it is clearly in this respect that jouissance is altogether real, for in the subject as a system, it is nowhere symbolized, nor is it symbolizable.

Hence the necessity of the myth that Freud proposes, and which resembles no other myth known to mythology. No one seems to be concerned about this shocking fact, except a few people like ol' [Alfred Louis] Kroeber and [Claude] Lévi-Strauss, both of whom clearly realize that it is not part of their universe and have no qualms about saying so. But it's as if they had said nothing, for everyone else continues to believe that the Oedipus complex is an acceptable myth.

It is acceptable, in a certain sense, but note that it designates nothing other than the place where we must situate the jouissance I just defined as absolute. The primal father of the myth is he who embraces [*confond*] all women in his jouissance. The mythical form of the statement indicates clearly enough, in and of itself, that we don't know what jouissance is involved. Is it the father's or that of all the women? Yet, as I also pointed out to you, it is feminine jouissance that has always remained an enigma in analytic theory.

Although it does not represent the subject, the phallic function nevertheless seems to signal a point of his determination qua limited field of the relation between jouissance and what is structured as the Other. It is in returning to our experience from these radical perspectives, and in examining it more closely, that we will immediately see how things translate clinically.

At what point does a neurosis arise? At the moment of the positive intrusion of an autoerotic jouissance, typified perfectly in the first sensations more or less linked to onanism – call it as you like – in children. In the cases that fall under our purview – that is, those that lead to a neurosis – it is at that precise point, [that is,] at the very moment at which the "positivization" of erotic jouissance occurs, that the positivization of the subject as dependent on the Other's desire correlatively occurs. This is the anaclitism I mentioned last time. We see here the entry point by which the subject's structure turns tragic [*fait drame*]. It is worth articulating the whole of the experience, for it confirms the seam [*jonction*] at which this tragedy arises. I believe I already sufficiently indicated last time the weight object *a* takes on there, not insofar as it is rendered present, but by demonstrating retroactively that it is object *a* that previously constituted the entirety of the subject's structure.

322

We will see the other frontiers at which the tragedy arises. But we can already say something about the upshot of these effects. Thanks to the positive relation of the subject to so-called sexual jouissance, the desire to know appears, but without sexual union being in any way assured.

The desire to know is designated as essential to the position(ing) of the subject. Essential to the psychoanalytic discovery is the decisive step Freud took by revealing the relationship between sexual curiosity and the entire realm of knowledge. He pointed to the welding [*jonction*] of *a*, on the one hand – namely the [place or thing] where the subject can find anew his real essence as nothing more than "failure to enjoy" [*manque-à-jouir*], regardless of the representative with which he must designate himself thereafter – to the field of the Other, on the other hand, insofar as knowledge is laid out therein. And we have, on the horizon, the domain of jouissance which is prohibited by its very nature, with which sexual jouissance introduces a minimum of diplomatic relations that, I will say, are quite difficult to maintain.

It is because something that I called tragic occurs that the signifier of the Other qua structured, and with a hole in it, is something other than what we can metaphorically call the signifier that makes a hole in it – that is, the phallus. It is because it is something else that we can see what occurs when a young subject must respond to the effects produced by the intrusion of sexual functioning into his subjective field.

I laid great stress on a certain game little Hans played, and those who were here when I did so still recall it.

The little Hans case study is an exemplary writeup of an absolutely discombobulated first exploration that went around in circles and was, up to a certain point, undirected – despite the imperialist direction of, first, the reference to the father who played a role whose shortcomings I pointed out, and which Freud did not hide, but second, the final reference to Freud himself as someone with supposedly absolute knowledge. I was careful, as I reminded you, to take up at great length everything that can be discerned in the chaos in order to show you the various strata. One of them is the game little Hans played which involved a confrontation between a big giraffe and a little giraffe.

I emphasized its importance by showing that his phobia fundamentally revealed that it was impossible to make the she-man [*hommelle*] – namely, the phallicized mother, the big giraffe being Hans' way of expressing his relationship with her – coexist with anything that might diminish her. He sketched a little giraffe to show, not that it was an image comparable to the big one, but that it was a writing on a piece of paper, which is why he *zerwurzelt* it, as Hans put it, he crumpled it up and sat on it. What was important was not the imaginary way in which Hans identified with the phallus, with that complement of his mother that was, in short, his great rival; it was that he managed to shift the phallus into the symbolic. For it was there that it could have its efficacy, and everyone knows what sort of efficacy there is in phobias.

If there is an expression that serves a purpose in political vocabulary, and not for no reason, at the seam between power and knowledge, it is clearly the one that was proposed in a place I alluded to earlier regarding language: "paper tiger." What could better qualify as a paper tiger than a phobia? A child's phobia often concerns tigers that are in a photo album, tigers that are truly made of paper. Yet, if politicians have such a hard time persuading the masses to put paper tigers in their place, what should be prescribed here is the exact opposite. We must give its full import to the fact that, in order to deal with [*combler*] a question that cannot be resolved owing to the intolerable anxiety it provokes, the subject has no other resource at his disposal than to create a fear of paper tigers. That is what is instructive – all the more so in that little Hans is not the type of subject psychoanalysts imagine phobics to be – for, as he himself puts it, it was convenient [*facilité de style*], he did all of that by putting it together as best he could.

There was a very close link between his structure as a subject and the fact that he dealt with the question via fear. It was when little Hans' entire person had become a symptom that the world, or, at least the she-man across from him, who was the foundation of his world, transformed into a paper tiger all by herself, suddenly becoming grimacing and beginning to scare him. Whether [a child alights upon] a tiger or a smaller animal like a cat is of no importance, for no analyst can overlook its true function.

324

If we were finally led to see the importance of lack, as regards the penis as an altogether real object, in every determination of the relationship between the sexes, it is because the way was paved for us by neurotics and the questions they raise. The castration complex is merely the result of the discourse by which we had to deal with their questions. They effectively create a place for lack in the field of signifiers. This means that it is necessary that, at the end of an analysis, what truly is and remains *angewachsen*, as little Hans put it, rooted – and, thank God, able to serve most analysands, at least we hope so – be *zerwurzelt* [crumpled up] at a certain level. It must be shown that what is involved is no more than a symbol.

This is what leads to a problem at the end of little Hans' treatment, as I already indicated.

It was necessary, of course, that he arrive – like any other neurotic – at the formulation that, in order to become a man, "I don't have the penis as a symbol [*à titre de symbole*]," for that is the castration complex. But we must realize that this sentence can be broken down in different ways. "I don't have the penis," which is what we mean when we say that an analysis ends with the realization of the castration complex, which pushes outside the pure and simple function [φ] of the penis, such as it functions – in other words, outside of the symbolized register. But the sentence can be broken down differently: "I don't have, as a symbol, the penis," meaning that the penis, qua signifier, cannot attest to [or: guarantee] my virility. This wasn't achieved with little Hans; it fell through the cracks.

Little Hans – who continued all the while to play the role of the one who has the penis with little girls – nevertheless maintained a view of sexual relationships that foregrounded the penis qua imaginary function. This is what led me at the time to voice my reservations regarding the end of his treatment. Otherwise stated, as heterosexual as he might have appeared to be, he was at exactly the same point as homosexuals – I mean those who recognize themselves to be homosexuals, for when relations between the sexes are involved, we cannot overly extend, in the field of apparently normal relations, the field that structurally corresponds to homosexuality.

325

Hence the importance of exploring and elucidating the junction [*joint*] of the imaginary and the symbolic that situates the function – or, more precisely, facets of the function – that we define as the castration complex in its rightful place.

Other forms of neurosis supply us still more experience with the junction of the Other and jouissance, and I will continue by broaching them in what follows.

May 14, 1969

XXI

RESPONSES TO APORIAS

The history of a *belle époque* pen
An alibi based on the impossibility in inadequacy
Biography in psychoanalysis
Choosing between impossibility and impotence
Hysteria and obsession

We need to lay out the nowhere system. Utopia will finally take on meaning thereby, but realized in the right way this time.

The old term "nullibiety" – which I long ago supplied with the renewed luster it deserves for having been invented by Bishop Wilkins [see *Écrits*, p. 16], and which designates the quality of what is nowhere – what is it? It concerns jouissance.

What psychoanalytic experience demonstrates is that, owing to a connection with what allows for the emergence of knowledge, jouissance is excluded and the circle closes. This exclusion is enunciated only by the system itself, insofar as it is the symbolic. It thereby asserts itself as the ultimate real of the functioning of the system that excludes it. From nowhere, it returns everywhere, owing to the very exclusion that is the whole of that by which it gets actualized. Our practice focuses on the following: when we deal with symptoms, we must unveil and unmask the relation to jouissance, which is our real because it is excluded.

This is why I propose the following three terms as props: "jouissance" insofar as it is excluded, the "Other" qua locus where that [exclusion] is known, and "object *a*" which is what is at stake in the matter.

Object *a* is the scrap [or: leftover, *chute*] that results from the fact that, in the play of the signifier, it is jouissance that is nevertheless aimed at. The subject – who, because he has received (from where?) the signifier qua means [*moyen*], has emerged from the unsayable relationship to jouissance – is thereby struck by a relationship to what assumes the form of the Other from that point on, avatars of which arise, it still being operative, and this is clearly what draws our attention.

These are the terms with which we must situate psychoanaly-
328   sis. Right from its very origin, it is the, as it were, wild experience thereof. Born, undoubtedly, in an exceptional flash, thanks to Freud, psychoanalysis has never stopped being at the mercy of the diversions [*versants*] available along its route, which are identical to the ones in the network in which the subject it deals with is caught up.

1

I would like to begin with something as close to home as possible.

Here is an object or device that I especially like – you can lecture me about it as you like, from an analytic standpoint please, or some other standpoint, it doesn't much matter. It is a pen.

It is as similar as possible to a feather pen [or: nib or quill holder, *porte-plume*], in the old antediluvian sense, because it is so slim. Very few people use them nowadays. As it can be closed, becoming something that fits in the palm of your hand, it holds very little ink. The upshot being that it is difficult to refill because osmotic effects occur, which are such that when one pours a drop of ink in it, the drop is exactly the same size as the opening. It is thus quite inconvenient. Still, I am quite attached to it because it constitutes a certain type of nib with a real feather. Indeed, it dates back to a time when people really used feathers, not the rigid devices they use today.

This feather pen was given to me by someone who knew I was looking for this sort of thing. The gift was sent (just a few minutes – or just a few hours or days, it doesn't really matter – before I received it) by someone who was certainly paying homage to me in a very precise, in short fetishistic, way. It was, moreover, an object which, as the giver told the person who handed it to me, came from the gift-giver's grandmother. That explains why it is not easy to find another one like it. There are, apparently, shops in New York where people sell pens from the *belle époque* [beginning of the twentieth century]. I acquired mine, as you see, through a different channel.

I thus have a glimpse into the history of this object, but it is dear to me for its own sake, quite independently of its history. For, to tell you the truth, I am not especially grateful to the person who gave me this present. My relation to this object is based on the fact that it is
329   certainly very close to what, for me, constitutes object *a*. I thus have a glimpse into the history of the object, but don't you see – owing to

the way I just brought it alive – that the history of an object is just as open to question as the history of a subject is?

How can we imagine who it is that knows that history and can answer for it, unless we establish the Other as the locus where it is known? And assuming we have begun to grasp this dimension, how can we avoid realizing that the dimension exists – at least for certain people, and I dare say for each of us? For certain people it is altogether predominant, but it constitutes a backdrop for all of us. There is a somewhere [or: a place, *un quelque part*] where everything that has happened is known. As soon as we begin to investigate in this vein, we recognize that the signifier of A qua whole is always implicit, and that it is far more implicit to the obsessive neurotic than to others.

It is via history – insofar as it is suggested, not at all directly on the basis of the subject, but on the basis of the fate of objects – that we realize how crazy it is to presuppose any sort of locus in which it is known. "It is known," in the neutral sense in which I just introduced it, immediately veers toward an interesting question: does the locus where it is known know itself [*ça se sait soi-même*]? Its reflexivity only arises from consciousness owing to this very detour, which must be verified if, where we assume it is known, it is known that it is known.

It is amusing to note, for instance, that mathematicians, when they do mathematical work, are well aware that they are doing so, but are utterly unable to say what allows them to determine it. They haven't said a word about it thus far. They can say what mathematical work is not, but not what it is.

Yet a mathematician with whom I was speaking about this quite recently told me that what characterizes a mathematical claim is its independence from its context. A theorem can be stated and justified all by itself, because it is sufficiently self-contained [*recouverture à soi-même*]. This frees it from the discourse that presents it, unlike what we see in other discourses where if we quote a part of it, we risk taking it out of context. We have here, perhaps, a first step along the path to be followed, which consists in organizing things that are said in such a way that they know themselves [*ça se sait soi-même*] at every moment and can attest to it.

We should look into this closely. Indeed, the subsistence of the instantaneous "it knows itself" as such is accompanied by the fact that it assumes that everything that attains this is also known, in the sense in which it overlaps itself [or: intersects itself, *se recouvre soi-même*], it knows itself as a whole [or: in its set, *dans son ensemble*]. Now what is revealing here is that what is presupposed by a discourse that aspires to completely intersect itself encounters limits, insofar as there are points that cannot be posited in it.

330

The first image of this is provided by the infinite series of whole numbers, where the number that is defined as being larger than any number cannot be posited. It is impossible to write a number that is greater than every other. Such a number is excluded, specifically qua symbol. It is owing to the impossibility of writing it that the entire series of whole numbers turns out not to be the simple written trace [*graphie*] of something that can be written, but something that is in the real. The real arises from this very impossibility.

It is this very mechanism that allows us to return to this sign – which cannot be posited in terms of the series of whole numbers, in other words, at the level of symbols – in order to posit it by writing it as a transfinite number [$\aleph$, aleph]. We can then begin to explore what can happen by using this sign or symbol. We note that it allows us, in fact, to handle in a new symbolic way relations [i.e., operations] that are admissible in the series of whole numbers, which constitute its reality. Not all of them can be taken up anew in this way, but some of them certainly can.

This has led to progress that is still ongoing in mathematical discourse, which, while knowing itself at every moment, never fails to encounter a combination of limits with holes known as infinite numbers – in other words, unfathomables – until we are able to reduce them to limits by taking them up in a different structure. An aporia here is never anything but the encounter with some facet of the Other's structure.

We see this quite clearly in set theory, in which we can in fact innocently make headway for a while. It especially interests us because, at the more radical level with which we deal, that of the impact of the signifier in repetition, nothing apparently objects to the fact that A is the complete inscription of all possible histories. Every signifier refers all the more to the Other as it can refer to itself only qua Other. Which means that nothing stops signifiers from being distributed in a circular manner.

331   This is what allows us to clearly state that there is a set of everything that is not identical to itself. It is perfectly conceivable that things are organized in such a way as to go around in a circle, even the catalog of all catalogs that don't include themselves. It is perfectly admissible on the sole condition that we know that no catalog contains itself, apart from its title. This doesn't stop the set of all catalogs from having the closed characteristic that each catalog, insofar as it does not include itself, can always be inscribed in another catalog that it itself includes.

If we draw the directed network of these things, the only one that is excluded is the circular path which implies that *b* refers to itself [see the circle on the left in Figure 21.1]. It suffices that *b* refer to *c* and that c refer back to b for there to be no obstacle to the correlative subsistence of b and c, or to them both being included in some larger whole [e.g., the schema on the right in Figure 21.1].

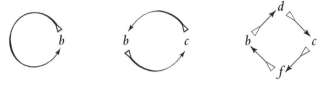

Figure 21.1: The First Pathway is Excluded

2

What psychoanalytic experience does is detect somewhere the "point at infinity" [also known in mathematics as the "ideal point"] of everything that is organized in the realm of signifying combinations. This point at infinity is irreducible, insofar as it concerns a certain jouissance that is left problematic, insofar as it raises the question of jouissance in a way that is no longer outside the system of knowledge.

The signifier of jouissance – a signifier that is excluded inasmuch as it is the one we promote, calling it the "phallic signifier" – is that around which all the biographies to which psychoanalytic literature tends to reduce neurosis revolve.

Indeed, once an analyst becomes accustomed to this, he begins to take for granted the strained infantile relations that develop between a subject and a certain number of terms – father, mother, and a baby brother or sister – and he considers them to be the earliest terms, even though they only take on meaning and weight owing to the place they occupy in the links between knowledge, jouissance, and a certain object. That, at least, is how I am formulating it today – I shall perhaps formulate it more elaborately hereafter, at least I hope so.

It is not enough to take a step back from the current "interpersonal relations," as they are called, that someone whom we call an adult (an adult who is, I must say, necessarily adulterated) comes to confide in us about and to point out a simple homology – even if it is as complete as possible – between them and his earliest relationships. The latter must all be situated with respect to these three terms whose presence, weight, and insistence in the course of the analysis we convey – whether we like it or not, and whether we know it or not – by the way in which we understand the second (or rather first) biography, said to concern childhood. We say that it is the

332

earliest, but often it is there merely to mask the question we really have to explore: what determines it.

Its sole mainspring is always, of course, found in the way in which the father's and mother's desires presented themselves – in other words, the way in which they in fact offered knowledge, jouissance, and object *a* to their child. This is what must consequently incite us to not merely explore the subject's history, but the way in which each of these terms was offered to him. Therein lies what we improperly call "the choice of neurosis," or even the choice between psychosis and neurosis. There was no choice, for the choice was already made at the level of what was presented to the subject, but that can only be located and perceived as a function of the three terms I have just tried to bring out for you.

Their import is not singular, and part of it is historical. We must indicate what psychoanalysis signifies in history where certain choices were offered to it, too, relations between knowledge and jouissance, considered on a community-wide scale, not being the same in our times as in Antiquity, for example. Could anyone possibly believe our position is akin to that of the Epicureans or another such school? A certain retreat from [or: suspension of, *retrait au regard de*] jouissance was possible for them, in a way that was in some sense innocent, whereas owing to the emergence of what we call capitalism, we are all included in the relation to jouissance in a way that is characterized by the ridgeline [*arête*] of its purity, as it were.

333

What is known as the "exploitation of workers" very precisely involves the fact that jouissance, being excluded from work, provides them – by dint of that very fact and in the same way I mentioned earlier regarding the point at infinity – with their entire reality [*réel*]. This is what brings on the sort of aporia that is suggested by the new meaning (which was absent from its Ancient context, and is without precedent) acquired by the word "revolution" with regard to the domination [*empire*] of society.

We have something to say about this, first of all to recall to mind the close, circular tie between this word and the system that brings it to us: the capitalist system. Marx saw this quite clearly, and it is even the only thing that he articulated that has thus far proven effective. But we as analysts perhaps also have something to propose regarding this. We could point, with a series of examples, to a seam where this circle could open up. This is what makes psychoanalysis of interest, I mean of historical interest. We could also quite miserably fail to do so.

If we examine the turning point that biographically constitutes the moment at which a neurosis is born, we see a choice being offered, being offered in a way that is all the more insistent in that it is itself what is determinant at that turning point.

The choice is between what is rendered present – namely, the point of impossibility or point at infinity that always enters the picture when one first encounters sexuality [*la conjonction sexuelle*] – and its correlate, which is the projection of this impossibility onto inadequacy stemming from the fact that it arises in childhood prior to puberty [*prémature*]. But how could this time not always be premature with regard to impossibility? This impossibility is masked by inadequacy and diverted from having to be executed, because the subject is not necessarily up to it qua living being when left to his own devices.

The alibi that is based on the impossibility in inadequacy is also a detour [*pente*], as I called it earlier, that psychoanalysis can take. After all, humanly speaking, we cannot fail to sense that we are ministers of succor and may, at one point or another, with one person or another, have the opportunity to do something beneficial.

Nevertheless, that is not what justifies psychoanalysis, nor is it where it comes from or where its meaning lies. This is so for a simple reason, which is that it is not what the neurotic attests to.

334

3

If we are willing to listen, what the neurotic tells us through all of his symptoms – which constitute the locus in which his discourse is situated – is that he seeks solely to be equal to the question he raises.

Whether hysteric or obsessive – I will establish later the link between these two facets of neurosis and object *a* as I expounded it in phobia's efficacity – the neurotic calls into question the truth of knowledge. He does so precisely because knowledge is attached to jouissance.

Is the neurotic right to raise this question anew? Of course he is, since we know that knowledge not only derives its earliest status from its dependence on jouissance, but articulates its distance from it in the course of its development. Yet, it is not because his discourse is, naturally, dependent on the truth of knowledge that, as I have already explained, it necessarily concerns [or: falls under, *relève de*] this truth. The fact that what he says may be true [or: in the right, *dans le vrai*] still does not make legible what, at a certain level, exposes the coherence or constitutive knot by which knowledge depends on the prohibition of jouissance.

Why wouldn't the neurotic constitute a certain form of aporia himself, the kind I showed earlier with a mathematical example, in the form of a stance adopted regarding the impasses that can be formulated as the Other's law in sexual matters?

After having reviewed as many of the facets distinguishing obsession from hysteria as I could, I would say that, in the final analysis, the best formulations that I can provide you of them proceed from what nature offers, from what is natural, as a solution to the impasse of the Other's law.

For man, insofar as he must identify with the so-called function of the symbolic Father – the only function that satisfies, which is why it is mythical – the position of virile jouissance in the sexual encounter [*la conjonction sexuelle*] is what nature offers. This is precisely what is known as "being the master." This was, and still quite adequately remains, within a person's grasp.

Well, I will say that the obsessive is the one who in fact refuses to consider himself a master, because – with regard to what is at stake, the truth of knowledge – what is of concern to him is the relationship between this knowledge and jouissance. What he knows about this knowledge is that he possesses nothing but what remains from the first impact of its prohibition – namely, object *a*. Jouissance is unthinkable to him except as a treaty [*traité*] with the Other, who is always imagined by him to be fundamentally whole. He negotiates [*traite*] with the Other. He is authorized to experience jouissance only if he pays over and over again, there being some sort of insatiable Danaides barrel, an account that can never be squared. This is what turns the terms and conditions of debt [repayment] into the only ceremony in which he encounters his jouissance.

It is no accident that we find the hysterical form of response to the impasses of jouissance at the other end of the spectrum.

Hysteria is characterized by not considering oneself to be the woman [or: a woman, *la femme*] – which is why we encounter hysteria more often in women – whereas in this aporia, "being the woman" – filling that role in the sexual encounter where the hysteric's lot is naturally quite fair [*une assez bonne part*] – is quite regularly open to her, as naturally as it is open to a man.

What the hysteric represses, they say, is sexual jouissance. In reality, she promotes [or: pursues (or holds out for herself), *promeut*] the point at infinity of jouissance as absolute. She promotes [*promeut*] castration at the level of the symbolic Name-of-the-Father, with regard to which she adopts the stance of wanting to be his ultimate jouissance. And it is because this jouissance cannot be attained that she refuses all others, which, with regard to the absolute relationship that she feels a need to establish, would seem lesser. This is true, moreover, because it is only tangentially related, being solely at the level of adequacy or inadequacy.

In light of these terms, I would recommend that you read and reread cases of hysteria, and you will see that they consist of something quite different from anecdotes and from a going around in biographical circles, which the transference, by repeating it, resolves in order to make it easier to deal with, but merely tempers. We undoubtedly strive to calm what we are presented with there by way of an opening or gap, but isn't it essential to locate the mainspring by which it arises? What the neurotic questions anew is nothing other than the border – a border that nothing can in fact suture – that opens up between knowledge and jouissance.

My discussion of 1 and *a* here was certainly not included at random, and it is not obsolete. This mathematical model is nothing but a sequence of numbers in which, on the sole condition that we write the relationship among them as involving addition, *a* as a function links up with the simple repetition of the 1. There is no reason to be surprised by this, for it is the first thing we encounter there.

$$1, 1, 2, 3, 5, 8, 13, 21, 34, \ldots$$

After two 1s we have a 2, and we continue on indefinitely. The second 1 added to the 2 makes 3. 3 plus 2 is 5. And after that, we have 8, 13, and so on and so forth. This sequence, as I told you, more and more closely approximates the ratio *a* as the numbers get bigger.

If we go in the opposite direction, the negative direction, proceeding by subtraction, the same series arrives at a limit [see Figure 8.4]. The sequence marked by the ratio *a* keeps getting smaller until it arrives – assuming we sum it all up – at a thoroughly finite limit, which can constitute a new point of departure.

What constitutes hysteria can be inscribed in this [negative] direction. Namely, the hysteric subtracts *a* from the absolute 1 of the Other because he or she interrogates it in order to see if it will deliver up the final 1 which would in some sense assure [or: insure] it. With the help of this model, it is easy to demonstrate that the entirety of the hysteric's effort to call *a* into question leads, in the process, at best to the subject being strictly equated with *a* and nothing else. This is the drama which – being transposed from the mathematical level, where it can be correctly stated, to another level – is translated by the irreducible gap of an actual castration.

At the level of statements, a level that I characterized with the term *famil* [see Chapter XVIII], the impasse created by the hysteric is in fact resolved through the encounter with castration. But there are other possible outcomes at the level of enunciation, which promote [*promeuvent*] the relationship between jouissance and knowledge.

336

Thanks to illustrious historical examples, everyone must know that the solution can be found in a subjective equilibrium, on the sole condition that the appropriate tribute is paid by the edifice of a [form of] knowledge – a knowledge that would like to be knowledge that is corroborated by [or: overlapped (or intersected) by, *se recouvrant d'un*] tried and true knowledge of sexual relations such as they are perceived only on the basis of the apprehension of the point at infinity, which constitutes an impasse and an aporia, certainly, but which also constitutes a limit.

Everyone knows that the same is true for the obsessive. We all know that an entire sector depends on the obsessive's productivity. Even those who are most blind, the most closed off to historical reality, have noticed his contribution to what we call thought. Isn't this also something that expresses its [or: his] limit and must be thoroughly de-exorcised?

This is the question Freud raised when he talked about the relation between obsessive rituals and religion. Religions obviously are not exhaustively accounted for by such practices. Pascal's wager is anxiety-provoking precisely because it forces us to see this.

Even if we consider things at the level of the promise, even if we turn out to be partisans of the God of Abraham, Isaac, and Jacob and reject the Other to such an extent that we say we don't know whether he is or, moreover, what he is, it is nevertheless clearly the Other that Pascal investigated in his wager in terms of even or odd, of "he is or he is not." For, indeed, given his era, he was caught up in this questioning of knowledge.

It is on that point that I will leave you today.

May 21, 1969

JOUISSANCE: ITS LOGIC

XXII

PARADOXES OF
PSYCHOANALYTIC ACTION

The two Gods
The nonexistence of the subject-supposed-to-know
Only repetition is interpretable
The psychoanalyst as a scapegoat
Comparison with masochistic practices

There are fewer people standing today. For their sake, I don't regret it, but it means that there are fewer people here today, which I do regret because I always say the most interesting things in the final meetings. That's my style.

Which reminds me that, last year, around the beginning of a certain memorable month of May [1968] and the events that took place then, I – of my own accord and for reasons that I don't repudiate – interrupted my Seminar. Whether my reasons were legitimate or not, the fact remains that what I said was left truncated.

The topic was "psychoanalytic action" [*l'acte psychanalytique*], which no one had even dreamt of naming before me, which makes it obvious that people hadn't even considered it. Had they thought that some kind of action takes place in psychoanalysis, all they had to do was name it. I cannot but believe that this truth remained veiled.

It's no accident, I think, that what I had to say about action got truncated that year. There is a relationship, which is naturally not one of causation, between the events of May and the failure of analysts regarding the topic of action, specifically psychoanalytic action. But there is also a relationship between what caused those events and the field in which psychoanalytic action is situated, such that one can say that it is undoubtedly owing to a lack of interest in this action on their part that analysts have not shown themselves up until now to be terribly disposed or available to provide any sort of take on these events, no matter how superficial.

On the other hand, it is, of course, merely accidental that those events interrupted what I had to say about action. I don't deplore the interruption, because it gave me an excuse not to say what, in short, "mustn't be said" on the topic of psychoanalytic action. Still, I view the latter as an appointment I need to keep.

You see here that, owing to what I proposed last time, we end up back at something that is not far from the field I discussed last year, since, in the wager, action is clearly involved, insofar as it is related to object *a*. You should realize that this object is included in the title of this year's Seminar, and that it is what is at stake in my discourse.

That is what I must provide a formal expression of in this year's final meetings.

1

For at least those of you who recall what I ended on last time, it may, it seems to me, be of interest to remind you that I emphasized object *a* in the field of Pascal's wager.

That is the approach I selected this year by which to indicate that it lies in the field of the Other and defines a certain game [*jeu*]: what I call the *en-Je* [in-I, a homonym of *enjeu*, stake(s)], with my usual play on words.

It may seem odd that I discussed Pascal's wager, given my position, which is not ambiguous in this regard and which is certainly not that of religious apologetics. For that wager is formulated as a response to a certain partner who is taken at his word, so to speak – at his word in speech that is attributed to him owing, good Lord, as is widely accepted, to the promise of eternal life he makes us. This is a point taken for granted by all believers who follow God's commandments, at least in the field of what constitutes this God's broadest religious reference – namely, the Church.

It is not unfitting to begin there, because it has an altogether clear relationship to something permanent in our structures, structures that go much further than what one might call "mental structures." The structures that are defined by everyday discourse and language obviously go much further than what can be reduced to the function of mentality. As I regularly stress, we are completely surrounded by it, even in areas that don't seem at first glance to be obviously related to it.

The structure I wish to begin with today is the earliest structure, the one I call "from an Other" [cf. the title of this Seminar]. We must indicate how far it goes, owing to the impact of psychoanalysis, and reveal that we can harbor no doubt about it, as it were, given

343

our horizon. This Other, who is clearly the God of the philosophers, is not as easy to eliminate as people think. In reality, it remains, in any case, stable on the horizon of all our thinking, and it is obviously not unrelated to the presence of the God of Abraham, Isaac, and Jacob.

Before returning to the structure of this Other – because it is quite necessary to spell out here what must be designated about it – it is worth recalling at the outset that, if this structure is present for us, on a certain structural horizon, as determined by everyday discourse (which is the field that Freud designates as "civilization," Western civilization, that is), the presence of the other God, the one who speaks – namely the God of the Jews, the God of Abraham, Isaac, and Jacob – clearly props him up.

This is not solely because the God of the philosophers, the Other with a capital O, is One. What distinguishes the God of the Jews – the one at the origin of monotheism – is not the fact that he posits himself as One (regardless of how our notion of the One has evolved since then). It is worth recalling that the God of the burning bush and on Mount Sinai never said he was the only God, but rather, "I am what I am." That's a horse of a different color. It does not mean He is the only god but that where He is there is no other god at the same time as Him. If you look closely, you will see that this is what it says in the Bible. Where He is, on His turf – namely, in the Holy Land – it is out of the question to obey any other god than Him. But the presence of other gods where He is not, where it is not His land, is never denied. Punishment never rains down except when tribute is paid to other gods where He who said "I am what I am" alone is supposed to reign.

Some people might think that this is merely of historical interest, but let me get to the point and make it clear that it is simply to return to what I first stated, which is that the God in question stands out owing to the fact that he speaks. Regardless of how this speech was distorted thereafter (for it is not clear that people say exactly the same thing in the Catholic Church, apostolic and Roman), this is what justifies us in saying, in any case, that He is the God who is defined by His relationship to speech, that we are dealing with a God who speaks. This is why prophets are preeminent in the Jewish tradition. The dimension of Revelation as such – namely, of speech as bearing truth within it – has never been as clearly highlighted outside of that tradition. Elsewhere, the place of truth, since it must clearly be covered [or: accounted for, *couverte*], is filled by myths, for example. It is not covered by prophecy, except in a thoroughly local manner known as oracular prophecy, which has an entirely different meaning than prophesizing as such.

344

That was a rather long introduction, but I needed to enumerate certain giant landmarks which must be kept in mind in order to clearly understand what is at stake when we say that, with respect to the field of truth – which interests us immensely even if we don't identify it with what has been revealed – knowledge lies elsewhere.

This is why, as soon as the dimension of Revelation is introduced, a traditional dimension in our culture is simultaneously introduced – which we should not believe is dead in our times – that of the "double truth," as it is improperly called. It refers to the distinction between truth and knowledge.

What psychoanalysis has revealed – which no one previously suspected – is what is produced in knowledge: namely, object *a*.

2

Psychoanalysis articulates object *a* for what it is: namely, the cause of desire, in other words, the cause of the subject's division, the cause of what ushers into the subject what the *cogito* masks, which is that next to this being who he believes assures his existence [*dont il croit s'assurer*], the *a* is, essentially and right from the outset, lack.

I am returning here to the way in which I felt I needed to introduce the paradox of psychoanalytic action last year.

345 Psychoanalytic action presents itself as inciting people to know. The rule we give analysands implies that they can say whatever they like. Lord knows how absurd that can seem at first. If they took us at our word, if those we initiate into this practice set about truly saying everything that goes through their minds – which truly means anything whatsoever – and found meaning in it, where would it take us? If we are able to trust them in this enterprise, it is precisely because of something that is implicit, even if they cannot articulate it, which is that regardless of what you say, there is the Other – the Other who knows what it means.

The God of the philosophers, however he may have been linked in the course of history to the God who speaks, is certainly no stranger to the latter. It was not illegitimate to turn the God of the philosophers into the throne, support, or seat of the One who spoke. Even when the God who speaks rose to take His leave, at least for certain people, the seat of the Other stayed behind, insofar as it situates the unifying and unified field that has a name for those who think. Let us call it, if you will, the "principle of sufficient reason."

The fact that at least a number of you did not suspect as much – a number that I presume to exist, for, after all, I do not know it exists – doesn't stop you from being underpinned by the principle of sufficient reason. Perhaps all of you are able to perceive this, but if you don't, it doesn't matter: you are nevertheless situated in the field in which the principle of sufficient reason underpins everything. It would certainly not be easy to conceptualize what would happen were things to be otherwise, even if it is perfectly conceivable.

I am stating this principle here before you as something that lies on the horizon of what makes psychoanalytic experience possible. Namely, that even if there seems to be no sufficient reason for something you say in looking no further than saying whatever is going through your mind, there will always be a sufficient reason for it. This is what suffices to situate the Other with a capital O, the one who knows, on the horizon. This is, in any case, altogether clear in the privileged subjects of this experience – neurotics. The neurotic seeks to know. We will try to figure out why more precisely, but he seeks to know, and at the outset of analytic experience, we have no trouble inciting him to, in short, trust in this Other as the locus in which knowledge is instated, that is, trust in the subject-supposed-to-know.

It is thus regarding the subject of what is articulated qua knowledge already at the most basic level, no matter how basic it may be, that we intervene by making an interpretation. The latter is distinguished from what this term designates everywhere else. In logic, for example, the interpretation of a logical system involves illustrating it, as they say, by providing a system of lesser scope that is, in this regard, more accessible. That goes no further than superimposing knowledge-based articulations. Psychoanalytic interpretation differs therefrom by the fact that – in linking up with what is already articulated qua knowledge, no matter how primitive – it aims at an effect, a knowledge effect, that it renders palpable owing to its truth.

This truth is, as I have said, related to desire – in other words, to the subject's division. Let me go straight to the point, as I cannot trace out anew the entire pathway now, and because what I have to discuss today is something else. The truth in question comes down to the following: the Freudian Thing, that is, this truth – the Freudian Thing and this truth are one and the same – is asexual, as opposed to what people say, namely, that Freud's theory is pansexualist. However, since the living being – who is that being by whom a truth is transmitted – has a sexual function and position, there is consequently no such thing as a sexual relationship, in the precise sense of the term in which a relationship [*rapport*] is a logically definable relation [or: operation, *relation*].

As I tried to formulate it for you not just one but two years ago this time [in Seminar XIV, *The Logic of Fantasy*], what we might call the sexual relationship is missing – namely, a relation [*relation*] that

346

is definable as such between the sign of the male and the sign of the female. The sexual relationship, referring here to what is commonly known by that term, can only be constructed on the basis of an act [or: action, *acte*]. This is what allowed me to propose two notions: that there is *no* such thing as a sexual act, in the sense in which that act is based on a true relationship, and conversely, that there are nothing *but* sexual acts [*acte*], in the sense in which the relationship can only be created through acts.

Psychoanalysis reveals to us that the true dimension of action – the true dimension of the sexual act, for sure, but of all other acts as well, and this has been obvious for a long time – is failure [*l'échec*]. Which is why, at the heart of the sexual relationship, there is what is known in psychoanalysis as castration.

I spoke earlier today about "what is produced in knowledge." You obviously didn't pay very close attention. I should have said "what knowledge produces." I couldn't say it just then because one mustn't jump the gun. In order for that to have a meaning, we have to look at it more closely and delineate the true dimension of production.

347

One might say that only a certain process of technological progress has allowed us to discern production as designating the fruit of labor, but is it as simple as all that? In order for production to be truly distinguished from what has always been known as poesis – making or working, like a potter does – it was necessary that the *means* of production become autonomous. This is quite clear in capitalism where everything revolves around the question of knowing who has these means at his disposal. It is on the basis of a similar homology that the distinction between the function of knowledge and the production of knowledge can be brought out. The production of knowledge qua knowledge is distinct – since it is a means of production, and not simply labor – from truth. It is in this sense that knowledge produces what I call object *a*.

Object *a* takes the place of the gap that is designated by the impasse of the sexual relationship, and it redoubles the subject's division by giving him his cause, which up until then could not in any way be grasped, for what is specific to castration is that nothing can truly enunciate it, because its cause is absent. Object *a* takes its place qua cause substituted for the radical gap [or: crack, *faille*] in the subject.

After defining the function of object *a* in this way two years ago, I told you last year that the psychoanalyst – because he has at his disposal this path, means, or trick known as the fundamental rule of psychoanalysis, which involves the incitement to know that I mentioned, whereas he doesn't know all that much himself – is he who takes upon himself the task of propping up the *subject-supposed-to-know*. I also told you, and in plenty of different ways, that the problem in our times, in the current situation of psychoanalysis, should merely be understood as one of the symptoms of the fact that it is clear this subject-supposed-to-know doesn't exist. Indeed, nothing indicates that the Other – this unique locus where knowledge supposedly comes together – constitutes a One, that the Other isn't, just like the subject, signifiable only on the basis of the signifier of a specific topology that can be summed up in terms of object *a*.

The psychoanalyst thus invites the subject, the neurotic in this case, to follow a path that leads him to encounter a subject-supposed-to-know, because this incitement to know should lead him to truth. At the end of this operation, object *a*, insofar as it represents the gap in truth, is evacuated; and it is the analyst himself who represents this evacuated object on the basis of his *en-soi* [in-himself], so to speak. In other words, the analyst falls away, he himself becoming the rejected fiction.

348

This is what led me to highlight the enigma and paradox of psychoanalytic action. If it is true that the psychoanalyst knows what an analysis is and what it leads to, how can he execute this action?

I mentioned the word "fiction" here. I proposed that truth has a fictional structure a long time ago already [see, for example, *Écrits*, pp. 11, 375–6, 625, and 684]. Should object *a* be taken simply as pointing to the subject of truth, who presents himself as divided, or must we, as it seems, accord it more substance? Don't you sense that we are faced here with a nasty knot, which already accounts in Aristotle's logic for the ambiguity between substance and subject, between *ousia* and *hypokeimenon*, that persists throughout his work, even if the two functions are distinguished, but as in a braid.

Hypokeimenon is clearly isolated by him insofar as, logically, it is nothing other than what mathematical logic was able to isolate later in the function of the variable – in other words, the function of something that can only be designated by a predicative proposition. As for the word *ousia*, honestly, it would be far better translated by *être* [being] or by *étance*, by Heidegger's *Wesen*, than by *substantia*, substance, a word that merely perpetuates the said ambiguity. It is there that we find ourselves when we try to articulate the function of object *a*.

An enigma or question remains regarding an act which – owing to the very person who inaugurates it, namely the psychoanalyst – can only be initiated by veiling what it will entail for him, not only at the terminus of the process, but, strictly speaking, its end [or: goal, *fin*], inasmuch as the terminus retroactively determines the meaning of the whole process, inasmuch as the terminus is truly the final cause.

The use of this term deserves no derision here, for nothing in the field of structure is conceivable without a final cause. What alone deserves to be derided in so-called finalism is the notion that the end has the slightest utility whatsoever.

Does the analyst know what he is doing when he acts? That is the precise point at which I broke off my Seminar last year, owing to the events I mentioned earlier today, on the horizon of a knot that was so seriously and rigorously investigated by calling psychoanalytic action into question. The interruption freed me from assuredly embarrassing resonances, which are nevertheless those around which both psychoanalytic theory and institutions can be questioned.

I will perhaps say a bit more about it in what will now follow.

3

Let us begin by recalling to mind what results from this way of positing, between knowledge and truth, the true field of production, where we see that it is, in short, the psychoanalyst himself who incarnates production.

It is in such terms that we must situate transference, for example.

Given that what we call transference is interpreted in psychoanalysis in terms of repetition, why could analysts – except those who are absolutely lost in this network such as I articulate it – possibly need to call into question its objective status and claim that it is the refusal to face something else, to face what is really at stake in the analysis? For indeed, analysis is a situation based solely on the structure within which nothing of the analyst's discourse can be enunciated that does not conform to the fact that structure rules [*commande*]. We can thus grasp nothing therein except what involves repetition.

I am not asking whether repetition is predominant in the [patient's] history. In a situation that is designed to investigate what presents itself on the basis of structure, no history is organized except by repetition. Let me repeat that what is at stake is what can be said at the level of putting the effects of knowledge in the analysis to the test. It is not correct to say that transference is itself defined by repetitive effects. Transference is defined by the relationship to the subject-supposed-to-know, insofar as it is structural and linked to the locus of the Other qua locus in which knowledge is illusorily articulated as One. To investigate in this way the functioning of he who seeks to know, everything that is articulated must be articulated in terms of repetition.

To whom do we owe such an experience? It is clear that it would never have been instated were there no neurotics. Who needs to know the truth? Only he who is bothered by knowledge. That is the very definition of the neurotic.

We are going to zero in on this more closely, but before leaving the topic – about which I have not come full circle, and for good reason – I still want to point out, in what might seem to be a tangent with regard to what I am tracing out today, a final landmark with which I am trying to correctly delineate this field.

If we operate in this field, as I just said we do, in a way that we admit to be incomplete [*partiale*], we must admit that repetition is the only thing in analysis that is interpretable, and that this is what we take transference to be. And the end [*fin*] that I designate as the taking up [*prise*] of the analyst in himself in the excavating of *a* [or: drilling for *a*, *forage d'a*] is very precisely what constitutes what is not interpretable. In short, what is uninterpretable in psychoanalysis is the analyst's presence. Which explains why, when people try to interpret his presence – as they do, and ink has even been spilled about it – they open the door to "acting out"*: they invite it to occupy that place [i.e., the place of the analyst's presence].

In order to designate the precise places of the analyst and the subject in psychoanalysis, I reminded you, in last year's Seminar, of the distinction we must make, regarding the Oedipal myth, between the heroic staging that serves analytic practice as a mythical reference point and what is articulated behind that: the knot of jouissance at the origin of all knowledge. The subject's division forms and modulates like the division between the spectator and the chorus in Greek tragedy. As for the analyst, he is in the place of what was played out onstage: he merely occupies the place of the actor, inasmuch as one single actor suffices to occupy that stage. This is what gives psychoanalytic action its meaning. The other striking paradox of psychoanalytic action is, as I reminded you last year, the actor who effaces himself by evacuating object *a*. That connects back up with what I said earlier.

This is what shows us that, if the fundamental rule of psychoanalysis demands that he who enters into analysis avoid a *passage à l'acte* [desperate action], it is precisely in order to privilege the place of "acting out"* for which the analyst alone takes and maintains responsibility.

"Say nothing, see nothing, hear nothing" – who can forget that these are the terms with which a certain wisdom tradition, not ours, indicates the path that should be followed by those who seek the truth? Isn't there something strange – assuming we recognize the meaning those commandments thus take on – about the fact that we

351   see something analogous in the analyst's position? Yet the analytic
           context makes it bear singular fruits. By *saying nothing*, the voice is
           detached [or: isolated], as the core of what constitutes words on the
           basis of saying [or: as the core of what, on the basis of what is said
           (or, on the basis of the act of saying), constitutes speech, *noyau de ce
           qui, du dire, fait parole*]. The gaze is detached [or: isolated] by *seeing
           nothing*, which is all too often true of analysts; the gaze is the tight
           knot around the sack that contains everything, at least everything
           that is seen. Lastly, by *hearing nothing* of the two demands in which
           desire has slipped and which summon it, we enfetter it in the func-
           tion of the breast or excrement.
               What reality could prompt the analyst to serve this function?
           What desire or satisfaction can he encounter there? I don't intend
           to designate it immediately, even if I must say more about it before
           leaving you today.
               We should emphasize a certain dimension here, that of the
           "scapegoat"* – it was one of Frazer's favorite themes – and high-
           light it properly. We know that its origin is Semitic. The scapegoat
           is the analyst who takes object *a* upon himself and who acts in such
           a way that he can forever be a reprieve [or: suspended sentence,
           sursis] for the subject, such that the fruit of a completed [*terminée*]
           analysis – as I called it last year – is a truth of which the subject
           can no longer be cured, precisely because one of its terms has been
           evacuated. Doesn't this explain the singular position occupied by
           the community of psychoanalysts in the social world, a community
           that takes the form of an International Association for the protec-
           tion of scapegoats? Scapegoats save themselves by forming a group
           and, even more so, by creating ranks. It is true that it is difficult to
           imagine a society of scapegoats. So one creates head scapegoats and
           scapegoats who are next in line to become head scapegoats. It is
           truly odd.
               Poking fun like that wouldn't be justified if, in the documents that
           I just received regarding an upcoming Congress that people have
           the gall to hold in Rome, there weren't [published] texts that make
           it clear that even if people ignore Lacan's discourse, they find them-
           selves faced with the very same difficulties I just articulated.
               They knock themselves out, for example, by attempting to define
           what is non-transferential in the analytic situation, and they come
           up with statements that are, strictly speaking, tantamount to an
           admission that they haven't the foggiest. They haven't the foggiest
           because they don't hold the key, and they don't hold the key because
           they don't want to look [at the texts] where I have formulated it.
           Similarly, they invent a term, the "self" – and it would be quite
           worthwhile if someone was curious enough to investigate how it

can be explained and resolved in a discourse like the one I have just pronounced today. If I have time in the meetings to come, I may say more about it. The error, or rather the ineptitude, of what is said on the topic of the analytic treatment of psychosis – the complete failure they evince to situate psychosis in a psychopathology that is analytic in nature – has the same mainspring.

352

I indicated that I could have articulated something more regarding analytic action, from which I was fortunately dispensed, as I said. It is in relation to masochism that this articulation should be provided. It would be instructive to compare psychoanalytic action and masochistic practices, assuredly not in order to conflate them. This was already indicated, and, in some sense, introduced, by what I said about the conjunction of the perverse subject with object *a*, which is literally displayed in masochistic practices.

One might, in a certain way, say that the masochist is the true master, as much as he wishes to be. He is the master of the real game. He can, of course, founder. It is even highly likely that he will, because he requires no less than the Other with a capital *O*. When the eternal Father is no longer there to play the role, there is no one to do so. If you address a woman, of course, if you address Wanda [the protagonist of Leopold von Sacher-Masoch's *Venus in Furs*], there is no chance – the poor girl hasn't the foggiest. But even if the masochist founders, he gets off on it anyway, such that one can say that he is the master of the real game.

I, naturally, wouldn't dream even for a second of imputing such success to the psychoanalyst. That would require me to trust in his ability to seek out his jouissance that I am far from granting. And it wouldn't, moreover, be very fitting. Let us say that the psychoanalyst plays the part of the master [*fait le maître*], in both senses of the word *faire* [creates and plays the part of]. I will return to this formulation, regarding – and there should be nothing surprising about this – obsessives.

Try to pay attention for another five minutes, because what I am saying is very condensed and subtle.

As I told you earlier, the question that arises regarding psychoanalytic action is that of the decisive act which, owing to the analysand, leads to the emergence and establishment of the psychoanalyst. Whereas the psychoanalyst is conflated with the production of the analysand's doing [*faire*] or work, we can say that the analysand creates [*fait*] the psychoanalyst, in the strongest sense of the term. But we can also say that at the precise moment at which the said psychoanalyst emerges, if it is so hard to grasp what can motivate him to do so, it is because his action comes down to

353   *faire* the psychoanalyst in the sense of simulation [or: posturing, *simagrée*], to playing the part of he who guarantees the subject-supposed-to-know. Who hasn't told the person who was willing to help him out early on in his career [i.e., his supervisor] that he has the impression he is acting a part, that of the analyst? Why devalue this testimony? Lastly, and taking up anew this time the two functions of the word *faire*, isn't leading someone to the terminus of his psychoanalysis – to the end of his incurable truth, to the point at which he knows that, although there truly is action, there is no sexual relationship – to somehow *faire* true mastery, even if it doesn't often happen?

Still, if the psychoanalyst can also be said to be involved in the game, he is certainly not the master [*maître*] thereof, unlike the masochist. And yet he props up and incarnates its trump card [or: strong suit, *atout-maître*], because he is the one who plays the role of object *a* – a weighty role, if ever there was one.

I have never before taken my discourse on psychoanalytic action this far. What is the status of the point at which this discourse itself can be situated – namely, the point from which I enunciate it? Is it the point where the subject-supposed-to-know is located? In speaking about analytic action, can I be its savant? Certainly not. Nothing is final about the investigation of this action that I am undertaking. Why wouldn't I be its logician, something that is confirmed by the fact that this logic makes me odious to so many? This logic is articulated on the basis of the very coordinates of our practice, and of the points from which it derives its motivation. Isn't knowledge – insofar as it is produced by truth – what a certain version of the relations between knowledge and jouissance imagines?

For the neurotic, knowledge is the subject-supposed-to-know's jouissance. It is in this respect that the neurotic is incapable of sublimation. Sublimation is characteristic of he who knows how to revolve around [*faire le tour de*] what the subject-supposed-to-know is reduced to [i.e., object *a*]. Every artistic creation involves closing in on [*cernement*] what remains irreducible in knowledge insofar as it is distinguished from jouissance. Something nevertheless comes to mark this enterprise, insofar as it forever designates that the subject is unfit to fully realize it.

Don't we find, at the threshold of knowledge, something analogous to the imputation that the work done by those who are exploited is presumed to contribute to the exploiter's jouissance? For the means knowledge creates make of those who possess those means the ones who take advantage of those who earn this knowl354   edge by the sweat of their truth. The analogy would undoubtedly fall flat when used in such distinct contexts, if knowledge hadn't shown itself for some time already to be thoroughly implicated in the field of what is known as the capitalist mode of exploitation.

It just so happens that excess exploitation displeases people. I say "displeases people" because there is nothing further to be said about it. The principle of revolutionary revolt is none other than the fact that there is a point at which things displease people. I hope you recall that, last year, I indicated that the analyst's position – assuming it has to rigorously coincide with his action – is such that, in the field of creation [*faire*] that he inaugurates with the help of this action, there is no room for anything that displeases him or even for what pleases him. If he makes room for that, he abandons his position.

Still, this doesn't mean he has nothing to say to those who, in the field of knowledge, have risen up against a certain deviating of this knowledge, both as regards what can limit them and divert them, and as regards the proper way to articulate knowledge, the only one that can allow knowledge to once again leave behind the field where it exploits people.

On that note, I will end today.

Next time I promise I will discuss in detail what is involved in the respective positions of the hysteric and the obsessive with regard to the Other with a capital *O*.

June 4, 1969

XXIII

HOW TO GENERATE SURPLUS JOUISSANCE LOGICALLY

On the empty set
On the one in the Other
Hegel with Pascal
The slave's jouissance
The body purified of jouissance

This little weekly festival not being fated to continue for all eternity, today I am going to try to give you an idea of the way in which, if we were in a more favorable, better structured context, we could endeavor to make the theory a bit more rigorous.

When I selected "From an Other to the other" as the title of my Seminar this year, one of the people who, I must say, stands out here owing to his fine ear – but who, like Saint Paul on the road to Damascus, was floored along the way by something that happened to us last year (you are all aware of it, for its memory lingers on) and found himself thrown off his theorizing horse by a Maoist illumination – this person heard my title and said to me, "Well . . . it sounds banal."

I would nevertheless like to point out, if you don't already suspect as much, that the title means something that necessitates my very explicit choice of these words, which are written as I dare to hope you see them in your mind's eye: "From an Other to the other." On several occasions this year, I have written capital A on sheets of paper on which I remind you from time to time of the existence of certain graphs, and "the other" involves what I write with a lower-case a.

One might have thought that these terms no longer resonated in the flabbergasted ear by any other sound than that of a little melody by which to stroll, like "from one to the other" – "From one to the other, taking a stroll."

1

Yet, "to say from one to the other" isn't insignificant. It stresses a displacement from here to there. Those of us who are not itching at every moment to take action can wonder why talking about two ones might be of interest. If the other is still a one, why one more than the other?

There is a certain prepositional use of the terms "one" and "other," which are inserted between a "from" and a "to," the effect of which is to establish between them what I called, at another time – you perhaps recall, at least I imagine you do – a "metonymic relationship." That is what I just designated by raising the question of what interest it can be if the other is still a "one." It nevertheless becomes interesting if you write it as follows, where the metonymic relationship is between two elements, each of which is 1.

$$\text{from the } \underline{\text{one}} \text{ to the } \underline{\text{other}}$$
$$\quad\quad\quad 1 \quad\quad\quad\quad 1$$

It is important to write it in that way. Written as 1, "one" is a privileged signified effect generally known as a number. This "one" is characterized by what is called numerical identity. Nothing is designated by these terms here – we are not at the level of some sort of unary identification, for example, that of a "one" that would be inscribed on the palm of your hand as a sort of tattoo with which to identify you in a certain context, as has happened. In each case here we are talking about a line [*trait*] that marks nothing. We are at the level of what is known as strict numerical identity, which marks pure difference insofar as nothing specifies [or: differentiates] it. The other is other in no respect, and this is precisely why it is the other.

We might wonder why there are these things lying around in "from the one to the other," things known in French as definite articles. This cannot be seen very clearly at the outset in the first case. Why "*the* one"? We would be tempted to qualify the "the" [*l'*] as euphonious if we hadn't been sufficiently warned by prior experience to mistrust such explanations. Let us see if it is any better justified in the second case.

The definite article in French differs from its use in English, for example, where its demonstrative accent is so strongly stressed. A main feature of the definite article in French is to highlight notoriety [*le notoire*], as it is known. In the phrase "from the one to the other" with which we began, are we talking about "the other among all" [or: "the other among many," *l'autre entre tous*]? Are we going to gently take it in that direction? Since we say "among all," does that mean there are others? Yet it is worth realizing here, worth "recalling," as it were, that, when I wrote "the Other" with a capital *O*, I also formulated that "there is no Other of the Other." As this is truly essential to my entire discourse, I am going to have to seek some other form of notoriety for the definite article. If there is no Other of the Other, does that mean there is only one of them? But that, too, is impossible, because otherwise it would not be *the* Other.

All of this may strike you as a bit rhetorical. It is. People speculated a great deal in Ancient times about these topics, which were spelled out a bit differently back then. People spoke about the Other and the Same, and Lord knows where that led a whole lineage known as Platonic. To speak, as I do, of "the one" and "the Other" is not the same thing. The Platonic lineage naturally could not do otherwise than end up raising the question of the One, but it did so in a way that we are going to investigate, in the end, in the sense of calling it into question. The "one" – as we take it up here at the level of numerical identity – is of a different order than the One elaborated by Platonism.

It is clear, to those of you who have listened attentively this year, that the relationship "of the one to the Other" is tantamount to conveying the function of the ordered pair. You observed, in passing, the major role played by this function in the introduction of what is bizarrely called "the theory of sets" [*la théorie des ensembles*]. Everyone seems to adapt quite easily to "sets" in the plural, whereas it is a burning question, which has yet to be completely resolved, to know whether to make it a plural or not. The question at least remains open whether we may say that an element can belong to two different sets while remaining the same.

This little aside is designed to remind you of the powerful logical innovation constituted by everything related to what I will call "ensemblissement" [a play on *ensemble*, set, and *établissement*, establishment]. I like this term better than *ensemblement* [at the same time] for its consonance, even though from time to time it happens that set theory gets bogged down [or: stuck in the sand, *s'ensable*]. Yet it reassembles itself [*se réensemblit*] quite easily. In referring to set theory, I would like to highlight, in passing, the radical innovation constituted by the fact that it introduces, and literally right from its very inception, the notion that we must not conflate any specific element with the set that has it as its only element. They are not at all the same thing.

This step in logical innovation can serve us as a fitting introduction to our problematic Other, about which I just questioned why we would grant it the notorious value of calling it *the* Other, using the definite article. The Other, in the sense in which I am introducing it, provided with a capital O, takes on notoriety, not because it is the Other among all, nor because it is the only one, but because there might not be an Other at all, and simply an empty set in its stead. That is what designates it as *the* Other.

This may remind you of the schema I have written on white sheets of paper several times this year, in order to designate the relationship between the S_1 and an S_2, the latter being the other signifier of the subject in the sense that the S_1 represents the subject to another signifier.

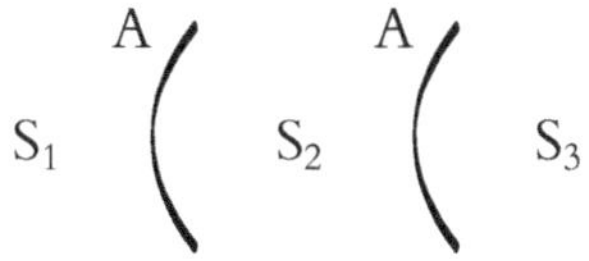

$$A \Big(\quad A \Big($$

$$S_1 \qquad S_2 \qquad S_3$$

Figure 23.1: S_1, S_2, S_3 ...

The S_1 is placed here outside of a circle, A, which precisely designates the limit of the field of the Other qua empty set. The S_2 is written in the field of the Other. This is what designates the relationship between the S_1 and the S_2.

I also emphasized that the limit of A, which is, let me repeat, the empty set, is renewed with S_3 and as many other signifiers that may come afterward, serving as a kind of relay.

We are going to explore this relay today. I have provided this reminder for those of you who might not see what I am going to designate, because you were absent when I wrote these formulas in this way.

Note that there is nothing arbitrary about identifying the limit traced out by the line here with the same repeated letter A, for it is hardly the strangest facet of set theory that, when you investigate a set, you can at any moment bring out the empty set as a subset, as they say, of it. Regardless of the level at which it is produced, it is the same empty set.

You are immediately going to be able to picture this very simply. Let us posit a set constituted by the element "one" and by the set whose only element is the element "one." This gives us a set with two distinct elements, since we cannot in any way confuse an element with the set that contains only that element.

$$\{1\{1\}\}$$

The play of so-called subsets is quite interesting in set theory, and perhaps, indeed, constitutes its main interest. I'm sorry to have

359

to provide the following reminder, but the ever-larger number of people attending here obliges me to do so.

Let us make x, y, z, and n, representing different entities, the elements of set E:

$$\{x, y, z, n\}$$

Included in set E is another set, known as a subset, which is the following:

$$\{x, y, z\}$$

There are other subsets as well, and the number of them grows quite quickly. There is the subset whose elements are $\{x, y, n\}$, the subset $\{y, z, n\}$, and so on and so forth. I need not, I think, stress this any further for it to be quite obvious to you.

At first glance, the subsets might seem to be parts [or: members] of the initial set. Yet they are nothing of the kind. It is clear that the number of subsets of the set E, from which we began in order to articulate them, is absolutely not equal to the number of elements in that set, namely 4, but goes well beyond it. It is even easy to imagine the exponential formula that gives the number of a set's constructible subsets as the number of elements in the set grows.

360   It is very important to remember this in order to shake up our belief in a supposedly natural geometry, and especially in a postulate – which, if I recall correctly, a guy by the name of Eudoxus [of Cnidus] made a great deal of – discussed somewhere in Euclid's Book X (I hope I am not mistaken). We will immediately see in passing how important this point is to us, too, by enumerating the subsets of our Other.

The Other is reduced here to its simplest function, that of being a set bearing the "one," the signifier that is necessary since it is the one to which the "one" of the subject [or: the subject as "one," *l'un du sujet*] will be represented, from the one to the Other. Later we will see within what limits it is legitimate to reduce these two Ss, S_1 and S_2, to the same "one." That is the purport of my remarks today.

$$1\{1\}$$

It is clear that by investigating the "one" inscribed in the field defined as the Other, as an actual set, its subsets will be the "one" and the following, which is the way in which we write the empty set:

$$\{1, \emptyset\}$$

This is the simplest illustration of the fact that the subsets of a set constitute a collection that is numerically greater than the number of elements in the set.

Need I stress this further?

$$\{1, \{\ \}\}$$

The double parenthesis you see here is clearly the same line as the one that designates A, exactly identical to the A qua empty set, in the two places on the schema we saw earlier [Figure 23.1].

This reminds us that, as soon as we conceptualize that something as simple as the unary trait is inscribed in the field of the Other, the function of ordered pairs arises owing to the nature of sets. Indeed, two "ones" can be inscribed here, which are distinguished owing to their different membership. The one on the left is the sole element of the initial set, which is empty prior to this inscription, whereas the one on the right fills the second empty set, if I may put it thusly, since, as an empty set, it is the same:

$$\{1, \{1\}\}$$

Herein lies the unheralded nature of the deceptively simple "from the one to the other" with which we began earlier, which served to remind us what is specific in the relation that inspired my title this year, "From an Other to the other." For everything that constitutes our experience can merely turn, return, and forever revolve around the question of the subject's subsistence – the never-to-be-lost-sight-of axis and indispensable axiomatic with which we have to deal concretely in the most effective manner possible.

If we don't, if this axis or axiom is not maintained, we fall into confusion – the kind of confusion we have been seeing all around us recently in everything that has been enunciated in the realm of psychoanalytic experience, especially when it includes, and in an ever more invasive way, the so-called function of "the self," which is especially present in current articulations of Anglo-American psychoanalysis.

2

The difference between [1] the signifier that represents the subject and [2] the signifier in relation to which it [*il*] will be inscribed in the field of the Other so that the subject of this very representation can emerge, is based, as you see, on a dissymmetry. What initial steps does that allow us to take?

This fundamental dissymmetry allows us to raise a question: What is the status of the Other? Does he know?

I am not asking you to respond with one voice. But why, after all, wouldn't you tell me the following? "No, he does not know. Everyone knows that. The subject-supposed-to-know – bang, bang, he's dead!"

If I had before me two rows of students of a certain type, who I fortunately don't have to consider to be typical, but that I can still call "amusing," they would say just that. For there are still plenty of people who believe it, and even teach it in places that are unexpected, even if they only came into being recently. But that is not at all what I said.

I didn't say that the Other does not know – those who say so don't know much about it in spite of all my efforts to teach them. I said that the Other knows – this is obvious since it is the place of the unconscious. Yet, the Other is not a subject. The negation in the formulation "there is no subject-supposed-to-know," assuming I ever said it in that negative form, bears on the subject, not on the knowledge. It is, moreover, easy to grasp if you've had a bit of experience with the unconscious, for it is characterized by the fact that we don't know who it is in there that knows [*qui c'est qui sait*].

That can be written in at least two different ways in French:

> *qui c'est qui sait* [who it is that knows]
> *qui sait qui c'est* [who knows who it is]

French is a beautiful language, especially when you know how to use it. As in every other language, double entendres aren't produced in it at random.

In my symbolism, the status of the Other is written S(A), which designates the signifier of the Other, of the Other which I characterized today as the empty set. I am specifying this, because I would not like it if – owing to the no-holds-barred style with which I earlier assumed you would reply (I am obviously obliged to imagine questions and answers here) that the Other does not know – you got it into your head that I am in the process of explaining to you what is found in the upper-left-hand corner of my graph, namely S(A̶), which is something else: the signifier of the *barred* Other. As we will have two more classes this year, I will have time to explain the difference to you. S(A) is what I just enunciated here regarding the status of the Other qua empty set. That means that the Other is in no wise One. It is not because there is no other [or: there aren't any other Others] that the Other is One.

I will assume, for the time being, that there is no confusion regarding a certain number of my notations. I am very slowly concluding that this is the case, but it is important to mention for reasons I will perhaps give you a glimpse of at the end of our meeting today. Did I really have to return to it yet again, when I have been speaking about nothing but that since the beginning? Still, I haven't yet seen proof that I have no need to return to it.

In order for the subject to come from the outside and get himself represented in the Other, he must thus find one other [or: another, *un autre*] signifier. He can only find it there [i.e., in the Other].

363

The source of the confusion is the painful necessity that makes it such that he must start from elsewhere, not for no reason of course. I cannot retrace his history for you every time – namely, how this animal with a fire lit under it [literally: with flames at its backside, *feu au derrière*] ends up needing to establish itself as a subject in the Other. It is quite clear that it is the fire lit under it that incites it to do so [laughter in the audience]. The fire lit under it is the only thing that interests you. Yet, I must be able to speak to you from time to time about what happens, leaving aside the fire, which is nevertheless, of course, the only thing that can incite he who I called an animal to get himself represented in this way.

In this perspective we must thus begin, not from the Other, but from this "one Other," the "one" of the signifier [or: the signifier as the "one," *l'un du signifiant*] inscribed in the Other, which is a necessary condition for the subject to be connected to it, and a fine occasion as well not to recall the (pre)condition of this "one" – in other words, the Other.

Well. I'm not sure you saw it coming, but if I spoke to you about Pascal and his wager at the beginning of the year, it was not merely to demonstrate an erudition – that I, moreover, hid altogether, as usual – concerning my Jansenist affinities and other such journalistic idiocies. That is not exactly what is at stake. It is, rather, to study what happens on the basis of what I just wrote on the board, and regarding which you should be at least three-quarters of an hour ahead of me.

What happens is that something must announce the subject prior to it becoming connected to the "one Other." This something is there in the simplest form, that of the same unary "one" to which, in the strictest of terms, we reduce what it can connect up with in the field of the Other.

I wrote the simplest mode of this on the board today, the mode of the subject himself counting himself as "one" [*se compter* un *lui-même*]. I must admit that it is tempting. It is even so tempting that there isn't a single one of you who doesn't do it. Despite all the psychoanalysis that has been dumped on your heads, there's nothing to be done about it. You will believe yourselves to be "one" for a long time. And it must be admitted that you have very strong reasons for doing so.

The mention of this "one" would instead make me vacillate and perhaps fall – even though I am not talking right now about mentality, cultural context, or other such trash – into the lamentable weakness of mentioning a fact that, in any case, you are incapable of understanding, because I am too: there are places in the world where the goal of religion is to avoid this "one Other." And yet, that involves such a different way of behaving toward the divinity that we cannot even say, like Pascal did, that we don't know what God is or even if He is. We cannot say so for, according to a Buddhist, that would already be saying too much about the divinity. It presupposes a discipline that is obviously required, based on the consequences that result therefrom, as you nevertheless suspect, in the relations between truth and jouissance. They spray some kind of DDT on the field of the Other, which obviously allows them to do certain things that we cannot allow ourselves to do.

The logic that arose among them at a certain moment in history, parallel to what Aristotle cooked up for us, must nevertheless bear some relation to what I am telling you here, and it would be amusing to see that relation. The preparation of the dish takes on a different form. Their logic is not so bad. It is full of things that have yet to be put to use. And instead of there simply being a major premise, a minor premise, and a conclusion, there are at least five terms. Still, in order to grasp it, you have to begin by doing a number of exercises that allow you to establish a different relationship between truth and jouissance than the one we usually find in a civilization that revolves to so great an extent around its neurotics.

Owing to that, the following is at stake: it is insofar as he is initially inscribed qua unary signifier that the subject announces himself to this "one Other" who is there, in the Other, and with respect to which he must posit himself as "one." There is a sort of double or nothing here for the subject. You thus see the import of my take on Pascal's wager which also involves just one gambler, since the Other, as I emphasized, is not a gambler but rather the empty set. The Other knows things, but since he is not a subject he cannot gamble.

Pascal articulates very clearly what is involved in this double or nothing. He even says that what is at stake is simply to have a second life after our first and that this is worth everything. That impresses us, and, as we are a civilization with neurotics at our core, we buy it, we believe it – indeed, we believe it wholeheartedly.

I believe it like you believe it. It would be worth chucking this life to receive another. Why? Because that would allow us to add them together, to make two. And we are all the more likely to win since there's no other choice. 365

I am not sure you grasp to what degree what I am saying coincides with a little schema found somewhere in the "Remarks" made on the presentation by Mr. So and So ["Remarks on Daniel Lagache's Presentation" in *Écrits*]. The schema is that of a mirrored relationship with the field of the Other, precisely constituted by the relationship to the ideal. To establish this ideal, it suffices to prop it up with the unary trait; the latter has a decisive impact, as the rest of the schema shows, on the way little *a* – which I situated in a place that allows it to be reflected in the mirror in the right manner – links up with it [*s'y accointer*]. In this figure, I am clearly forced to instate little *a* as completely given [*comme tout donné*], but this was merely a stage of the explanation, for what is at stake is to know from whence emerges this *a*, which is closely related to the unary trait in the Other, insofar as it is the basis of what, in the schema, takes on its import qua ego-ideal.

Haven't you noticed that what is at stake in the double or nothing is also found in a certain text about which I have been speaking to you for a very long time, so long that some of you must all the same have opened up Hegel's *Phenomenology of Spirit*?

To reintroduce the little story of master and slave, with its somewhat overly dramatic charge, in this way allows us to isolate the crux of the proof, as it were. Hegel was writing at a time when Germany was altogether shaken up in the wake of people who, fortunately, represented something else, soldiers commanded by someone who was rather clever, who had no need to come to my Seminar to know how he needed to operate politically in Europe. So, master and slave, the struggle to death of pure prestige – he really knocks our socks off with that!

There is no struggle to the death since the slave doesn't die – otherwise he couldn't serve as a slave. There is no need for struggle, whether to the death or not. One need but think and, regarding this struggle, to think means that, yes, indeed, if you have to do it, you do it – one constitutes a unary trait with what is, after all, the only thing, if you think about it carefully, with which a living being can do so, with someone who is alive. In that way, things are clear: you'll only have one life, in any case. Deep down, everybody knows it, but that does not stop there from being but one interesting thing, which is to believe that you have an infinity of lives and that these lives are, moreover, destined to be infinitely happy – God only knows who made such a promise and why. We shall try to elucidate that. 366

It must really have been quite something to be Pascal! What he wrote on those little scraps of paper not intended for publication has a certain structure that converges with the struggle, which is only to the death insofar as it transforms one's life into a signifier limited to the unary trait. This is what constitutes pure prestige and it is, moreover, chock-full of effects that take their rightful place at the level of animals.

The struggle is no more to the death in animals than it is in men. We need but consider what happens in the struggle among males that Konrad Lorenz described so well for us. Weekly papers are still making much of it 20 years after I showed its importance in my Seminars at Saint Anne Hospital, at the time of the mirror stage and I don't know what else, the migratory locust and the stickleback. When people asked, "What is a stickleback?" I drew them a picture. Sticklebacks and other species don't necessarily kill each other; they intimidate each other. Lorenz showed us astonishing things on that score – what happens among wolves, for example. A male wolf that is intimidated offers up his throat to be bitten by the threatening wolf. The gesture suffices; the other male has no need to rip his throat out. Yet the victorious wolf does not thereafter believe he is two wolves. The speaking being, on the other hand, believes he is two – namely, as they say, "master of himself." That is the pure prestige that is created in this business. Were there no signifier, you could never imagine such a thing.

It is enough to talk to anyone at all to realize that, at a minimum, he believes himself to be two. That's because the first thing someone always tells you is that, if things hadn't happened the way they did, they would have been otherwise, and they would have been so much better because they would have corresponded to his true nature, to his ideal. The exploitation of one man by another begins at the level of ethics, except that we see more clearly what is at stake at the level of ethics – in other words, that it is the slave who is the master's ideal. It is the slave who brings the master what he needs, his "one-extra" [un-en-plus]. That is the ideal: scrupulously performed services [service service].

This makes what happens to the master at the end of history in Hegel's work much less astonishing. It suffices to look at it to realize that the master is as thoroughly enslaved as you can get. Whence the formulation I proffered about him at a certain turning point, at Saint Anne Hospital – that he is history's cuckold. But he is cuckolded right from the outset; he is a magnificent cuckold. That is the ideal, and the ego-ideal: a body that obeys. The master looks for it in the slave. But, naturally, he does not know what the slave's position is. For nothing, in all of that, proves that the slave doesn't

367

know perfectly well what he wants right from the outset. As I have very often pointed out, the question of the relations between the slave and jouissance is not at all elucidated [by Hegel]. Whatever the case may be, it leaves his own choice in this matter completely in the dark.

After all, nothing proves that the slave has refused the struggle, or even that he was intimidated by it. If, indeed, this double or nothing between the "one" and the "one" costs something, nothing proves that it doesn't also encroach on entirely different situations than animal situations in which we see the possible point of connection, even though the latter is not necessarily unique. One can thus imagine a slave who views things altogether differently. The Stoics even tried to do something like that. But the Church painted them green and hung them on the wall, which made it such that we can no longer grasp what was at stake – they are no more recognizable than the lobster in [Aesop's] fable. The Stoics provided a certain solution to the double or nothing, which was the slave's position. Others might continue their struggles as they liked; the Stoics concerned themselves with something else.

All of which merely repeats what I said earlier: the exploitation of one man by another must be taken up at a level that is, let us say, ethical. The game involved in my right to imagine myself to be two, and in constituting my pure prestige, deserves to take on its import from the reminder of all these coordinates, because it is closely related to what is known as the discontent in civilization. The struggle to the death is perhaps a bit more complicated than its point of departure; we can gauge how far it goes in a civilization that is characterized precisely by having taken it as its point of departure.

Indeed, to return to the subject, Hegel's ideal master, represented by "one," wins, naturally, because he alone wagers. It is precisely because he signified himself as "two" that, having won, he can latch on to the relationship that then gets established between the "two" and the "one." Since he laid the "one" on the table in the field of the Other, there is no reason for him to stop. Against this "one," he will wager the "two."

368

1) 1) 2) 3)

In other words, he enters into action, assisted by his slave, against anyone who has the same obsession as him and who believes himself to be a master. And that goes on in this way, according to the series about which I spoke to you some time back, because it can't be said that I don't spoon-feed things to you:

$$1\ 2\ 3\ 5\ 8\ 13\ 21$$

And that continues up to 89 or some other remarkable number like that. It is the Fibonacci series, characterized by the following:

$$U_0 = 1$$
$$U_1 = 1$$
$$U_n = U_{n-1} + U_{n-2}$$

What is involved here is not very far from what our civilization leads to – namely, that there are always people who are willing to take up the position of mastery, and that it is not surprising that, as of the last count, we now have [a U_n of] somewhere around 900 million people on our hands who became masters at the preceding stage.

What is interesting about the Fibonacci series is not at all, of course, that it crudely reminds us of the present. If I am speaking to you about it, it is because, as the numbers get bigger, the value of U_{n-1}/U_n gets closer and closer to what is designated – and this is no accident even though the context is different – by the same sign as the one with which I designate object a. This little irrational a is equal to:

$$\frac{\sqrt{5} - 1}{2}$$

This ratio is ever more closely approximated the further we go in the representation of the subject by one numerical signifier to another numerical signifier. A close approximation is obtained very quickly – there is no need to go up into the millions. When you are merely at the level of 21 or 34 and so on, you already obtain a value that is quite close to that of little a.

369

I am providing this example because the point is to try to understand – via something other than the reference to the fire lit under one that I spoke about earlier, namely, via the process itself – what happens when the game of the subject's representation is played out.

3

At the outset, there is thus the double or nothing of "one" against "one" in order for that to make "two." After which the process does not stop until the end, until it has as its only result – a result that is no slim pickings – the strict definition of a certain proportion, which is difference functioning at the level of the apparatus I designated of *a* as a number [*mis en chiffres*].

If we wish to explain this incredible point of departure, we can say that the master has, in short, sacrificed his pinkie. In the end, the pure prestige of constituting a "one" does not cost him very much. This little finger was his life, but at this level it is not clear whether we know the import of what we are doing, as is demonstrated by the fact that we must, in fact, know a great deal about it to do a double take. So he staked his pinkie once and then the whole operation was set in motion. I mean that the master, along with his slave, has to undergo, in his turn, the same fate.

The Trojans knew quite a bit about this. Don't you find that this Other, this empty set, can serve as some sort of representation, indeed a fine representation, of the Trojan horse? Except that it doesn't have the exact same function as the one this image shows us, that of pouring out warriors in the heart of a group of humans who can't take it anymore. Here it is the opposite. Through this appeal, through this procedure of the 1 that is equal to the 1 in the game of mastery, the Trojan horse absorbs more and more of them into its belly, and that is ever more costly. That is the discontent in civilization.

But I must go further without indulging in little poems. I will thus leave the whole population that celebrates the Trojan horse to line up in front of Kafka's castle, and I will indicate that this makes sense only if we take little *a* into account.

Only *a* accounts for the fact that the wager is initially established as a double or nothing, since it is a "one" against "one." Why play at double or nothing since we already have what can be won, as someone points out quite correctly in Pascal's dialogue? Except that we must believe that the *a* that is isolated when the process is followed out to the bitter end is already there at the outset and that when one wagers "one" against "one," there is a difference:

$$1 + a - 1 = a$$

If the master wagers the "one" against the theoretical "one" which is a life different from his, it is because between the two "ones" – between <1 + *a*> and the other – there is a difference. That difference can be seen afterward, since, regardless of how you take it, whether you begin with the "one" or not, assuming you obey the law according to which the third term is formed by the addition of the preceding two terms, you obtain the following series:

370

$$1$$

$$1 + a$$
$$2 + a$$
$$3 + 2a$$
$$5 + 3a$$

What is remarkable about this series is that the number of as – that is, the numerical coefficient in front of little a – reproduces the whole number of the preceding stage. This number is, if you will, the number of slaves involved. The series on the right-hand side, that of the coefficients of little a, since that is the series that is enslaved, grows with a slight delay compared to the series on the left. The delayed series is that of little a.

I have called this little a "surplus jouissance," insofar as it is what is sought out in the actual enslaving of the other, although nothing clear is said about the slave's own jouissance. The function of little a as surplus jouissance resides here in the relationship of risk and wager, in the fact that the master has the other's body at his disposal yet cannot do anything about its jouissance.

371   It is important to highlight this, not in order to illustrate the constant status of a's function – the function of the a privileged by the inaugural function of the ideal – but to demonstrate that we can, at the level of surplus jouissance, generate a in a purely logical way.

This is, strictly speaking, the only thing of value in what I am proposing today. But it nevertheless retains its illustrative character, owing to the link between a and what I called having the other's body at one's disposal.

It is no accident that Lévi-Strauss closely likened, and not at all viciously, our so-called liberal civilization – for the ravages it brings with it – to Aztec civilization. Among the Aztecs, things were more blatant: they ripped a out of their victims' chests for you on the altar. That at least had a value, about which it is conceivable that it could serve in a religion that was strictly based on jouissance.

I am not in the process of saying that everything in our culture boils down to the master/slave dialectic. Let us not forget that in the Judeo-Christian tradition, the first murder is one that I need not recall to mind. But no one seems to have observed that Cain killed Abel in order to act just like Abel did. The lambs that Abel sacrificed to God pleased God greatly, tickling His nostrils quite palpably – for, in the end, the God of the Jews has a body. What was the column of smoke that preceded the Israelites as they wandered through the desert, if not a body? Cain sees Abel fostering God's jouissance so much through his sacrifice – how could he not but take the step of sacrificing the sacrificer in his turn?

We find ourselves here at a level where we can put our finger on the relationship to jouissance that a can have, a relationship that is masked by the ridiculous hope we have in lives we will have after this one, which is such that we completely leave aside the question of the jouissance that is there, there behind the empty set, behind the field of the Other scrubbed [or: wiped] clean of this jouissance. This assuredly provides the value taken on in general, in what I earlier called our civilization, by a watchword like that of *habeas corpus*. You have your body; it belongs to you; only you can dispose of it by tossing it into the frying pan.

That will no doubt allow us to see that it is not uninteresting that in this dialectic, the rate of bodies, if I may put it thus, that get exploited is related, in the same way, to the logically prior rate of surplus jouissance. $<5 + 3a>$ may or may not come to "possess," as they say, $<3 + 2a>$, but the fact remains that $<3>$ nevertheless had its $<2a>$ passed down from the $<2>$ at an even earlier stage. The body, the body that is idealized and purified of jouissance, demands a bodily sacrifice [*réclame du sacrifice de corps*]. This is an important point if we are to understand what I told you last time, a point I will merely summarize today – namely, the structure of obsession.

We will talk about hysteria next time, since today I was only able to describe this series to you in the increasing direction – namely, double or nothing. But there is another direction, the one in which the subject might – why not? – get himself represented as the empty set in relation to the "one" that is in the Other. This is what is generally called castration. Psychoanalysis is designed to clarify this other direction of experience, which, as you will see, leads to totally different results. Let me indicate right away that it is where the structure of hysteria will be inscribed.

I will confine myself here to indicating that the structure of obsession can be thoroughly situated in relation to the numerical ratios that I articulated for you today, insofar as they are based on a series that is quite specific. This, let me repeat, is merely an example, in conformity with the essence of the neurotic – who himself is but an example for us: an example of the way in which the structure of the subject should be dealt with.

The obsessive does not want to take himself to be the master. He takes the master as an example only in his way of escaping from what? From death? Of course. At a certain superficial level, one might say that I have stated that. The obsessive is very clever, taking the place of little a himself, which, in any case, always survives the struggle. Whatever happens, surplus jouissance is always there. But

372

we have to know whose it is. Surplus jouissance is the true stakes of the wager, and I have no need to remind you what I said about it in order for it to take on its full import. This is where the obsessive seeks out his place in the Other. And he finds it, since it is at the level of the Other that, in this way of generating ethics, the *a* is situated. That is how it is constructed.

But what about the obsessive's goal [*fin*]? It is not so much to escape death, which is certainly present in all of this, but is never graspable as such in any logical articulation. The struggle to the death, as I presented it to you earlier, is a function of the ideal and not of death, the latter never being perceived, if not written on the basis of a limit that is well beyond the play of the logical field. What is at stake, and it is just as inaccessible in this dialectic, is jouissance. That is what the obsessive intends to escape from, and I hope to be able to articulate it clinically enough to show you that it is the crux of his position.

Since I wasn't able to take things any further today, and not even to the point of communicating something to you that I wanted to illustrate with a letter, I will stop there. I will simply indicate that if you come next time, you will know why, if I hope to continue to give these classes next year to you and with you, it will not, in any case, be in this auditorium.

June 11, 1969

XXIV

ON THE ONE-EXTRA

On the intersubjectivity of the one-extra
The perverse statue
Object *a* is structure
The master and woman
Coalescence and cut

I would be in a still more excellent mood if I didn't want to yawn, as you just saw me do, owing to the fact that I got – I know not why, purely by accident – little sleep last night.

My excellent mood is based on one of those fleeting things known as a hope, and in this case it is the hope that, if things go a certain way, I'll be freed from this weekly sublimation my relations with you involve.

In one of my earlier Seminars, I proffered, "You do not see me from where I am looking at you," in order to characterize a type of object *a* insofar as it is based on the gaze, or rather is nothing but the gaze. "You owe me nothing from where I devour you" – such is the message that I could easily receive from you in the form that I call "inverted," insofar as it is my own message. Then I wouldn't have to make the two-way trip here every week around an object *a* that is clearly what I just designated with a formulation that – as you must sense from my use of the words "owe" and "devour" – is inscribed in what is known as the oral drive; yet, we would do better to relate it to the placental thing, the thing by which I plaster myself [*je me plaque*], however I can, onto the great big body you all constitute in order to create something with my substance that can be a satisfying object to you. "Ô ma mère Intelligence" ["Oh Intelligence, my mother," Paul Valéry, *Poésie* (1920)], as someone, I no longer recall who, once said.

Today I will thus only half-keep the promise I made you last time, since it is merely in the form of a guessing game that I will quickly

376   question you regarding what can be sketched out in your minds
regarding the following.

What could possibly justify the fact that starting next year I will
no longer have this auditorium at my disposal, an auditorium to
which you come en masse, honoring me owing to what I produce
here?

When I was asked to be a lecturer at a rather noble school, the one
known as the École des Hautes Études, I was offered space by that
school in another school, the one we are at here, the École Normale
Supérieure (ENS), which is a well-protected place that garners
all sorts of privileges within the university system. An eminent
philosopher – whose name this adjective will, I believe, allow you to
deduce since there aren't that many of them – an eminent philosopher who teaches here [Louis Althusser] interceded on my behalf
with the ENS administration so that I could use this auditorium. Is
the fact that I occupy this space the very reason why I will no longer
have it at my disposal? I don't believe that I use it at a time of day
that could be coveted by anyone else.

Could it be that my presence here generates confusion by making
people believe that my teaching is authorized by the ENS, which I
just characterized by the eminent position it enjoys in the university
system by being, in a certain sense, excluded from it? I must note
that I have only ever authorized myself on the basis of the field
whose structure I endeavor to maintain in its authenticity. In truth,
I have never authorized myself on the basis of anything else, and
certainly not on the fact that I am speaking at the ENS. Perhaps my
presence here has led to a certain movement in the school – a rather
limited, brief movement, moreover – which cannot, in any case, be
written in the debit [or: liability, *déficit*] column. The *Cahiers pour
l'analyse*, a journal which has come out owing to the induction, as it
were, of the field of my teaching, can hardly be considered a deficit,
even if it might be said that I am not at all the one who worked on
it. Thus there are many reasons why it is not urgent that I be distinguished from the ENS.

A single person was, it is true, confused about this, and he
published false statements in an article I discussed with you on
January 8. The paper was rather funny, I must say, and it came
out in a journal that was the perfect place for it, the *Nouvelle Revue
Française*. It discussed something that was called an extract or even
an exercise in my style, and it stated that I was a professor, which I
most certainly am not, especially not at the ENS.

377   If it was because of this confusion, I would note first that the
article contained plenty of other confusions. It proposed, for
example, that my teaching was founded on a commentary on

Saussure's work, which it wasn't, since I never used Saussure otherwise than one might use an instrument or a device, and for very different ends than Saussure's, since my ends are those of the field I just designated. The article claims that I had merely read Saussure's work *en diagonale* [skimmed through it], which just goes to show that its author is surprisingly ignorant of the use that can be made of the word "diagonale." It is altogether clear that I did not read Saussure *en diagonale* like I read articles in the newspaper *Le Monde*, which are designed to be read that way, whereas Saussure's *Course* [*in General Linguistics*] certainly is not. Moreover, the so-called diagonal method is well known for its usefulness in mathematics – namely, for revealing that, in every seriation that claims to be exhaustive, one can extract some other entity that is not included in its series. In this sense, I would willingly accept the idea that I had made "diagonal" use of Saussure's work.

But the idea that, on that basis – in other words, on the basis of a lack of perspicacity – people would point out an oversight (to put it kindly) that goes well beyond this lack of perspicacity, in order to seek out something by which to imagine that some third party could find justification to take precautionary measures (whereas it would suffice quite simply to point out that this oversight was nothing but that, especially on the part of someone who included quite a few oversights in his text) – well, there is obviously something rather odd here. It suggests that, in the final analysis, one is not allowed to discuss knowledge in universities. For you can admit that, if an author, who manifestly makes a mistake regarding one point can, regarding another point, incorrectly characterize [me as a professor at the ENS], no further action need be taken than to tell the author that he is obviously mistaken.

This is the conclusion that I am indicating right now, a conclusion that deserves to be drawn.

I will leave things there and – keeping you in suspense because I can't say any more about it today – plan to meet with you next week. Assuming it will, in any case, be the last class of the year, I promise I will distribute a certain number of little papers that I already prepared for you and that I have in my briefcase. Should things take a turn for the worse, these papers will at least mark something. They will obviously not be diplomas, but little signs that will serve as reminders of your presence here this year.

Having said that, I will now return to what I said last time.

378

1

Last time, I managed to give a certain structural form to something that is implied by what I intended to articulate this year with the terms "From an Other to the other."

It involves, in short, the fact that nothing that allows itself to be taken up in the signifying function can ever be "two" again without something being excavated in the so-called locus of the Other, to which I attributed the status of the empty set last time.

That, at least, is the way in which what in this case changes the topography of the real can be written, given the present state of our logic, and without excluding the possibility that it can be written differently.

Once again I am writing the "one," and then the circle (which first served to inscribe the Other). Next, in this circle [the one on the right in Figure 24.1], taken here as a set, I am writing two elements: on the left the "one" and on the right something which, if it is the Other once again, should be taken as a set here. This [Ø] is the symbol that designates the empty set. Owing to mathematical usage, it would be wrong to use a zero; it would be more accurate to represent it, as is classic in set theory, by crossing the zero with an oblique line which, as you know, I use for my own purposes as well.

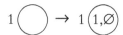

Figure 24.1: From the First to the Second Schema

379

Everything that allows itself to be taken up in the signifying function can no longer be "two" without something – which is located all the way to the right – being excavated, and in a way that organizes the field on the basis of this dyadic relation in such a way that nothing can enter into it any more without being obliged to go around what I just called the empty set. The latter is, strictly speaking – let it be said for those who have taken some time to grasp this – what I have always designated, in my writings and in my propositions, as the "one-extra" [or: "extra one," *un-en-plus*].

If at the outset I had – in order to lay out the functioning of the unconscious in the function and field of speech and language – to resort to the fragile and highly problematic term "intersubjectivity" (which is necessitated by Freud's second topography, in which nothing plays out, functions, or is regulated except on the basis of intra-subjective correlates), my discourse has, so to speak, made headway, and I am stressing here the decisive function of the "one-extra" qua outside of the subjective realm.

Let us examine the drawing I proposed last time, on which I based what I wanted to tell you regarding the topic I am taking up anew today.

"A [*Un*] subject," I said, inserting it in the formulation that "a signifier represents him to another signifier," and who can fail to see that the words "From an Other" in my title are already inscribed in this formulation? The signifier to which the subject is represented is, strictly speaking, this "Other one" [or: this "one Other," *cet* un Autre]. You see it inscribed here [in Figure 24.1] as "one," insofar as it is the resource to which what must function as a subject is represented in the field of the Other. As such, this "one in the Other" cannot but include the empty set qua "one-extra."

These three basic signifiers – the first "one," the second "one," and the "one-extra" – are written here in a way that is not self-evident. It took me months and years of explanations, designed for the very people whose practice cannot hold up for even a second without relying on this structure – I mean psychoanalysts. It suffices that these three signifiers be written in this specific form for them to already bring signifying effects with them, and for them to, in and of themselves, constitute a structure, owing to what they already imply, even before there is any question of showing how the subject arises from them. By virtue of their articulation, they already constitute a form of knowledge [*un savoir*].

The "Other one" [L'*un Autre*] inscribed here as the "one" which is on the left inside the circle, proves to be what it is – namely, the "one in the Other," the "one" to which the subject is able to get himself represented on the basis of the first "one" (the one that is all the way to the left outside of the circle). What does that mean? Where does this "one" – to which the subject is going to be represented by the first "one" – come from? It is clear that it comes from the same place as the first "one," the one that represents the subject.

This is the first stage [*temps*] of the constitution of the Other. Last time, I compared the Other qua locus to a sort of reverse Trojan horse – one that constantly swallows up new units in its stomach instead of letting them swarm out into the hushed city – because the entrance of the first "one" is foundational, in the very simple sense that it is the minimum necessary in order for us to be able to assert that the Other cannot in any way include itself, except as a subset.

2

Let me make this clear.

Can we say that the Other includes itself, if I fill out the empty set by repeating these two elements therein: a "one" and the empty set?

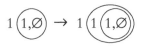

Figure 24.2: From the Second to the Third Schema

We can't truthfully say that this amounts to including itself. The set transformed in this way, written with the elements I just mentioned, is not the same as the first set, which has as its sole elements the couple made up of the element "one" and the empty set. The elements "one" and the empty set are now reproduced in this empty set.

There is no question of the set of all sets that do not include themselves here, for the simple reason that no set ever includes itself. It does not suffice to speak of the set of all the sets that do not include themselves in order to constitute it. The very question whether a set can include itself or not cannot even be raised until after it has absorbed the "Other one," so that the empty set, in being included, appears qua "one-extra." This is the very reason why the latter is not in any way two. There is no empty set that contains an empty set. There aren't two [different] empty sets; there is only one empty set.

The inclusion of the first "one" is thus what requires that the simplest formula for the inscription of the "two" in the field of the Other be the couple made up of the "one," qua element, and the empty set, inasmuch as the latter is nothing other than what is produced when we distinguish the subsets of a set with one element.

This stems from the very structure of sets. Even if we posit a set that has just one element, the "one-extra" known as the empty set arises as a subset thereof. It is because this structure was misrecognized that people were long content with the "one" all alone, a confusion that led people to say that the Other is the One.

In other words, in order to become the "one-extra" – that is what it itself is, the empty set – the Other needs an other [or: one other]. It is a second signifier, an other "one" which, unlike the first, is included in the Other. It is this other "one" that I called the "Other one."

The relationship between the "one" and the other "one" is such that the subject can only come to be represented at the level of the second "one," at the level of S_2 if you wish to write it thusly. The first "one," S_1, certainly intervenes as representing the subject, but this intervention only implies the appearance of the subject as such at the level of S_2.

Thus, as I pointed out last time, the "one-extra" or empty set is S(A) – in other words, the signifier of the Other, the signifier of the inaugural A.

What you see on the board [Figure 24.2] shows the structure thus defined, which is based on the relationship between the "one" inscribed in the first circle, that of the Other, and the second circle, which is that of the "one-extra," which itself can contain the "one" plus the "one-extra." This "one-extra" can only be distinguished with reference to the "one" – it is only in this way that it is not the same empty set.

This structure can be repeated indefinitely: "one," circle, "one," circle, "one," and so on and so forth. It is what defines the Other.

And it is the very thing that constitutes the instance of object *a* as such.

3

It is indispensable, as I just told you, that there be in the Other at least one element, reduced to the element "one," and this is what long made people mistake the Other for the One.

Now, there is a psychical structure that restores, as it were, the Other's apparent integrity, and that grounds S(A) in an effective relation which is not marked by what is designated by the bar in S(Ⱥ) – the signifier of the barred Other. (The latter, located in the upper left-hand corner of my graph, is nothing but the identification of the indefinitely repeated structure designated by object *a*.) That psychical structure is perverse structure.

In order to designate the apparent restoration of the Other's integrity – insofar as it is object *a* here – as perverse structure, I will employ a metaphor: it is in some sense the imaginary cast [or: mold(ing), *moulage*] of signifying structure.

Later today, we will see what plays the role of this *a* in the game of psychical identification. Well, no, let us look at it right away. Let us spell it out, taking up the first case that presents itself as one of hysteria. We will see how Freud, who gives this economy its first explanation, stays hot on its heels [*lui emboîte le pas*].

How can we fail to investigate the status of the relationship between such narratives – between the "talking cure"* as Anna O. herself dubbed it – and the particularly clear symptom we find in cases of hysteria: something that is emptied out in the body, a field

in which sensitivity disappears, and another field – whether it is connected to the first or not – where motor movement vanishes?

Nothing but a signifying unit [*unité*] can explain this. Freud
himself clearly pointed out the anti-anatomical aspect of hysterical symptoms. For, if the arm of a hysteric is paralyzed, it is solely
because it is called an "arm," for nothing in the real distribution of
nerve impulses [*influx*] can explain the limits of its field. The body
clearly comes to serve here as a prop [or: medium, *support*] for the
earliest and most typical symptoms we have ever investigated, they
having been at the very origin of psychoanalytic experience.

Even if we knew nothing more about hysteria – which is not the
case, for we know a great deal more about it, I mean that we know
that it is necessary to outline this structure differently than Freud
did – how could we stay as close to the text as possible and fail to
see that Freud is, with respect to the progress made by the talking
cure*, in the place of the "Other one," the "one" inside the circle in
the schema [Figure 24.1]? Indeed, it is at the level of Freud that a
certain subject is established. Without Freud as listener, that subject
would not have appeared, and a question remains: How could
Freud submit to listening to narratives every evening for a year or
two that were recounted while in an altered state of consciousness,
a state that marked the sectioning or cut [*la coupe, la coupure*] with
which a symptomatic Anna separated herself from her own subject
(as did someone like Dora)?

Recall to mind the case study. It revolves around a fact [*trait*],
which is not lost in the shadows of something forgotten, but which
was simply cut off from the prior year and narrated by the patient
in the form of a historical reprisal. As Freud comes to be informed
of it, with a delay that must in and of itself take on meaning for us,
the symptom – which is quite far removed from it, and quite forced
with respect to what gets articulated – lifts. If we take things as they
are presented, it suffices that a subject come to know a fact [*trait*] of
this kind. How then can we fail to investigate the hidden relationship at work here between what is articulated and what constitutes
a symptom?

The foundation [*assise*] of a subject who is transformed into
knowledge in the field of the Other, and her relationship with something that is hollowed out at the level of the body – that is the first
sketch of a structure that we have sufficiently developed for decades,
in order to [1] be able to bring this structure together in its unicity,
as what functions as the object called little *a*, which is this very structure, and [2] say that, with regard to the body that is emptied out so
as to function as a signifier, there is something that can flow into a
mold [or: become molded, *s'y mouler*] there.

This metaphor will help us conceptualize what ends up, in the case of the pervert, functioning in such a way as to restore the Other to its plenitude, qua A without the bar. It is, strictly speaking, a statue.

In order to assess the imaginary relation involved in perversion, it suffices to grasp this statue at the level of Baroque contortion. Can anyone overlook the fact that the latter encourages voyeurism, insofar as voyeurism represents phallic exhibition? How can we fail to see that – as it was used by a religion concerned with regaining its power over souls at the very moment at which that power was being contested [during the Protestant Reformation] – a Baroque statue (whatever it may be, whatever male or female saint it represents, even if it is the Virgin Mary herself) is strictly speaking a gaze, a gaze designed in such a way that, when we stand before it, the soul opens up?

384

We must take advantage of this exemplary connection between a single feature [*trait*] of perverse structure and some kind of capturing – which must truly be called idolatrous – of faith, because it brings us right to the heart of what took the form in the West of a war of images.

4

I said that I would discuss neurosis today. Last time, you heard me approach it by articulating that nothing about obsession can be conceptualized unless it is linked to the following structure.

The master, insofar as he functions qua "one," a signifier, subsists only by being represented to a second "one" – which corresponds to the slave – that is in the Other, the only place where the subjective function of the master resides. The one and the other have nothing in common, except what I said was initially articulated by Hegel as the master's wagering of his own life. The act of mastery consists in risking one's life.

In the booklet that constitutes the first issue of the journal *Scilicet*, I felt I needed to cite the miraculous words of a child, which I heard from his father. The child had told his father that he had "cheated (his way through) life" [*qu'il était* un tricheur de vie]. It is a prodigious formulation, like those that we can hear only from those whose speech has not yet been expurgated.

Risking one's life is the crux of what we might call the act of mastery, and its guarantor is none other than the slave in the Other – the slave as the only signifier in relation to which the master can prop himself up as a subject. The support the master finds therein is that provided by the slave's body, insofar as it is *perinde ac cadaver* [like a corpse; figuratively, totally submissive or obedient], let it be said, adopting a formulation that came to the fore in spiritual life, which was hardly an accident. The slave thus lies solely in the field with which the master props himself up as a subject.

Something remains outside the limits of this machinery, which is precisely what Hegel wrongly brought into it – namely, death. For death, as has often been pointed out, shows up here only insofar as it contests the whole of the structure as concerns the slave alone. In the entire phenomenology of master and slave, only the slave is real. This is what Hegel realized, and it is such that nothing need go any further in this dialectic. The situation is altogether stable. Should the slave die, there is nothing more. Should the master die, everyone knows that the slave is still a slave. And as history tells us, no one was ever freed from slavery by the death of his master.

Note that the same is true when it is the neurotic who initiates the dialectic. Indeed, the entire dialectic involved in the relationship between master and slave is enunciated where? At the level of the slave himself, because it is insofar as the master is represented at the level of the slave that the dialectic continues. Where is it heading? Toward absolute knowledge, and for good reason. If we can see it progress toward and arrive at this goal, it is because absolute knowledge was already placed there at the outset, like a rabbit in a hat, in the form of the subject-supposed-to-know, which is immediately on the horizon. The function of knowledge remains uncritiqued here, for nowhere is the fact that the subject subtends [or: is implicit in, *sous-jacence*] knowledge investigated.

What we cannot fail to see is that the master himself knows nothing. Everyone knows that the master is an idiot. He would never have entered into this whole adventure – given the elimination of his function that the future has in store for him – had he (even for an instant) been for himself the subject that, owing to some sort of ease of enunciation, Hegel imputes him to be. Could the function of the so-called struggle to the death, the struggle for pure prestige, that makes him depend so thoroughly on his partner, have been instated if the master were truly nothing but what we call the unconscious – namely, what is not known by the subject [or: not known about the subject, *l'insu du sujet*] as such, I mean the unknown from which the subject is absent and is merely represented elsewhere?

I am saying this solely to present the following step, which involves what I have to articulate today about hysteria.

I said that we cannot articulate anything about obsession unless we inject into the dialectic of the master subject what is necessitated by the truth of this process, and, along the pathway of this truth, the susception or bringing into play of the subject-supposed-to-know.

The obsessive takes the model of the master as his point of reference. We can say that he does not view himself as a master, but presumes that the master knows what he wants. This is the machinery that I am now taking up anew in order to situate its analogue at the heart of the other neurosis, hysteria.

I have already spoken to you about the analogue that the hysteric derives from her point of reference, woman – not that hysterics must necessarily be women, nor obsessives necessarily men. I am going to enunciate now the status of the model in which woman establishes something for the hysteric that is far more central, as you will see, to analytic experience.

When I proposed this somewhere around May 21, someone asked me a question afterward, "But do we know what woman is?" Of course, we do not know what woman is any more than we know what the master is. Yet we can sketch out woman's status in the field of the Other.

It is just as idiotic [*con*] – that's the word for it! [*con* is also a slang term for "cunt"] – as the master's status. I'm not talking about women for the moment, I'm talking about "woman" as a point of reference for the hysteric. Don't you already see the status of our two "ones" when woman is at stake? It strikes me as in no way doubtful that the inner "one" – that is, the S_2 – is what has to be erected, that's the word for it! What we thus need to know is why the "one" with which the woman subject props herself up is so ordinarily the Phallus with a capital *P*. It is at the level of the "one" that we must elicit woman's identification in the dyadic mirage, inasmuch as at its horizon lies the Other, the empty set, namely, a body – a body emptied out of what? Of jouissance.

Where the master subject risks his life in the wager that inaugurates the dialectic, woman – I didn't say the hysteric, I said woman, for the hysteric, like the obsessive earlier, can be explained only with woman as point of reference – woman risks and wagers jouissance.

This jouissance is not her jouissance, about which everyone knows that it is inaugural and existent for her, and that she not only obtains it without any of the efforts and detours that characterize autoeroticism in men, but that it always subsists in her as distinct from and parallel to the jouissance she obtains from being the man's woman, the one that contents itself with man's jouissance [or: confines itself to (or is satisfied with) man's jouissance, *qui se satisfait de la jouissance de l'homme*]. What is at stake in the game is the man's jouissance, by which woman is captured and captivated like the master is by the slave.

The man's jouissance provides the radical origin of what plays the same role in hysteria as is played by death in obsession, something that is just as inaccessible. To say that woman identifies with it is just as false and empty as to say that the master identifies with death. On the other hand, just as the slave is bound up with death – subsisting only on the basis of his relation to it, and making the whole system subsist on the basis of this relation – similarly woman's relationship to castration is what holds the whole machine together. Having mentioned *perinde ac cadaver* regarding the master, I will thus mention, regarding woman, the dimension – which is rather remarkable as it is caught up in the field of the signifier – known as necrophilia, otherwise stated, eroticism that very clearly involves a dead body. Shall I mention here, on the horizon, the figure of Jeanne la Folle [Mad Joan] and the fact that she lugged around the corpse of Philip the Handsome [her husband] for two weeks?

These inaugurating structures or functions – which correspond strictly to our dependence on the signifier that analytic experience has allowed us to articulate – show us here that, just as the obsessive does not view himself as a master, as I said, the hysteric does not view herself as woman. In what respect doesn't she take herself to be woman? Precisely in the respect that the hysteric constitutes the woman subject, whose structure I just articulated, as "supposed to know." In other words – and you might think of Dora here – the hysteric is interested in and captivated by woman insofar as she believes that woman is the one who knows how to give a man jouissance.

Now something is missing from this model – namely, the fact that what therefore sustains the woman subject leads to the man's castration. The woman functioning in the model does not know it, praised be God [*Dieu soit loué*] – that's the word for it! On the other hand, the hysteric knows it full well, which is why she looks further. I already said this about Dora in my first take on transference ["Presentation on Transference" in *Écrits*]. Reread Freud's case study, along with everything that, in his prior case studies, those found in *Studies on Hysteria*, allows us to see this simple correlation: according to the hysteric, woman is supposed to know, whereas in the model it is unconsciously that she knows it.

The two models, those of the hysteric and the obsessive, cannot be distinguished on the basis of the factor that I just introduced, because it brings both types together under the heading of neurosis. This is why you can also observe that death, which is the correlate of this factor, is also at play in the way the hysteric broaches woman [or: in the aspect of woman that the hysteric broaches, *dans ce que l'hystérique aborde de la femme*].

The hysteric creates the man who assumes that woman knows [or: The hysteric plays the part of the man who would like to presume woman knows, *L'hystérique fait l'homme qui supposerait la femme savoir*]. That is why she is brought into this game from an angle which always involves a man's death. Need I remind you that Anna O.'s hysteria arose in close connection with her father's death? Must I highlight the correlate, in Dora's two dreams, of death insofar as it is implied by her mother's jewelry box? In the first dream, the father says, "I refuse to let myself and my two children be burnt for the sake of your jewel-case," and in the second dream we hear that the father has been laid to rest. Neuroses assume hidden truths to be known. Neurotics must be relieved of this assumption in order to stop representing that truth in their flesh.

The hysteric is already an analysand, as it were, in other words already on the road to a solution. She seeks it out on the basis of the following: her point of reference involves the subject-supposed-to-know, which is why she encounters a contradiction – assuming her analyst does not practice in such a way as to cut what we see on the board, on the one hand, which is the unconscious structure (namely, the models that I have suitably articulated, both at the level of the master and at the level of woman, with these three elements, "one," "one," and "empty set"), from the supposition of the subject-supposed-to-know, on the other hand, which makes the neurotic into a natural analysand, because this opposition already in and of itself constitutes transference, prior to any analysis.

The coalescence of structure with the subject-supposed-to-know attests to the following in the neurotic: that he questions the truth of his structure and that he himself becomes this questioning in the flesh. In short, he himself is a symptom. If there is something that can put a stop to that, it is the analyst's way of operating, which consists in practicing a form of cutting [*pratiquer la coupure*] thanks to which the supposition of the subject-supposed-to-know is detached and separated from structure. The supposition locates structure accurately, except that neither the master nor woman can be assumed to know what they are doing.

The game of analytic treatment revolves around this cut [*coupure*]. It is a subjective cut, since assuredly, everything we say about unconscious desire always boils down to assuming that a subject ends up knowing what he wants. What does that mean? Are we, in providing such formulations, merely preserving once again something which implies that there is knowledge and there is what one wants, and never the twain shall meet? There is certainly a place where that is the case. It is when we have to say yes or no to what I called "what one wants." That is what is known as the will. But as for "knowing what he wants," for the master and woman it is desire itself. Just as I turned two words into one earlier with my "one-extra," here I am turning "knowing-what-he-wants" into a single word, and the latter is desire itself.

What the hysteric presumes is that woman knows what she wants, in the sense in which she desires it [or: would like to desire it, *le désirerait*]. This is why the hysteric only manages to identify with woman at the cost of an unsatisfied desire. Similarly, the obsessive – with regard to the master who allows him, in a game of hide and seek, to pretend that only the slave dies – is he who identifies only the following, which is the real, about the master: namely, that his desire is impossible.

June 18, 1969

EVACUATION

XXV

THE RAVISHING IGNOMINY OF THE *HOMMELLE*

The master's accession to knowledge
Alma mater
The student's servile position
A little permutational system
Distributing diplomas

1

Try not to let go of the handrail regarding what we are qua effect of knowledge.

Qua effect of knowledge, we are shattered. In the fundamental fantasy ($ \$ \lozenge a$) – S barred, lozenge, little *a* – we are, strange as this may seem, self-caused. And yet there is no self. Or, rather, there is a divided self.

The only true political revolution can stem from following this path. Knowledge serves the master. I will return to it again today to highlight that knowledge is born of the slave.

If you remember the formulations I provided last time, you will recall that I also claim that knowledge serves woman, because it turns her into the cause of desire.

That is what I indicated last time, in my commentary on the schema that I am putting back up on the board today. I believe that I must take it up again, especially for those who might have been preoccupied with what they considered to be more pressing matters last time.

$$1 \left(1, \varnothing \right)$$

Figure 25.1: Schema of the One-Extra

394 This schema stems from the logical definition I gave in our second to last meeting of the Other as the empty set, and from the indispensable absorption by the Other of a unary trait, the one on the right, in order for the subject, in the form of a signifier, to be able to be represented to this unary trait.

Where does the signifier [S₁] that represents the subject to another signifier [S₂] come from? From nowhere, because it appears in that place only by virtue of the retroactive efficacy of repetition. It is because the unary trait aims at the repetition of a jouissance that another unary trait arises after the fact, *nachträglich*.

I was the first to extract this latter term from Freud's work and highlight it as such – let this be said for anyone who, wishing to translate a certain *Vocabulaire* [*de la psychanalyse; The Language of Psychoanalysis* (New York: Norton, 1973)], might notice that under the heading of *après-coup* [*ex post facto* action; *Nachträglichkeit*], which wouldn't even exist without my discourse, I am not mentioned.

The unary trait arises after the fact, in the place, therefore, of S₁ – the signifier insofar as it represents a subject to another signifier.

Here, all the way to the right, we have the sign of the empty set, which is A's form-taking [or: the form A takes, *l'enforme de A*].

What I am saying here is that everything that arises from repetition – from the repeated reproduction of this *enforme* – is, every time, this *enforme* itself. And this is object *a*.

$$1 \left(1, a \right)$$

Figure 25.2: The Object that has Arisen from Repetition

This is where people get alarmed. "You are thus providing a purely formal definition of object *a*," they say.

No, I am not. For all of this is produced solely on the basis of the fact that, in the place of the "one" on the left, the S₁, there is what there is: the enigmatic jouissance attested to by the fact that – at every level at which that jouissance is found and that I will reproduce – we know nothing about it except that it wants another, another jouissance.

This is always true. It is true in "four, two, three," the question in the little fable to which Oedipus gives the ridiculous answer that everyone knows. Let's try a different one. In this Oedipal scenario, it was the hysteric who gave the answer, and she [or: he, *il*] must have told the truth about woman there for the Sphinx to disappear. This is why, in accordance with the hysteric's fate, she [or: he, *il*] played the part of [or: created, *fait*] man thereafter.

395

Since some time will pass before we meet again, I will tell you that the hysteric brings me great joy. She assures me – more than she assured Freud, who was not able to hear her – that woman's jouissance is perfectly adequate to her. If she nevertheless erects this mythical woman, the Sphinx, it is because she needs something else – namely, to enjoy the man [*jouir de l'homme*], who to her is but the erect penis, owing to which she knows herself qua Other – that is, as the phallus of which she is deprived, otherwise stated, as castrated. This is the initial game she articulates.

This is the truth that allows us to dissipate certain illusions, and that recalls that it is suitable to posit little *a* as I did this year – namely, as surplus jouissance, in other words, as the stakes of the wager to win the other jouissance.

This is why last time I wrote the master/slave dialectic differently, clearly pointing out that the slave is the master's ideal, and that he is also the signifier to which the master subject is represented by another signifier. As for the third term, I gave a representation of it that was not formal – here it is [see Figure 25.2] in the form of the stakes constituted by *a*.

In this dialectic, as a philosopher by the name of Hegel noticed, the stakes are clearly what can be contained in a signifying *enforme* like "one" – namely, one life. It is true that we have but one. Yet that is an idiotic formulation of what is at stake, because we cannot formulate that we have but one except on the basis of the notion that we could have others, which clearly does not apply [*hors de jeu*].

Hegel clearly spoke about a life, but he was mistaken about which one it was. What is at stake is not the master's life but the slave's. The master's other jouissance is that of the slave's life. This is what is enveloped by the formulation of the struggle to the death, which is so completely closed off. This is what we find in the box.

As for the struggle to the death itself, it is a [or: one] signifier. This is so clear that we can probably assume it is nothing but the signifier [or: signifying system] itself. Everyone knows that death is not part of the game [or: not applicable, *hors de jeu*]. We don't know what it is. But the death verdict is what the master qua subject is: a signifying verdict, perhaps the only true one.

What the master lives off is a life – not his but his slave's. This is why, whenever life is wagered, it is the master who is speaking. Pascal was a master and, as everyone knows, a pioneer of capitalism, having worked on calculating devices and omnibuses. You've heard about that somewhere, and I am not going to provide a bibliography here.

That sounds dramatic. And it became dramatic up to a certain point. In the beginning, it wasn't, because the first master had no idea what he was doing. And the master subject is the unconscious. In Ancient comedy, whose indicative value for us cannot be overstated, it is the slave who tells the imbecilic master, or the master's son – which is still better than the Son of Man – what people are saying in the town, for example, where he has just arrived like an oddball. He also tells him what magic words to say. It is even better to read Plautus than Terence: Antiquity's slave is a legal expert and a PR man, to boot. The slave was no slouch [or: random fool, *le dernier venu*] in Antiquity.

Need I make in passing two or three little points that will perhaps be heard by an ear or two here?

There were, of course, masters who tried their hand at knowledge. But why, after all, wouldn't Plato's knowledge be an unconscious philosophy? Perhaps that is why it is so profitable to us.

When it comes to Aristotle, we shift to a different level. He served a master, Alexander the Great, who assuredly hadn't the slightest idea what he was doing. He did it all the same, and very well at that. Aristotle, who worked for him, wrote the best natural history there ever was, and initiated logic, which is no trifling matter.

How, then, did the master come to know what he was doing? According to the schema I put up on the board earlier, it was by following the hysteric's pathway, by playing the part of the slave, the wretched of the earth. He worked hard at it. He replaced the slave with surplus value, which wasn't easy to find, but it led to the master waking up to his own essence. Naturally, the master qua subject could only be articulated at the level of the slave qua signifier. Yet, the master's accession to knowledge allowed for the establishment of the most absolute masters ever seen since the beginning of history.

The slave is left with class consciousness. Which means that he must simply keep his mouth shut. Everyone knows that what I am saying is true, and that the problem of the relations between class consciousness and the party involves the relations between the educated and the educator. If anything gives meaning to what is known as Maoism, it is the revival [or: repeat, *reprise*] of the relations between slave and knowledge. But let's not get ahead of ourselves here.

Prior to that, the proletariat – as the master's philosophy, which was the first, had the gall to call it – had the right to do what you know: abstain. As you hear in misleading places designed for this precise purpose, if I dare say so, psychoanalysis simply ignores class struggle. This is perhaps not entirely clear, for psychoanalysis could even give it back its true meaning.

Don't imagine that speaking out [*prise de parole*], whereby you

397

express yourself, frees you in any way, on the pretext that the master himself speaks and even talks a great deal. The fantasy that, for the matter to be resolved, it suffices to speak out instead of the master, is sheer childishness. Need I recall to mind that I began my discourse on psychoanalysis this year by saying that psychoanalysis is a discourse without speech?

Knowledge shakes things up, and not necessarily for the benefit of those for whom it claims to work. It merely claims to do so, moreover, for, as I told you, knowledge is not work.

The only solution is to enter the defile without letting go of the handrail, and to work at being the truth of knowledge.

2

I believe that I have already sufficiently commented on the three terms that are up on the board – S_1, S_2, and a.

I will take them up again at two different levels: that of the master on the top line and of the slave on the bottom line. I will complete them with a line in the middle where I add what I already wrote on the board in a different form last time, something that concerns the relationship of woman to her other jouissance, such as I articulated it earlier.

$$\begin{matrix} S_1 & S_2 & a \\ S_2 & a & S_1 \\ a & S_1 & S_2 \end{matrix}$$

Figure 25.3: Master, Woman, and Slave

Reread a bit of the Bible – who would ever tell you to "read the whole thing"? Woman, at S_2 here, who makes herself into the cause of desire, a, is the subject who, we must say, manages to create demand with supply [*l'offre*]. Man would never have taken the bait if he hadn't first been offered the apple – namely, object a. What is the signifier S_1 at the end of the line? Capital Phi, Φ, the sign of what woman is certainly lacking in this business, which is why man must provide her with it.

It is amusing that after 70 years of psychoanalysis, no one has yet formulated what man is. I am talking about *vir*, the male sex. I'm not talking about the human being here and other nonsense regarding anti-humanism and all that structuralist stuff – I'm talking about what a man is. Freud tells us he is active. There are, indeed, reasons to say so. For he has to work pretty hard not to disappear

398

into a pit. Well, thanks to psychoanalysis, he knows that, in the end, he will be castrated.

Well, it's true that he knows this, yet he has been castrated since the outset. Now he can learn it, which is a change introduced by knowledge.

As you have seen, there is something odd here. There is a sort of gap. "Two" has been dropped, and we have jumped from S_1 to a.

Why wouldn't this schema be made one by one? There would have first been the series S_2, then a, then S_1. We should be able to situate ourselves with respect to what that means.

I'm going to immediately give you the key, especially since you must be prepared for it, since I spoke to you earlier about the shift from master to schoolmaster. Wherever the S_2 is, that is where knowledge is situated, and it is located here in the place of a master [à une place de maître].

That is perhaps what is at stake in the middle line. The hysteric is characterized by what remained in the middle of the top line, S_2. Let us note that the first place is that of enunciation. I have spoken to you about the "she-man" [hommelle; homme means man and elle means she]. Doesn't everything converge on her, she who is both master and knowledge? She speaks, she proffers.

If you'd like to see an example of her, go watch something, but go in at the right moment like I did. It is a horrible movie called If – God only knows why, my word. In it we see British academia in its most seductive forms, those that confirm everything psychoanalysis was able to articulate, and nothing more, about the society of men – a society in the sense I mentioned earlier, a society of homosexuals.

399   You'll see the she-man there. She's the housemaster's wife. She is ravishingly and exemplarily ignominious. But the real find – indeed, it is the sole flash of genius evinced by the film's author – is the moment she takes a stroll all alone, naked (and Lord knows there is a lot there), among the basins of knowledge in the kitchen, she being sure she is the queen of the realm, while the whole little homosexual brothel is carrying out a military drill in the courtyard.

You are perhaps beginning to see what I mean. The she-man is the true face of the alma mater, in other words the University, the place where, because you have executed a certain number of knowledge-related schemes, you have a stable institution under the leadership of a spouse.

We can perhaps rather easily identify what a represents on this line [the middle line in Figure 25.3]. They are the pupils, the dear little children in our charge, who are themselves created by their parents' desires. In any case, that is what they are asked to wager: the way in which they arose from their parents' desires.

As for the ante, which is in slot three, and which is S_1 here, we should identify it with that around which what we call student uprisings revolve. It seems very important that students agree to play the game, given the way they argue about the sheepskin that is sloughed off at the end. If you don't play the game, you won't receive a diploma this year. That may well bear some relation to S_1.

So, good God, we see on the board a little system that gives us at least a first approximation of the meaning of things regarding which people usually get completely lost, concerning what is happening these days in certain places. I do not claim to be supplying any sort of historical key. What I am saying is that refusing to play the game has no meaning unless a question is raised about the relations between knowledge and the subject, the very terms on which psychoanalysis focuses.

What is the effect of knowledge on the subject or subjection? Students have no vocation to revolt. You can believe someone who ventured into academic territory for historical reasons, very precisely because there was no way to get psychoanalysts to know anything whatsoever. So I had a little hope that, as an effect of reflection, university training might have made them reason differently. In short, a sounding [*résonance*] board for the drum, when the drum itself does not reason [*raisonne*] – that's the word for it!

So you see, I have encountered students for years. Being a student is normally an altogether servile position. Don't think for a minute that because you have spoken out in a few little venues, the matter has been resolved. In short, students continue to believe in their professors. There can be no doubt about what they think of what the latter say: the well-established opinion is, in most cases, that what they say is not worth much. But they are the professors, so the students nevertheless expect from them what is found at the level of S_1, what is going to make them into masters on paper, paper tigers.

Certain students have come to see me to say, "You know, it's scandalous: so and so's book is copied right out of your Seminar." That's what students do. But let me tell you that I didn't even open the book in question, because I already knew that's all it contained. Still, students came to tell me about it. (To write such a book is an altogether different matter.) They told me because they were students.

Well, what could possibly have happened such that, all of the sudden, there was this uprising? What is that called? "It is a revolt, Sire." What would it take for it to become a revolution? The question would have to be broached, not by needling [or: flattering, *chatouillages*] a few professors, but by examining the relations between the student qua subject and knowledge.

400

People have long linked the subject with knowledge, believing that all knowledge implies a subject, leading them to slip substance, too, in there quite easily. But no, things don't work that way. Even *hypokeimenon* can be separate from knowledge, as psychoanalysis has demonstrated.

Yet knowledge that is not known to the subject [or: unbeknownst to the subject, *à l'insu du sujet*] is not a concept, as opposed to what I was saddened to read in an account of what is said in a certain place where psychoanalysis is put to the test – not for no reason, naturally. Psychoanalysis, under such conditions, would do better not to try to charm people, not to claim that there is, in short, but one single Freudian concept, the unconscious – nor even to call it what I just called it, knowledge that is not known to the subject, for that is not a concept at either of the two levels. It is a paradigm on the basis of which concepts exist, thank God, with which we can delineate the Freudian field. And Freud provided other concepts that, whether they are acceptable or not, arose from the first moment of psychoanalytic experience, from the unconscious qua example discovered by him in neurotics.

401

The neurotic is $s(A)$. This means that the neurotic teaches us that the subject is always an Other, but that, moreover, this Other is not the right one. It is not the right one if we want to know what causes the subject, or what the subject himself causes. So, people try as hard as they can to reunify the barred A and tailor it to any significant statement [or: cut it down to size so it fits any significant statement, *le retailler à la mesure de tout énoncé significatif*] – in other words, to rewrite it as $s(A)$, which is found to the left on the bottom line of my graph [Figure 16.3]. That, we must state, is where people know what they are saying, and that is where psychoanalysis stops, whereas what should, on the contrary, be done is to connect up with what is in the upper left-hand corner, S(A), capital S qua signifier of barred A.

It is the same for the pervert. He is the signifier of A qua intact, S(A), as I told you. People try to reduce him to the lowercase s of the same uppercase A – it's always the same deal – in order to make sense of him.

3

Do you think I'm going to keep speaking like this for a long time today? And because it is my last class, continue to tell you things so that at the end you applaud, for once, because you know that after that – look out, I'm off?

The discourse I'm talking about has no need for such glorious endings. It is not a classical *oratio*. Indeed, my discourse offends classical oration.

A man – who is the head administrator of this establishment, which is privileged within the university system, and in which it would seem that, owing to this fact, the said establishment must comply with certain external reviews of what happens inside of it, which does not seem at all true, however – this man apparently has the right to tell me, after having hospitably welcomed me here, that that's enough now.

Which is fine with me, just fine with me, because, first of all, it's true, I have merely been granted hospitality here. Moreover, he was right to remind me of something I have known for a long time, which is that my teaching seems to him to be exactly what it is – namely, anti-academic [*anti-universitaire*], in the sense in which I just defined it.

402

He nevertheless took quite a while to tell me so. He did rather recently, during a last little phone call to him that I felt I needed to make, because there was, I sensed, a sort of misunderstanding that I absolutely wanted to dispel before telling him, "Of course, there is no question of . . ., etc." It's quite curious that he spilled the beans at that point, telling me that that was precisely why. "Your teaching," he told me, "is very trendy" [*dans le vent*, literally "in the wind"]. You hear that: "the wind." I would have thought that I was going against the wind here, but whatever.

So. I have no reason to doubt that he has the right to do this to me. To do it to you might be a separate matter. But that's your business. The fact that a certain number of you have been in the habit of coming here for the past six years doesn't count – you are being evacuated. That is very explicitly what is involved.

In this regard, I must apologize to you, not because you are being evacuated – I have had no hand in that – but I could have told you sooner. I received a little piece of paper on the subject on March 19.

It's very funny that on March 19 I did not give a lecture. I have tried by every means imaginable not to do so since then, because I was lazy [or: I couldn't be bothered, *j'avais la flemme*]. And, moreover, you understand, I am not moved by the idea of providing you a last lecture, because every time I come here, I tell myself that this may finally be the last time.

So one day I'm asking myself, or asking you, why you flock here in droves, and [upon returning home or] the very next morning – I can't even say which it was – I received a brief letter that I'm going to read to you. I didn't share it with you because I told myself, "If, by chance, it stirred them up, things could get even more complicated!"

I was already in a similar predicament once for two years [the "excommunication" from the SFP and the IPA]. There were people who strove to liquidate me. I let them continue their chicanery, in order that my Seminar continue, I mean so that certain things I had to say would be heard. The same is true this year.

Thanks to which I thus received this on March 20 – it's dated March 18. There is thus no connection. I even kept the envelope. At first I ripped it up, then I picked it back up, and it is clearly stamped March 18. Trust abounds, as you see.

[Lacan reads:]

403   Doctor Lacan
          5, rue de Lille [Lacan comments: "as some of you know"]
          Paris, 7th arrondissement

Doctor,

At the request of the 6th division of the École Pratique des Hautes Études, the École Normale has provided you with an auditorium in which to hold your class for over five years.

The reorganization of the École's studies, which is a consequence of the general reform of universities and the recent law regarding the orientation of higher education, and the expansion of teaching in several disciplines, will make it impossible for us to lend you the Dussane auditorium, or any other auditorium in the school, for your course starting in October 1969.

I am letting you know in plenty of time [Lacan comments: "that is true"] for you to be able to begin to look for another establishment at which to hold your class during the 1969/1970 academic year.

I really like that. I really do. It is historically accurate and altogether true. The request in fact came from the 6th division of the École Pratique des Hautes Études, owing to the transfer of a personal debt. There was an eminent man by the name of Lucien Febvre who had, I can't say the regrettable idea, for he had nothing to do with it, of dying before he could give me what he had promised me: a place in that École. Others gleaned what he had promised me. The university operates in a very feudal manner; things still work in that way. In the university system, one is still a liege man [homme lige]. Liege man, she-man [hommelle] – all of that hangs together. So it is on the basis of a request, as they say, that I was here. Fine.

It doesn't bother me that the reform was the reason given. I am, as you know, no babe in arms – I know very well that on Wednesdays at 12:30 p.m., no one wants the Dussane auditorium. We had to work very hard, moreover, to get the sound system in this room working . . .

Let me mention that I felt that what I just read you was worth photocopying for everyone who is here today. A few people are going to hand out copies to you.

Please only take one each. You never know what will come of it in the future. You understand that it is S_1. You will all be united by something, you will know that you were here in 1969 on the 25th of June. And the fact that you were here that day might even attest to the fact that you were here all year long. It is a diploma.

You never know, it might help us reunite. Because, who knows, if I wander off into the bush and come back someday, it could serve us as a sign of recognition or symbol. I could very well say one day that anyone who has one of these sheets of paper can enter into such and such a room for a confidential communication regarding the functions of psychoanalysis in the political realm.

You can't imagine how much people wonder about them. For, indeed, there is a true question there, which, who knows, psychoanalysts, and maybe even the university system, could someday benefit from learning something about. I would be inclined to say that, if someone asked *me* if he could say something about it, I would arrange to meet with you in this room so that you could have a last class of the year – the one you didn't have, in short, because I stopped early, so as not to hold a last class. I didn't feel like it.

So you have this little object in hand. And there are, all the same, some 300 of us who are being evacuated.

Now that everyone has a diploma, it's time for me to leave you amongst yourselves for a while. That isn't so bad, because when I am here none of you speak up, in spite of my efforts to get you to. Who knows – you might well have things to say to each other.

Your smoking habits, for example, played a role in this evacuation. The janitors here – for in an affair like this, everyone gets consulted, as you know – have told me straight out that I have a strange audience. It even seems that they had to repair some of the seats. Something happened. Jean-Jacques Lebel, didn't you bring a band saw? That little noise we hear now and then must be you sawing off the arms of the chairs. You learn something new every day.

With this paper in hand, you will be able to open up to each other when I say "good day" in a moment. The odor of what is written on it will replace the smell of smoke.

What would be great, you see, is if you gave it the only fate that would truly be worthy of what it is – a signifying fate. You will make up a meaning for the word *flacelière* [the last name of the man who wrote the letter Lacan just read aloud]. I am putting it in the feminine, just for fun. I won't say that it is a penchant, but it sounds rather feminine to me, like *cordelière* [rope belt or draw-string] or *flatulencière*. What if it caught on? "Do you take me for a *flacelière?*" That could be useful in our times. "Don't pull too hard on the *flacelière!*" I'll let you find your own. I've always taught you that it is the signifiers that create the signifieds.

This piece of paper gave me pause for thought. I realized plenty of things, and specifically our complete ignorance about when a certain use of paper [as toilet paper] began. It obviously could only begin once paper existed. Prior to that, people didn't do it with parchment or papyrus. I called the headquarters of a few [toilet] paper makers, and they didn't know. It must have begun very shortly after paper did, since it is a question that came to me when reading Chapter 13 of Rabelais' *Gargantua*. Someone could perhaps enlighten me on this score.

Well, don't use it for that. I'm not giving you a whole roll of paper, after all, just one sheet each.

I am going to leave you now, my dear friends. Let me point out that your papers are signed. I didn't want to put my signature on the back of the paper, but I put the date there. On 191 copies, I wrote the date myself; on the other 150, it was Gloria, my faithful secretary, who was willing to do it for me – as you know, it leads to writer's cramp. While it's very graphic to write 25.5.69 191 times, I nevertheless took the trouble to do so.

So, if you'd like to exchange a few comments amongst yourselves, or send me a message, I will leave you in the hands of my faithful Gloria, who will collect any such messages. Those who would like to say whatever might seem opportune to them to say have at least 20 minutes to do so.

As for me, I bid you adieu and thank you for your loyalty.

June 25, 1969

[The stenography of the session mentions abundant laughter and applause; the text is chock-full of exclamation marks.]

APPENDICES

FIBONACCI AS USED BY LACAN

A Few Mathematical Observations

by Luc Miller

On the topic of Fibonacci sequences and the golden ratio [or: golden number, *nombre d'or*] that Lacan discusses in Chapters VIII and IX of Seminar XVI, the reader can consult fruitfully and with pleasure the book by H. E. Huntley, *The Divine Proportion: A Study in Mathematical Beauty* (New York: Dover, 1970).

The best website on Fibonacci is the one by Ron Knott at the University of Surrey: http://www.mcs.surrey.ac.uk/Personal/R. Knott/Fibonacci/fib.html.

[As of 2022, see, instead: http://www.maths.surrey.ac.uk/hosted-sites/R.Knott/Fibonacci/fib.html.]

Terminology

Lacan often uses the terms "sequence" [*suite*] and "series" [*série*] indiscriminately (as does Huntley). Today people prefer the word "sequence" and only use the word "series" for the sum of the terms of a sequence. We thus talk about a Fibonacci "sequence" when we consider 1, 1, 2, 3, 5, 8, 13, etc., and a Fibonacci "series" when we consider the sequence of the partial sums: 1, 1 + 1, 1 + 1 + 2, 1 + 1 + 2 + 3, 1 + 1 + 2 + 3 + 5, 1 + 1 + 2 + 3 + 5 + 8, 1 + 1 + 2 + 3 + 5 + 8 + 13, etc.

The distinction can be important, especially when we are dealing with convergence on a limit (in other words, and all too briefly, what the terms of a sequence indefinitely approach). Thus the sequence on the left in Figure 8.2 (the so-called decreasing series) converges on the limit 0, but its series converges on $1 + a$. As in the paradox of Achilles and the tortoise, adding together an infinity of smaller and smaller numbers yields a finite sum.

Lacan illustrates this series using a schema that is reproduced here [Figure 8.6]. We divide a segment of length $1 + a$ into segments whose lengths are the odd powers of a (namely, a, a^3, a^5, a^7, etc.), on the one hand, and the even powers of a (namely, a^2, a^4, a^6, etc.), on the other hand. Each half-circle of the schema corresponds to a "rotation," as described by Lacan. We can, in fact, transfer a segment of a given length end to end by placing the point of a compass at the shared end of the given segment and its duplicate: the half-circle is then the trace left by the compass in its movement from the opposite extremity of the given segment to the opposite extremity of its thus constructed duplicate.

Fibonacci

The term "Fibonacci sequence" is usually reserved for those sequences that begin with 1, 1, and that are sometimes preceded by the term 0. More generally speaking, this term designates all sequences that satisfy the same rule of formation, namely: each new term is obtained by adding together the two preceding ones. In mathematics, such a rule of formation is known as "a formula of recurrence" (here, it is "linear, second order"; this is currently studied [in France] in the scientific curricula just prior to or just after the completion of high school). If we call u_n the nth term of the sequence, this formula of recurrence is written: $u_{n+2} = u_{n+1} + u_n$.

Lacan seems to think that all Fibonacci sequences are identical because a appears as the limit of the ratio between one term and the next (it is in this sense that all Fibonacci sequences are homologous, Lacan says). This property is, in fact, deduced from the preceding formula of recurrence, with the exception (omitted by Lacan as by Huntley, pp. 36–7) of those sequences that begin with two terms where the ratio of the first to the second is $-1/a$ (the ratio of a term of one of these "exceptional" sequences to the following term is always $-1/a$, and thus cannot converge toward the limit a). Among the Fibonacci sequences (in other words, those that satisfy the preceding formula of recurrence), the sequence on the right [in Figure 8.2] is the only one (apart from those including a multiplier of each term, or, what amounts to the same thing, those beginning with 1) in which the ratio of one term to the next is exactly a. In his book, Huntley qualifies this sequence as the "golden series" (p. 49).

411   The formula of recurrence that determines the formation of the sequence on the right is Fibonacci's. Yet a minus sign must be introduced in front of the middle term, that is, u_{n+1}, to obtain the formula of recurrence of the sequence on the left. Lacan points

out that it is nevertheless the same formula of recurrence if one inverts the order of the terms in the sequence on the left. Let us note that the same formula of recurrence is at work if we change the sign of one term out of two. This explains in what respect the sequence on the left is almost a Fibonacci sequence, and in particular why the coefficients that appear in it are the terms of the Fibonacci sequence with alternating signs (we shall return to this).

Note that we can add a supplementary first term to the two "parallel" sequences without violating the rules by which they are generated. The one on the left then begins with 1, a, and the one on the right with a, 1.

The Number a and the Golden Ratio

Lacan introduces the number a as the positive solution of the equation $1/a = 1 + a$. This equation naturally appears in the search for sequences that verify the formula of recurrence of the sequence on the left. In particular, for those sequences where the relationship between any one term and its preceding term is constant (in mathematics, we talk about a "geometrical sequence," and the relationship is referred to as its "ratio" [raison]), the values of this ratio are the solutions to the equation. For example, the sequence on the left is such a sequence and the ratio there is equal to a.

For the sequence on the right, the analogous equation is $\varphi = (1 + \varphi)/\varphi$. Its only positive solution is the golden ratio, which is often written φ. In that respect, a, in the formula of recurrence of the sequence on the left, is analogous to φ in Fibonacci sequences. One can calculate that $a = (\sqrt{5} - 1)/2$, and that $\varphi = (\sqrt{5} + 1)/2$; thus a is expressed as a function of the golden ratio by the formulas $a = \varphi - 1$ and $a = 1/\varphi$.

The golden ratio is also known as the "divine proportion," for it rules the division of a quantity into two parts such that the smaller part (1) is to the larger part (φ) what the latter (φ) is to the total ($1 + \varphi$). In this division, φ is the ratio of the larger part to the smaller. Since a is the inverse of φ [$a = 1/\varphi$], it is the ratio of the smaller part to the larger. The following figure is the classic representation of φ by means of a rectangle, and the analogous representation of a.

412

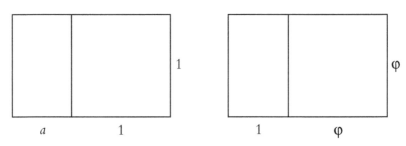

Figure A1.1: Little *a* and the Golden Ratio φ

Vectorial Space

The natural rules with which we operate on sequences verifying the same formula of recurrence are obtained by considering the sequences as vectors – namely, the addition of two sequences and the multiplication of one sequence by a number. In school, we learn to operate on two-dimensional vectors represented by arrows and indicated by two coordinates (x, y). The addition involves placing two arrows end to end – $(x, y) + (x', y') = (x + x', y + y')$ – whereas the multiplication involves modifying the length while preserving the direction: $a \times (x, y) = (a \times x, a \times y)$. Here the vectors have an infinite number of coordinates $(u_1, u_2, u_3, u_4, \ldots)$, but the same operations apply to each coordinate. Indeed, the result of these operations is a sequence that verifies the same formula of recurrence.

Lacan's comments on the status of the numbers 1 and *a* in the formation of these parallel sequences reminds us of the vectorial space structure of the Fibonacci sequences. In fact, coefficients appear in these sequences that are exactly the same terms as in the Fibonacci sequence. This is explained by the Fibonacci formula of recurrence by adopting the vectorial point of view. I have already indicated how to modify the sequence on the left in order for it to also verify this formula: I will henceforth call the "modified sequence on the left" the sequence on the left by which the first, third, and all the other odd terms are multiplied by −1.

Let us recall that the sequence on the right is formed by beginning with 1, 1 + *a*, and then by applying the Fibonacci formula of recurrence. Adding up the Fibonacci sequence that begins with 1, 1 is the same as adding to it *a* times the Fibonacci sequence that begins with 0, 1 (in other words, the same sequence preceded by 0). Indeed, the result of this operation verifies the same formula of recurrence, and the first term is calculated as follows: $1 + a \times 0 = 1$; the second term is calculated as follows: $1 + a \times 1 = 1 + a$; this clearly gives us the sequence on the right. From the vectorial standpoint, each term in the sequence is thus formed by the sum of a multiple of 1 and a multiple of a, and these coefficients are the terms of the Fibonacci sequence.

Similarly, the modified sequence on the left is formed by beginning with $-a$ and $1 - a$, and then applying the Fibonacci formula of recurrence. Since $(0, 1) - a \times (1, 1) = (-a, 1 - a)$, it is the same to add the Fibonacci sequence that begins with 0, 1 as to subtract a times the Fibonacci sequence that begins with 1, 1 (in other words, the same sequence without its first term). From the vectorial standpoint, we see that the coefficients before a and -1 in the modified sequence on the left are the terms of the Fibonacci sequence with the shift mentioned by Lacan. The shift from the modified sequence on the left to the sequence on the left in the Seminar explains the alternation of the plus and minus signs mentioned by Lacan.

Partial Sum

Lacan makes a comment about the addition of the powers of $1/a$ up to $1/a^{100}$, which is also the sum of the first 101 terms of the series on the right (it is not clear whether Lacan also means to add the initial 1, but it is a negligible quantity with regard to the total). As Lacan says, this sum is close to 2 followed by 21 zeros, namely 2×10^{21} (more precisely, this total is greater than 2×10^{21} but it does not exceed it by more than 10^{20}). Close to two thousand billion billions, as [Tintin's friend] Captain Haddock would say.

This sum is not easy to calculate precisely by hand. As it is a sum of successive powers, we can easily conclude that it is equal to $1/a^{102} - 1/a$. (More generally speaking, the recurrence formula $u_{n+2} = u_{n+1} + u_n$ implies that $u_1 + u_2 + u_3 + \ldots + u_{n-1} + u_n = u_{n+2} - u_2$.) We then must calculate the precise values of the powers of $1/a$, the golden ratio. Another possibility consists in utilizing our remark regarding the vectorial expression of the sequence on the right, in order to link this sum to the Fibonacci sequence, a gigantic number (far more than 100) of whose terms are included in tables. We thus find that this sum is equal to the 103rd term of the Fibonacci sequence plus a times the 102nd term of the Fibonacci sequence minus $1/a$. Using the value of the 102nd and 103rd terms of the Fibonacci sequence (respectively 927372692193078999176 and 1500520536206896083277) and the approximate value for a (0.618) given by Lacan in the preceding formula and neglecting $1/a$, we obtain a very fine approximation of the value of this sum.

January 2006

414

READER'S GUIDE
by Jacques-Alain Miller

[Paragraph numbers here refer to the chapter numbers in the Seminar.]

1. Who is the "publicist" mentioned here by Lacan? It is not, I hope, Roland Barthes, even if he knew how to get the general public interested in structuralism. The garbage can: Samuel Beckett's is mentioned at the beginning of "Lituraterre" (the first article in the collection entitled *Autres Écrits*). The mustard pot is mentioned on page 647 of *Écrits*. Lacan's Hegel derives, as is well known, from Kojève (see his *Introduction to the Reading of Hegel* [New York: Basic Books, 1969]). The topic of embarrassment [or: quandary, *embarras*] was discussed in the first chapter of Seminar X, *Anxiety*.

2. Speaking out [*prise de parole*]: see the book by Michel de Certeau, SJ, member of the École Freudienne de Paris. Mudger Muddle: a Bugs Bunny-style nickname given by Lacan to Lucien Goldmann (personal communication), author of *The Hidden God: A Study of Tragic Vision in the* Pensées *of Pascal and the Tragedies of Racine* (New York: Routledge, 2013 [1955]). The book, which had its moment of glory, was devoted to Jansenism as a tragic worldview shared by Pascal and Racine. A Marxist thinker and well-known figure in the Latin Quarter, Goldmann (1913–70) had a habit of frequenting colloquia, heckling everyone, and promising to submit them to a Lukácsian analysis (Lukács was a great Hungarian Marxist philosopher). People sometimes say "fudge," "mudge," or "muddle" in English to revile work that has been botched or mucked up. One of Henry James' characters (in *In the Cage*) is named Mr. Mudge; in our times, it is the name of a character in a children's story [*Henry and Mudge and the Forever Sea*]. Did Lacan expect Goldmann to show up at his Seminar?

3. "Suture": a talk given by Jacques-Alain Miller [on February 24, 1965] at Lacan's Seminar XII, *Les problèmes cruciaux de la psychanalyse* (1964/65). In 1968, he was 24 years old, which was precisely the "average age" of the new generation mentioned by Lacan here. Famillionaire: see Seminar V, the first chapter and following. The graph: see its construction in Seminar V and in *Écrits*, pp. 804–15. *The Devil in Love* by Jacques Cazotte (1772) was recently reissued in French by the Mille et Une Nuits publishing house. Russell's paradox, that of the catalog of catalogs that do not include themselves (does it include itself or not?) is a *pons asinorum* of mathematical logic and set theory – there are innumerable references to it.

4. *Qu'est-ce que le structuralisme?* ("What Is Structuralism?") was published by Seuil [Paris: 1968]. Michel Henry's *L'Essence de la manifestation* was published by Presses Universitaires de France [Paris: 1963; second edition 2011]. The message sent to Lacan regarding the ordered pair came from Daniel Sibony, a mathematician who would go on to become a psychoanalyst.

5. Gödel: see, for example, Raymond Smullyan's *Gödel's Incompleteness Theorems* (Oxford: Oxford University Press, 1992).

6. Quine: *Word and Object* (Cambridge, MA: The MIT Press, 2013 [1960]). Georges Brunet's *Le Pari de Pascal* was published by Desclée De Brouwer (Paris: 1956).

7. Georges Bataille's well-known essay, *The Accursed Share*, was published in English by Zone Books (New York: 1988). Regarding Terence, see *Terence: The Comedies* (Oxford: Oxford University Press, 2006). In the list of works by Georges-Théodule Guilbaud, a mathematician who was a friend of Lacan's, I located several texts referring to Pascal, but none of which provide a formalization of the wager as in game theory; that formalization, which became common in the 1970s, can be found today on many websites.

8. The "Que sais-je?" book on Jansenism was written by Louis Cognet (Paris: Presses Universitaires de France, 1961), a highly erudite man treated rather offhandedly here. See the following two books regarding *convulsionnaires*: B. Robert Kaiser, *Miracles, Convulsions, and Ecclesiastical Politics in Early Eighteenth-Century Paris* (Princeton, NJ: Princeton University Press, 1978), and Ephraim Radner [*Spirit and Nature: The Saint-Médard Miracles in 18th-Century Jansenism* (New York: Herder & Herder, 2002), a book based on his dissertation], "A Pneumatological Investigation of the Miracles of Saint-Médard and Their Rejection" (Yale University, 1994). Two recent

books have returned to the topic of Jansenism by displacing its button tie to the French Revolution: Dale K. Van Kley, *The Religious Origins of the French Revolution: From Calvin to the Civil Constitution, 1560–1791* (New Haven, CT: Yale University Press, 1996), and Catherine-Laurence Maire, *De la cause de Dieu à la cause de la nation. Le Jansénisme au XVIIIe siècle* (Paris: Gallimard, 1998). The two authors vehemently disagree with each other: see Maire's review of Van Kley's book in the journal *Le Débat*, 130 (2004) and his reply in *Commentaire*, 108 (2004–2005). See, also, Monique Cottret's *Jansénisme et lumières. Pour un autre XVIIIe siècle* (Paris: Albin Michel, 1998).

417

9. On Fibonacci, see the preceding appendix.

10. See Edmund Bergler's *The Basic Neurosis* [*: Oral Regression and Psychic Masochism* (New York: Grune & Stratton, 1949)]. Charles Blondel, an anti-Freudian professor of psychology, was the author of *La Conscience morbide. Essai de psychopathologie générale* (Paris: Félix Alcan, 1914), among other works.

11. The letter Lacan received was the work of two schoolboys in Lyon who decided not to continue this exchange (personal communication with Jacques Borie). Maud Mannoni, member of the École Freudienne de Paris, was the author of *L'Enfant arriéré et sa mère* (Paris: Seuil, 1964) [*The Backward Child and His Mother: A Psychoanalytic Study* (New York: Pantheon Books, 1972)].

12. Lacan mentions his reworking of the text of Seminar VII, *The Ethics of Psychoanalysis*, "perhaps in view of publishing it," and speaks further on about "endeavoring to write [it] up." This undoubtedly corresponds to the pages posthumously published in the journal *Ornicar?* 28 (January 1984) [*: 7–18*], entitled "Compte rendu avec interpolations du Séminaire de *L'Éthique.*" Foucault's talk can be found in *Dits et Écrits I* (Paris: Gallimard, 2001 [1994]), pp. 789–821. In it, there is a trace of Lacan's response to it (preceded, moreover, by one by someone mentioned earlier, Lucien Goldmann).

13. "The logic of the signifier" is a term that the young Jacques-Alain Miller had highlighted in Lacan's discourse. The commentary that follows (on p. 209 in the French edition) makes obvious reference to the journal published by the École Normale Supérieure, *Cahiers pour l'analyse*, which was devoted to the concept of discourse (cf. Jacques-Alain Miller's "Action de la structure" in issue 9 [1968]; [translated as "Action of the Structure" in *The Symptom*, 10 (2016)]); the same journal had also brought out an issue (number 7) entitled "What is a Novel?" and had just published its tenth and final issue on

"Formalization," the first article of which inspired Lacan to come up with the term "pas-tout." The reverie regarding the "Lacan theorem" evokes that regarding the "Lacan knot" in Seminar XXIII. Georg Simmel (1858–1918), a philosopher and sociologist in Berlin, had always been sidelined by German universities; many of his works have been translated into French in the last 20 years, the main one of which is *The Philosophy of Money* [London & New York: Routledge, 2011 (1900)].

14. Deleuze published the following books: *Difference and Repetition* (New York: Columbia University Press, 1994 [1968]); *Expressionism in Philosophy: Spinoza* (New York: Zone Books, 1990 [1968]); and *The Logic of Sense* (New York: Columbia University Press, 1990 [1969]). The dismantling [*démontage*] of the drive: see chapter 13 in Seminar XI. The note on curl flux is found on p. 721 (n. 3) in *Écrits*. François Jacob and the bacteriophage: see, for example, *The Emergence of Bacterial Genetics* by Thomas D. Brock (Cold Spring Harbor, NY: Cold Spring Harbor Laboratory Press, 1990). Lacan often refers to the *Mammaries of Tiresias*, "a surrealist drama" by Apollinaire.   418

15. "Trapped youth": this text can be found in the archives of *Le Nouvel Observateur*; I didn't look for it. Johnny: the nickname of Giovanni Agnelli, the famous boss of Fiat who was quite a jetsetter in his youth, and who was taken to be an emblematic figure of Italy during his lifetime; Lacan spent time with him during the postwar years in Paris.

16. Lacan likes to refer to the passage on the gaze in *Being and Nothingness*. When he mentions certain "little scenarios" involving torture, one cannot fail to think of Sartre's play, *Morts sans sépulture* [see "Men without Shadows" in *Three Plays: Altona, Men without Shadows, and the Flies* (Harmondsworth, UK: Penguin, 1962)]. Deleuze's book on masochism and sadism is his *Masochism: Coldness and Cruelty & Venus in Furs* (New York: Zone Books, 1989 [1967]).

17. The book decried at the beginning of the chapter is *L'Univers contestationnaire*, by "André Stéphane," a pseudonym. Originally published by Payot, it was reissued in 2004 by In Press with the names of its real authors on the cover, a couple of "training analysts" at the Société Psychanalytique de Paris, Béla Grunberger and Janine Chasseguet-Smirgel. Thomas Moore is the author of *Utopia* (1516), a title maintained in several languages. Protagoras: Lacan's viewpoint is that of Walter Burkert in his 1962 book, *Weisheit und Wissenschaft: Studien zu Pythagoras, Philolaos und Plato* (Nuremberg: Verlag Hans Carl, 1962) [*Lore and Science in Ancient Pythagoreanism* (Cambridge,

MA: Harvard University Press, 1972)]. Giuseppe Peano gave a purely axiomatic definition of the set of natural numbers in 1889; since that time, people have been speaking of "Peano arithmetic."

18. Lacan likes to cite Einstein's quip "God does not play dice" [the French, "Dieu non trompeur," means the "God who doesn't deceive"]; on this topic, see, for example, the article by Françoise Balabar, "Dieu et Einstein," in *Ornicar?* 51 (Paris: Navarin, 2005). Which of Berkeley's works had Lacan read? He undoubtedly knew *An Essay towards a New Theory of Vision* (1709), *A Treatise concerning the Principles of Human Knowledge*, Part I (1710), *Three Dialogues between Hylas and Philonous* (1713), and *Siris* (1744). The camera obscura was first used in astronomy. In Aristotle's time, it took the form of a darkened room with an orifice in one wall allowing light to enter so as to form the inverted image of a solar eclipse on the opposite wall. In 1515, Leonardo da Vinci described a dark room that he called *Oculus artificialis* [the artificial eye]. In the sixteenth century, people were advised to add a lens for better image quality. See, on the subject, *La Vision chez Platon et Aristote* by Anne Merker (Louvain-la-Neuve: Academia, 2003).

19. "Anxiety is not without an object" [or: "Anxiety is not devoid of an object" (or "Anxiety does involve an object")]: see Chapter 7 of Seminar X, *Anxiety* (Cambridge: Polity Press, 2014). On Angelus Silesius, see Seminar III. On Helene Deutsch, see *Neuroses and Character Types: Clinical Psychoanalytic Studies* (Madison, CT: International Universities Press, 1965). "To think is to say no": see *Propos sur les pouvoirs* [: *Eléments d'éthique politique* (Paris: Gallimard, 1985)] by Alain, "L'homme devant l'apparence," dated January 19, 1924. Here is what Alain says: "To think is to say no. Note that the sign of yes is that of a man who is nodding off; on the contrary, one shakes one's head upon awakening and says no. No to what? To the world, a tyrant, a preacher? That is merely what it appears to be. In all such cases, thought is saying no to itself. It is breaking with happy acquiescence. It is separating from itself. It is fighting with itself. There is no other battle in the world. If the world can fool me with its perspectives, fogs, and diversionary shocks, it is because I consent and seek nothing further. And if a tyrant can become my master, it is because I respect instead of examining. Even a true doctrine falls into error owing to this somnolence. Men become slaves by believing. To reflect is to gainsay [*nier*] what we believe. He who believes no longer even realizes *that* he believes. He who contents himself with his thought has stopped thinking altogether."

419

20. Alfred L. Kroeber (1876–1960) was the most famous American anthropologist after Boaz, under whom he studied. He became friendly with Ishi, who was reputed to be the last of the Yahi Indians in California, and who he got to wear a suit and tie. The "paper tiger" is a famous metaphor borrowed from tradition and used by Chairman Mao in the 1960s to convey the idea that the strength of the imperialists is only apparent and to encourage the masses to fight fearlessly under the direction of the Communist Party. In Hong Kong, you can buy little paper tigers made out of papier-mâché.

21. There would be a great deal to say about Bishop Wilkins. Or one could do what I will do: refer the reader to Borges, who devotes one of his most bewitching *Ostras Inquisiciones* to "The Analytical Language of John Wilkins." See *Other Inquisitions, 1937–1952* (Austin, TX: University of Texas Press, 1964).

22. It occurs to me that at the moment that Lacan was giving this class on June 4, he was busy writing up the summary of the Seminar he gave the prior year for the yearbook of the École des Hautes Études, which he finished on June 10. You can find it in *Autres Écrits*, "L'acte psychanalytique" [Paris: Seuil, 2001], pp. 375–83. James Frazer (1854–1941) is the well-known author of *The Golden Bough*, whose influence can be felt, according to Wikipedia, in the work of Yates, Joyce, D. H. Lawrence, T. S. Eliot (*The Waste Land*), Robert Graves (*The White Goddess*, quoted by Lacan in *Autres Écrits*, p. 563), Ezra Pound, Mary Renault, Joseph Campbell, and Camille Paglia. The theory of the scapegoat was taken up by René Girard. The Rome Congress that offended Lacan was an IPA event.

23. Who said to Lacan, "Yes . . . it's banal"? None other than Jacques-Alain Miller. Lacan's reference to Euclid's Book X, accompanied by the mention of a postulate by Eudoxus [of Cnidus], seems to me to concern the first proposition of that book, which introduces the method of exhaustion, which is put to use in Book XII. This proposition is equivalent to the so-called Archimedes' principle and comes from Eudoxus: in short, for all values A and B, there is a whole number n such that nA is greater than B. A researcher from Palermo by the name of Spagnolo considers "the Eudoxus–Archimedes postulate" to be an epistemological obstacle in Bachelard's sense (1995). The "self" is also discussed in "L'acte psychanalytique" [mentioned in the previous note]. Konrad Lorenz mentions, in *On Aggression* (1963), the ritualization of animal behavior and its shift to symbolization and simulation; the example he gives is the simulation of domination. *Habeas corpus*: the "great writ"

420

in common law is *habeas corpus ad subjiciendum*, which allows a prisoner to demand to appear before a court in order for a decision to be handed down regarding the lawfulness of his imprisonment.

24. Another reference to *Cahiers pour l'analyse*. The child who [told his father he had] "cheated (his way through) life" later turned out to be the eldest son, little Pierre, of Jacques and Marguerite Derrida.

25. *If* is a movie by Lindsay Anderson (1968); it recounts the revolt of students at a private British high school. The hero is played by Malcolm McDowell who, three years later, played Alex in *A Clockwork Orange*. Gargantua: Chapter 13 explains the invention by the hero of a very effective form of asswipe.

DOSSIER ON THE EVACUATION

June 25, 1969: After the 25th class was over and Lacan had left, the audience occupied the home of the head of the École Normale. They were forcibly kicked out of it by the police two hours later.

June 26: The newspaper *Le Monde* published an account of the facts, and relayed critical remarks made by "someone in charge of the École."

June 27: In the same newspaper columns, Mr. Flacelière denied having made those remarks and complained of "vandalism and the theft of several objects."

July 5: *Le Monde* published a letter by Lacan, followed by a note from the editor confirming Mr. Flacelière's denial.

November 8: Mr. Flacelière wrote a letter to *Le Monde*, responding to Lacan's letter.

The latter took the trouble to write a second letter, which the newspaper published, the editor indicating that it put an end to the debate.

Two other articles published by *Le Monde* are part and parcel of this debate: a declaration of support for Lacan signed by "over 85 people"; and an invitation to Lacan, made public in November, to come teach in the philosophy department of the Vincennes Experimental Center.

Below the reader will find the two letters by Lacan and the declaration of support. My friend François Regnault kindly furnished these archival texts, which he had managed to keep.

J.-A. M.

Lacan's First Letter to *Le Monde* [July 5, 1969]

Please publish these lines in their entirety, in accordance with my rights.

The edition of *Le Monde* that appeared on Thursday, June 26, included a change in its usual format, adding – to the account of the incidents caused at the École Normale Supérieure by the interruption of my course – in bold letters "remarks" made by that school's administration.

My lectures are, according to them, "fashionable [*mondaines*] and incomprehensible to any normal person," a remark that is so dubious that it makes one laugh, not necessarily at my expense.

The very same day, owing to reactions that will be brought to light, Mr. [Robert] Flacelière retracted what he had said as head of the École, a school for which he is obviously responsible. In the guise of a denial, he submitted a text including outright slander, which *Le Monde* nevertheless published the next day, Friday.

To indicate to the public that it was a forgery did not actually disavow the content, but amounted, instead, to publishing the text.

It is, however, slander to speak of provocation on the part of the adversary, and, furthermore, to claim that thefts were committed in the private apartment of the head of the ENS by those who he calls my disciples owing to this very fact.

Le Monde, in the pages of which Mr. Flacelière is known better than elsewhere (without prejudice to what his envoy understood), never doubted the authenticity of the remarks that were retracted (I would add that I was told they were considered "too marvelous" to require any confirmation).

It was not simply at *Le Monde* that it was held [or: from *Le Monde* that it was withheld, *au* Monde *qu'on retenait*] that these remarks had clearly been made by him.

Shouldn't *Le Monde*, after admitting later that they had been too quick to judge, have decided not to publish the declaration it received, signed this time by Mr. Flacelière, if they weren't going to ask him to indicate what thefts – that is, exactly what objects were stolen – he wanted to pin on the people who went to his home to ask for an explanation which he refused to give?

This is what supposedly justified Mr. Flacelière in calling the police, who immediately arrived in force.

I am hereby summoning Mr. Flacelière to tell us the extent of the thefts that he is attributing to his indiscreet visitors.

Declaration of Support

423

A declaration made by the "administration" of the École Normale Supérieure in the rue d'Ulm [in Paris], which came out in your paper on June 27 – for whose authorship no one seems to be willing to accept responsibility today, but which seemed plausible enough to the editors of *Le Monde* that they did not hesitate to publish it – a declaration that followed the barring of Doctor Lacan's Seminar, justified the latter by qualifying his teaching as "fashionable," "incomprehensible to any normal person," and "unscientific."

It is impossible not to mention, given such a declaration, the theoretical debt that all of the work being done today in France owes to Jacques Lacan's teaching – not just in psychoanalysis, but in all of the disciplines that come under the heading of the human sciences, and in philosophy and literary criticism as well. When we see that a venue where science is obviously being done is insistently designated as "unscientific," it is difficult not to believe that the official argument of the "reorganization of studies" is being used above all as a pretext for repressive, censorial acts. Knowledge here is thus all too visibly nothing but an ideology that allows people to endorse what is "normal." We, the undersigned, whose mere names should suffice to indicate that we know the current state of the fields we are talking about, wish to show here our solidarity as theoreticians with Jacques Lacan's teaching. It would be extremely regrettable and worrisome should Doctor Lacan be deprived of a place to teach at a university.

Lacan's Second Letter

Please communicate to your readers my position regarding this matter.

I have emphasized it just enough for them to be able to judge what constitutes the argument made by the man who heads a *grande École*. Having honored the shelter that *École* offered me for six years with my work, I owe thanks to its head: such is the feudal regime in our present-day university system.

The only justification he gave for the expulsion of my teaching from that *École* is that he found it objectionable [*indésirable*], yet it took him four and a half years to realize this, when assuredly – and this is an integral part of his complaint – my teaching did not go unnoticed.

424

I will return elsewhere to the scorn that has been shown, here and elsewhere, to an audience that does not conform to his criteria, and testimonies will appear that indicate that his refusal to provide any explanation is based on just that.

For my part, the fact that I did not avoid informing my audience that something was up – as I did, at the last minute, in order to do my duty right up until the end – precisely indicates a response which, had it been followed up on, should have given rise to a song.

Index

Page numbers in *italics* refer to figures